MW00913783

ASSET FORFEITURE

PRACTICE AND PROCEDURE IN STATE AND FEDERAL COURTS

SECOND EDITION

DEE R. EDGEWORTH

AMERICAN BAR ASSOCIATION
**Defending Liberty
Pursuing Justice**

CRIMINAL JUSTICE SECTION

Cover design by ABA Publishing

12 11 10 09 08   5 4 3 2 1

ISBN: 978-1-60442-063-0
         1-60442-063-4

Asset Forfeiture: Practice and Procedure in State and Federal Courts / Edgeworth, Dee

Discounts are available for books ordered in bulk. Special consideration is given to state bars, CLE programs, and other bar-related organizations. Inquire at Book Publishing, ABA Publishing, American Bar Association, 321 North Clark Street, Chicago, Illinois 60654.

www.ababooks.org

Contents

Tables

Foreword to the Second Edition

Before the First United States Congress passed the Judiciary Act of 1789 and the Bill of Rights, it passed the Hamilton Tariff and with it the first forfeiture provisions in U.S. law to enforce these tariff provisions against smuggling. Despite this pedigree and long history in American law, it was not until the 1980s that law enforcement began to broadly and vigorously utilize asset forfeiture as a weapon against commercial and economic criminal enterprises.

As a young, enthusiastic major narcotics prosecutor for the California Attorney General's Office in those days, I marveled as the detectives and specials agents I worked with in Southern California hauled in boxes, suitcases, car and truckload, and eventually rooms full of cash. The joke in those days was that the drug cartels did not count their money, they weighed it; but it was a joke with a great deal of truth to it. Yet, in those "early" days, cash was seized only because it was found alongside the drugs, and other assets of these drug organizations, with the exception of the occasional expensive sports car, were, for the most part, left behind. There was little or no effort at the investigative stage to target drug assets for seizure and no mechanism to systematically seize, forfeit, and convert drug assets to dismantle the drug enterprise and to simultaneously enhance the law enforcement effort. In those days, when cash was seized, we called in a state tax agent who conducted a "jeopardy assessment," hauled the cash away, and dumped it into the state general fund, never to be seen again.

Beginning in the 1980s, federal, state, and local law enforcement and prosecution officials began to appreciate that to successfully attack narcotics and other criminal enterprises, merely making arrests and putting violators in prison was not sufficient. Members of any organized criminal venture were fungible and could easily be replaced so long as the organization and its infrastructure survived. Likewise, a prison term was a small price to pay—the "cost of doing business," in relation to the staggering profits to be reaped from narcotics, vice, and other racketeering activity.

Asset forfeiture emerged as a potent weapon to both strip the criminal enterprise of its infrastructure—the cars, houses, and equipment which facilitated the criminal activity—and to capture and deny to the organization and its hierarchy the immense profits or proceeds of the criminal activity. Both the federal and state legislatures began to enact a host of civil and criminal asset forfeiture statutes aimed at an ever-widening category of commercial and economic criminal activity. Armed with these statutes, law enforcement and prosecutors began to employ asset seizure and forfeiture as an essential and integral part of its strategy in attacking and dismantling criminal enterprises.

By the end of the 1980s, I found myself in Holland working with Dutch authorities to round up assets and records that would allow us to prosecute members of the largest marijuana distribution operation in the United States and to seize and forfeit the assets of that organization found both in the United States and overseas. One of the assets of that organization was a large "ranch" on the border of Orange and Riverside Counties in Southern California, which once seized and forfeited, became parkland and required the reshaping of the borders between the two counties. Clearly, we had come a long way from simply handing over boxes of cash to the agents from the state Franchise Tax Board.

In the ensuing years, the utilization of asset forfeiture as a critical enforcement strategy gave rise to a host of significant legal issues in the courts. The federal and state trial and appellate courts were soon confronting issues going to both the proper interpretation, scope, and operation of the various forfeiture provisions and to the requisites for the procedures for the seizure of assets and adjudication of forfeiture cases. It was not long before weighty constitutional issues arising in asset forfeiture proceedings were on the docket of the United States Supreme Court, including claims affecting the right to counsel, "excessive fines," search and seizure, double jeopardy, and procedural due process. While many of the more significant legal issues affecting asset forfeiture have been resolved, some critical issues have yet to an addressed by our highest court, such as the application of the Exclusionary Rule in a civil asset forfeiture proceeding. Likewise, other legal claims and questions continue to be litigated and decided in the federal and state appellate courts.

Asset forfeiture has become a permanent and central feature of law enforcement and prosecution efforts targeted on commercial and economic crimes. The proliferation of forfeiture statutes and case law makes a resource such as this book an essential tool in the fair and effective application of these laws. This second edition not only updates the relevant statutory and case law but gathers together in a comparative form the various state forfeiture provisions. There is also an expanded treatment of trial procedures and evidentiary issues in asset forfeiture litigation. Understanding this unique and important area of law, being conversant in its nomenclature and aware of its powerful reach and potential pitfalls is important to anyone involved in the enforcement and prosecution of the criminal laws in the 21st Century. This volume provides both a primer and a deep and wide treatment of this critical subject matter.

Gary W. Schons
Senior Assistant Attorney General
Office of the California Attorney General
San Diego

Gary Schons has headed the Criminal Division of the California Attorney General's Office in San Diego since 1992. In the 1980s he was assigned *to the office's Special Prosecutions Unit, where he prosecuted organized* crime, major narcotics and major fraud cases in both the state and federal *courts, the later as a cross-designated federal prosecutor. He drafted California's asset forfeiture and money-laundering statutes, served on the* staff of the President's Commission on Model State Drug Laws, and coauthored the Model Asset Forfeiture Law. He has testified before the United States Congress and California legislature and lectured throughout *the country on asset forfeiture, money laundering, and financial investigations.*

Foreword to the First Edition

The past 15 years were a very exciting time to be in the law enforcement profession, especially in New York City. As crime plummeted to historic lows across the country, police agencies were well positioned to test different ideas and strategies like never before. In the summer of 1995, as a newly promoted captain in the New York City Police Department, Commissioner William J. Bratton tasked me to implement an asset forfeiture strategy for the department. This included the creation of an Asset Forfeiture Unit, developing training curricula, and implementing new policies and procedures for the rank and file.

As a New York City cop serving in a variety of patrol, administrative, and investigative assignments, I thought I was up to this challenge. Little did I know how much there was to learn and accomplish. It was early on in our quest that I met Dee Edgeworth and a group of terrific professionals from the Asset Forfeiture & Money Laundering Section of the United States Department of Justice. Over the years they provided indispensable training, support, and advice throughout our developmental journey and laid the groundwork for our continued long-term success.

Defining the problem was easy. What we had done in the past made little difference. Arrests moved people off the streets for varying periods, but not much really changed over time. New faces appeared doing the same old thing. So our first task was to start from scratch and reinvent the way we attacked old problems. Realizing that we were not going to arrest our way out of the chronic conditions that plagued our city, we searched for a better way. We had for too many years missed something. People were involved in certain types of crime for one thing, money, and we had to become more effective in going after that money.

Asset forfeiture provided a perfect tool to do just that. It allowed us to move away from our routine. Instead of effecting multiple arrests at the same old problem spots, we would now target the most nefarious drug organizations with a tag-team approach. Coupling a vigorous criminal investigation and prosecution with a comprehensive asset forfeiture strategy allowed us to get people's attention. Criminals were stunned to find out that we not only found their money but also seized it. Police and the community were also amazed at these notable results. Organizations started to fade away and crime dropped. Things started to look different, and that was good.

Not only were criminals brought to justice, but also their ability to re-establish criminal activity was impaired. The successes of an effective asset forfeiture program paid many rewards. The lessons we learned were rolled into other types of investigations, including prostitution, gambling, auto theft rings, trademark infringement, gangs, and organized crime, and continued to pay big rewards. The concept was simple and could be applied in many different scenarios.

The asset forfeiture field proved to be an interesting and rewarding assignment, and the learning process was an ongoing endeavor. It was important to keep current on legal issues, procedural changes, crime, and money-laundering trends. It was equally important to build and maintain a rapport with other asset forfeiture practitioners locally, regionally, and nationally. Making new contacts and establishing relationships was part of the job. Law enforcement and business sector contacts were crucial to our development and were a part of our planning. As we hit the ground running, we experimented, learned, and made daily progress. I was truly amazed at the enthusiasm, tenacity, and professionalism that the investigators assigned to the NYPD Asset Forfeiture Unit brought to their new assignment. I am proud to have been part of this dynamic team. They did yeoman's work learning and applying their new craft. I am thankful for the tremendous effort they brought to their assignment.

One essential nugget we learned quickly was that in order to succeed, we had to learn more and become intimately familiar with the various forfeiture laws. Properly defining the framework of our new forfeiture world was the key to establishing an effective law enforcement tool. Knowing the triggers for various provisions of the federal, state or local laws allowed us to tailor our investigations to ensure a successful prosecution while crippling the criminal organization through forfeiture. Knocking these criminal groups out, one by one, became much easier as we became more and more familiar with identifying and attacking the financial base. We made a difference, and it is my wish that this book helps you make a difference as well.

John J. Murphy, M.A.
Managing Director
Murphy Partners, LLC

John Murphy manages Murphy Partners, a consulting firm tailored to meet the needs of the law enforcement community, specializing in asset forfeiture for state and local agencies. He retired in 2000 as a deputy inspector from the New York City Police Department, where he commanded the Organized Crime Investigation Division, the Joint Organized Crime Task Force (FBI) and the Asset Forfeiture Unit. He later received a two-year appointment to serve as a magistrate in the Fifth Judicial District of North Carolina in Wilmington. He continues to advise and train for the United States Department of Justice, Criminal Division, Asset Forfeiture & Money Laundering Section.

Preface

    My first exposure to asset forfeiture litigation occurred in 1987, when I was assigned to the major narcotics prosecution program of our county. In addition to my criminal caseload, I was asked to handle any corresponding civil asset forfeiture litigation that pertained to my cases. I quickly discovered that the statutes were new, there was very little case law defining them, and the constitutional parameters were virtually untouched. I determined that a successful asset forfeiture litigator required not only my skills as a criminal prosecutor, but also the prior civil litigation experience that I acquired prior to joining the district attorney's office. What I foresaw as a dull and dreary duty has developed into one of the most interesting and challenging assignments of my career.

    Several years ago, I was asked to teach at a national law enforcement conference on asset forfeiture. The topic was the application of the Double Jeopardy Clause to civil asset forfeiture cases, which at that time was a major area of unresolved litigation because of two federal appellate decisions which had determined that civil asset forfeiture cases were multiple punishments in violation of the Fifth Amendment Double Jeopardy Clause. *See United States v. $405,089.23 U.S. Currency*, 33 F.3d 1210 (9th Cir. 1994), *reversed at* 518 U.S. 267 (1996), and *United States v. Ursery*, 59 F.3d 568 (6th Cir. 1995), *reversed at* 518 U.S. 267 (1996). I felt that the one-hour time block that had been allocated for my presentation was inadequate for such a complex topic, and I called the course facilitator to plead for additional time. She gave me this counsel: "Think of your presentation as a cruise along a river and you are the tour guide. Although you do not have sufficient time to describe everything, you can point out the main points of interest as well as where to avoid the submerged rocks, undertow, and other hazards along the way. If you tailor your presentation in this format, you will be able to cover the items of real importance and still remain within the time allocation." This has become my approach to asset forfeiture: to take a very complex topic and to break it down into its basic principles.

When I was asked to write this book, I began by reviewing the published materials in this area. I noted several excellent treatises, but they were too lengthy or detailed for the average practitioner. I did not find any work that a criminal prosecutor, defense attorney, or layman could use as a practice guide: a "how-to" book that could be pulled off the shelf when confronted with a common, practical question.

The purpose of this manual is not to be a detailed, comprehensive examination of a potentially complicated area of law, but rather to set out the common legal and practical issues faced by the asset forfeiture litigator. I have attempted to review the federal statutes and the laws of the 50 states and the District of Columbia to find common principles and then break those down into understandable, logical steps and procedures. Consequently, this book is painted with very broad brushstrokes and does not replace a thorough reading of the relevant statutes or reference to the scholarly treatises.

I hope that this tour down the river will give the reader a better understanding and appreciation of asset forfeiture as an economic remedy in the 21st Century.

Acknowledgments

I first met California Deputy Attorney General Gary W. Schons in 1987 when he was the head of the California Department of Justice Attorney General's Office Special Prosecutions Unit in San Diego, California. Having recently authored the *State of California Asset Seizure and Forfeiture Manual,* he was crisscrossing the state holding small training meetings for prosecutors and law enforcement officers on how to implement the new law. I was impressed by his immense knowledge of the topic and his indefatigable dedication to the use of civil forfeiture as a tool in effective law enforcement. He subsequently authored two subsequent revisions of his state forfeiture practice manual and organized the first statewide asset forfeiture training conference in San Diego in 1989. For his efforts, Gary is affectionately known among California prosecutors as the "Father of California Asset Forfeiture." He is currently Supervising Deputy Attorney General in the San Diego office and a true friend and mentor.

Recognizing the need for consistent professional training, in 1990 Gary Schons and the California Attorney General's Office teamed up with the California District Attorneys Association to hold a second statewide training conference in San Francisco. In organizing that conference, Gary called and asked me to be one of the presenters. That was my first opportunity to teach asset forfeiture and has led to a wonderful long-term relationship with my colleagues and friends of the California law enforcement community.

The torch for asset forfeiture training and publications passed to the California District Attorney's Association when Gary Schons was promoted to Supervising Deputy Attorney General. Since 1990, CDAA has assumed the responsibility for state-wide asset forfeiture instruction and training consultant Ursula Donofrio has been instrumental in overseeing the development of this curricula. Additionally, when revisions to the *State of California Asset Forfeiture and Seizure Manual* became necessary, under Ursula's gentle prodding

Armando Cuellar, Jr. of the Alameda County District Attorney's Office and I updated the previous work of Gary Schons in three subsequent publications in 1996, 2000, and 2006. My association with Ursula Donofrio and other members of the CDAA Asset Forfeiture Training and Education Committee in offering one of the most comprehensive state asset forfeiture training and publications programs in the country has been most pleasant and rewarding.

My first opportunity for national training occurred in 1993 when Merri Hankins, then the director of Training Development for the National District Attorneys Association American Prosecutor's Research Institute, invited me to serve on the faculty of a regional asset forfeiture course that she was holding in Park City, Utah. It was through Merri that I was introduced to the national ethical codes relating to asset forfeiture and given the opportunity to develop training plans on that important topic. Since that date I have taught asset forfeiture ethics to thousands of law enforcement agents and prosecutors throughout the country. This has become the core of my fundamental belief in the values underlying the asset forfeiture program.

In April 1994, through my association with Merri Hankins, I was invited to attend and teach at a State and Local Model Asset Forfeiture Training program at the FBI Academy in Quantico, Virginia. It was here that I first met Alice Dery and Araceli Carrigan, now of the U.S. Department of Justice, Criminal Division, Asset Forfeiture and Money Laundering Section. Alice and Celi have long been interested in developing asset forfeiture training programs for federal, state, and local law enforcement agents and prosecutors. Subsequently, they have kindly invited me as a presenter to many of their federal and state asset forfeiture training programs, and this has led to a long-term teaching relationship with appearances in areas as diverse as New York City to Lafayette, Louisiana, and Honolulu, Hawaii, to Oklahoma City, Oklahoma. In these programs I teach the "Introduction to Forfeiture," which includes an overview of the federal law as well as the state asset forfeiture statute. In preparing this overview I have always reviewed the relevant state statute(s) for the area that we were teaching in, and thus began my interest in the similarities and contrasts between the federal and state forfeiture systems. It was through this study that my interest in preparing this book commenced. I cannot overstate my appreciation to Alice Dery and Araceli Carrigan for their continued professional support and friendship.

I have greatly profited from my relationship with the attorneys and staff of the U.S. Department of Justice, Criminal Division, Asset Forfeiture and Money Laundering Section in Washington, D.C. They have always been helpful and encouraging to me in any request that I have made of them. I especially give credit to the Publications Unit for the excellent resources such as *Quick Release, Asset Forfeiture News,* and other publications that have permitted me to better understand the federal forfeiture program.

I want to pay a special note of appreciation to Stefan D. Cassella of the U.S. Department of Justice Asset Forfeiture and Money Laundering Section for reviewing the initial draft of the first edition of this book. I have always had the highest esteem for Stef's scholarship and legal acumen, and sincerely appreciate a person with his national reputation and stature conducting a critical review of this work. He made significant recommendations to that initial draft and this final product is a much better work on account of his keen eye and legal knowledge.

I also want to express appreciation to Sandra Janzen of the Arizona Attorney General's Office for making specific corrections to the sections relating to the Arizona statute. She has been a long-time friend and teaching colleague in the asset forfeiture community.

Steve Welk, chief of the Asset Forfeiture Unit of the U.S. Attorney's Office in the Central District of California, and his assistant, Monica Tait, have been invaluable resources in tutoring me in federal forfeiture practice during my service as a Special Assistant United States Attorney in their office.

Tim Brandhorst, executive editor of the ABA, has been extremely supportive of this project and has always believed in the value of this work.

Developing my expertise in the area of asset forfeiture would not have been possible without the support of my employer, the San Bernardino County District Attorney's Office. From when I received this assignment in 1990 through March 2008 I have had the full support of my administration to improve and to share my skills in this complex area. I am grateful to all of the elected district attorneys, namely Dennis Kottmeier, Dennis Stout, and Michael Ramos, who have given me the opportunity to serve in this assignment in the office.

The production of this book has been a family affair. Researching the state codes of the 50 states and preparing a final manuscript are arduous tasks. I want to acknowledge the work of my son Jeremy and daughters Emily and Marcie, for their assistance in the research of the state codes, preparation of many of the tables, and citation checking in the first edition. My son Kyle became the prime statute researcher for the second edition, and he did an excellent job.

Finally, I want to give credit to my wife, Nadine, for her unswerving support of my work in asset forfeiture. After thousands of miles of travel and hundreds of hours of research and writing, she continues to stand by my side encouraging me in my professional goals.

Introduction

Follow the Money

On June 17, 1972, the world paid little notice when it was reported that five men had broken into the offices of the Democratic National Committee at the Watergate Hotel in Washington, D.C.[1] However, when it was later discovered that a $25,000 cashiers check earmarked for President Nixon's re-election campaign had been deposited into the bank account of one of the five men arrested in the Watergate break-in, the case took a new direction.[2] Additionally, it was determined that a large number of hundred-dollar bills had been withdrawn from the same account and that several of these bills were found on the five men when they were arrested. A full-scale criminal and congressional investigation was launched in an effort to determine whether the Nixon administration was connected to the illegal break-in.

In their 1974 book, *All the President's Men, Washington Post* reporters Bob Woodward and Carl Bernstein describe a key informant who provided critical information concerning their investigation and was given the code name of "Deep Throat." These meetings between Woodward and Deep Throat were later dramatized in the 1975 film, which depicted Deep Throat in an underground garage uttering the famous words, "Follow the money."

By following the money investigators were able to connect a bungled commercial burglary to the Campaign to Re-elect the President by uncovering a secret slush fund that was being used to fund covert political operations and was managed by high-ranking officials in the White House. This culminated in the eventual resignation of the President of the United States. Following the money was a key development in the investigation and underscored the essential role of money in the underlying criminal activity.

The impact of financial crime on American society is staggering. In 2000, Americans spent $62.4 billion on illegal drugs, and illegal drug trafficking costs our society $110 billion per year in expenses and lost revenue.[3] White-collar crime including health care, bank, government, contract, and telemarketing fraud exacts an even higher cost. The Association of Certified

Fraud Examiners estimates that fraud cost American businesses $600 billion in 2002.[4] The National Fraud Information Center estimates losses of $5.6 million dollars in telemarketing fraud alone.[5] On the international front, Canadian authorities estimate that organized economic crime costs Canadians $5-9 billion each year, illegal drugs another $7-10 billion, and another $5-17 billion per year is involved in money laundering.[6]

Realizing the impact of financial crime on society and the limited success of conventional law enforcement strategies of arrest and incarceration, in 1993 the National District Attorneys Association issued the following statement:

> "Crime in America is a multibillion-dollar industry that has a devastating effect on legitimate economic enterprise by diverting money from lawful commerce while rewarding and financing ongoing illegal activity. Asset forfeiture destroys the money base necessary for the continuation of illegal enterprises and attacks the economic incentive to engage in and to facilitate criminal activity. Asset forfeiture programs then rededicate the money from illegal activity to the public good. The National District Attorneys Association strongly believes that law enforcement and prosecutors should aggressively pursue forfeiture actions to eliminate the instrumentalities of crime and to confiscate the proceeds from criminal acts."[7]

Hence, law enforcement realized that, to stem the mounting societal costs associated with financially motivated crime and to take the financial incentive out of criminal activity, new strategies needed to be developed. This included the freezing, seizing, and confiscation of assets better known as asset forfeiture.

As detailed in the NDAA proclamation asset forfeiture has four main goals:

1. Destroy the money base of illegal enterprises;
2. Deter individuals from using their property to facilitate criminal activity;
3. Confiscate the proceeds of criminal activity;
4. Rededicate the money to the public good.

The importance of financial remedies, including asset forfeiture, was clearly demonstrated in the aftermath of the terrorist attacks of September 11, 2001. One of the first steps taken by President George W. Bush in response to the unprecedented terrorist attacks on American soil was the issuance of an Executive Order freezing any assets belonging to Osama Bin Laden and other groups suspected of funding terrorism.[8] In announcing the role of asset seizure in the war on terrorism, President Bush emphasized that the war on terrorism must be fought on many fronts to "starve the terrorists of funding."[9] More than $104 million of property linked to the al-Qaeda and Taliban groups was frozen and 191 individuals and organizations suspected of terrorism were identified.[10]

What was the difference between the failed 1993 World Trade Center bombing and the devastating strike of September 11? The answer is that the September 11 attack was more disciplined, well organized, and substantially better financed. Whereas the failed 1993 World Trade Center bombing was financed with only $20,000,[11] the September 11 attacks were funded with between $400,000 and $500,000 in overseas funding traced to the al-Qaeda organization, which paid for the hijackers' pilot training, living expenses and airline tickets.[12]

Terrorist experts allege that groups such as al Qaeda and the Taliban fund their illegal activities through a combination of legitimate and illegitimate sources as diverse as credit card fraud, trading in illegal weapons, and drug trafficking, and the sale of diamonds and honey.[13]

A direct connection between United States drug trafficking and the funding of Middle East terrorist groups, including purchasing Stinger surface-to-air missiles for al-Qaeda, was established by DEA in two cases that documented a significant portion of drug proceeds exceeding $4.5 million being transferred overseas. [14]

In 2002, corporate giant Enron collapsed into bankruptcy, wiping out thousands of jobs, more than $60 billion in market value and $2 billion in pension plans.[15] Once the seventh-largest company in America, Enron was destroyed by fraudulent accounting schemes, heaping misery on scores of investors and employees. The government filed forfeiture actions to seize bank accounts, homes, and vehicles from former high-ranking Enron officials to help repay investors part of their losses.[16] This strategy was repeated as federal prosecutors took on cable giant Adelphia and other high-publicity corporate financial fraud cases.[17]

The White House, DEA, and federal prosecutors have discovered that the only way to successfully wage a war against terrorism, drug trafficking or corporate fraud is to attack the money base of the underlying organizations, prevent individuals from using their funds to promote or facilitate the criminal acts, and confiscate the profits of the illegal activity.[18] These are precisely the goals of asset forfeiture as articulated by the National District Attorneys Association.

The September 11 attacks and Enron case remind our nation that most criminal acts have a financial motivation, and until we take away the financial incentive to commit the particular criminal act it will continue. This is why asset forfeiture is such a vital key to the future of law enforcement in a civilized society. Whether the criminal act is terrorism, drug trafficking, child pornography or an array of other financially motivated offenses, asset forfeiture attacks crime at the lowest common denominator: money. Criminals need money either to promote the crime or in an attempt to obtain more money. Americans are familiar with the saying that "Crime does not pay," but in reality it does pay...handsomely. If criminal suspects merely face the threat of incarceration but are allowed to retain the proceeds of their illegal conduct what disincentive is there to prevent recidivism when they realize that their criminal activity reaps such handsome material profits?

The United States Supreme Court has consistently upheld the use of asset forfeiture to prevent illegal activity by stripping offenders of their operating tools and economic base (see *Caplin & Drysdale v. United States*, 491 U.S. 617, 630 (1989)) and to ensure that persons do not profit from their illegal acts. *United States v. Ursery*, 518 U.S. 267, 291 (1996).

Just as following the money changed the course of the Watergate investigation, the use of asset forfeiture is becoming a key element in criminal investigations and prosecutions in the 21st century as governments strive to protect themselves and their citizens against threats to their personal security and economic financial stability.

Understanding the principles and practice of asset forfeiture litigation is vital for every law enforcement investigator or prosecutor who handles any type of financially motivated crime to understand the interrelationship between the underlying criminal action and any corresponding criminal or civil forfeiture sanctions. It is also critical that counsel from the defense bar that represent criminal clients and potential third party interests comprehend the legal issues and procedures that may be facing their clients. Finally, the general public is entitled to some basic facts relating to the application of asset forfeiture in the American legal system and the impact on their individual Constitutional rights. The intent of the author is to prepare a work that may be useful to each group as they strive to understand this increasingly utilized and oft-times misunderstood legal tool.

Notes

1. *5 Held in Plot to Bug Democrats' Office Here*, WASHINGTON POST, June 18, 1972, A01.
2. *Bug Suspects Got Campaign Funds*, WASHINGTON POST, Aug. 1, 1972, A01.
3. National Drug Control Strategy: 2001 Annual Report, Office of National Drug Control Policy, p. 30.
4. *Occupational Fraud: The Audit as Deterrent*, JOURNAL OF ACCOUNTANCY, April 2002, p. 24.
5. National Fraud Information Center: http://www.fraud.org/telemarketing/00statsfinal.htm.
6. Bill 155 – Remedies for Organized Crime and Other Unlawful Activities Act, 2000 at http://www.newswire.ca/government/ontario/english/releases/February2001/20/c4929.html.
7. Resolution of the Board of Directors National District Attorneys Association President's Commission on Model State Drug Laws Economic Remedies, December 1993, p. A-75.
8. Executive Order 13224, Sept. 23, 2001.
9. *Bush Moves to Cut Terrorists' Support*, WASHINGTON POST, Sept.25, 2001, A01.
10. Associated Press, March 11, 2002, at http://news.findlaw.com/ap/o/1110/3-11-2002/200203111015867507.html.
11. *U.S. Ties Hijackers' Money to Al Qaeda*, WASHINGTON POST, Oct. 7, 2001, A01.
12. *U.S. Probe of Sept. 11 Financing Wraps Up*, WASHINGTON POST, Jan. 7, 2002, A01, THE 9-11 COMMISSION REPORT (New York: W.W. Norton & Co. 2004) p. 169.
13. WASHINGTON POST, Jan. 7, 2002, A01; USA TODAY, Oct. 4, 2001 http://www.usatoday.com/news/attack/2001/10/04/assets.html; http://www.msnbc.com/news/633205.asp?pne=msn. The 9-11 Commission found no reliable connection between Bin Laden and drug trafficking or that al Qaeda funded itself through the diamond trade. THE 9-11 COMMISSION REPORT, *Id.* at 171-72.
14. *Drug profits in U.S. linked to terrorists*, VICTOR VALLEY (CAL.) DAILY PRESS, Sept, 2, 2002, A1; *U.S. arrests four in drugs-for-arms plot*, VICTOR VALLEY (CAL.) DAILY PRESS, Nov. 7, 2002, A3.
15. *Associated Press*, Nov. 29, 2007, at http://news.practice. findlaw.com/ap/f/66/11-29-2007/20aa0033e221155.html
16. *Associated Press*, Aug. 22, 2002, at http://news.findlaw.com/ap/f/1310/8-2-2002/20020822051501_02.html; *Federal Officials Target Assets of Enron*

Principals, Houston Chronicle, Aug. 22, 2002, at http://www.highbeam.com/doc/1G1-120225101.html; *Former Enron treasurer argues against money forfeiture,* USA Today, Dec. 30, 2002.

17.   *Associated Press,* Nov. 6, 2002, at http://news.findlaw.com/ap/f/1310/11-6-2002/20021106034501_05.html; *Adelphia founder sentenced to 15 years,* CNNMoney, June 20, 2005, at http://money.cnn.com/2005/06/20/news/newsmakers/rigas_sentencing.

18.   In a recent federal criminal conviction against a wealthy Long Island, New York, couple involving imprisonment, torture, and forced labor, the jury determined that the couple's 5,898-square-foot home worth between $1.6 and $2.8 million should be forfeited. *See Slavery Conviction to Cost N.Y. Couple Their Lavish Home,* Victor Valley (Cal.) Daily Press, Dec. 19, 2007 at B3.

1 Forfeiture Terminology

A. Introduction

One of the most challenging aspects of asset forfeiture is mastering the various legal concepts and principles that are its foundation. With roots in Biblical and English common law, the unwary practitioner can become bewildered when confronted with concepts that he has not heard discussed since he left the halls of law school, if even then. This chapter will review some of the basic terms and concepts utilized in asset forfeiture practice.

B. Definition

Asset forfeiture has been described as the divestiture without compensation of property used in a manner contrary to the laws of the sovereign. *See United States v. Eight Rhodesian Statues*, 449 F. Supp. 193, 195 (C.D. Cal. 1978). In other words, the government confiscates the property because it has been used in violation of the law and to require disgorgement of the fruits of the illegal conduct. *See United States v. Ursery*, 518 U.S. 267, 284 (1996).

C. Jurisdiction

Remember the law school discussions about types of jurisdiction? Hopefully you paid attention enough to discern the difference between *in personam* and *in rem* jurisdiction.

1. *In Personam* Jurisdiction

In personam jurisdiction is simple to comprehend as it is against a specific individual. *See Black's Law Dictionary*, 4th edition, West Publishing, St. Paul, Minn., 1968 p. 899. In this type of jurisdiction the person or individual becomes the party to the lawsuit. The prosecuting authority files charges against the defendant *in personam* and that is reflected in the caption of the pleading (i.e., *People v. Orenthal James Simpson*). For example, in criminal actions, the court obtains jurisdiction over the defendant when she is arraigned in court. From that point on until the conclusion of the action the court has jurisdiction over the defendant and she is personally liable to comply with the orders of the court. If she fails to appear in court, the magistrate issues a bench warrant for her arrest. If she is convicted of the criminal offense the judge may impose a sentence over the defendant such as a fine, probation terms or jail time because he has *in personam* jurisdiction over her.

The same principle applies to civil actions. In a civil *in personam* action the case is filed against a specific individual whose name is listed in the pleading caption (i.e., *Fredrick Goldman v. Orenthal James Simpson*). Once the lawsuit is filed, the first action is to serve the defendant with notice of the lawsuit and a summons ordering him to file a response with the court. That action gives the court *in personam* jurisdiction over the defendant and he becomes subject to the power of the court. Failure to comply with the orders of the court can subject him to an adverse judgment enforceable against him personally.

2. *In Rem* Jurisdiction

In rem jurisdiction is not against a specific individual but is designed with reference to all whom it may concern i.e. "all the world." *See Black's Law Dictionary*, 4th edition, *Ibid.* Here the court obtains jurisdiction against the property rather than the wrongdoer based on the legal fiction that the property is "guilty." The subject of the lawsuit is the property itself and it becomes the party of the litigation. Hence the legal pleading caption may contain such interesting parties as "*United States v. One Assortment of 89 Firearms.*" *See* 465 U.S. 354 (1984) or "*One 1958 Plymouth Sedan v. Pennsylvania.*" *See* 380 U.S. 693 (1965). Notice is given to all potential individuals who may have a legal interest in the property and if they desire to contest the *in rem* action they must file a legal response as "claimants." Since the court has jurisdiction over the property, it will decide which party has the superior legal claim to the property.

D. Methods of Forfeiture

There are various methods that are utilized to implement asset forfeiture which **include non-judicial forfeiture** such as **summary** and **administrative** forfeiture and **judicial forfeiture** comprising **criminal** and **civil** forfeitures.

1. Summary Forfeiture

This forfeiture works by operation of law. It applies to items that the law has declared to have no lawful or legitimate purpose and is therefore characterized as contraband per se. These forfeitures are generally effectuated without formal legal process. When the property that has been seized has no further evidentiary value the law permits the law enforcement agents to destroy it. Examples of items subject to summary forfeiture include controlled substances. *See N.C. Gen. Stat.* § 90-112(e)) and drug paraphernalia (*Ark. Code Ann.* § 5-64-505(b).

2. Administrative Forfeiture

Administrative forfeiture entails forfeiture of property without formal court action. When statutorily authorized it permits a law enforcement or prosecutorial agency to give notice to potential claimants that property has been seized based on probable cause that it is subject to forfeiture and unless a claim is filed opposing the administrative forfeiture action, the agency will declare the property forfeit to the Government.

The rationale for granting administrative forfeiture authority is that it is faster and less expensive than judicial cases and conserves judicial time and resources on uncontested matters. *See In re Application for Warrant to Seize One 1988 Chevrolet Monte Carlo,* 861 F.2d 307, 310 (1st Cir. 1988); *United States v. $57,960.00 in U.S. Currency,* 58 F. Supp. 2d 660, 664-65 (D.S.C. 1999); *United States v. Ninety-Three (93) Firearms,* 330 F.3d 414, 422 (6th Cir. 2003); *People v. Angeloni,* 40 Cal. App. 4th 1267, 1271 (1995).

There are four basic elements for administrative forfeiture actions.

1. Notice of the forfeiture action must be served on all potentially interested parties;
2. Notice of the forfeiture proceeding must be published in a newspaper of general circulation;
3. If no claim opposing forfeiture is filed during the statutorily required period of actual or published notice the item is declared forfeit by the administrative agency.
4. If a claim opposing forfeiture is filed, then the administrative forfeiture proceeding halts and the matter is converted into a judicial forfeiture action.

These are civil actions and when they are uncontested, probable cause is sufficient to sustain the forfeiture. Examples of administrative forfeitures are found at 19 U.S.C. § 1602 et seq. (federal customs statutes) and *Georgia Code Annotated* § 16-13-49(n).

For a list of states that authorize administrative or uncontested forfeiture see Table 1-1.

Table 1-1
Summary of State Asset Forfeiture Statutes
Administrative/Uncontested Forfeiture

State	Statute
Alaska*	Ak. Stat. § 17.30.116
Arizona*	Ariz. Rev. Stat. Ann. § 13-4309
California	Cal. Health & Safety Code § 11488.4 (j)
Delaware	Del. Code Ann. Title 16 § 4784 (b) & § 4791 (c)
District of Columbia	D.C. Code § 48-905.02 (d)(3)
Georgia	Ga. Code Ann. § 16-13-49 (n)
Hawaii	Hawaii Rev. Stat. § 712A-10
Illinois	725 ILCS 150/6
Iowa	Iowa Code Ann. § 809A.8
Kansas*	Kan. Stat. Ann. § 60-4109
Louisiana*	La. Rev. Stat. Ann. § 40:2608
Michigan	Mich. Comp. Laws §§ 333.7523; 600.4707
Minnesota	Minn. Stat. Ann. § 609.5314
Mississippi	Miss. Code Ann. § 41-29-176
New Hampshire	N.H. Rev. Stat. Ann. Title 30 § 318B:17-d
Oregon*	Ore. Rev. Stat. Ann. § 475A.055
Rhode Island	R.I. Gen. Laws § 21-28-5.04.2 (h)
Tennessee	Tenn. Code Ann. § 53-11-201
Washington	Wash. Rev. Code Ann. § 69.50.505 (3)

* Uncontested forfeiture (See Chapter 2, section G.2)

3. Criminal Forfeiture

Criminal forfeitures are *in personam* actions filed in conjunction with criminal charges. Therefore, it is the defendant's *interest* in the property that is forfeited rather than the actual property itself. *See United States v. Gilbert,* 244 F.3d 888, 919-20 (11th Cir. 2001). Generally the forfeiture count or allegation is included on the criminal indictment or information but could also be initiated by a separately filed petition. Criminal forfeiture requires that the defendant be convicted of the related criminal offense. *See United States v. Aramony,* 88 F.3d 1369, 1387 n. 11 (4th Cir. 1996). If the underlying criminal conviction is reversed, or the defendant dies prior to sentencing there can be no criminal forfeiture. *United States v. Cherry,* 330 F.3d 658, 670 (4th Cir. 2003); *United States v. Lay,* 456 F. Supp. 2d 869, 875 (S.D. Tex. 2006). Some jurisdictions require that the forfeiture action be proven beyond a reasonable doubt. *See Cal. Penal Code* § 186.5(d), but others permit forfeiture by a preponderance of the evidence. *See Tenn. Code Ann.* § 39-11-708(d). Under federal law criminal forfeiture is considered part of the sentence and may be proven by preponderance of the evidence. *See Libretti v. United States,* 516 U.S. 29, 36 (1995); *United States v. Dicter,* 198 F.3d 1284, 1289 (11th Cir. 1999); *United States v. Garcia-Guizar,* 160 F.3d 511, 517-18 (9th Cir. 1998); *United States v. Ferrario-Pozzi,* 368 F.3d 5, 8 (1st Cir. 2004).

There are a few unique features of criminal forfeiture. Since it is an *in personam* action, prior seizure of the property is not required for court jurisdiction and the right to possession remains with the owner. This poses obvious risks, especially if the owner is also a defendant and knows of the impending forfeiture action. If the defendant/owner is allowed to retain possession of the property pending the conclusion of the criminal action there is a concern that it will be sold, concealed or diminished in value prior to the criminal forfeiture judgment. Therefore the government will seek to obtain some type of restraining order to protect its interest. *See* 21 U.S.C. § 853(e).

Most criminal forfeiture statutes provide for a bifurcated trial that determines the defendant's guilt followed by a special finding by the court or jury on whether his interest in the assets is subject to forfeiture. *See Fed. R. Crim. P.* 32.2(b). Since it is an *in personam* action and limited to the defendant's interest in the property, an ancillary proceeding is necessary to forfeit all third party interests. Therefore, the preliminary order of forfeiture is followed by an ancillary hearing held before the same criminal court where third parties may litigate their interest in the property prior to the final order of forfeiture. *See Fed. R. Crim. P.* 32.2(c).

A criminal forfeiture order has a long reach as it may be entered as a money judgment against the defendant, directly against the defendant's interest in specific assets or against the defendant's substitute assets. *See United States v. Candelaria-Silva,* 166 F.3d 19, 42 (1st Cir. 1999). One of the prime advantages of criminal forfeiture is that it permits the forfeiture of substitute assets. This means that if the property subject to forfeiture cannot be found, or is beyond the jurisdiction of the court, other property owned by the defendant of equal value to the forfeitable property can be ordered forfeited. *See* 18 U.S.C. § 1963(m). Additionally all defendants subject to the criminal forfeiture judgment are jointly and severally liable. *See United States v. Simmons,* 154 F.3d 765, 769 (8th Cir. 1998); *United States v. Corrado,* 227 F.3d 543, 553 (6th Cir. 2000); *United States v. Faulk,* 340 F. Supp. 2d 1312, 1313 (M.D. Ala. 2004). Examples of criminal forfeiture statutes are found at 21 U.S.C. § 853 (federal) and *Ohio Rev. Code Ann.* § 2925.42. For a list of states that have criminal forfeiture statutes see Table 1-2.

Table 1-2
Summary of State Asset Forfeiture Statutes
Criminal Forfeiture

State	Statute
Alaska	Ak. Stat. § 17.30.112
Arizona	Ariz. Rev. Stat. Ann. § 13-4312
California	Cal. Penal Code § 186.2 *et seq.*
Colorado	Colo. Rev. Stat. § 18-17-102 to 18-17-109
Florida	Fla. Stat. Ann. § 895.05
Georgia	Ga. Code Ann. § 16-13-49 (j)
Hawaii	Haw. Rev. Stat. § 712A-13
Idaho	Idaho Code §§ 37-2801 to 37-2815
Kentucky	Ky. Rev. Stat. Ann. § 500.090
Maine	Me. Rev. Stat. Ann. Title 15 ch. 57 § 5826
Maryland	Md. Code Crim. Proc. §§ 13-101 to 13-206
Minnesota	Minn. Stat. Ann. §§ 609.905 to 609.908
Nebraska	Neb. Rev. Stat. § 28-431
Nevada	Nev. Rev. Stat. §§ 207.420 to 207.450; 207.490
New York	N.Y. Penal Code Law §§ 480.00 to 480.35
North Carolina	N.C. Gen. Stat. §§ 90-112 to 90-113.2
Ohio	Ohio Rev. Code Ann. §§ 2925.42 and 2923.32
Oregon	Or. Rev. Stat. §§ 131-550 to 131-602
Rhode Island	R.I. Gen. Laws § 21-28.5.04.1
Tennessee	Tenn. Code Ann. § 39-11-708 (d)
Virginia	Va. Code Ann. §§ 19.2-368.19 to 19.2-386
Wisconsin	Wis. Stat. Ann. § 973.075

4. Civil Forfeiture

There are two forms of civil forfeitures: civil *in rem* and civil *in personam*. Each will be discussed separately.

Civil *In Rem* Forfeiture

This is a civil *in rem* action against the property. To initiate the forfeiture action the court should obtain actual or constructive control over the property. *See Republic National Bank v. United States,* 506 U.S. 80, 84 (1992); *United States v. One Oil Painting,* 362 F. Supp. 2d 1175, 1180 (C.D. Cal. 2005); *Matter of One Hundred Thirteen Thousand Eight Hundred Eighty-eight Dollars ($113,888.00) U.S. Currency,* 168 Ariz. 229, 812 P.2d 1047, 1050 (Ariz. App. 1990). Control signifies that the court has the power to direct or manage the property. *People v. Thirty-Three Thousand Two Hundred and Twelve Dollars,* 83 P.3d 1206, 1210 (Colo. App. 2003). Civil *in rem* forfeiture statutes permit law enforcement to immediately seize and retain possession of the property pending the resolution of the proceedings. Most statutes provide for seizure of the property by issuance of an arrest warrant *in rem,* seizure warrant, or permit warrantless seizure based on probable cause.

Since it is a civil action, a lower burden of proof such as probable cause or preponderance of the evidence is sufficient to establish the forfeiture. No criminal conviction is required. *See The Palmyra,* 25 U.S. 1, 15 (1827). Even if the defendant is acquitted of the underlying criminal case, the government can still proceed on the related civil forfeiture case provided it has sufficient evidence to meet the civil burden of proof. *See United States v. One Assortment of 89 Firearms,* 465 U.S. 354, 366 (1984); *One Lot of Emerald Cut Stones v. United States,* 409 U.S. 232, 234-35 (1972). Also, hearsay evidence may be used to establish probable cause. *See United States v. Property at 4492 S. Livonia Road,* 889 F.2d 1258, 1267 (2d Cir. 1989).

Examples of civil *in rem* forfeiture statutes are found at 21 U.S.C. § 881 (federal) and *Mass. Ann. Laws* Ch. 94C § 47.

A list of state jurisdictions that utilize civil *in rem* forfeiture statutes is included as Table 1-3.

Table 1-3
Summary of State Asset Forfeiture Statutes Civil In Rem Forfeiture

State	Statute
Alabama	Ala. Code § 20-2-93
Alaska	Ak. Stat. § 17.30.112
Arizona	Ariz. Rev. Stat. Ann. § 13-4311
Arkansas	Ark. Code Ann. § 5-64-505
California	Cal. Health and Safety Code §§ 11469 to 11495
Colorado	Colo. Rev. Stat. §§ 16-13-301 to 16-13-702
Connecticut	Conn. Gen. Stat. Ann. § 54-36h
Delaware	Del. Code Ann. Title 16 §§ 4784 to 4791
District of Columbia	D.C. Code Ann. § 48-905.02
Florida	Fla. Stat. Ann. §§ 932.701 to 932.707
Georgia	Ga. Code Ann. § 16-13-49 (o)
Hawaii	Haw. Rev. Stat. § 712A-12
Idaho	Idaho Code §§ 37-2744 to 37-2751
Illinois	720 ILCS 550/12; 725 ILCS 150/1-14; 725 ILCS 175/1-11
Indiana	Ind. Code Ann. §§ 34-24-1-1 to 34-24-1-9
Iowa	Iowa Code Ann. § 809A.13
Kansas	Kan. Stat. Ann. § 60-4113
Kentucky	Ky. Rev. Stat. Ann. § 218A.405 to 460
Louisiana	La. Rev. Stat. Ann. §§ 40:2611 to 40:2612
Maine	Me. Rev. Stat. Ann. Title 15, ch. 517 §§ 5821 to 5825
Maryland	Md. Ann. Code Crim. Proc. §§ 12-101 to 12-505
Massachusetts	Mass. Ann. Laws ch. 94C § 47
Michigan	Mich. Comp. Laws §§ 333.7521 to 333.7525; §§ 600.4701 to 600.4709
Minnesota	Minn. Stat. Ann. § 609.531 (6a)

Table 1-3 (continued)
Summary of State Asset Forfeiture Statutes Civil In Rem Forfeiture

State	Statute
Mississippi	Miss. Code Ann. §§ 41-29-153 to 41-29-185
Missouri	Mo. Ann. Stat. § 513.607
Montana	Mont. Code Ann. §§ 44-12-101 to 44-12-206
Nevada	Nev. Rev. Stat. §§ 179.1156 to 179.121; § 453.301
New Hampshire	N.H. Rev. Stat. Ann. §§ 318-B:17-b to 318-B:17-f
New Jersey	N.J. Stat. Ann. §§ 2C:64-1 to 2C:64-9
New Mexico	N.M. Code Ann. Section §§ 30-31-34 to 30-31-37
North Dakota	N.D. Cent. Code §§ 19-03.1-36.1 to 19-03.1-38
Ohio	Ohio Rev. Code Ann. § 2925.43
Oklahoma	Okla. Stat. Ann. §§ 63-2-503 to 63-2-508
Oregon	Ore. Rev. Stat. §§ 475A.005 to 475A.160
Pennsylvania	Pa. Consol. Stat. Ann. Title 35 §§ 831.1 to 831.5; Title 42 §§ 6801-6802
Rhode Island	R.I. Gen. Laws § 21-28-5.04.2
South Carolina	S.C. Code Ann. §§ 44-53-520 to 44-53-590
South Dakota	S.D. Codified Laws Ann. §§ 34-20B-70 to 34-20B-92
Tennessee	Tenn. Code § 39-11-708 (a); § 53-11-201 to 203; §§ 53-11-451 to 452; §§ 40-33-101 to 215
Texas	Tex. Code of Crim Proc. §§ 59.01 to 59.11
Utah	Utah Code Ann § 24-1-4
Vermont	Vt. Stat. Ann. Title 18 §§ 4241 to 4248
Virginia	Va. Code Ann. §§ 19.2-386.1 to 19.2-386.31
Washington	Wash. Rev. Code Ann. §§ 69.50.505 to 69.50.520
West Virginia	W. Va. Code § 60A-7-701 to 707
Wisconsin	Wis. Stat. Ann. § 961.555 (1)
Wyoming	Wyo. Stat. § 35-7-1049 to 1053

Civil *In Personam* Forfeiture

These are civil actions brought against a person for the assets acquired or maintained through the conduct giving rise to the forfeiture. They are *in personam* actions that determine **liability** rather than **criminal culpability**. Therefore no criminal conviction is required as a predicate to this forfeiture. Once the court makes a determination of liability it enters a judgment of forfeiture for the property found subject to forfeiture. Property interests held by third parties may be resolved in an ancillary hearing or a separately filed *in rem* action. *See* The White House President's Commission on Model State Drug Laws, *Economic Remedies, Commission Forfeiture Reform Act (CFRA)*, December 1993, p. A-56 to A-58.

One aspect of civil *in personam* forfeiture that it shares in common with criminal forfeiture is that it provides for money judgments and the forfeiture of substitute assets if the forfeitable property cannot be located or is beyond the jurisdiction of the court.

Civil *in personam* forfeitures are rarely found in the federal forfeiture statutes[1] but do exist in ten states. See Table 1-4. States with civil *in personam* forfeiture statutes include Arizona, *See Ariz. Rev. Stat. Ann.* § 13-4312, and New York, *See N.Y. Civil Practice Law* § 1310-1352.

Table 1-4
Summary of State Asset Forfeiture Statutes
Civil In Personam Forfeiture

State	Statute
Arizona	Ariz. Rev. Stat. Ann. § 13-4312
Arkansas	Ark. Code Ann. § 5-64-505 (j)
Georgia	Ga. Code Ann. § 16-13-49 (p)
Hawaii	Haw. Rev. Stat. § 712A-13
Iowa	Iowa Code Ann. § 809A.14
Kansas	Kan. Stat. Ann. § 60-4114
Louisiana	La. Rev. Stat. Ann. § 40:2613
Missouri	Mo. Ann. Stat. § 513.607 5
New York	N.Y. C.P.L.R. § 1310 to 1352
Wisconsin	Wis. Stat. Ann. § 961.555 (1)

E. Theories of Forfeiture

There are four basic theories that subject property to forfeiture. They are contraband, proceeds, facilitation, and enterprise forfeitures.

1. Contraband Forfeiture

Contraband per se is property that is illegal to possess because the legislature has determined that it has no lawful purpose. No one can have a legal right in contraband and any property interest is extinguished by operation of law. See Cooper v. Greenwood, 904 F.2d 302, 304-05 (5th Cir. 1990); Helton v. Hunt, 330 F.3d 242, 247 (4th Cir. 2003). Thus, there is no innocent owner exemption for contraband forfeitures. United States v. 144,774 Pounds of Blue King Crab, 410 F.3d 1131, 1136 (9th Cir. 2005). Examples of contraband per se include illegal narcotics, State v. One Hundred Seventy-Five Thousand Eight Hundred Dollars U.S. Currency, 942 P.2d 343, 349 (Utah 1997), and counterfeit currency. See 49 U.S.C. § 80302.

Some statutes make reference to **derivative contraband**. This is property that is lawful to possess but is subject to forfeiture because it has been used in some manner to facilitate the underlying crime involving contraband per se. (i.e., Scales and plastic baggies found along with controlled substances, car used to transport illegal drugs or a firearm involved in a drug trafficking offense.) Since the property has a legitimate purpose it can only be forfeited upon proper due process and a finding of its nexus to the underlying criminal activity. See United States v. Rodriguez-Aguirre, 264 F.3d 1195, 1213 n. 13 (10th Cir. 2001); State v. Giles, 697 So.2d 699, 703 (La. App. 1997). Derivative contraband will be discussed under facilitation forfeitures.

2. Proceeds Forfeiture

This is one of the most powerful tools in the prosecutor's arsenal of weapons as it forfeits property that is traceable directly or indirectly to the illegal activity. It includes all interest, dividends, income or property derived from the original illegal transaction, See United States v. One 1980 Rolls Royce, 905 F.2d 89, 91 (5th Cir. 1990), including the appreciation in the value of the property. See United States v. Hawkey, 148 F.3d 920, 928 (8th Cir. 1998); United States v. Real Estate Located at 116 Villa Rella Dr., 675 F. Supp. 645, 646 (S.D. Fla. 1987).

There is no requirement to trace the proceeds to a particular criminal transaction. It is sufficient to connect the item to the criminal offense in general. See United States v. Four Million Two Hundred Fifty-Five Thousand, 762

F.2d 895, 903 (11th Cir. 1985). It is not necessary to prove that the item seized was "directly" purchased with illicit proceeds. No matter how many times the property changes form it is still subject to forfeiture. *See United States v. $33,000 U.S. Currency,* 640 F. Supp. 898, 900 (D. Md. 1986); *United States v. Swanson,* 394 F.3d 520, 529 n. 4 (7th Cir. 2005). Traceable proceeds includes an asset indirectly exchanged for the illicit funds in one or more "intervening legitimate transactions, or otherwise changed in form . . ." *See United States v. Banco Cafetero Panama,* 797 F.2d 1154, 1158 (2d Cir. 1986).

The government is required to establish a nexus between the property to be forfeited and the criminal violation. If the theory of forfeiture is that the money is related to drug sales, it is essential to produce sufficient evidence to connect the seized property to a narcotic transaction or trafficking. A general suspicion of criminal activity is not enough. *See United States v. $191,910.00 U.S.* Currency, 16 F.3d 1051, 1071 (9th Cir. 1994); *United States v. $30,060.00,* 39 F.3d 1039, 1044 (9th Cir. 1994); *People v. $47,050,* 17 Cal.App.4th 1319, 1324 (1993). The evidence produced must be sufficient to meet the applicable burden of proof required under the statute. *See* 19 U.S.C. § 1615 "probable cause" versus 18 U.S.C. § 983(c) "preponderance of the evidence."

The government carries the burden of tracing the illicit funds to the seized asset. *See United States v. Gonzalez,* 240 F.3d 14, 17 (1st Cir. 2001). If an asset has been purchased with commingled legitimate and illegitimate funds, forfeiture is limited to the portion traceable to the illegal activity. *See United States v. Pole No. 3172 (Hopkinton),* 852 F.2d 636, 639-40 (1st Cir. 1988); *United States v. One 1980 Rolls Royce,* 905 F.2d 89, 91 (5th Cir. 1990); *United States v. One Parcel Known as 352 Northrup St.,* 40 F.Supp. 2d 74, 78 (D. R.I. 1999).

One state statute uses the term "substitute proceeds." *See New York Civil Practice Law* § 1310.3. This is another way of distinguishing proceeds directly traced to the illicit activity and assets indirectly obtained in the sale or exchange of the proceed property in subsequent intervening transactions. *District Atty. of Queens County v. McAulifee,* 129 Misc.2d 416; 493 N.Y.S.2d 406, 409 (N.Y. Sup. 1985). Most forfeiture statutes do not delineate between "proceeds" and "substitute proceeds." *See* 21 U.S.C. § 881(a)(6). In order to not confuse the reader between this term and "substitute assets" the term "substitute proceeds" will not be used in this work.

3. Facilitation Forfeiture

Forfeitable property used in criminal activity is often referred to as "instrumentality" or "facilitation" forfeitures. Although these words are often used interchangeably there are subtle yet important differences between the two terms.

Instrumentality forfeitures are defined as property that "contributes directly and materially to the commission of the crime." *See N.Y. Civil Practice Law* § 1310.4. The term refers to the actual means by which the offense was committed and limits forfeiture to that property and no more. *See United States v. Bajakajian,* 524 U.S. 321, 333, n. 8 (1998). Therefore, property forfeited as an instrumentality is directly related to the offense. Examples include actual funds laundered in a money laundering offense. *See* 18 U.S.C. § 981 (a)(1)(A); obscene materials. *See* 18 U.S.C. § 1467(a)(1); and child pornography. *See* 18 U.S.C. § 2253(a)(1).

Some statutes use the term "contraband" to refer to property that is subject to forfeiture because it has been used as an instrumentality in the commission of a criminal offense. *See Fla. Stat. Ann.* § 932.701(2)(a)(5) (1997). This property is not really being forfeited as "contraband per se" on the theory that it is illegal to possess, but rather as "**derivative contraband**" on an instrumentality theory that it was directly involved in the criminal offense. *See Florida v. White,* 526 U.S. 559, 564 n. 3 (1999); *State v. One 1994 Ford Thunderbird,* 349 N.J. Super. 352; 793 A.2d 792, 803 (N.J. Super. A.D. 2002). Thus the court in *One 1958 Plymouth Sedan v. Pennsylvania,* 380 U.S. 693, 699 (1965) declined to uphold the forfeiture of a vehicle used to transport illegal liquor as "contraband per se" reasoning that: "There is nothing even remotely criminal in possessing an automobile" and categorized the property forfeitable under the statute as "derivative contraband." The courts consider property forfeited as an "instrumentality" or "derivative contraband" to be the same category. *See Bennis v. Michigan,* 516 U.S. 442, 460 (1996).

Facilitation forfeitures apply to property that has been used or intended to be used in the unlawful activity. It is property that makes it easier to conduct the illegal activity. *See United States v. One 1977 Lincoln Mark V Coupe,* 643 F.2d 154, 157 (3d Cir. 1981); *Burmila v. One 1988 Chevrolet Auto,* 211 Ill.App.3d 238, 239; 581 N.E.2d 757 (Ill. App. 1991). The property need not be integral, essential or indispensable to the illicit offense, but merely make the prohibited conduct less difficult or free from obstruction. *United States v. Schifferli,* 895 F.2d 987, 990 (4th Cir. 1990). A vehicle used for transportation to and from a crime scene, or to obtain drugs for sale are examples of facilitation theory forfeitures. *City of Worthington Police Dept. v. One 1988 Chevrolet Berretta,* 516 N.W.2d 581, 584 (Mn. App. 1994); *Com. v. One 1975 Pontiac Coupe,* 18 Pa. D. & C.3d 236, 238 (Pa. Com. Pl. 1981).

Facilitating forfeitures have a much broader sweep than instrumentality forfeitures as they may include property that "is used or intended to be used *in any manner or part* to commit or facilitate the commission of a violation. . . ." *See* 21 U.S.C. § 881 (a)(7). Facilitation forfeiture statutes put property owners on notice that they must not allow their property to be used to assist criminal offenses. *See Bennis v. Michigan,* 516 U.S. 442, 452 (1996).

How strong must the connection be between the criminal offense and the facilitation property? Although earlier federal appellate opinions were not uniform on this point *(see United States v. Daccarett,* 6 F.3d 37, 56 (2d Cir. 1993) "nexus" versus *United States v. One 1986 Ford Pickup,* 56 F.3d 1181, 1187 (9th Cir. 1995) "substantial connection"), it appears that the current trend is to require that the government show a **substantial** connection between the property to be forfeited and the criminal activity. This is certainly the case in federal forfeiture. With the enactment of the Civil Asset Forfeiture Reform Act of 2000 (106 P.L. 185; 114 Stat. 202) federal law now requires a substantial connection between the property and the offense. *See* 18 U.S.C. § 983(c)(3); *United States v. Real Property in Section 9,* 308 F. Supp. 2d 791, 806 (E.D. Mich. 2004).

State courts have also struggled with this issue with some requiring only "some nexus" or "more than incidental or fortuitous connection" between the property and the illegal use, *People v. $1,124,905 U.S. Currency,* 177 Ill.2d 314, 685 N.E.2d 1370, 1382 (Ill. 1997); *Katner v. State,* 655 N.E.2d 345, 349-50 (Ind. 1995) but the vast majority requiring a "substantial connection." *Matter of Kaster,* 454 N.W.2d 876, 879 (Iowa 1990); *In re Forfeiture of 301 Cass Street,* 194 Mich. App. 381; 487 N.W.2d 795, 797 (Mich. App. 1992); *Riley v. 1987 Station Wagon,* 650 N.W.2d 441, 445 (Minn. 2002); *$9,050.00 in U.S. Currency. v. State,* 874 S.W.2d 158, 161 (Tex. App. 1994); *Lee v. Com.,* 253 Va. 222, 225; 482 S.E.2d 802 (Va. 1997).

The distinction between facilitation, and instrumentality or derivative contraband forfeitures may have significance in constitutional analysis under the Eighth Amendment excessive fines clause. *See* Chapter 12 Section B.

Recent federal legislation now subjects property **"Involved in"** criminal offenses such as money laundering, 18 U.S.C. § 981(a)(1); currency transaction report violations 31 U.S.C. § 5317(c), and terrorism, 18 U.S.C. § 981(a)(1)(G) to forfeiture.

Courts have defined property "Involved in" to include the actual funds laundered, or corpus of the offense, plus any facilitating property. *See United States v. Tencer,* 107 F.3d 1120, 1134 (5th Cir. 1997); *United States v. All*

Monies ($477,048.62), 754 F. Supp. 1467, 1473 (D. Haw. 1991); *United States v. Modi*, 178 F. Supp. 2d 658, 663 (D.W. Va. 2001).[2]

Examples of property forfeited under this theory include the actual funds transferred through a bank account, *United States v. Voigt*, 89 F.3d 1050, 1084-85 (3d Cir. 1996); all property acquired with the funds of the financial transaction, *United States v. One 1988 Prevost Liberty Motor Home*, 952 F. Supp. 1180, 1210 (S.D. Tex. 1996); and property used to facilitate the underlying criminal offense, *United States v. Wyly*, 193 F.3d 289, 302 (5th Cir. 1999). It is the most expansive version of the facilitation forfeiture theory and can be used to reach property that may not otherwise be completely forfeitable under other theories such as proceeds. *See United States v. McGauley*, 279 F.3d 62, 76-77 (1st Cir. 2002).

4. Enterprise Forfeiture

One final theory is enterprise forfeiture. This permits the government to forfeit the interest or control of any enterprise that a person has conducted or operated in conjunction with the criminal offense giving rise to the forfeiture. It is commonly used in federal and state RICO actions. *United States v. Cauble*, 706 F.2d 1322, 1346 (5th Cir. 1983). The goal is to reach the assets of corrupt organizations beyond those actually tainted by the illegal racketeering activity. *United States v. Segal*, 495 F.3d 826, 838-39 (7th Cir. 2007). The State of Arizona used this theory to forfeit the prospective royalties that "Sammy the Bull" Gravano was anticipating from a book detailing his criminal activities as a member of the Gambino organized crime family. *State ex rel. Napolitano v. Gravano*, 204 Ariz. 106, 60 P.3d 246, 256 (Ariz. App. 2002). This theory of forfeiture is not used extensively and is basically limited to federal racketeering violations under 18 U.S.C. § 1963(a)(2) and states with RICO and civil *in personam* forfeiture statutes.

F. Concepts of Forfeiture

In analyzing forfeiture statutes it is important to identify whether the statute is punitive or remedial as the courts may look at this distinction in determining which Constitutional protections apply.[3]

1. Punitive Statutes

A punitive statute is defined as a penalty intended to punish an individual based on his criminal culpability. Criminal punishment includes incarceration, fine, parole, and probation. *See Witte v. United States*, 515 U.S. 389

(1995). Criminal forfeiture is considered punitive. *See Alexander v. United States*, 509 U.S. 544, 558 (1993); *United States v. Bajakajian*, 524 U.S. 321, 325 (1998).

2. Remedial Statutes

A remedial law is defined as a sanction intended as a remedy to compensate society for damages due to the illegal activity. Some of the underlying bases for remedial statutes include removing dangerous or illegal items from society (*United States v. One Assortment of 89 Firearms*, 465 U.S. 354, 364 (1984)); protecting the nation against smuggled goods (*One Lot of Emerald Cut Stones v. United* States, 409 U.S. 232, 237 (1972)); reducing the financial incentive to commit the crime, compensating society for the economic damage due to the illegal activity, lessening economic and political power (*Caplin & Drysdale v. United States*, 491 U.S. 617, 630 (1989)); and restoring economic integrity to the marketplace.

Courts are now analyzing whether forfeiture statutes are punitive or remedial in determining if certain constitutional protections apply. *Serchion v. State*, 230 Ga. App. 336; 496 S.E.2d 333, 338 (Ga. App. 1998) (Georgia statute non-punitive); *State v. Eleven Thousand Five Hundred Sixty-Six ($11,566.00) Dollars*, 919 P.2d 34, 38 (Okla. App. 1996) (Oklahoma statute civil and remedial); *Katner v. State*, 655 N.E.2d 345, 347 (Ind. 1995) (Indiana statute non-punitive and remedial); *Jenkins v. Com.*, 13 Va. App. 420; 411 S.E.2d 841, 842, (Va. App. 1991) (Virginia statute is civil and not punishment).

In general, contraband and proceed theory forfeitures have been determined to be remedial. *See United States v. One Assortment of Firearms*, 465 U.S. at 364; *United States v. Ursery*, 518 U.S. 267, 291 (1996), and facilitation forfeitures have been found to be punitive. *See Austin v. United States*, 509 U.S. 602, 621 (1993). A complete discussion of this issue is found in Chapter 12 on Constitutional Protections.

G. Comparison of Forfeiture Laws

Determining which type of forfeiture action to file is a strategic decision that requires the prosecutor to balance several factors of benefits and weaknesses. This section will be a summary of the various methods of forfeiture and a discussion of the relative advantages and drawbacks of each form. The reader is directed to the comparison chart listed in Table 1-5.

Table 1-5
Summary of Asset Forfeiture Legal Terminology

Method of Forfeiture	Jurisdiction	Theory of Forfeiture	Concept of Forfeiture	Benefits	Weaknesses
Summary (Non-judicial)	In Rem	1. Contraband	Remedial	1. By operation of law 2. Requires no formal process 3. No innocent owner exemption	1. Limited to contraband forfeitures
Administrative (Non-judicial)	In Rem	1. Contraband 2. Proceeds 3. Facilitation	Remedial	1. Immediate possession of property 2. No criminal conviction required 3. Conserves judicial resources 4. Quick resolution for uncontested matters	1. Recognition of legal title without judicial orders
Criminal (Judicial)	In Personam	1. Contraband 2. Proceeds 3. Facilitation 4. Enterprise	Punitive	1. Substitute assets 2. Joint & several liability 3. Resolution of criminal and forfeiture in criminal proceeding	1. Restraining Orders required 2. Criminal conviction required
Civil (Judicial)	In Rem	1. Contraband 2. Proceeds 3. Facilitation	Remedial Remedial Punitive	1. Immediate possession of property 2. Lower burden of proof 3. Civil discovery available 4. No criminal conviction required 5. Resolution of all property rights in one civil hearing	1. No substitute assets 2. Pre-seizure hearings for real property 3. Adverse civil discovery considerations 4. Coordinating parallel proceedings
Civil (Judicial)	In Personam	1. Contraband 2. Proceeds 3. Facilitation 4. Enterprise	Punitive	1. No criminal conviction required 2. Lower burden of proof 3. Civil discovery available 4. Substitute assets 5. Joint & several liability	1. Restraining Orders required 2. May require separate in rem action to determine third-party interests

1. Summary Forfeiture

The benefits of summary forfeiture include that it functions by operation of law and does not require formal legal process to meet due process concerns. Since it operates *in rem* against property declared to be contraband per se it is a remedial statute so it should not raise any constitutional issues and innocent owner exemptions do not apply. Its weakness is that it is restricted to contraband per se property so it has limited use.

2. Administrative Forfeiture

Administrative forfeitures carry the advantages common to civil *in rem* forfeiture that they permit the seizing agency to obtain possession of the property and to retain custody during the pendency of the action, nor is there a criminal conviction requirement. The main benefit of this forfeiture is that it conserves judicial resources and provides quick resolution for uncontested matters. They are *in rem* matters that are considered remedial and not subject to Constitutional challenges outside of the issue of due process. *See Dusenbery v. United States*, 534 U.S. 161, 167 (2002). One potential drawback is that since the forfeiture is non-judicial, completed by an administrative agency pursuant to its executive powers, no court orders are issued and recognition of legal title may be questioned by entities unfamiliar with the government's administrative forfeiture authority.

3. Criminal Forfeiture

Some of the advantages of criminal forfeiture include the availability of a money judgment that is jointly and severally liable on all criminal defendants, access to substitute assets when the original forfeitable property cannot be located or is beyond the jurisdiction of the court, and the resolution of the criminal case and the forfeiture action in one criminal forum.

Weaknesses of the criminal forfeiture process include the criminal conviction requirement. Unless the defendant is convicted there can be no forfeiture. Therefore, if the defendant is acquitted, becomes a fugitive or dies prior to judgment that will prevent the completion of the criminal forfeiture action. *United States v. Lay*, 456 F. Supp. 2d 869 (S.D. Tex. 2006). Additionally, the prosecutor must take steps to protect the assets pending the criminal forfeiture judgment. This may require restraining orders to prevent the defendant from hiding, dissipating or damaging the property until the forfeiture judgment is obtained.

Since criminal forfeitures are *in personam* they are generally considered punitive and are subject to the full array of Constitutional protections afforded criminal defendants.

4. Civil *In Rem* Forfeiture

Advantages of civil *in rem* forfeiture include immediate possession of the property. The law enforcement agency obtains actual or constructive possession of the property and retains custody on behalf of the court pending the resolution of the forfeiture action. There is no criminal conviction requirement and the lower civil burden of proof applies. Hearsay evidence may be used to establish probable cause. Civil discovery is available and civil law and motion practice may be applied to challenge the validity of claims. Also, all of the property rights to the property are litigated in one civil proceeding. Property forfeited under the contraband and proceeds theories are considered remedial thereby limiting constitutional attacks.

One major weakness of civil *in rem* forfeiture is the lack of substitute assets. Unless the actual property subject to forfeiture is located there can be no forfeiture. Claimants may attempt to use civil discovery to gain information concerning the criminal case that would not be accessible through criminal discovery procedures. Although civil *in rem* statutes permit warrantless seizure, real property may not be seized without a noticed adversarial hearing. *See United States v. James Daniel Good Real Property,* 510 U.S. 43, 62 (1993); Discussed in Chapter 11 Real Property forfeitures. Coordinating separately filed criminal and civil actions can be challenging when handled by separate prosecutors and can lead to adverse consequences. See Chapter 9 on Parallel Proceedings. Property forfeited in a civil *in rem* proceeding on a facilitation theory has been determined to be punitive and is subject to constitutional attack.

5. Civil *In Personam* Forfeiture

These are unique because they blend the advantages of the criminal and civil forfeiture processes and avoid most of the pitfalls. They provide for the forfeiture of substitute assets and joint and several liability of the parties on the forfeiture judgment without the criminal conviction requirement. Since they are civil actions they have the lower civil burden of proof and allow civil discovery. They also permit the forfeiture of assets of corrupt organizations on the enterprise theory in addition to the contraband, proceeds and facilitation theories.

There are a few downsides to civil *in personam* forfeitures. Restraining orders and seizure warrants may be required to seize and protect the forfeitable property (*Ariz. Rev. Stat. Ann.* § 13-4312.C) and may be unavailable against substitute assets (*Ariz. Rev. Stat. Ann.* § 13-4305.D; 13-4313.A). A separate *in rem* action may be necessary to determine the rights of third party claimants and since it is an *in personam* action, it may be punitive and subject to constitutional challenges similar to criminal actions. *See State v. Leyva,* 195 Ariz. 13, 19; 985 P.2d 498, 505 (Ariz. App. 1999).

H. Summary

With this background whenever a practitioner is confronted with an asset forfeiture case, he or she should ask the following preliminary questions:

1. What type of jurisdiction is being asserted in this action? (*In Rem* or *In Personam*)
2. What type of forfeiture is this? (Non-judicial including Summary & Administrative forfeiture or Judicial including Civil *In Rem*, Criminal *In Personam* or Civil *In Personam*).
3. What is the legal theory that the government is asserting to forfeit this asset? (Contraband, Proceeds, Facilitation or Enterprise)
4. Under applicable statutory and case law is this type of forfeiture punitive or remedial?
5. What are the relative strengths and weaknesses of this type of forfeiture?

Notes

1. 18 U.S.C. § 545 permits the forfeiture of smuggled goods "or the value thereof" without a criminal conviction. Therefore, the forfeiture of the smuggled merchandise would be civil *in rem* (*see* United States v. Brigance, 472 F. Supp. 1177, 1181 (S.D. Tex. 1979), but an action personally against the party to recover the value of the merchandise would be civil *in personam*. (*See* United States v. A Lot of Precious Stones & Jewelry, 134 F. 61, 63 (6th Cir. 1905).) This is the only federal civil *in personam* forfeiture provision to the knowledge of the author.

2. The "Involved in" theory of forfeiture in federal money laundering cases is discussed in detail in *Establishing Probable Cause for Forfeiture in Money Laundering Cases* Stefan D. Cassella, 39 N.Y.L. Sch. L. Rev. 163 (1994).

3. See Mary M. Cheh, *Can Something This Easy, Quick and Profitable Also Be Fair? Runaway Civil Forfeiture Stumbles on the Constitution,* 39 N.Y.L. Sch. L. Rev. 1, 8 (1994).

2 Property Subject to Forfeiture

A. Introduction

The world was stunned when President John F. Kennedy was assassinated in 1963. In the grim aftermath of that event, the federal government filed a forfeiture action against the rifle and pistol found by the Warren Commission to have been used by Lee Harvey Oswald in assassinating the president and killing Dallas Police Officer Tippit. The government's forfeiture theory was that the firearms had been used in violation of the Federal Firearms Act. 15 U.S.C. § 903(d). Obviously the government was interested in retaining the weapons for their historic value. The government was chagrined when the appellate court reversed the forfeiture, finding that the evidence did not warrant forfeiture under the Act. *See King v. United States*, 364 F.2d 235, 241 (5th Cir. 1966). The *King* case highlights two important principles pertaining to forfeiture litigation. First, there must be a specific statute authorizing forfeiture of the property and, second, there must be sufficient evidence to establish that the property is subject to forfeiture as defined in the statute. *Richardson v. One 1972 GMC Pickup*, 121 Idaho 599, 826 P.2d 1311, 1315 (Idaho 1992) (firearms not included within statute).

This chapter will discuss the property subject to forfeiture as defined in the federal and state statutes.

B. History of Federal Forfeiture

American forfeiture is rooted in biblical and pre-Judeo-Christian law. During the 17th century, colonial courts enforced English and local forfeiture statutes. After ratification of the U.S. Constitution, one of the initial acts of the First U.S. Congress in 1790 was to enact forfeiture statutes for vessels and cargoes involved in customs violations. *See Calero-Toledo v. Pearson Yacht Leasing,* 416 U.S. 663, 683 (1974). From those early beginnings, federal forfeiture statutes migrated into such diverse areas as property used in connection with an illegal distillery, *see Dobbins Distillery v. United States,* 96 U.S. 395, 399 (1878), tax fraud, *see Goldsmith-Grant Co. v. United States,* 254 U.S. 505, 508 (1921), and criminal racketeering, *see* 18 U.S.C. § 1963.

This growth of forfeiture statutes led the U.S. Supreme Court in *Calero-Toledo* to opine: "[t]he enactment of forfeiture statutes has not abated; contemporary federal and state forfeiture statutes reach virtually any type of property that might be used in the conduct of a criminal enterprise." *Calero-Toledo,* 416 U.S. at 683.

A review of recently enacted federal forfeiture statutes demonstrates the reality of this statement. In 1998, the U.S. Department of Justice estimated that there were more than 140 federal civil forfeiture statutes. *See* U.S. Department of Justice, Criminal Division, Asset Forfeiture and Money Laundering Section, *Asset Forfeiture Law and Practice Manual* Ch. 1, Sec. II (1998), at 1-1. With the enactment of the Civil Asset Forfeiture Reform Act of 2000, also known as "CAFRA," Pub. L. No. 106-185, 114 Stat. 202 (2000), Congress authorized the addition of over 247 specified unlawful activities contained in the federal money laundering statute, *see* 18 U.S.C. § 1956(c)(7), as subject to forfeiture on a proceeds theory. *See* 18 U.S.C. § 981(a)(1)(C). The USA PATRIOT Act of 2001, Pub. L. No. 107-56, 115 Stat. 272 (2001), added an additional 18 statutes related to terrorism as predicates of the criminal racketeering statute, making them forfeitable on a proceeds theory as well. *See* 18 U.S.C. § 2332b(g)(5)(B); 18 U.S.C. § 1961(1). The expanse of federal forfeiture statutes is extensive.

C. Types of Federal Forfeiture

The federal forfeiture system uses summary, administrative, criminal, and civil *in rem* procedures (see Chapter 1). Civil *in personam* forfeitures are rarely used in the federal statutes.[1] Although the federal statutes utilize both criminal and civil procedures, their use has been far from uniform. Table 2-1 is a summary of selected federal asset forfeiture statutes in effect prior to 2000.

Table 2-1 demonstrates the inconsistencies that existed among the statutory authorities to forfeit property under various federal offenses. Although copyright infringement, 17 U.S.C. § 509, firearms, 18 U.S.C. § 922, and gambling offenses, 18 U.S.C. § 1955, authorized the forfeiture of facilitating property

Table 2-1
Summary of Selected Federal Asset Forfeiture Statutes
Pre-CAFRA

Offense	Statute	Civil Proceeds	Civil Facilitation	Criminal Proceeds	Criminal Facilitation
Copyright Infringement	17 USC § 509		17 USC § 509		
Counterfeiting	18 USC §§ 471-473	18 USC § 981(a)(1)(C)	18 USC § 492	18 USC § 982(a)(2)(B)	
Firearms	18 USC § 922		18 USC § 924(d)		
Identity Theft	18 USC § 1028	18 USC § 981(a)(1)(C)		18 USC § 982(a)(2)(B)	18 USC § 982(a)(8)
Mail Fraud	18 USC § 1341	18 USC § 981(a)(1)(C)		18 USC § 982(a)(2)(A)	
Wire Fraud	18 USC § 1343	18 USC § 981(a)(1)(C)		18 USC § 982(a)(2)(A)	
Bank Fraud	18 USC § 1344	18 USC § 981(a)(1)(C)		18 USC § 982(a)(2)(A)	
Health Care Fraud	18 USC § 1347			18 USC § 982(a)(7)	

Table 2-1 (continued)
Summary of Selected Federal Asset Forfeiture Statutes
Pre-CAFRA

Offense	Statute	Civil Proceeds	Civil Facilitation	Criminal Proceeds	Criminal Facilitation
Obscenity	18 USC §§ 1461-1466, 1468			18 USC § 1467	18 USC § 1467
Gambling	18 USC § 1955		18 USC § 1955(d)		
Money Remitters	18 USC § 1960			18 USC § 982(a)(1)	18 USC § 982(a)(1)
RICO	18 USC § 1962			18 USC § 1963(a)(3)	18 USC §§ 1963(a)(1) & (2)
Child Sexual Exploitation	18 USC §§ 2251-2252	18 USC § 2254(a)(3)	18 USC § 2254(a)(2)	18 USC § 2253(a)(2)	18 USC § 2253(a)(3)
Prostitution	18 USC §§ 2421-2424	18 USC § 2254(c)	18 USC § 2254(b)	18 USC § 2253(a)(2)	18 USC § 2253(a)(3)
Narcotics Trafficking	21 USC §§ 841-846	21 USC § 881(a)(6)	21 USC § 881(a) (2)-(7); (9); (11)	21 USC § 853(a)(1)	21 USC § 853(a)(2)
Continuing Criminal Enterprise	21 USC § 848	21 USC § 881(a)(6); 18 USC § 981(a)(1)(c)	21 USC § 881(a)	21 USC § 853(a)(3)	21 USC §§ 848, 853(a)(3)
Bank Secrecy Act	31 USC §§ 5313, 5316, 5324		18 USC § 981(a)(1)(A); 31 USC § 5317(c)		18 USC § 982(a)(1)

using civil forfeiture procedures, there was no power to forfeit the same property using criminal forfeiture. Conversely, health care fraud, 18 U.S.C. § 1347, obscenity, 18 U.S.C. §§ 1461–1466, 1468, and money remitter, 18 U.S.C. § 1960, offenses could forfeit proceeds of the crimes using criminal procedures, but there was no corresponding authority to use the civil forfeiture statutes. There were other offenses, such as narcotics trafficking, 21 U.S.C. §§ 841-846, prostitution, 18 U.S.C. §§ 2421–2424, and child sexual exploitation, 18 U.S.C. §§ 2251–2252, that had full authority to forfeit property civilly or criminally on both a proceeds and facilitation theory. The result was confusion and limited application of certain forfeiture laws to various criminal offenses.

The passage of CAFRA in 2000 helped rectify this hodgepodge of forfeiture authority with two simple paragraphs. Section 16, 106 Pub. L. No. 185, 114 Stat. 202, 221, amended 28 U.S.C. § 2461 to allow criminal forfeiture anytime there is a civil forfeiture provision but no corresponding criminal forfeiture statute, and the defendant is charged and convicted of the underlying crime. *United States v. Razmilovic*, 419 F.3d 134, 136 (2d Cir. 2005). Section 20, 106 Pub. L. No. 185, 114 Stat. 202, 224, amended 18 U.S.C. § 981(a)(1)(C) to permit the forfeiture of the proceeds of any offense listed as a specified unlawful activity or conspiracy to commit that offense as contained in 18 U.S.C. § 1956(c)(7). *United States v. All Funds*, 345 F.3d 49, 53 n.2 (2d Cir. 2003).

These two paragraphs have substantially enhanced the property subject to forfeiture under the federal system. The reader is directed to Table 2-2, Summary of Selected Federal Asset Forfeiture Statutes Post-CAFRA and Post-USA PATRIOT Act. The items in bold print indicate new powers to forfeit property after CAFRA was enacted. The result of these two legislative amendments is to make virtually all of the selected offenses listed in the table subject to both civil and criminal forfeiture, with the exception of the federal RICO or criminal racketeering statute found at 18 U.S.C. § 1962, which remains subject solely to criminal forfeiture. The reader also is directed to a new offense entitled Bulk Cash Smuggling, 31 U.S.C. § 5332, which was added by the USA PATRIOT Act in 2001 and provides for both criminal and civil forfeiture. These recent amendments help clarify federal forfeiture practice by making criminal and civil procedures applicable to many federal criminal violations.

Table 2-2
Summary of Selected Federal Asset Forfeiture Statutes Post-CAFRA & USA PATRIOT Act

Offense	Statute	Specified Unlawful Activity	Civil Proceeds	Civil Facilitation	Criminal Proceeds	Criminal Facilitation
Copyright Infringement	17 USC § 509			17 USC § 509		17 USC § 509 & 28 USC § 2461
Counterfeiting	8 USC §§ 471-473	18 USC § 1961(1)(B)	18 USC § 981(a)(1)(C)	18 USC § 492	18 USC § 982(a)(2)(B)	18 USC § 492 & 28 USC § 2461
Firearms	18 USC § 922			18 USC § 924(d)		18 USC § 924(d) & 28 USC § 2461
Identity Theft	18 USC § 1028	18 USC § 1961(1)(B)	18 USC § 981(a)(1)(C)		18 USC § 982(a)(2)(B)	18 USC § 982(a)(8)
Mail Fraud	18 USC § 1341	18 USC § 1961(1)(B)	18 USC § 981(a)(1)(C)		18 USC § 982(a)(2)(A)	
Wire Fraud	18 USC §1343	18 USC § 1961(1)(B)	18 USC § 981(a)(1)(C)		18 USC § 982(a)(2)(A)	
Bank Fraud	18 USC § 1344	18 USC § 1961(1)(B)	18 USC § 981(a)(1)(C)		18 USC § 982(a)(2)(A)	
Health Care Fraud	18 USC § 1347	18 USC § 1956(c)(7)(F)	18 USC § 981(a)(1)(C)		18 USC § 981(a)(7)	
Obscenity	18 USC §§ 1461-1466, 1468	18 USC § 1961(1)(B)	18 USC § 981(a)(1)(C)		18 USC § 1467	18 USC § 1467
Gambling	18 USC § 1955	18 USC §1961(1)(B)	18 USC § 981(a)(1)(C)	18 USC § 1955(d)	18 USC § 981(a)(1)(C) & 28 USC § 2461	18 USC § 1955(d) & 28 USC § 2461

Table 2-2 (continued)
Summary of Selected Federal Asset Forfeiture Statutes
Post-CAFRA & USA PATRIOT Act

Offense	Statute	Specified Unlawful Activity	Civil Proceeds	Civil Facilitation	Criminal Proceeds	Criminal Facilitation
Money Remitters	18 USC § 1960		18 USC § 981(a)(1)(A)	18 USC § 981(a)(1)(A)	18 USC § 982(a)(1)	18 USC § 982(a)(1)
RICO	18 USC § 1962				18 USC § 1963(a)(3)	18 USC §§ 1963 (a)(1) & (2)
Child Sexual Exploitation	18 USC §§ 2251-2252	18 USC § 1961(1)(B)	18 USC § 2254(a)(3)	18 USC § 2254(a)(2)	18 USC § 2253(a)(2)	18 USC § 2253(a)(3)
Prostitution	18 USC §§ 2421-2424	18 USC § 1961(1)(B)	18 USC § 2254(c)	18 USC § 2254(b)	18 USC § 2253(a)(2)	18 USC § 2253(a)(3)
Narcotics Trafficking	21 USC §§ 841-846	18 USC § 1961(1)(D); 18 USC § 1956(c)(7)(D)	21 USC § 881(a)(6)	21 USC § 881(a)(2)-(7); (9); (11)	21 USC § 853(a)(1)	21 USC § 853(a)(2)
Continuing Criminal Enterprise	21 USC § 848	18 USC § 1961(1)(D); 18 USC § 1956(c)(7)(C)	21 USC § 881(a)(6); 18 USC § 981(C)	21 USC § 881(a)	21 USC § 853(a)(3)	21 USC §§ 848, 853(a)(3)
Bank Secrecy Act	31 USC §§ 5313, 5316, 5324		18 USC § 981(a)(1)(A); 31 USC § 5317(c)(2)	18 USC § 981(a)(1)(A) 31 USC § 5317(c)(2)	31 USC § 5317(c)(1)	31 USC § 5317(c)(1) Previously under 18 USC § 982(a)(1)
Bulk Cash Smuggling	31 USC § 5332		31 USC § 5332(c)	31 USC § 5332(c)	31 USC § 5332(b)	31 USC § 5332(b)

The federal criminal offenses with forfeiture provisions number in the hundreds and range from environmental, *see* 33 U.S.C. §§ 1411–1421, hunting, *see* 16 U.S.C. § 26, and endangered species violations, *see* 16 U.S.C. § 1540, to murder, *see* 18 U.S.C. § 1114, fraud, *see* 18 U.S.C. § 1344, and smuggling, *see* 19 U.S.C. § 1526. The offenses listed on Tables 2-1 and 2-2 merely are representative of some of the major offenses. A detailed review of these statutes is beyond the purview of this publication, and readers are directed to the specific statutes or other treatises for an analysis of these sections. However, there are a few civil and criminal forfeiture statutes that merit a little more attention and are discussed in the sections that follow.

D. Federal Civil Forfeiture

1. Narcotics Trafficking, 21 U.S.C. § 881

The federal drug trafficking forfeiture statute, 21 U.S.C. § 881, is one of the most-utilized federal civil forfeiture statutes. It provides for the forfeiture of such items as controlled substances, 21 U.S.C. § 881(a)(1); conveyances that include aircraft, boats, and vehicles, 21 U.S.C. § 881(a)(4); money or things of value, 21 U.S.C. § 881(a)(6); and real property, 21 U.S.C. § 881(a)(7). The property may be forfeited on either a facilitation, 21 U.S.C. § 881(a)(4), or proceeds theory, 21 U.S.C. § 881(a)(6).

One contribution of 21 U.S.C. § 881 is that it has been used as a template by many states in drafting their own civil narcotic forfeiture statutes. For example, the chart below compares the federal and Maryland civil drug forfeiture statutes listing property subject to forfeiture:

Federal Forfeiture	Maryland State Forfeiture
21 U.S.C. § 881(a)	Md. Code Ann., Crim. Proc. § 12-102
Controlled Substances	Controlled Substances
Raw Materials	Raw Materials
Container	Container
Conveyances	Conveyances
Books/Records	Books/Records
Money and Things of Value	Money and Things of Value
Real Property	Real Property

At least 36 states have modeled their list of property subject to forfeiture under their state drug forfeiture law after the federal drug forfeiture statute. See Table 2-3. Many states have relied on the federal narcotic forfeiture statute in drafting their own state statute; therefore, federal case law interpreting that statute may be persuasive authority in state court. *See 725 Ill. Comp. Stat. 150/2; People v. Superior Court (Moraza)*, 210 Cal. App. 3d 592, 598 (1989); *People ex rel. Wayne County Prosecutor v. $176,598.00 U.S. Currency*, 465 Mich. 382; 633 N.W. 2d 367, 370 n.10 (Mich. 2001); *City of Bellevue v. Cashier's Checks*, 70 Wash. App. 697; 855 P.2d 330, 332 (Wash. App. 1993). However, some state statutes are more restrictive in their provisions enabling the seizure and forfeiture of property under certain theories than the federal drug statute. For example, three states impose minimum quantities of drugs that must be involved before conveyances may be forfeited on a facilitation theory. *See Cal. Health & Safety Code* § 11470(e); *S.C. Code Ann.*§ 44-53-520(a)(6); *S.D. Codified Laws* § 34-20B-74.

Table 2-3
Summary of State Asset Forfeiture Statutes
Comparison to 21 U.S.C. § 881(a)

State	Statute
Alabama	Ala. Code § 20-2-93(a)
Alaska	Ak. Stat. § 17.30.110
Arkansas	Ark. Code Ann. § 5-64-505 (a)
California	Cal. Health & Safety Code § 11470(a)-(g)
Delaware	Del. Code Ann. Title 16 § 4784(a)
District of Columbia	D.C. Code Ann. § 48-905.02 (a)
Idaho	Idaho Code § 37-2744 (a)
Illinois	720 ILCS 550/12 (a)
Kentucky	Ky. Rev. Stat. Ann. § 218A.410
Louisiana	La. Rev. Stat. Ann. § 40:2604
Maine	Me. Rev. Stat. Ann. Title 15 ch. 517 § 5821
Maryland	Md. Ann. Code Crim. Proc. § 12-102
Massachusetts	Mass. Ann. Laws ch. 94C § 47 (a)
Michigan	Mich. Comp. Laws § 333.7521

Table 2-3 (continued)
Summary of State Asset Forfeiture Statutes
Comparison to 21 U.S.C. § 881(a)

State	Statute
Mississippi	Miss. Code Ann. § 41-29-153 (a)
Montana	Mont. Code Ann. § 44-12-102 (1)
Nebraska	Neb. Rev. Stat. § 28-431(1)
Nevada	Nev. Rev. Stat. § 453.301
New Hampshire	N.H. Rev. Stat. Ann. § 318-B:17-b I
New Mexico	N.M. Code Ann. § 30-31-34
North Carolina	N.C. Gen. Stat. § 90-112 (a)
North Dakota	N.D. Cent. Code § 19-03.1-36 1
Oklahoma	Okla. Stat. Ann. § 63-2-503 A
Oregon	Ore. Rev. Stat. § 475A.020
Pennsylvania	Pa. Consol. Stat. Ann. Title 35 § 6801 (a)
Rhode Island	R.I. Gen. Laws §§ 21-28-5.04 & 21-28-5.05
South Carolina	S.C. Code Ann. § 44-53-520 (a)
South Dakota	S.D. Codified Laws Ann. § 34-20B-70
Tennessee	Tenn. Code Ann. § 53-11-451 (a)
Utah	Utah Code Ann. § 58-37-13(2)
Vermont	Vt. Stat. Ann. Title 18 § 4241 (a)
Virginia	Va. Code Ann. § 19.2-386-22a
Washington	Wash. Rev. Code Ann. § 69.50.505 (a)
West Virginia	W. Va. Code § 60A-7-703(a)
Wisconsin	Wis. Stat. Ann. § 961.55 (1)
Wyoming	Wyo. Stat. § 35-7-1049(a)

2. General Forfeiture Statute, 18 U.S.C. § 981

The general civil forfeiture statute is found at 18 U.S.C. § 981 and makes subject to forfeiture any real or personal property involved in violations of the federal money laundering statutes, 18 U.S.C. §§ 1956, 1957, 1960 (see 18 U.S.C. § 981(a)(1)(A)), and terrorism, 18 U.S.C. § 2331 (see 18 U.S.C. § 981(a)(1)(G)). The general civil forfeiture statute further reaches the proceeds of property traceable to violations of federal financial institution fraud (FIRREA), Pub. L. No. 101-73, 103 Stat. 183 (1989) (see 18 U.S.C. § 981(a)(1)(C)–(D)), and federal carjacking violations, Pub. L. No. 102-519, 106 Stat. 3384 (1992) (see 18 U.S.C. § 981(a)(1)(F).

With the enactment of CAFRA, 18 U.S.C. § 981(a)(1)(C) was amended to include as proceeds all of the specified unlawful activities contained in 18 U.S.C. § 1956(c)(7), which also incorporates all of the offenses listed in the criminal racketeering statute found in 18 U.S.C. § 1961(1). This extends the proceeds theory of civil forfeiture to an additional 247 federal offenses, making 18 U.S.C. § 981 the most prevalent civil forfeiture section utilized by federal prosecutors in forfeiture actions.

For a discussion of federal civil administrative forfeiture authority, see Chapter 4, Sections C.1 through C.3.

E. Federal Criminal Forfeiture

Criminal forfeiture is fast becoming a popular method of forfeiture in the federal system. This is due in part to past constitutional challenges alleging double jeopardy violations, see United States v. Ursery, 518 U.S. 267, 275 (1996), and to Congress expressing a preference for criminal forfeiture.[2]

In an effort to encourage prosecutors to use criminal forfeiture in lieu of civil forfeiture statutes, Congress enacted Section 16 of CAFRA, 106 Pub. L. No. 185, 114 Stat. 202, 221, which amended 28 U.S.C. § 2461 by authorizing criminal forfeiture for any property that is subject to civil forfeiture. United States v. Vampire Nation, 451 F.3d 189, 200 (3d Cir. 2006). Table 2-2 demonstrates that this effectively has added criminal forfeiture authority on both proceeds and facilitation theories for many offenses that previously were limited to civil forfeiture. This section will review three of the main federal criminal forfeiture statutes.

1. RICO, 18 U.S.C. § 1963

Enacted in 1970, the criminal racketeering forfeiture statute forfeits all real property, tangible personal property, and intangible personal property of the defendant acquired in violation of the racketeering statute. 18 U.S.C. § 1963(b). The theories of forfeiture include proceeds, 18 U.S.C. § 1963(a)(3), and that the defendant had a source of influence over the illegal enterprise, 18 U.S.C. § 1963(a)(2)(D).

This is a powerful section because the definition of racketeering includes over 143 federal and state criminal offenses as detailed in 18 U.S.C. § 1961. It is one of the few forfeiture sections that did not obtain a corresponding civil forfeiture provision as part of the CAFRA amendments (see Table 2-2). The burden of proof for federal RICO forfeitures is beyond a reasonable doubt. *United States v. Pelullo*, 14 F.3d 881, 903 (3d Cir. 1994).

2. Narcotic Offenses, 21 U.S.C. § 853

This statute is a companion to the civil narcotic forfeiture statute at 21 U.S.C. § 881 and provides for criminal forfeiture for all real property, tangible personal property, and intangible personal property interests of the defendant. 21 U.S.C. § 853(b). The theories of forfeiture include proceeds, 21 U.S.C. § 853(a)(1), facilitation, 21 U.S.C. § 853(a)(2), and, in one limited instance, enterprise interest, 21 U.S.C. § 848, 853(a)(3). Unique items forfeited under this provision include a medical license used to distribute controlled substances, *United States v. Singh*, 390 F.3d 168, 189–191 (2d Cir. 2004), and a winning lottery ticket purchased with drug proceeds. United *States v. Betancourt*, 422 F.3d 240, 251–52 (5th Cir. 2005).

3. General Offenses, 18 U.S.C. § 982

This section corresponds to the civil general forfeiture statute, 18 U.S.C. § 981, and requires forfeiture of all real or personal property involved in or traceable to a money laundering offense under 18 U.S.C. §§ 1956, 1957 or 1960, *see* 18 U.S.C. § 982(a)(1), proceeds traceable to federal financial institution fraud (FIRREA), *see* 18 U.S.C. § 982(a)(2)–(4), and federal carjacking offenses, *see* 18 U.S.C. § 982(a)(5). It incorporates the seizure, distribution, and general procedures of the federal criminal narcotic forfeiture statute under 21 U.S.C. § 853. *See* 18 U.S.C. § 982(b)(1).

A review of state asset forfeiture laws and procedures follows, concluding with a comparison of the federal and state forfeiture systems.

F. History of State Forfeiture

In 1942 the U.S. Supreme Court reviewed a case in which the State of California seized and forfeited a fishing net used in violation of its Fish and

Game Code. *C.J. Hendry Co. v. Moore,* 318 U.S. 133 (1942). The question facing the court was whether the state could enforce its forfeiture statute given that admiralty jurisdiction belongs exclusively to the federal courts.

In its opinion the U.S. Supreme Court discussed at length the historical underpinnings of asset forfeiture in America. The court observed that, before the adoption of the U.S. Constitution, the common law courts of the colonies, and later as states, during the Confederation, were enforcing forfeiture statutes. Shortly after ratification of the U.S. Constitution, state legislation was enacted authorizing forfeiture of nets and boats illegally used in fishing, and similar legislation subsequently was enacted in half the states. The court concluded that the common law prior to the adoption of the U.S. Constitution gave *in rem* forfeiture authority to the states and upheld the forfeiture judgment.

As demonstrated in the *Hendry* opinion, state forfeiture authority preceded the U.S. Constitution and the states retained common law authority after the Constitution was adopted. The only area in which the federal courts have exclusive jurisdiction is the enforcement of admiralty law. *See* 28 U.S.C. § 1333.

G. Types of State Forfeiture

Given that state forfeiture has such a long history, it is not surprising to find the use of summary, civil *in rem,* administrative, civil *in personam,* and criminal forfeitures in various state statutes. Additionally, many states have statutes that provide for the forfeiture of property as a nuisance.

Due to the overwhelming number of state forfeiture statutes, it is not feasible to review each state in any detail. However, three charts comparing some common characteristics are included for reference in this section.

1. Civil *In Rem* Statutes

Civil *in rem* jurisdiction is widely used in the state forfeiture system as demonstrated by Table 1-3. Forty-seven states and the District of Columbia all have civil *in rem* forfeiture statutes. Most of these provisions are drug forfeiture statutes patterned after the federal civil *in rem* narcotic forfeiture law, 21 U.S.C. § 881.

2. Administrative Forfeiture

Administrative or nonjudicial forfeiture does not have widespread use within the state forfeiture system. Only 18 states and the District of Columbia authorize its use (see Table 1-1). The main difference between administrative forfeiture in the state and federal systems is that, in the federal system, administrative forfeitures are initiated by the federal law enforcement agencies; whereas, in the state system most are under the purview of the state prosecutor as part of his or her executive power. Additionally, many state statutes cap the value of property that can be forfeited administratively. *See Mich. Comp. Laws* § 600.5314 ($100,000); *Miss. Code Ann.* § 41-29-176 ($10,000). The federal District of Columbia permits administrative forfeiture up to $250,000. *D.C. Code Ann.* § 33-552(C). These state statutory caps are much lower than the federal authority, which permits administrative forfeiture of up to $500,000 value, *see* 19 U.S.C. § 1607(a)(1), or unlimited value for conveyances used in controlled substances offenses or monetary instruments as defined by 31 U.S.C. § 5312(a)(3). *See* 19 U.S.C. § 1607(a)(2)–(4). *See also Chapter* 4, Sections C.1 through C.3. Neither the state nor the federal systems permit the forfeiture of real property administratively. *See* 18 U.S.C. § 985(a); Haw. *Rev. Stat.* § 712A-10.

Five states provide for **uncontested forfeiture** rather than administrative forfeiture. See Table 1-1. Uncontested forfeiture actions are similar to administrative forfeiture actions with the exception that, once the property is unclaimed, a judicial order is obtained, rather than the executive agency, declaring the property forfeited. *See Alaska Stat.* § 17.30.116; *Ariz. Rev. Stat. Ann.* § 13-4314; *Kan. Stat. Ann.* § 60-4116; *La. Rev. Stat. Ann.* § 40:2615; *Ore. Rev. Stat.* § 475A.055(4). This permits the court to confirm that proper notice of the forfeiture action was given and that probable cause exists for the forfeiture of the property. *See Ariz. Rev. Stat. Ann.* § 13-4314.A; *Kan. Stat. Ann.* § 60-4116.

3. Criminal Forfeiture

Criminal forfeiture authority is contained in 22 state statutes. See Table 1-2. Nebraska[3] and North Carolina[4] are the only states to rely on criminal forfeiture as their primary drug forfeiture statutes. Most states use the criminal forfeiture statute as an alternative to the civil *in rem* forfeiture statutes. *See Utah Code Ann.* § 24-1-8.

4. Civil *In Personam* Forfeiture

A handful of states have forfeiture statutes that allow for civil *in personam* forfeiture of property. See Table 1-4. Most notable on the list is New York, which uses this as its primary drug forfeiture statute because it does not have a corresponding civil *in rem* drug forfeiture statute. *See N.Y. C.P.L.R.* § 1311. The New York statute contains some additional restrictions, such as a criminal conviction requirement and a higher burden of proof, that incorporate some of the elements common to criminal forfeitures and distinguishes it from other state *in personam* forfeiture statutes.

All other states that authorize civil *in personam* statutes use it as an alternative to the civil *in rem* or criminal procedures, thus giving prosecutors many options in bringing forfeiture actions in those states. The strategic advantages and disadvantages of each type of forfeiture must be analyzed in connection with the facts of the underlying seizure before the charging decision is made. See Chapter 1.

5. RICO Forfeitures

Several states have enacted criminal racketeering statutes based on the federal model contained at 18 U.S.C. § 1963. A list of states with RICO forfeiture statutes is listed in Table 2-4. Although several states statutes are consistent with federal practice limiting RICO forfeitures to criminal procedures, *see Cal. Penal Code* § 186.2; *Idaho Code* § 18-7804(i), several of the state statutes utilize civil *in rem*, *see Colo. Rev. Stat. Ann.* § 18-17-106(2); *N.J. Rev. Stat.* § 2C:64-3(a), and civil *in personam* actions, *see Fla. Stat. Ann.* § 895.05(2); 725 *Ill. Comp. Stat.* § 175/6(b), including the lower civil burden of proof. *See Colo. Rev. Stat. Ann.* § 18-17-106(11) (preponderance); 725 *Ill. Comp. Stat.* § 175/5(9)(b) (preponderance).

A detailed explanation of RICO forfeitures is beyond the scope of this work. Practitioners should be aware of these provisions and utilize them in significant cases involving criminal racketeering.

Table 2-4
Summary of State Asset Forfeiture Statutes
State RICO Statutes

State	Civil	Criminal	Statute
Arizona	X		Ariz. Rev. Stat. Ann. §§ 13-2314(D)(6); (G)(1)-(3)
California		X	Cal. Penal Code § 186.2 et seq.
Colorado	X	X	Colo. Rev. Stat. §§ 18-17-102 through 109
Connecticut		X	Conn. Gen. Stat. § 53-397(b)(1)
Delaware	X		11 Del. Code Ann. § 1506
Florida	X	X	Fla. Stat. Ann. § 895.05(2), (10)
Georgia	X		Ga. Code Ann § 16-14-7(a), (c), (m)
Hawaii		X	Haw. Rev. Stat. § 842-3
Idaho		X	Idaho Code § 18-7804(i)
Illinois	X	X	725 ILCS 175/6(d)
Indiana	X		Indiana Code §§ 34-24-2-1 through 34-24-2-8
Louisiana	X		La. Rev. Stat. Ann 15 § 1356(A)(1)
Michigan	X	X	Mich. Comp. Laws § 750.159j(4); 750.159n(1)
Minnesota		X	Minn. Stat. Ann. § 609.905(1)
Mississippi	X		Miss. Code Ann. § 97-43-9
Nevada	X	X	Nev. Rev. Stat. §§ 207.420(1), 207.460
New Jersey	X	X	N.J. Rev. Stat. §§ 2C:41-3(b); 4(a)(9)
New York	X	X	N.Y. Penal Code § 460.30; N.Y. Civ.Prac. L. & R. 13-A
North Carolina	X		N.C. Gen. Stat. § 75D-5(a);(c);(k)
North Dakota	X		N.D. Cent. Code §§ 12.1-06.1-05(4)(f), (5)
Ohio		X	Ohio Rev. Code Ann. § 2923.32(B)(3)
Oklahoma		X	Okla. Stat. Ann. Tit. 22 § 1405(A)
Oregon	X		Or. Rev. Stat. § 166.725(2)
Rhode Island	X	X	R.I. Gen. Laws § 7-15-3.1; 4(e)
Tennessee	X		Tenn. Code Ann. § 39-12-206(b)
Utah		X	Utah Code Ann. § 76-10-1603.5(1)
Virginia	X		Va. Code Ann. § 18.2-515B
Washington	X		Wash. Rev. Code Ann. §§ 9A.82.100(4)-(5)
Wisconsin	X	X	Wis. Stat. Ann. §§ 946.86; 946.87

6. State Nuisance Forfeiture Statutes

Certain states and municipalities also permit forfeiture of property as a nuisance. The theory of this type of forfeiture is that the property is related to some sort of criminal activity that has been specifically declared dangerous or injurious to the public good and is therefore forfeit to the government to abate the nuisance. In other words, the property is forfeit not only because it was used to facilitate the criminal activity but also to prevent the continued use of the property in the illegal activity. *See Cal. Veh. Code* § 14607.4(f); *City of Albuquerque v. One 1984 White Chevy*, 132 N.M. 187; 46 P.3d 94, 99 (N.M. 2002).

Some of the crimes that have been declared nuisances under state or local ordinances include prostitution, gambling, sales of controlled substances (*see Mich. Comp. Laws* §§ 600.3801, 600.3825), repeat offender driving on a suspended drivers license, *see Cal. Veh.* Code § 14607.6; *Tenn. Code Ann.* § 55-50-504(h), and multiple-offense driving under the influence. *See N.Y.C. Code* § 14-140; *Albuquerque, N.M., Code of Ordinances,* ch. 7, art. 6, §§ 7-6-1 to -6. Property subject to forfeiture under these sections generally is limited to the instrumentality of the offense, such as the vehicle. *People v. One 1979 VW*, 773 P.2d 619, 621 (Colo. App. 1989) (vehicle used in prostitution); *State v. Edwards*, 752 So. 2d 395, 396 (La. App. 2000) (vehicle used by driving-under-the-influence repeat offender).

H. Analysis of State Forfeiture Statutes

Some state statutes contain a section listing all of the criminal offenses that are subject to forfeiture. *See Kan. Stat. Ann.* § 60-4104; *Mich. Comp. Laws* § 600.4701; *Mo. Ann. Stat.* § 513.605. Criminal offenses contained within these lists include narcotics, money laundering, gambling, see *Kan. Stat. Ann.* § 60-4104, such white-collar crimes as embezzlement, insurance fraud, and securities fraud, *see Mich. Comp. Laws* § 600.4701, and sexual offenses including prostitution, pornography, and child obscenity. *See Mo. Ann. Stat.* § 513.605. The reach of state forfeiture can be as extensive as the federal power.

Other states have similar comprehensive forfeiture authority, but it is scattered throughout their codes. It may be difficult to find all of the statutes and determine the type of forfeiture and correct procedures to follow. A case in point is California. Table 2-5 is a summary of selected California state asset forfeiture statutes that shows the offense, statute, and whether the forfeiture is

Table 2-5
Summary of Selected California State Asset Forfeiture Statutes

Offense	Statute	Civil Proceeds	Civil Facilitation	Criminal Proceeds	Criminal Facilitation
Animal Cruelty	Pen. Code §§ 597(b); 597.1; 597.5; 599(b)		Pen. Code §§ 597(f)(1); 597.1(k); 599aa		
Arson	Pen. Code § 451			Pen. Code § 186.2(a)(1)	
Assault	Pen. Code § 245		Pen. Code § 245.3	Pen. Code § 186.2(a)(4)	
Beverage Container Recycling Fraud	Public Resource Code § 14500 et seq.			Pen. Code § 186.2(a)(27)	
Bribery	Pen. Code §§ 67-68			Pen. Code § 186.2(a)(2)	
Child Pornography	Pen. Code §§ 311.2; 311.3; 311.4		Pen. Code § 312.3	Pen. Code § 186.2(a)(3)	
Computer Crime	Pen. Code § 502		Pen. Code § 502.01	Pen. Code § 186.2(a)(24)	
Concealed Weapons	Pen. Code §§ 12020; 12025; 653K		Pen. Code § 12028		
Conspiracy	Pen. Code § 182			Pen. Code § 186.2(a)(25)	
Counterfeiting	Pen. Code §§ 477-480; 527		Pen. Code §§ 480; 502.01; 527		
Counterfeit Trademark	Pen. Code § 350		Pen. Code § 350	Pen. Code § 186.2(a)(23)	

Table 2-5 (continued)
Summary of Selected California State Asset Forfeiture Statutes

Offense	Statute	Civil Proceeds	Civil Facilitation	Criminal Proceeds	Criminal Facilitation
DUI (Repeat Offender)	Pen. Code § 191.5; Veh. Code §§ 23152; 23153		Veh. Code § 23596		
Extortion	Pen. Code § 518			Pen. Code § 186.2(a)(6)	
Fishing & Hunting	Fish & Game Code § 12008; Pen. Code § 597		Fish & Game Code §§ 12157-12160		
Forgery	Pen. Code § 470			Pen. Code § 186.2(a)(7)	
Fraud & Embezzlement	Pen. Code §§ 424; 503			Pen. Code § 186.2(a)(5); Pen. Code § 186.11	
Gambling	Pen. Code §§ 337; 320; 335		Pen. Code §§ 325; 335a	Pen. Code § 186.2(a)(8)	
Gang Activity	Pen. Code § 186.22		Pen. Code § 246; Pen. Code § 186.22(a)	Pen. Code § 186.2(a)(26)	
Grand Theft & Stolen Property	Pen. Code §§ 487; 496			Pen. Code § 186.2(a)(13); Pen. Code § 186.2(a)(16)	
Health Care Fraud	Wel. & Inst. Code § 14107			Pen. Code § 186.2(a)(21)	
Human Trafficking	Pen. Code § 236.1			Pen. Code § 186.2(a)(28)	
Identity Theft	Pen. Code § 530.5			Pen. Code § 186.2(a)(29)	
Insurance Fraud	Pen. Code § 550			Pen. Code § 186.2(a)(20)	

Table 2-5 (continued)
Summary of Selected California State Asset Forfeiture Statutes

Offense	Statute	Civil Proceeds	Civil Facilitation	Criminal Proceeds	Criminal Facilitation
Kidnapping	Pen. Code § 207			Pen. Code § 186.2(a)(9)	
Mayhem	Pen. Code § 203			Pen. Code § 186.2(a)(10)	
Mental Disorder	Wel. & Inst. Code §§ 5150, 5250, 5300		Wel. & Inst. Code § 8102		
Money Laundering	Pen. Code § 186.10			Pen. Code § 186.2(a)(22)	
Murder	Pen. Code § 187			Pen. Code § 186.2(a)(11)	
Narcotics Trafficking	Health & Safety Code § 11351 et seq.	Health & Safety Code § 11470(f)	Health & Safety Code §§ 11470(e); (f); (g)	Pen. Code § 186.2(a)(17)	
Obscenity	Pen. Code § 311		Pen. Code § 312	Pen. Code § 186.2(a)(19)	
Prostitution	Pen. Code § 266			Pen. Code § 186.2(a)(12)	
Robbery	Pen. Code § 211			Pen. Code § 186.2(a)(14)	
Securities Fraud	Corp. Code § 25541			Pen. Code § 186.2(a)(18)	

Table 2-5 (continued)
Summary of Selected California State Asset Forfeiture Statutes

Offense	Statute	Civil Proceeds	Civil Facilitation	Criminal Proceeds	Criminal Facilitation
Solicitation to Commit Felonies	Pen. Code § 653f			Pen. Code § 186.2(a)(15)	
Unlicensed Drivers	Veh. Code §§ 14601; 12500		Veh. Code § 14607.6		
Vehicle Theft	Veh. Code § 10851			Pen. Code § 186.2(a)(30)	

civil or criminal and on a proceeds or facilitation theory. The table demonstrates that 36 criminal offenses have forfeiture provisions. Although that may seem impressive, further analysis shows the limited effect of those statutes. The only statute allowing civil forfeiture of proceeds property is the narcotic forfeiture. *Cal. Health & Safety Code* § 11470 *et seq.* The remaining property is only civilly forfeitable on a facilitation or nuisance theory. Criminal forfeiture authority is even more restricted. The California criminal profiteering statute, *Cal. Penal Code* § 186 *et seq.*, authorizes forfeiture of the proceeds of 30 criminal offenses but has no authority to forfeit on a facilitation theory. The criminal and civil forfeiture statutes are strewn throughout voluminous state codes and are difficult to find. In addition, many do not contain statutory procedures on how to conduct the forfeiture proceeding, i.e., *Cal. Penal Code* § 325. Consequently, most are not used or enforced by state prosecutors.

Recently, the State of New Mexico has attempted to correct similar statutory deficiencies by enacting uniform procedures governing state forfeiture practice. *See N.M. Stat. Ann.* §§ 31-27-1 to 31-27-8. This bill establishes general rules and procedures related to state forfeiture actions. These procedures apply to forfeiture provisions contained in such diverse state offenses as illegal hunting, *N.M. Code Ann.* § 17-2-20.10, desecration or destruction of state historic or cultural sites, *N.M. Code Ann.* § 18-6-9.3, shooting from motor vehicles, *N.M. Code Ann.* § 30-3-8.1, firearms, *N.M. Code Ann.* § 30-7-2.3, gambling, *N.M. Code Ann.* § 30-19-10, controlled substances, *N.M. Code Ann.* § 30-31-35, racketeering, *N.M. Code Ann.* § 30-42-4, computer crimes, *N.M. Code Ann.* § 30-45-7, and alcoholic beverage sales, *N.M. Code Ann.* § 60-7A-4.1. It is hoped that other states will follow this example in drafting a uniform statute governing state asset forfeiture practice.

I. Comparison of Federal and State Forfeiture Statutes

Generally, federal statutes are more numerous and comprehensive than most companion state statutes. This is especially true in cases that involve assets located in foreign countries or in multiple states, or that are related to federal crimes or interstate commerce. However, several states have excellent statutory authority to seize and forfeit property using criminal, civil *in rem*, and civil *in personam* procedures attacking a large number of financially motivated offenses. *See Haw. Rev. Stat.* § 712A-1 to 712A-20; *Ariz. Rev. Stat. Ann.* §§ 13-4301 to 13-4315.) The decision whether to utilize the federal or state forfeiture system is discussed in Chapter 4. However, when contemplating any forfeiture action the practitioner should ask this preliminary question: Is there a forfeiture statute authorizing the forfeiture of this property?

Notes

1.   See Chapter 1, Forfeiture Terminology, note 1.

2.   During the congressional debate on the Civil Asset Forfeiture Reform Act on June 24, 1999, Congressman Henry Hyde, the author of H.R. 1658 made the following statement: "There are two kinds of forfeiture, criminal asset forfeiture and civil asset forfeiture. What is the difference? The difference is in criminal forfeiture you must be indicted and convicted. Once that happens, the government then may seize your property if your property was used, however indirectly, in facilitating the crime for which you have been convicted. You are a criminal, you are convicted, and they seize your property. I have no problem with that. I think that is useful in deterring drug deals and extortionists and terrorists. *I have no problem with criminal asset forfeiture."* 145 Cong. Rec. H4854-02, 1999 WL 419756.

3.   The question whether the Nebraska drug forfeiture statute was civil or criminal was resolved by the Nebraska Supreme Court in *Nebraska v. Juan Franco, Jr.,* 257 Neb 15; 594 N.W.2d 633 (Neb. 1999), with the court determining that it was a criminal statute.

4.   There is some debate about whether North Carolina's drug statute at N.C. Gen. Stat. § 90-112 should be determined as criminal or civil. One state court called it a civil statute, *State v. Honaker,* 111 N.C. App. 216, 431 S.E. 2d 869 (1993), and another determined that it is a criminal statute, *State v. Johnson,* 124 N.C. App. 462, 476, 478 S.E. 2d 16, 25 (N.C. App. 1996). A federal district court determined that it was criminal in nature and an *in personam* proceeding. United States v. Winston-Salem/Forsyth County Bd of Educ., 902 F.2d 267 (1990). A noted forfeiture treatise concludes that the statute is criminal *in personam. See* Kessler, Civil and Criminal Forfeiture § 9:13 (2001).

3 Seizure of Property for Civil Forfeiture

A. General Principles

Between January 1999 and May 2000, the *Kansas City Star* newspaper ran numerous articles concerning the seizure of property by state law enforcement officials and the transfer of that property to federal authorities for processing under the federal forfeiture statutes.[1] These articles highlight one of the most controversial aspects of civil asset forfeiture cases: a law enforcement agency is permitted to seize property based on probable cause and retain possession of the property pending final resolution of the matter. *See Republic National Bank v. United States,* 506 U.S. 80, 84 (1992).

With this background, there are three questions that should be addressed whenever property is seized for civil forfeiture:

1. What is the legal authority for seizure of the property?
2. What constitutional issues are involved?
3. How is property transferred from one jurisdiction to another (state to federal or vice versa)?

B. Judicial Authorization

Federal and state statutes generally provide for the seizure of property by judicial process. These are divided into two types of orders called **seizure orders,** or **seizure warrants,** and **arrest warrants** *in rem.*

1. Seizure Order/Warrant

A seizure order, or seizure warrant, authorizes the seizure of property *prior* to the filing of the forfeiture complaint or petition. *See In re Application for Warrant to Seize One 1988 Chevrolet Monte Carlo,* 861 F.2d 307, 312 (1st Cir. 1988). This judicial authority is specifically provided for in the enabling forfeiture statutes. *See* 18 U.S.C. § 981(b)(2); *Cal. Health & Safety Code* § 11471. It generally is presented to the magistrate in the same manner as a search warrant—an ex-parte order based on a sworn affidavit of probable cause that the property is subject to forfeiture. *United States v. Approximately 600 Sacks of Green Coffee Beans,* 381 F. Supp. 2d 57, 64 (D. P.R. 2005). It is useful in seizing property not amenable to physical seizure, such as the proceeds of illicit criminal activity held in financial institution accounts under the names of the perpetrators.

Most state statutes contain specific, judicially authorized pre-filing seizing authority within their forfeiture provisions. See Table 3-1. Because the New York statute is civil *in personam* rather than civil *in rem,* it does not provide for judicial seizure warrants, however, because seizure of the property is not required for the court to obtain jurisdiction. The New York statute does provide for subpoena authority to locate assets precomplaint, *see N.Y. C.P.L.R.* § 1311, and for provisional remedies to protect and preserve the property post-filing. *See N.Y. C.P.L.R.* § 1312.

Table 3-1
Summary of State Asset Forfeiture Statutes
Civil Seizure Authority—Court Order

State	Statute
Alabama	Ala. Code § 20-2-93 (b)
Alaska	Ak. Stat. §17.30.114 (a)
Arizona	Ariz. Rev. Stat. Ann. § 13-4305 A.1
Arkansas	Ark. Code Ann. § 5-64-505 (c)
California	Cal. Health & Safety Code § 11471
Colorado	Co. Rev. Stat. § 16-13-315 (1)(a)
Connecticut	Con. Gen. Stat. Ann. § 54-36a
Delaware	Del. Code Ann. Title 16 § 4784 (c)
District of Columbia	D.C. Code Ann. § 48-905.02 (b)
Florida	Fla. Stat. Ann. § 895.05 (3)
Georgia	Ga. Code Ann. § 16-13-49 (g)(1)
Hawaii	Hawaii Rev. Stat. § 712A-6(1)(a)-(b)
Idaho	Idaho Code § 37-2744 (b)
Illinois	720 ILCS 550/12 (b)
Indiana	Ind. Code Ann. § 34-24-1-2(a)(3)
Iowa	Iowa Code Ann. § 809A.6 1
Kansas	Kan. Stat. Ann. § 60-4107 (a)
Kentucky	Ky. Rev. Stat. Ann. § 218A.415(1)
Louisiana	La. Rev. Stat. Ann. § 40:2606 A
Maine	Me. Rev. Stat. Ann. Title 15 § 5822.6
Maryland	Md. Criminal Procedure Act § 12-202 (a)(1)
Massachusetts	Mass. Ann. Laws Ch.94C-47 (f)(1)
Michigan	Mich. Comp. Laws § 600.4703 (1);333.7522
Minnesota	Minn. Stat. Ann. § 609.531 Subd.4
Mississippi	Miss. Code Ann. § 41-29-153 (b)
Missouri	Mo. Ann. Stat. § 513.607.6(1)
Montana	Mont. Code Ann. § 44-12-103 (2)
Nevada	Nev. Rev. Stat. § 179.1165.1
New Hampshire	N.H. Rev. Stat. Ann. § 318-B:17-b I-b.(a)

Table 3-1 (continued)
Summary of State Asset Forfeiture Statutes
Civil Seizure Authority—Court Order

State	Statute
New Jersey	N.J. Stat. Ann. § 2C: 64-1 b
New Mexico	N.M. Code Ann. § 30-31-35 A
North Dakota	N.D. Cent. Code § 19-03.1-36 2
Ohio	Ohio Rev. Code Ann. § 2925.43 (C)(1)
Oklahoma	Okla. Stat. Ann. § 63-2-504
Oregon	Ore. Rev. Stat. § 475A.035 (5)(a)
Pennsylvania	Pa. Consol. Stat. Ann. Title 35 § 6801 (b)
Rhode Island	R.I. Gen. Laws § 21-28-5.04.2 (c)(1)-(2)
South Carolina	S.C. Code Ann. § 44-53-520 (b)
South Dakota	S.D. Codified Laws Ann. § 34-20B-74
Tennessee	Tenn. Code Ann. § 40-33-102 (a);53-11-451(b)
Texas	Tx. Code of Crim. Proc. § 59.03 (a)
Utah	Utah Code Ann. § 58-37-13 (3)
Vermont	Vt. Stat. Ann. Title 18 § 4242 (a)
Virginia	Va. Code Ann. § 19.2-386.2A(2)
Washington	Wash. Rev. Code Ann. § 69-50-505 (b)
West Virginia	W. Va. Code § 60A-7-704 (a)
Wisconsin	Wis. Stat. Ann. § 961.55 (2)
Wyoming	Wyo. Stat. § 35-7-1049 (b)

2. Arrest Warrant *In Rem*

An arrest warrant *in rem* differs from a seizure order/warrant because it is issued *after* the filing of the civil forfeiture action by the court. Once issued and served, the property either is actually or constructively seized, thereafter vesting the court with *in rem* jurisdiction over the res. *See American Bank of Wag Cl. v. Registry of Dist. Ct. of Guam,* 431 F.2d 1215, 1218 (9th Cir. 1970); *Strong v. United States,* 46 F.2d 257, 260 (1st Cir. 1931); *Ventura Packers, Inc. v. F/V Jeanine Kathleen,* 424 F.3d 852, 859-61 (9th Cir. 2005).

The arrest warrant *in rem* has its genesis in the law of admiralty and is specifically provided for under Rule G(3) of the Supplemental Rules for Certain Admiralty and Maritime Claims (Supplemental Rules) and federal statutes. *See* 18 U.S.C. § 981(b)(2)(A).

There is no requirement that the magistrate conduct a probable cause hearing before issuing the arrest warrant *in rem* for property that is already in government custody or is subject to a judicial restraining order, Supplemental Rule G(3)(b)(i). (iii), as it is merely a ministerial duty that may be performed by a clerk. *See United States v. Real Property 874 Gartel Drive*, 79 F.3d 918, 922 (9th Cir. 1996). If property is not in government custody or subject to a judicial restraining order, a probable cause finding is mandated. Supplemental Rule G(3)(b)(ii).

The use of the arrest warrant *in rem* has limited applicability in state forfeiture practice because only two states authorize its use in their state forfeiture procedures. *See Va. Code Ann.* § 19.2-372; *Md. Ann. Code Crim. Proc.* § 12-306.

3. Warrantless Seizure

Both federal and state statutes specifically authorize the warrantless seizure of property for forfeiture. Prior to August 2000, the seminal federal statute for seizure without a warrant was contained in the narcotic forfeiture statute at 21 U.S.C. § 881(b) and authorized seizure without process under four conditions:

(1)   The seizure was incident to an arrest or search warrant;
(2)   The property was subject to a prior forfeiture judgment in favor of the government;
(3)   There was probable cause to believe that the property was directly or indirectly dangerous to health or safety; or
(4)   There was probable cause to believe that the property was subject to civil forfeiture. *See* 21 U.S.C. § 881(b)(1)-(4).

This provision became the pattern followed by virtually all state narcotic forfeiture statutes, and 47 states and the District of Columbia have comparable civil warrantless seizure authority. See Table 3-2.

Table 3-2
Summary of State Asset Forfeiture Statutes
Civil Seizure Authority—Warrantless

State	Statute
Alabama	Ala. Code § 20-2-93 (b)
Alaska	Ak. Stat. §17.30.114 (a)
Arizona	Ariz. Rev. Stat. Ann. § 13-4305 A.3
Arkansas	Ark. Code Ann. § 5-64-505 (c)
California	Cal. Health & Safety Code § 11471
Colorado	Co. Rev. Stat. § 16-13-315 (1)(c)
Connecticut	Con. Gen. Stat. Ann. § 54-36a
Delaware	Del. Code Ann. Title 16 § 4784 (c)
District of Columbia	D.C. Code Ann. § 48-905.02 (b)
Florida	Fla. Stat. Ann. § 932.703 (2)(a)
Georgia	Ga. Code Ann. § 16-13-49 (g)(2)
Hawaii	Hawaii Rev. Stat. § 712A-6(c)
Idaho	Idaho Code § 37-2744 (b)
Illinois	720 ILCS 550/12 (b)
Indiana	Ind. Code Ann. § 34-24-1-2(a)(1)
Iowa	Iowa Code Ann. § 809A.6 2
Kansas	Kan. Stat. Ann. § 60-4107 (b)
Kentucky	Ky. Rev. Stat. Ann. § 218A.415 (1)
Louisiana	La. Rev. Stat. Ann. § 40:2606.A
Maine	Me. Rev. Stat. Ann. Title 15 § 5822.6
Maryland	Md. Criminal Procedure Act § 12-202 (a)(2)
Massachusetts	Mass. Ann. Laws ch. § 94C-47 (f)(1)
Michigan	Mich. Comp. Laws § 600.4703 (2); 333.7522
Minnesota	Minn. Stat. Ann. § 609.531 Subd.4
Mississippi	Miss. Code Ann. § 41-29-153 (b)

Table 3-2 (continued)
Summary of State Asset Forfeiture Statutes
Civil Seizure Authority—Warrantless

State	Statute
Missouri	Mo. Ann. Stat. § 513.607.6(2)
Montana	Mont. Code Ann. § 44-12-103 (2)
Nevada	Nev. Rev. Stat. § 179.1165.2
New Hampshire	N.H. Rev. Stat. Ann. § 318-B:17-b I-b.(b)-(c)
New Jersey	N.J. Stat. Ann. § 2C: 64-1 b
New Mexico	N.M. Code Ann. § 30-31-30 B
North Dakota	N.D. Cent. Code § 19-03.1-36 2
Ohio	Ohio Rev. Code Ann. § 2925.43 (C)(1)
Oklahoma	Okla. Stat. Ann. § 63-2-504
Oregon	Ore. Rev. Stat. § 475A.035(2)
Pennsylvania	Pa. Consol. Stat. Ann. Title 35 § 6801 (b)
Rhode Island	R.I. Gen. Laws § 21-28-5.04.2 (c)(3)
South Carolina	S.C. Code Ann. § 44-53-520 (b)
South Dakota	S.D. Codified Laws Ann. § 34-20B-75
Tennessee	Tenn. Code Ann. § 40-33-102 (b); 53-11-451(b)
Texas	Tx. Code of Crim. Proc. § 59.03 (b)
Utah	Utah Code Ann. § 58-37-13 (3)
Vermont	Vt. Stat. Ann. Title 18 § 4242 (b)
Virginia	Va. Code Ann. § 19.2-386.22A
Washington	Wash. Rev. Code Ann. § 69-50-505 (2)
West Virginia	W. Va. Code § 60A-7-704 (b)
Wisconsin	Wis. Stat. Ann. § 961.55 (2)
Wyoming	Wyo. Stat. § 35-7-1049 (b)

However, with the enactment of the Civil Asset Forfeiture Reform Act of 2000 (CAFRA) Section 5, 106 Pub. L. No. 185, 114 Stat. 202, 213, Congress effectively repealed 21 U.S.C. § 881(b) and revised 18 U.S.C. § 981(b)(2) to permit seizure without a warrant if:

(1) A complaint for forfeiture has been filed and the court has issued an arrest warrant *in rem,* 18 U.S.C. § 981(b)(2)(A);

(2) There is probable cause to believe that the property is subject to forfeiture, 18 U.S.C. § 981(b)(2)(B); AND

  a. The seizure is made pursuant to a lawful arrest or search, 18 U.S.C. § 981(b)(2)(B)(i); OR

  b. Another exception to the Fourth Amendment warrant requirement would apply, 18 U.S.C. § 981(b)(2)(B)(ii); OR

(3) The property was lawfully seized by a state or local law enforcement agency and transferred to a federal agency, 18 U.S.C. § 981(b)(2)(C).

In comparing the old and new versions of the statute, it appears that the new section is more restrictive because it does not allow a total exemption from the warrant requirement for probable cause seizures; however, it does permit any seizure that can be justified as an exception to the Fourth Amendment of the Constitution. Therefore, warrantless seizures under the automobile, *Florida v. White,* 526 U.S. 559, 566 (1999), plain view, *United States v. Dixon,* 1 F.3d 1080, 1084 (10th Cir. 1993), exigent circumstances, *United States v. Daccarett,* 6 F.3d 37, 49 (2d Cir. 1993), and search incident to execution of a search or arrest warrant exceptions would all apply. *United States v. $149,442.43 in U.S. Currency,* 965 F.2d 868, 875-76 (10th Cir. 1992). In essence, it does not appear that there has been any significant limitation on the ability of the federal government to seize property without a warrant for civil forfeiture under the new CAFRA amendments.

Likewise, state warrantless seizures have been upheld in the following situations:

• Vehicle stops, *State v. $113,871 in U.S. Currency,* 152 Or. App. 770, 954 P.2d 218, 221 (Or. App. 1998); *Crowley v. State,* 25 Md. App. 417; 334 A.2d 557, 563 (Md. App. 1975);

• Search incident to a lawful arrest or search warrant, *In re Forfeiture of $1,159,420,* 194 Mich. App. 134; 486 N.W.2d 326, 331 (Mich. App. 1992); *State ex rel. Boling v. Malone,* 952 S.W.2d 308, 312 (Mo. App. 1997);

- Probable cause that the property is forfeitable, *Frail v. $24,900.00 in U.S. Currency*, 192 W.Va. 473; 453 S.E.2d 307, 310 (W.Va. 1994); *In re U.S. Currency in Amount of $26,980*, 193 Ariz. 427, 973 P.2d 1184, 1187 (Ariz. App. 1998);
- Evidence, *Dragutsky v. Tate*, 262 N.J. Super. 257, 620 A.2d 1065, 1006 (N.J. Super. A.D. 1993).

C. Constitutional Considerations

Two constitutional issues that may arise in the seizure of property for civil forfeiture are Fourth Amendment privacy and Fifth Amendment due process rights.

1. Fourth Amendment Privacy

If an officer is in a public place, he or she may seize any property without a warrant where there is probable cause to believe that the property is forfeitable. *United States v. Gaskin*, 364 F.3d 438, 458-59 (2d Cir. 2004). There is no requirement that the seizure be contemporaneous with the act subjecting the property to forfeiture. *See Florida v. White*, 526 U.S. at 566; *Jones v. State*, 56 Md. App. 101, 466 A.2d 895, 904 (Md. App. 1983); *State v. Hall*, 52 N.C. App. 492, 279 S.E.2d 111, 114 (N.C. App. 1981).

However, if the seizure involves intruding into an area that has an expectation of privacy, such as a residence or business, then judicial process must be obtained. *See G.M. Leasing Corp. v. United States*, 429 U.S. 338, 358 (1977); *United States v. Mendoza*, 438 F.3d 792, 795 (7th Cir. 2006) (vehicle on private land in plain view subject to seizure unless expectation of privacy demonstrated).

2. Fifth Amendment Due Process Clause

The U.S. Supreme Court has determined that a claimant is not entitled to preseizure notice or a hearing before property subject to civil forfeiture is seized. *See Calero-Toledo v. Pearson Yacht Leasing*, 416 U.S. 663, 678-79 (1974); *United States v. Eight Thousand, Eight Hundred Fifty Dollars ($8,850) in United States Currency*, 461 U.S. 555, 563 n.12 (1983); *United States v. Monsanto*, 491 U.S. 600, 615 (1989). This is premised on the need for the government to exercise *in rem* jurisdiction over the property, curtail the continued use of the property in the illicit activity, and prevent it from being removed from the jurisdiction, destroyed, or concealed. For these reasons, postponement of notice and hearing until after seizure does not deny due process. *See Calero-Toledo,* 416 U.S. at 679-80; *State v. Richardson,* 23 N.C. App. 33; 208 S.E.2d 274, 276 (N.C. App. 1974); *In re Forfeiture of One 1981 Chevrolet El Camino,* 468 So. 2d 1093, 1094 (Fla. App. 1985); *Boyd v. Hickman,* 114 Md. App. 108, 689 A.2d 106, 115 (Md. App. 1997).

However, preseizure notice is required if real property is involved. See Chapter 3, Section G. This also does not preclude the claimant from challenging the seizure in a post-seizure hearing. For more discussion, see Chapter 5.

D. Forfeiture Receipts

Several state statutes require that, when property is seized for forfeiture, either by judicial process or warrantless seizure, a forfeiture receipt must be given to the person from whom the property was seized, or who was in possession of the premises on which the property was seized. *See Iowa Code Ann.* § 809.2; *Conn. Gen. Stat. Ann.* § 54-36f. This is not to be confused with the notice of forfeiture that initiates the forfeiture proceeding by administrative process, *see Tenn. Code Ann.* § 53-11-201(a), but merely is intended to advise the property owner that the property has been seized by the law enforcement agency, which intends to seek forfeiture of the seized property. It is similar to a property receipt that an agency would issue when seizing property for evidence in a criminal case. *See Cal. Penal Code* § 1412.

E. Special Circumstances

There are some situations where it is physically impractical, or economically unfeasible, to seize the actual property for forfeiture. These include real property forfeitures, funds kept in financial institutions, on-going businesses, and attorney fees. In these situations the agency may constructively seize the property by the use of court-ordered provisional remedies, such as restraining orders and other protective orders.

1. Federal Authority

Federal law permits the prosecutor to apply for court orders to protect and preserve property subject to forfeiture upon the filing of a civil forfeiture complaint OR prior to the filing of the complaint upon notice to the opposing side, and

(1) A finding by the court that there is a substantial probability that the government will prevail; and

(2) Unless the order is issued, the property may be destroyed or removed from court jurisdiction; and

(3) The need to preserve the property outweighs the hardship on the opponent. *See* 18 U.S.C. § 983(j)(1).

The order is valid for 90 days unless extended by the court. *See* 18 U.S.C. § 983(j)(2).

The government may also obtain a precomplaint ex-parte temporary restraining order without notice that is effective for 10 days upon a finding that notice would jeopardize the availability of the property. *See* 18 U.S.C. § 983(j)(3). Therefore, court-ordered process is available in the federal system both prefiling and post-complaint.

The types of provisional remedies provided by the federal statute include restraining orders, injunctions, performance bonds, receiverships, conservators, custodians, appraisers, accountants, or trustees or **any other action to seize, secure, maintain, or preserve the availability of property for forfeiture.** *See* 18 U.S.C. § 983(j)(1). It is clear from the bolded wording that relief is not limited to the items specifically mentioned in the statute.

Similar federal authority to preserve and protect property is contained in Supplemental Rule G(7), including the use of interlocutory sales for deteriorating or encumbered assets. *See* Supplemental Rule G(7)(b); 19 U.S.C. § 1612; *Merchant's Nat'l Bank v. Dredge General G. L. Gillespie,* 663 F.2d 1338, 1342 (5th Cir. 1981); *United States v. Pelullo,* 178 F.3d 196, 198-99 (3d Cir. 1999).

2. State Authority

State statutes also provide for provisional remedies similar to the federal statute authorizing restraining orders, *People v. Taube,* 843 P.2d 79, 82-83 (Colo. App. 1992), and the appointment of receivers and custodians. *See Mass. Ann. Laws* Ch. 94C § 47(f)(1). Some states also permit an interlocutory sale of the seized property upon notice and a showing that the property is liable to significantly depreciate and that the cost of maintaining the property is disproportionate to the value of the property. *See Ak. Stat.* § 17.30.120; *Kan. Stat. Ann.* § 60-4108; *Va. Code Ann.* § 19.2-386.7.

F. Substitute Res/Release and Bond Out

Another option that could be pursued is called a substitute res or release and bond out provision. Here the seizing authority agrees to return the seized property to the claimant upon obtaining a bond or payment of money equal to the value of the seized property that thereafter would be deposited with the court as a substitute for the res subject to forfeiture. *See Ala. Code* 28-4-287; *Ak. Stat.* § 17.30.118(b)(2); *Md. Ann. Code Crim. Proc.* § 12-208; *Va. Code Ann.* § 19.2-386.6. The claimant has a duty not to harm or diminish the value of the asset while it is in his custody or he may be liable for damages. *In re Forfeiture of One 1978 Glastron Carlson Motor Boat,* 97 Ohio App. 3d 278, 646 N.E.2d 560, 561 (Ohio. App. 1994).

If the court finds the property forfeitable, the substituted funds are ordered forfeited, but if the claimant prevails, the bond or substitute res is returned. This eliminates property-management issues for the seizing agency and allows the claimant to regain possession of the property, yet still litigate the ultimate forfeiture decision. It can be useful in the seizure of ongoing businesses, real property, or conveyances such as vehicles, boats, or airplanes where the costs of maintenance can be expensive and the risk of protracted litigation can cause severe depreciation of the asset.

G. Real Property Seizures

Because the seizure of real property implicates serious challenges to the rights of property owners, tenants, and secured creditors, the courts have given added constitutional protections to these cases. In *United States v. James Daniel Good Real Property,* 510 U.S. 43, 62 (1993), the U.S. Supreme Court ruled that, under the due process clause of the U.S. Constitution, real property cannot be seized for civil forfeiture without notice and an adversarial hearing in which the government must show exigent circumstances that justify the seizure. At the hearing, the government must demonstrate that less-restrictive measures, such as filing a lis pendens, restraining order, or bond, would not be sufficient to protect their interest. The *James Daniel Good* case has been codified into federal, *see* 18 U.S.C. § 985, and state law. *See Cal. Health & Safety Code* § 11471(e); *Fla. Stat. Ann.* § 932.703(2)(b).

Consequently, real property cannot be seized without a noticed hearing and exigent circumstances justifying the seizure. *Levingston v. Washoe County By and Through Sheriff of Washoe County,* 112 Nev. 479; 916 P.2d 163, 167

(Nev. 1996). In practice, most prosecutors file a lis pendens simultaneously with the forfeiture complaint giving constructive notice of the pending civil litigation and clouding the marketability of the title until the forfeiture case is resolved. *See Va. Code Ann.* § 19.2-386.2.

H. Status Quo or Freeze Orders

There are times when the seizing agency encounters an asset that it desires to forfeit but not physically seize on account of adverse financial consequences in the event that the forfeiture is not successful. This includes the seizure of securities and equity accounts, such as stocks and mutual funds that have values that can fluctuate daily or secured investment accounts, such as IRAs or certificates of deposit, that assess a penalty upon early withdrawal.

In these instances, law enforcement can make an application to the court to freeze the account or maintain the status quo. This can be done either pre-filing with a seizure warrant/order, *see* 18 U.S.C. § 981(b)(2), or post-complaint with protective orders as provided by the statute. *See* 18 U.S.C. § 983(j)(1). The purpose is to prevent the claimant from selling, transferring, or taking any action that would dissipate the asset pending a future court order. The orders should be drafted to grant the court flexibility to prevent the liquidation of the asset, yet permit the parties to manage the asset to retain the highest possible value. *See Ore. Rev. Stat.* § 475A.045(7).

I. Attorney Fees

The U.S. Supreme Court has determined that a defendant cannot compensate counsel with funds that represent illicit proceeds, and such funds are forfeitable. *See Caplin & Drysdale v. United States,* 491 U.S. 617, 631 (1989). State courts also concur that attorney fees cannot be paid with funds traceable to illicit activity. *Com. v. Hess,* 532 Pa. 607; 617 A.2d 307, 312-14; (Pa. 1992); *Vergari v. Lockhart,* 144 Misc.2d 860, 545 N.Y.S.2d 223, 229-30 (N.Y. Sup. 1989).

Additionally, the trial court has statutory authority to enter a pretrial restraining order freezing assets even when the claimant intends to use those funds to pay an attorney. *See United States v. Monsanto,* 491 U.S. 600, 616 (1989); *People v. Jackson,* 138 Misc. 2d 1015, 525 N.Y.S.2d 1002, 1004 (N.Y. Co. Ct. 1988).

In one state case, the prosecutor obtained an ex-parte temporary restraining order, followed by an application for a permanent injunction, to prevent disposal or transfer of the funds in an attorney trust account without actually seizing them. *See People v. Superior Court (Rishwain, Hakeem & Ellis),* 215 Cal. App. 3d 1411, 1414 (1989). This essentially froze or maintained the status quo without requiring the attorney to relinquish actual custody of the funds.

There are a few states that statutorily exempt funds used, or intended to be used, to pay reasonable attorneys fees in connection with the criminal defense from forfeiture. *See Conn. Gen. Stat. Ann.* § 54-36h(d); 725 *Ill. Comp. Stat.* 150/12; *Kan. Stat. Ann.* § 60-4106(a)(5); N.Y.C.P.L.R. § 1311.12.

Obviously, the pretrial seizure of attorney fees should be approached with caution due to the attorney-client privilege. The U.S. Department of Justice Criminal Division has promulgated a directive requiring approval of the Assistant Attorney General before civil forfeiture proceedings may be instituted against attorney fees. *See Asset Forfeiture Policy Manual,* Chap. 9, Sec. II (1996), at 9-14.

J. Turnover Orders

One of the rules pertaining to *in rem* jurisdiction is that two courts cannot concurrently exercise jurisdiction over the same res. This is to avoid conflicts between the federal and state court systems. Therefore, the court first asserting jurisdiction over the property may maintain that jurisdiction to the exclusion of the other. *See Penn General Casualty Co. v. Pennsylvania,* 294 U.S. 189, 194 (1935). Consequently, a federal court will not exercise jurisdiction over property that is subject to a state asset forfeiture proceeding. *See United States v. One 1985 Cadillac Seville,* 866 F.2d 1142, 1145 (9th Cir. 1989); *In re: Seizure of Approx. 28 Grams of Marijuana,* 278 F. Supp. 2d 1097, 1101 (N.D. Cal. 2003).

There are times, however, when a state law enforcement agency might seize an asset but desire to turn the property over to the federal authorities for forfeiture under the federal system. This is to enable the state agency to participate in the federal equitable sharing program. This is discussed further in Chapter 4.

Additionally, there may be times when property is seized pursuant to the federal forfeiture authority, but it would be more advantageous to turn possession of the seized property to a state or local official for initiation of forfeiture proceedings under state or local law. *See* 18 U.S.C. § 981(e)(7).

The legal process by which property is transferred from one legal jurisdiction to another (state to federal or vice versa) is called a turnover order. It is issued by a court from the judicial system that has first exercised some form of jurisdiction over the property, authorizing the release of the property to another court or jurisdiction for legal proceedings pursuant to its statute. This generally is an ex parte order, *People v. $25,000 U.S. Currency*, 131 Cal. App. 4th 127, 134 (2005), but notice may be required in certain jurisdictions. *See Mo. Ann. Stat.* § 513.647; *Utah Code Ann.* § 24-1-15(2)(c).

The determination of when a turnover order is required is a sticky issue, but there appear to be a couple of principles practitioners should follow.

The first principle is that, whenever property is seized pursuant to a state warrant, a turnover order should be obtained before it is transferred to federal custody. *See Scarabin v. DEA*, 966 F.2d 989, 995 (5th Cir. 1992); *United States v. $490,920 U.S. Currency*, 911 F. Supp. 720, 724 (S.D.N.Y. 1996). Under most state statutes, all property taken under the authority of the state warrant remains subject to the jurisdiction of the issuing magistrate. *See Cal. Penal Code* § 1536; *Hibbard v. City of Anaheim*, 162 Cal. App. 3d 270, 275-76 (1984). Release of any property seized under the warrant without court approval could subject the officers who executed the warrant to contempt of court. *See City of San Jose v. Superior Court*, 195 Cal. App. 3d 743, 745 (1987); *People v. Icenogle*, 164 Cal. App. 3d 620, 623-24 (1985). A turnover order releasing property from state to federal jurisdiction furthers the orderly transfer of property from one jurisdiction to the other and shows deference to the issuing magistrate.

The second principle is that a turnover order should be sought whenever property has been seized by a state law enforcement agency in a warrantless seizure if state jurisdiction has attached.

The question of when jurisdiction attaches may be difficult to discern. Some cases hold that jurisdiction attaches at the time of seizure by state authorities. *See In re Matter of $3,166,199.00*, 337 Ark. 74; 987 S.W.2d 663, 668 (Ark. 1999) (Arkansas statute 5-64-505); *Scarabin v. DEA*, 966 F.2d 989, 994 (5th Cir. 1992) (Louisiana state statute La. C. Cr. P. art. 167). Some states specifically make that demarcation in their statute. *See Mo. Ann. Stat.* §§ 513.605(8), (9); *Utah Code Ann.* § 24-1-15(1). Other courts hold that jurisdiction does not attach until the state initiates the forfeiture action. *See United States v. Certain Real Property 566 Henrickson Blvd.*, 986 F.2d 990, 994 (6th Cir. 1993) (Michigan statute); *United States v. $639,470*, 919 F. Supp. 1405, 1410 (C.D. Cal. 1996) (California statute.); *State v. Terry*, 159 Vt. 531; 621 A.2d 1285, 1286 (Vt. 1993) (Vermont statute). Clearly, no general rule can be gleaned from these cases, and the underlying state statute and case law must be carefully reviewed before determining the appropriate procedure to follow.

Failure to obtain the requisite turnover order may result in dismissal of the action for lack of *in rem* jurisdiction. *See United States v. One 1979 Chevrolet*

C-20 Van, 924 F.2d 120, 123 (7th Cir. 1991); *United States v. One 1987 Mercedes Benz Roadster*, 2 F.3d 241, 244-45 (7th Cir. 1993). In some jurisdictions, the transferring party could be subject to a civil penalty of treble damages. *See Or. Const.* art. XV, § 10(10); *Utah Code Ann.* § 24-1-15(9)(a). Legal actions against offending officers and law enforcement agencies for conversion and contempt of court are also possible. *Lightfoot v. Floyd*, 667 So. 2d 56, 67 (Alaska 1995); *Tony v. City of Anchorage*, 950 P.2d 123 (Alaska 1997); *People v. Keys*, 324 Ill. App. 3d 630, 756 N.E.2d 414, 420 (Ill. App. 2001); *Karpierz v. Easley*, 68 S.W.3d 565, 571 (Mo. App. 2002); *Albin v. Banks*, 141 N.M. 742; 160 P.3d 923, 926-27 (N.M. App. 2007).

Strategies to avoid this problem include filing federal charges but deferring the actual seizure of the property until the state action has been dismissed, *see United States v. One Parcel Lot 85*, 100 F.3d 740, 743 (10th Cir. 1996); *United States v. $3,000,000 Obligation of Bank of Qatar*, 810 F. Supp. 116, 118-19 (S.D.N.Y. 1993), or releasing the property to the claimant and subsequently having the federal agents reseize the property for forfeiture under federal law. *See United States v. One 1987 Jeep Wrangler*, 972 F.2d 472, 477-78 (2d Cir. 1992); *United States v. One Black 1999 Ford Crown Victoria LX*, 118 F. Supp. 2d 115, 118-19 (D. Mass 2000).

There are 12 states with specific statutes or case law requiring turnover orders in forfeiture actions. See Table 3-3. Turnover orders are not required in three states. *Kan. Stat. Ann* § 60-4107(j);[2] *DeSantis v. State*, 384 Md. 656, 866 A.2d 143, 151 (Md. App. 2005); *United States v. $84,940 U.S. Currency*, 86 Fed. Appx. 978, 984 (7th Cir. 2004) (Wisconsin statute). Even where a state court refuses to issue the turnover order, the same asset can be forfeited in a federal criminal forfeiture action. *United States v. Timley*, 443 F.3d 615, 628 (8th Cir. 2006).

It is mandatory that law enforcement agents and prosecutors in these jurisdictions strictly comply with these provisions. Even in jurisdictions that do not statutorily require turnover orders, however, their use is highly recommended when appropriate to foster better communication, cooperation, and comity between the federal and state judicial systems and eliminate confusion and competition.[3]

Table 3-3
Summary of State Asset Forfeiture Statutes
Seizure Authority—Turnover Orders

State	Statute
Alaska	Ak. Stat. § 17.30.114 (b)(4)
Arkansas	Ark. Code Ann. § 5-64-505 (d)
California	*In re: Seizure of Approx. 28 grams of Marijuana*, 278 F. Supp. 2d 1097 (N.D.Cal. 2003); *People v. $25,000 U.S. Currency*, 131 Cal. App. 4th 127 (2005)
Colorado	Co. Rev. Stat. § 16-13-307 (2.5)
Illinois	*People v. Keys*, 324 Ill. App. 3d 630, 756 N.E. 2d 414 (2001)
Indiana	Ind. Code Ann. § 34-24-1-9
Minnesota	*Strange v. 1997 Jeep Cherokee*, 597 N.W. 2d 355 (Minn. App. 1999)
Missouri	Mo. Ann. Stat. § 513.647
New York	N.Y. Crim. Proc. § 690.55; *United States v. $490,920 in U.S. Currency*, 911 F.Supp 720 (S.D.N.Y. 1996)
Oregon	Ore. Rev. Stat. § 475A-045(4)(a)
Utah	Utah Code Ann. § 24-1-15
Washington	*Espinoza v. City of Everett*, 87 Wash. App. 857, 943 P.2d 387 (Wash. App. 1997)

Notes

1. These articles are grouped under the project name *Taking Cash into Custody—A Special Report on Police and Drug Money Seizures*, available at www.kcstar.com/projects/drugforfeit.

2. Kansas law specifically states that a turnover order is *not required*, provided the county or district attorney approves of such transfer. *See* KAN. STAT. ANN §§ 60-4107(j).

3. Two articles by state prosecutors that discuss the thorny issue of competing federal and state jurisdiction in civil forfeiture actions and strongly

recommend the use of turnover orders are Jeffrey J. Koch, *Adoptive Seizures and Judicial and Legislative Challenges to Jurisdiction,* FIN. CRIMES REPORT (Nat'l Ass'n of Attorneys Gen., Washington D.C. Sept./Oct.1993), at 7-8 and Mike Moore & Jim Hood, *The Challenge to States Posed by Federal Adoptive Drug Forfeitures,* CIVIL REMEDIES IN DRUG ENFORCEMENT REPORT (Nat'l Ass'n of Attorneys Gen., Washington, D.C., June/July 1992), at 1-2.

4 Initiation of Civil Forfeiture Proceedings

A. Introduction

Once property has been seized, it is time to initiate the civil forfeiture proceeding. This requires the seizing agency to confront two issues:

(1) Should the case be filed as a state or a federal forfeiture action?
(2) What type of forfeiture should be filed? Judicial or Administrative?

Although it would appear that the filing decision should be governed by whether the property was seized by a federal or state law enforcement agency, federal law permits property seized by state agencies to be adopted by federal law enforcement agencies and litigated in the federal system. *See* 21 C.F.R. § 1316.91(1); *Madewell v. Downs*, 68 F.3d 1030, 1037 (8th Cir. 1995). This allows the state agency to participate in the federal equitable sharing program.

B. Federal Equitable Sharing

One of the unique aspects of federal forfeiture is that it provides for the sharing of forfeited assets with state and local law enforcement agencies that assisted in the federal forfeiture. This is specifically authorized in the statutes, *see* 21 U.S.C. §§ 881(e)(1)(A), (e)(3); 18 U.S.C. § 981(e)(2); 19 U.S.C. § 1616(a), and is intended to "encourage further cooperation between the recipient State or local agency and Federal law enforcement agencies." *See* 21 U.S.C. § 881(e)(3)(B). To assist in this sharing decision the federal government classifies forfeitures into two types: (1) joint investigations; and (2) adoptive forfeitures.

1. Joint Investigation

"Joint investigation" is defined as a case in which federal agencies work together with state or local law enforcement agencies to enforce federal criminal laws. *See A Guide to Equitable Sharing of Federally Forfeited Property for State and Local Law Enforcement Agencies, U.S. Department of Justice,* March 1994, at 3. A task force comprised of federal, state, and local law enforcement agencies is an example of a joint investigation.

2. Adoptive Forfeiture

Generally, when a state or local agency seizes property as part of an ongoing state criminal investigation, and criminal charges are being prosecuted in state court, the forfeiture should also be pursued in a state action. There are certain factors, however, that may make federal forfeiture more appropriate. These include:

(1) State laws are inadequate, making a successful forfeiture action unfeasible or unsuccessful;

(2) The seized item poses unique property-management problems;

(3) State laws will result in a delay in the forfeiture that may lead to significant diminution of the value of the asset; and

(4) The state or local prosecutor has declined to initiate forfeiture proceedings. *See Asset Forfeiture Policy Manual* (1996) Ch. 6, Sec. I.E, at 6-3 through 6-4.

The state or local law enforcement agency may then request that one of the federal law enforcement agencies adopt the seizure and proceed with federal forfeiture. *State v. Gray,* 21 S.W.3d 847, 851 (Mo. App. 2000) (small agency with limited investigative resources made federal forfeiture more appropriate). This cloaks the initial seizure with federal authority as if federal officials made the seizure. *DeSantis v. State,* 384 Md. 656, 866 A.2d 143, 145-46 (Md. App. 2005). Seizing property under state law and forfeiting the asset federally does not violate the owner's due process rights. *North Carolina ex rel. Haywood v. Barrington,* 256 F. Supp. 2d 452, 466 (M.D.N.C. 2003).

Before a case will be adopted, the federal law enforcement agency must determine that the conduct giving rise to the forfeiture is a violation of federal law and that there is a federal statute authorizing the forfeiture. *See Guide to Equitable Sharing,* at 3. Additionally, federal agencies have set up minimum monetary thresholds that apply to various categories of assets (i.e., conveyances, real property, or cash) that should be met before it will be accepted into the federal program. These thresholds vary between the Department of Justice and Treasury programs; accordingly, the guidebooks of each agency should be reviewed to determine whether property will qualify for adoption. *See The Department of Treasury Guide to Equitable Sharing for Foreign Countries and Federal, State, Local Law Enforcement Agencies,* Oct. 1, 1993.

On joint investigations, contributing agencies are entitled to request a share of the asset that reflects the degree of their direct participation resulting in the forfeiture. *See Guide to Equitable Sharing,* at 7. On adoptive forfeitures where all of the preseizure activity was performed by the state or local agency, the federal government returns the net proceeds after deducting a flat rate of at least 20% for processing the forfeiture. *Guide to Equitable Sharing,* at 8. Therefore, if the state or local law enforcement agency seizes an asset while part of a joint federal investigation or that meets the criteria for adoptive forfeiture, it may desire that the property be filed as a federal forfeiture.

With this background we will now examine the available civil forfeiture procedures within the federal and state systems.

C. Administrative Forfeiture

One of the filing options in the federal and state jurisdictions with enabling statutes is to initiate the seizure as an administrative, or nonjudicial, forfeiture. Where authorized, most jurisdictions prefer to use the administrative procedure because it identifies contested claims early in the process, allowing uncontested property to be processed quickly and reserving the judicial court system for contested matters.

1. Federal Administrative Forfeiture

Rooted in customs laws, administrative forfeitures have a long history in the federal system, but they have been significantly altered by the recent enactment of the Civil Asset Forfeiture Reform Act of 2000 (CAFRA).

2. Federal Administrative Forfeiture under the Customs Laws, 19 U.S.C. § 1602 *et seq.*

Administrative forfeitures under the customs law are found at 19 U.S.C. § 1602 through § 1621. They permit the seizing agency to proceed nonjudicially against property that does not exceed $500,000; is illegally imported; or a conveyance used in controlled substances offenses or monetary instruments as defined by 31 U.S.C. § 5312(a)(3). *See* 19 U.S.C. § 1607.

Written notice of the seizure and intent to forfeit the property is given to all persons with an interest in the seized property that can reasonably be ascertained. *See Vance v. United States,* 676 F.2d 183, 186 (5th Cir. 1982). Notice must be published once a week for three weeks in a newspaper of general circulation. *See* 19 U.S.C. § 1607(a). Claimants have 20 days from the date of first publication notice to file a claim and post a cost bond. *See* 19 U.S.C. § 1608. If no claim is timely filed, the seizing agency declares the property forfeit and issues a declaration of forfeiture. *See* 19 U.S.C. § 1609. If a claim is filed, the administrative proceeding is terminated, and the seizing agency refers the matter to the U.S. Attorney to initiate judicial forfeiture proceedings. *See* 19 U.S.C. § 1608. The administrative forfeiture provisions of 19 U.S.C. § 1602 *et seq.* have been incorporated by reference as an authorized procedure in other federal civil forfeiture statutes. *See* 18 U.S.C. § 981(d); 21 U.S.C. § 881(d).

3. Federal Administrative Forfeiture under CAFRA, 18 U.S.C. § 983

With the passage of CAFRA, Section 2, 106 Pub. L. No. 185, 114 Stat. 202, 203, Congress significantly amended the administrative forfeiture process. CAFRA Section 2 applies to cases initiated on or after August 23, 2000. *United States v. One "Piper" Aztec "F" Deluxe Model,* 321 F.3d 355, 358 (3d Cir. 2003). Instead of amending the customs administrative procedures, however, it created a new provision found at 18 U.S.C. § 983 containing administrative forfeiture provisions that override the customs procedures where they are inconsistent.[1] The new CAFRA provisions apply to all civil forfeiture actions under federal law except the customs forfeiture provisions at title 19 and four other limited sections.[2] This is called the "Customs Carve-Out" because it exempts certain offenses investigated by the U.S. Customs and other treasury departments.[3]

Some of the changes to the deadlines and procedures of federal administrative forfeiture under CAFRA include:

(1) A deadline of 60 days from the date of seizure to send notice of administrative forfeiture to interested parties, 18 U.S.C. § 983(a)(1)(A)(i), unless the forfeiture is an adopted forfeiture where the deadline is extended to 90 days. 18 U.S.C. § 983(a)(1)(A)(iv).

(2) This deadline may be extended by 30 days upon request by federal supervisory personnel, 18 U.S.C. § 983(a)(1)(B), or 60 days by court

order. 18 U.S.C. § 983(a)(1)(C).

(3) If the government fails to meet this deadline, it must return the property without prejudice to the right to commence the forfeiture action at a later time. 18 U.S.C. § 983(a)(1)(F); *but see Manjarrez v. United States,* 2002 WL 31870533 (N.D. Ill. 2002).

(4) The claimant has 35 days after the date of mailing of the notice letter to file a claim, 18 U.S.C. § 983(a)(2)(B); Supplemental Rule G(5)(a)(ii)(A), or 30 days from the date of last publication. 18 U.S.C. § 983(a)(2)(B); Supplemental Rule G(5)(a)(ii)(B).

(5) The cost bond requirement is waived. 18 U.S.C. § 983(a)(2)(E).

(6) The government has 90 days after a claim is filed to initiate a judicial forfeiture action. 18 U.S.C. § 983(a)(3)(A).

A claim filed in opposition to an administrative forfeiture must be timely filed, verified by the claimant, identify the specific property claimed, and articulate the claimant's interest in the property. Supplemental Rule G(5)(a)(i); *United States v. Thompson,* 351 F. Supp. 2d 692, 694 (E.D. Mich. 2005).

Upon verifying that the claim complies with the mandated requirements, the administrative law enforcement agency forwards the claim and supporting documents to the U.S. Attorneys Office for filing within 90 days of receipt of the claim. 18 U.S.C. § 983(a)(3)(A).

The new CAFRA amendments are designed to insure that administrative forfeiture actions are initiated as expeditiously as possible by the seizing federal law enforcement agency, relieve the claimant of the burden of paying for a cost bond to contest the forfeiture, and give additional time to file the claim. Further, it puts a deadline on the federal prosecutor so that the judicial case will be timely filed. This prevents the government agencies from seizing and delaying implementation of the forfeiture action, depriving claimants of their property for an unwarranted period of time without some legal process.

For a discussion on motions to set aside federal administrative forfeitures, see Chapter 5, Section K.1.

4. State Administrative Forfeiture

As indicated by Table 1-1, several states provide for administrative or uncontested forfeiture actions. The value of property that may be forfeited administratively ranges from $10,000, *see Miss. Code Ann.* § 41-29-176, to $250,000, *see D.C. Code Ann.* § 48-905.02(3). Most state statutes differ from the federal system because the authority to initiate the administrative forfeiture is given to the state prosecutor rather than the law enforcement agency. *See Ga. Code*

Ann. § 16-13-49(n); *Iowa Code Ann.* § 809A.8. However, some states do allow law enforcement agency-generated administrative forfeitures. *See Mich. Comp. Laws* § 333.7523; *Miss. Code Ann.* § 41-29-176.

The state procedures generally follow the federal system with notice of the seizure and intended forfeiture served on interested parties and publication in a newspaper of general circulation. Claimants are directed to file the claim either with the law enforcement agency and prosecutor, *see Kan. Stat. Ann.* § 60-4111; *La. Rev. Stat. Ann.* § 40:2610, or directly with the court. *See Minn. Stat. Ann.* § 609.5314 Subd. 3(a). A cost bond may also be required. *See Hawaii Rev. Stat.* § 712A-10(9); 725 *Ill. Comp. Stat.* 150/6.

The claim must be verified, *Shannon v. North Mississippi Narcotics Unit*, 815 So. 2d 1255, 1259-60 (Miss. App. 2002), and specify the claimant's interest in the property. *Mitchell v. State*, 217 Ga. App. 282, 457 S.E.2d 237 (Ga. App. 1995).

After service on all interested parties and expiration of the time specified in the publication notice, if no timely claim is filed, the property is declared forfeited. *Craigo v. North Mississippi Narcotics Unit*, 762 So. 2d 349, 350 (Miss. App. 2000).

If a claim is filed, the prosecutor files a complaint or petition with the court initiating the judicial forfeiture action. *See Cal. Health & Safety Code* § 11488.4(j).

A few states do provide for an actual administrative hearing before a state commissioner or chief law enforcement officer to rule on whether the law enforcement agency can establish the necessary nexus and burden of proof that the seized property is subject to forfeiture. *See Tenn. Code Ann.* § 53-11-201(c); *Wash. Rev. Code Ann.* § 69.50.505(e).

D. Petition for Remission or Mitigation

One method of resolving an administrative forfeiture in the federal and certain state systems is to file a petition for remission or mitigation.

1. Federal Remission or Mitigation

Remission or mitigation is specifically authorized in the customs laws at 19 U.S.C. §§ 1613 and 1618 and has been part of American jurisprudence since 1790. *See Calero-Toledo v. Pearson Yacht Leasing*, 416 U.S. 663, 689, n.27. It is designed to ameliorate the harsh effects of forfeiture against individuals who are without willful negligence or intent to commit the offense. *Id.*

Because it is an exercise of the Executive branch of the government, the procedures and guidelines are established by each federal agency and are published in the Code of Federal Regulations.[4]

A notice of administrative forfeiture should contain language advising the claimant that, if he or she desires to seek remission or mitigation of the forfeiture, a petition must be submitted to the seizing agency within 30 days of receipt of the notice. See 28 C.F.R. § 9.3(a). This essentially is the same time limit that a claimant has to file a verified claim opposing a forfeiture action governed by CAFRA. See 18 U.S.C. § 983(a)(2)(B) (35 days if mailed and 30 days from publication).[5] Thus, when a claimant receives notice of the administrative action he or she has three options:

(1) File a claim opposing the forfeiture, 19 U.S.C. § 1608;
(2) File a petition for remission or mitigation, 19 U.S.C. § 1613); or
(3) File both.

The filing of a petition for remission or mitigation does not waive or suspend the requirement for filing a claim opposing the forfeiture; therefore, a claimant who desires to preserve the right to seek a judicial determination of the forfeiture should file both. See In re Forfeiture of $34,905.00 in U.S. Currency, 96 F. Supp. 2d 1116, 1119-20 (D. Or. 2000).

The petition must include a full description of the property, 28 C.F.R. § 9.3(c)(iii), as well as petitioner's ownership interest in the property supported by original or certified documentary evidence, 28 C.F.R. § 9.3(c)(iv), and it must be sworn to by the petitioner or his or her attorney. 28 C.F.R. § 9.3(e)(2).

To be eligible for remission, the petitioner must establish: (1) a valid legally cognizable interest in the property as owner or lienholder; AND (2) that he or she is innocent within the applicable innocent-owner provision contained in the civil forfeiture statute. 28 C.F.R. § 9.5(a). This would entitle petitioner to complete release of the property.

To qualify for mitigation of the amount of the forfeiture, the petitioner must show that, although the minimum conditions for remission have not been met, some relief is warranted, OR that, even if petitioner has met the minimum conditions for remission under the circumstances, complete relief is not warranted. 28 C.F.R. § 9.5(b). Under this section, the decision maker may reduce or lower the amount of the forfeiture based on a showing of extreme hardship or other extenuating circumstances. See 28 C.F.R. § 9.5(b).

There is no right to a hearing. *See* 28 C.F.R. § 9.3(g). An official of the seizing agency reviews the petition and makes the decision to grant or deny the request. Because the petition for remission and mitigation process is a discretionary act of the executive branch of the government, the merits of the decisions generally are not subject to judicial review. *See United States v. One 1972 Mercedes-Benz* 250, 545 F.2d 1233, 1236 (9th Cir. 1977); *United States v. One 1970 Buick Riviera, Ser. 494870H910774,* 463 F.2d 1168, 1170 (5th Cir.), *cert. denied,* 409 U.S. 980 (1972). In addition, appellate review is limited to whether the agency complied with statutory and procedural requirements. *See Yskamp v. DEA,* 163 F.3d 767, 770 (3d Cir. 1998).

Although there is no specific time requirement by which the government must rule on the petition, the decision should be timely and without unreasonable delay. *See United States v. Von Neumann,* 474 U.S. 242, 251 (1986).

Table 4-1
Summary of State Asset Forfeiture Statutes
Remission and Mitigation Procedures

State	Statute
Arizona	Ariz. Rev. Stat. § 13-4309.2
District of Columbia	D.C. Code § 48-905.02(d)(3)(F)
Hawaii	Hawaii Rev. Stat. § 712A-10(5)
Iowa	Iowa Code Ann. § 809A.11
Kansas	Kan. Stat. Ann. § 60-4110
Louisiana	La. Rev. Stat. § 40:2609
New Hampshire	N.H. Rev. Stat. Ann. § 318-B:17-d II(d)
Ohio	Ohio Rev. Code Ann. § 2925.42(E)(2)(a)
Rhode Island	R.I. Gen. Laws § 21-28-5.04.2(h)(4)
Tennessee*	Tenn. Code Ann. § 39-11-704(b)

*   The Tennessee statute does not contained detailed procedures for remission but merely provides that the state may stipulate to the exemption which it thereafter files with the court and no further claim, answer or pleading is required from the claimant.

2. State Remission or Mitigation

Several states also provide for petition for remission or mitigation similar to the federal statutes. See Table 4-1.

In the state system, the petitions are filed with the state or county prosecutor, not the seizing agency. *See Ariz. Rev. Stat. Ann.* § 13-4309.2; *Kan. Stat. Ann.* § 60-4110. Further, the state statutes set a specific time limit by which the prosecutor must make the decision, ranging from 60 days, *see N.H. Rev. Stat. Ann.* § 318-B:17-d II (f), to 120 days, *see La. Rev. Stat. Ann.* § 40:2609. Additionally, several states specifically prohibit filing both a claim opposing forfeiture and a petition for remission and mitigation at the same time. *See Ariz. Rev. Stat. Ann.* § 13-4309 2; *Hawaii Rev. Stat.* § 712A-10(4). Most opt instead to extend the time for filing a claim until after a decision on the petition for remission and mitigation has been received. *See Iowa Code Ann.* § 809A.8.

Granting the petition is discretionary, and the state may proceed with filing a judicial forfeiture at any time. *State v. Property Located at No. 70 Oakland Street,* 727 So. 2d 1240, 1244 (La. App. 1999).

The remission and mitigation process is an excellent way to resolve cases quickly and without extensive litigation where the facts will demonstrate that the claimant has a legally cognizable interest in the seized asset and is an innocent party, or where there are other extenuating circumstances that merit mitigation of the forfeiture. Practitioners in the federal and state systems with access to this process are encouraged to become acquainted with the relevant statutes and agency regulations and to use it.

E. Federal Judicial Forfeiture

Generally, a judicial forfeiture is required in federal cases involving property exceeding $500,000 in value, other than monetary instruments or conveyances used in controlled substance offenses, *see* 19 U.S.C. § 1607, real property actions, 18 U.S.C. § 985(a), or contested administrative forfeitures, 19 U.S.C. §§ 1603-1604. There is no statutory deadline mandating the time period within which a judicial action must be initiated except contested administrative forfeiture actions. If a claim is filed contesting an administrative forfeiture, the government must either file the complaint or take some other action[6] within 90 days of the filing of a claim with the federal administrative agency. *See* 18 U.S.C. § 983(a)(3)(A). Otherwise, the government will be required to release the property and not take any further action to forfeit the property pursuant to that offense. *See* 18 U.S.C. § 983(a)(3)(B); *but see United States v. $39,480.00 in U.S. Currency,* 190 F. Supp. 2d 929, 932 (W.D. Tex. 2002).

The complaint must be filed in compliance the Supplemental Rules of Certain Admiralty, which require it be verified, contain a description of the property, and allege sufficient facts to support a reasonable belief that the government can meet its burden of proof at trial. *See* Supplemental Rule G(2); *United States v. Mondragon,* 313 F.3d 862, 865 (4th Cir. 2002). However, there is no requirement that the government have sufficient evidence at the time of filing the complaint to establish the eventual forfeitability of the property. *See* 18 U.S.C. § 983(a)(3)(D); Supplemental Rule G(8)(b)(ii). Such evidence may be gathered after the case has been filed. *See* 18 U.S.C. § 983(c)(2); *United States v. Lopez-Burgos,* 435 F.3d 1, 2-3 (1st Cir. 2006).

After filing the complaint, the court clerk issues an arrest warrant *in rem, see* Supplemental Rule G(3)(a), and the complaint and notice of the forfeiture are served on interested parties advising them of the pending forfeiture action and the time requirements for filing a claim and answer. *See* Supplemental Rule G(4)(b).

Notice of the forfeiture action must be given to all persons who may have an interest in the property, preferably by personal service or registered mail. Actual notice is not required, *see Dusenbery v. United* States, 534 U.S. 161, 170 (2002), provided that the method of service is reasonably calculated to apprise the parties of the proceedings and of their opportunity to present their objections. *See* Supplemental Rule G(4)(b)(iii)(A); *Mullane v. Central Hanover Bank & Trust Co.,* 339 U.S. 306, 314 (1950); *Robinson v. Hanrahan,* 409 U.S. 38, 40 (1972). Publication in a newspaper of general circulation or posting on an official government forfeiture Internet site also is required. *See* Supplemental Rule G(4(a)(iii)-(iv).

A claimant must file a claim or statement of interest within 30 days from the date of service of the complaint or last publication in compliance with the Supplemental Rules. *See* 18 U.S.C. § 983(a)(4)(A); Supplemental Rule G(4)(b); G(5)(a)(ii)(B); *United States v. $138,381 in U.S. Currency,* 240 F. Supp. 2d 220, 227-28 (E.D.N.Y. 2003). The claim or statement of interest must be verified and state the nature of the claimant's interest. Supplemental Rule G(5)(a)(i); *United States v. 175,918.00 in U.S. Currency,* 755 F. Supp. 630, 632 (S.D.N.Y. 1991). A prior claim filed with a law enforcement agency to contest an administrative forfeiture under 19 U.S.C. § 1608 is not sufficient to meet this requirement under Supplemental Rule G(5), and failure to file a new claim pursuant to Supplemental Rule G(5) may lead to entry of default against the claimant.[7] *See United States v. One 1990 Mercedes Benz 300 CE,* 926 F. Supp. 1, 3 (D.D.C. 1996); *United States v. $88,260.00 in U.S. Currency,* 925 F. Supp. 838,

841 (D.D.C. 1996); *United States v. $50,200 in U.S. Currency*, 76 F. Supp. 2d 1247, 1251 (D. Wyo. 1999). An answer to the complaint must then be filed within 20 days after the filing of the claim. *See* 18 U.S.C. § 983(a)(4)(B); Supplemental Rule G(5)(b).

In addition to filing a claim and answer, a claimant, victim, or other interested party has the option of filing a petition for remission or mitigation on a judicial civil forfeiture action within 30 days of receipt of the notice of forfeiture. *See* 28 C.F.R. § 9.4(a). In contrast to the administrative remission process, this is filed directly with the U.S. Attorney for the district in which the judicial proceedings are brought. *See* 28 C.F.R. § 9.4(e). The U.S. Attorney then forwards the agency investigation and recommendation to the Chief of the Asset Forfeiture and Money Laundering Section in Washington D.C. for a ruling. *See* 28 C.F.R. § 9.4(f)-(g). This does not toll or replace the requirement to file a claim and an answer pursuant to 18 U.S.C. § 983(a)(4)(A)-(B), which should always be filed to preserve the right to a judicial determination of the merits of the case if the request for remission is denied. *See United States v. Tracts 10 and 11 of Lakeview Heights*, 51 F.3d 117, 120 (8th Cir. 1995); *United States v. United States Currency in the Amount of $2,857.00*, 754 F.2d 208, 213-14 (7th Cir. 1985); *United States v. One 1980 Ford Mustang*, 648 F. Supp. 1305, 1306-07 (N.D. Ind. 1986).

If no verified claim or answer is filed, the prosecutor may seek a default judgment against all parties who were served but did not respond. *See United States v. Commodity Account No. 54954930 at Saul Stone & Co.*, 219 F.3d 595, 597 (7th Cir. 2000); *United States v. $487,825.00*, 484 F.3d 662, 665-66 (3d Cir. 2007). In the federal system, a request for entry of default is filed with the clerk, *see* Fed. R. Civ. Pro. 55(a), followed by a default judgment of forfeiture. *See* Fed. R. Civ. Pro. 55(b).

F. State Judicial Civil Forfeiture

Under the state forfeiture systems, prosecutors may have the option of filing the matter as a civil *in rem* case, civil *in personam,* or both.

1. State Civil *In Rem* Judicial Forfeiture

Most states provide for civil *in rem* judicial forfeiture actions (see Table 1-3), and several have administrative forfeiture authority (see Table 1-1). In states with administrative forfeiture authority, a judicial forfeiture action is filed whenever the property seized exceeds the maximum value permitted under the statute for administrative forfeiture, *see R.I. Gen. Laws* 21-28-5.04.2(h) ($20,000 limit), in response to a claim filed in an administrative action, *see Ga. Code Ann.* § 16-13-49(n)(5), or in any real property case. *See Ore. Rev. Stat.* § 475A.075). For states without administrative process, all civil forfeiture actions are commenced with a judicial filing. *See S.D. Codified Laws Ann.* § 34-20B-84.

The initial document filed with the court may be called a complaint, *see Ga. Code Ann.* § 16-13-49(o); *Fla. Stat. Ann.* § 932.704, petition, *see Mass. Ann. Laws* Ch. 94C § 47(d); *W. Va. Code* § 60A-7-705, information, *see Va. Code Ann.* § 19.2-386.1, or notice of seizure and intended forfeiture, *see Tex. Code of Crim. Proc.* § 59.04(b); *Okla. Stat. Ann.* § 63-2-506B, but they all serve the same purpose, which is to be the charging document that outlines the jurisdiction of the court, the basis of the lawsuit, and the request for relief. For purposes of this discussion it will be referred to as a forfeiture complaint. The forfeiture complaint should: (1) list the property seized and the date and place the property was seized; (2) allege that the property is subject to forfeiture; (3) state the material facts on which the forfeiture is based; and (4) pray that the property be forfeited to the state. *See Pa. Consol. Stat. Ann.* Title 42 § 6802(a); *Howard County v. Connolley*, 137 Md. App. 99; 767 A.2d 926, 935 (Md. App. 2001); *White v. State*, 258 Ga. App. 700, 574 S.E.2d 892, 894 (Ga. App. 2002). The specific violation of state law that subjects the property to forfeiture should be cited. *State v. Eighteen Thousand Six Hundred Sixty-Three Dollars and Twenty-Five Cents ($18,663.25) Cash*, 11 P.3d 1253, 1255 (Okla. Civ. App. 2000). Some states require that the forfeiture complaint be verified. *See N.J. Stat. Ann.* § 2C:64-3b; *Md. Ann. Code Crim. Proc.* § 12-305(a)(10); *State v. $7,139.00 U.S. Currency*, 228 N.J. Super. 103, 548 A.2d 1175, 1177 (N.J. Super. 1988); *McMichen v. State*, 209 Ga. App. 169, 433 S.E.2d 92, 94 (Ga. App. 1993).

The statutory time requirement for filing the complaint varies from 14 days, *see Vt. Stat. Ann.* tit. 18 § 4243, to 180 days, *see Ind. Code Ann.* § 34-24-1-3, from the date of seizure. See Table 4-2. The fact that most states provide a specific time limit for initiating the judicial forfeiture action demonstrates the concern of the state legislatures that forfeiture proceedings be instituted promptly. *See Wyo. Stat.* § 35-7-1049(c).

Table 4-2
Summary of State Asset Forfeiture Statutes
Civil Judicial Forfeiture Filing Deadlines

State	Initiation Date from Seizure	Claimant Response Date	Statute
Alabama	Promptly		*Adams v. State ex rel. Whetstone*, 598 So.2d 967 (Ala.Civ.App. 1992)
Alaska	20 days	30 days	Alaska Stat. 17.30.116(a)-(b)
Arizona	60 days	30 days	Ariz. Rev. Stat. Ann. § 13-4308; 4311D
Arkansas	60 days		Ark. Code Ann. § 5-64-505(g)
California	As soon as practicable	30 days	Cal. Health & Safety Code § 11488.4 (a); 11488.5(a)(1)
Colorado	60 days	30-60 days	Co. Rev. Stat. § 16-13-505
Connecticut	90 days		Con. Gen. Stat. Ann. §54-36 (h)
District of Columbia	Promptly	30 days	D.C. Code Ann. § 48-905.02(c)-(d)(3)
Florida	45 days	20 days	Fla. Stat. Ann. §§ 932.701(1)(c); 932.704(5)(c)
Georgia	60 days	30 days	Ga. Code Ann. § 16-13-49(h)(2); 16-13-49(o)(3)
Hawaii	45 days	30 days	Hawaii Rev. Stat. § 712A-9; 712A-12
Idaho	30 days	20 days	Idaho Code § 37-2744(c)-(d)
Illinois	45 days	45 days	725 Ill. Compiled Statutes 150/9

Table 4-2 (continued)
Summary of State Asset Forfeiture Statutes
Civil Judicial Forfeiture Filing Deadlines

State	Initiation Date from Seizure	Claimant Response Date	Statute
Indiana	180 days	20 days	Ind. Code Ann. § 34-24-1-3
Iowa	90 days	20 days	Iowa Code Ann. § 809A.8; 809A.13
Kansas	90 days	20 days	Kan Stat. Ann § 60-4109; 4113
Louisiana	45 days	30 days	La. Rev. Stat. Ann. § 40:2608 (1); 2610A
Maine	21 days		15 Me. Rev. Stat. Ann. tit. 15, ch. 517 § 5823
Maryland	90 days 45 days – vehicles	30 days	Md. Code Ann. Crim. Proc. § 12-304(a)(1); Md. Rules 2-231
Massachusetts	Reasonable Dispatch		*Com. v. One 1978 Ketch Named Snow White,* 502 N.E.2d 570 (1987)
Michigan	Promptly 7 days	20 days 21 days	Mich. Comp. Laws § 33.7523(1)(c); 600.4707(1)-(2)
Minnesota	Reasonable Time	60 days	Minn. Stat. Ann. § 609.5314 sub. 2(a); sub. 3(a)
Mississippi	30 days	30 days	Miss. Code Ann. § 41-29-177; 41-29-179
Missouri	14 days		Mo. Stat. Ann. § 513.607.6(2)

Table 4-2 (continued)
Summary of State Asset Forfeiture Statutes
Civil Judicial Forfeiture Filing Deadlines

State	Initiation Date from Seizure	Claimant Response Date	Statute
Montana	45 days	20 days	Mont. Code Ann. § 44-12-201; 44-12-202
Nevada	60 days	20 days	Nev. Rev. Stat. § 79.1171.2; 179.1171.5
New Hampshire	60 days	30 days	N.H. Rev. Stat. Ann. § 318-B:17-b II (e); 318-B:17-d II (d)
New Jersey	90 days		N.J. Stat. Ann. § 2C:64-3
New Mexico	30 days	30 days	N.M. Code Ann. § 31-27-5; 31-27-6
North Dakota	Promptly	20 days	N.D. Cent. Code § 19-03.1-36 3; 19-03.1-36.4
Ohio	Promptly	30 days	Ohio Rev. Code § 2925.43(C)(3) 2925.43(E)(3)
Oklahoma	1 year	45 days	*State ex rel. Dept. of Public Safety v. Five Hundred Forty-Eight Dollars and Thirteen Cents ($548.13) in U.S. Currency,* 877 P.2d 1179 (Okla.App. 1994);Okla. Stat. Ann. § 63-2-506.D
Oregon	15 days 30 days	21 days 30 days	Ore. Rev. Stat. § 475A.055 (1), (3) Ore. Rev. Stat. § 475.075(1), (2)(d)
Pennsylvania		15 days	Pa. Consol. Stat. Ann Title 35 § 831.5(3);
	Forthwith	30 days	Pa. Consol. Stat. Ann. Title 42 § 6801(c); 6802

Table 4-2 (continued)
Summary of State Asset Forfeiture Statutes
Civil Judicial Forfeiture Filing Deadlines

State	Initiation Date from Seizure	Claimant Response Date	Statute
Rhode Island	30 days + immediately 30 days + 20 days	30 days 30 days	R.I. Gen. Laws § 21-28-5.04.2(f); (g) & (h)(4) R.I. Gen. Laws § 21-28-5.04(f); (i) & (l)
South Carolina	Reasonable time		S.C. Code Ann. § 44-53-530 (a)
South Dakota	30 days	30 days	S.D. Codified Laws Ann. § 34-20B-76;34-20B-86
Tennessee	Promptly	15 days 30 days	Tenn. Code. Ann. § 40-33-103; § 53-11-451(c); 40-33-201 § 40-33-107(3) § 40-33-206(a)
Texas	30 days		Code of Crim. Proc. § 59.04 (a)
Utah	60 days	30 days	Utah Code Ann. § 24-1-4
Vermont	Promptly-14 days		Vt. Stat. Ann. Title 18 § 4243(a)
Virginia	21 days	30 days	Va. Code Ann. § 19.2-386.3
Washington	15 days	45 days 90 days real property	Wash. Rev. Code Ann. § 69.50.505(3)-(4)
West Virginia	90 days	30 days	W.Va. Code § 60A-7-705 (a)(4); (d)
Wisconsin	30 days		Wis. Stat. Ann. § 961.555 (2) (a)
Wyoming	Promptly		Wyo. Stat. § 35-7-1049 (c)

Some state forfeiture statutes have provisions that may require a criminal conviction as a prerequisite to obtain a civil *in rem* forfeiture judgment. *See Cal. Health & Safety Code* § 11488.4(i)(3); *Colo. Rev. Stat.* § 16-13-307; *Ky. Rev. Stat. Ann.* § 218A.460; *N.M. Code Ann.* § 31-27-6E(2); *Ore. Constitution* Article XV Sec. 10(3); *Utah Code Ann.* § 24-1-8(1); *Vt. Stat. Ann.* tit. 18 § 4244. In these jurisdictions, the forfeiture prosecutor will need to correlate the filing of a civil *in rem* forfeiture action in conjunction with the underlying criminal prosecution.

In contrast to the federal forfeiture system, most states do not make provision for the issuance of an arrest warrant *in rem* upon the filing of the complaint commanding the seizure of the property. This likely is because most states do not base their jurisdiction and procedures on the Supplemental Rules of Certain Admiralty and Maritime Claim, as in the federal arena. Two states that do provide for the arrest warrant *in rem* process are Virginia, *Va. Code Ann.* § 19.2-372, and Maryland, *Md. Ann. Code Crim. Proc.* § 12-306. The fact that these two states were part of the original colonies, have a rich maritime history, and are part of the Washington D.C. beltway may have had an influence on the drafters of these state provisions. In these states, the clerk issues the warrant or notice that is immediately executed or posted by the sheriff.

Although the arrest warrant *in rem* is unavailable to most state prosecutors, they are not powerless to protect the property subject to the forfeiture action. If the property is not already in law enforcement custody pursuant to a precomplaint seizure warrant or warrantless seizure, almost all states authorize some form of court process granting provisional orders upon the issuance of the forfeiture complaint. *See Mass. Ann. Laws* Ch, 94C § 47(f)(1); *Cal. Health & Safety Code* § 11492. Other states provide for the issuance of ex parte seizure warrants after the filing of the forfeiture complaint, *see Ariz. Rev. Stat. Ann.* § 13-4310; *Kan. Stat. Ann.* § 60-4112, or the filing of forfeiture liens against the property. *See Mo. Ann. Stat.* § 513.640; *Ky. Rev. Stat. Ann.* § 218A.450(2). A few states also require that, when law enforcement seizes property pursuant to the warrantless seizure exceptions, it must immediately obtain a court-authorized forfeiture warrant based on probable cause to continue to hold the property during the forfeiture proceeding. *See La. Rev. Stat. Ann.* § 40:2606; *Tenn. Code Ann.* § 39-11-707(c); *Vt. Stat. Ann.* Title 18 § 4242.

Notice must be given to all potential interested parties of the pending forfeiture action. In some jurisdictions this is achieved by serving the complaint and a summons on all parties, similar to a civil lawsuit. *See Nev. Rev. Stat.* § 179.1171; *N.D. Cent. Code* § 19-03.1-36.3. In other states it is achieved by giving notice of the seizure and intended forfeiture along with a copy of the petition. *See Cal. Health & Safety Code* § 11488.4(c).

The response that must be filed by a claimant varies widely among the states. Some require the filing of a claim, *see Cal. Health & Safety Code* § 11488.5(a)(1); *R.I. Gen. Laws* § 21-28-5.04.2(l), an answer, *see 725 Ill. Comp. Stat.* 150/9; *Pa. Consol. Stat. Ann.* Title 42 § 6802(b), or both a claim and an answer. *See Kan. Stat. Ann.* § 60-4113; *La. Rev. Stat. Ann.* § 40:2612; *Utah Code Ann.* § 24-1-4(5). Specific provisions for each state must be reviewed to determine the precise requirements and timelines. See Table 4-2.

If no response is timely filed, the prosecutor may apply for a default judgment pursuant to the Civil Rules of Procedure. *See Ind. Code Ann.* § 34-24-1-3; *Ark. Code Ann.* § 5-64-505(g)(5)(A); *Tenn. Code Ann.* § 39-11-708(b). Unverified claims or answers or responsive documents not in compliance with statutory requirements may be stricken. *Munoz v. City of Coral Gables,* 695 So. 2d 1283, 1287 (Fla. App. 1997) (unverified claim); *State ex rel. McDougall v. Superior Court (Maricopa),* 173 Ariz. 385, 843 P.2d 1277, 1279 (Ariz. App. 1992) (no personal verification); *State v. Albritton,* 610 So. 2d 209, 212 (La. App. 1992) (no answer filed); *Holmes v. State,* 233 Ga. App. 872, 506 S.E.2d 157, 158 (Ga. App. 1998) (failed to state ownership interest). A default judgment may be obtained on a showing of minimal burden of proof such as probable cause, *see La. Rev. Stat. Ann.* § 40:2612G; *State v. Fifteen Thousand Four Hundred Thirty-One Dollars & Other Property,* 670 So. 2d 693, 696 (La. App. 1996), or prima facie evidence. *See Cal. Health & Safety Code* § 11488.5(b)(1).

2. State Civil *In Personam* Forfeiture

A few states have civil *in personam* forfeiture statutes and use them in addition to or in lieu of the *in rem* forfeiture statute. See Table 1-4. In initiating these actions, three basic steps to consider are: (1) filing the complaint or petition; (2) restraining the assets; and (3) giving notice to potential interested parties.

Most states provide for filing the complaint or petition as a civil action. *See Ark. Code Ann.* § 5-64-505(j). The complaint should name the individual against whom the action is directed and specify the assets sought to be forfeited. This typically is the defendant in a criminal action. In one jurisdiction, notice of the forfeiture allegation may be included on the criminal complaint, information, or indictment. *See Ariz. Rev. Stat. Ann.* § 13-4312.B.

Concurrent with the filing of the forfeiture petition, the prosecutor may seek to obtain ex-parte restraining orders without notice by demonstrating probable cause that the property would be subject to forfeiture and that notice would jeopardize the availability of the property for forfeiture. *See La. Rev. Stat. Ann.* § 40:2613.B. If the restraining orders are issued, notice must be given to potential interested parties of the issuance of the restraining orders and of their right to an expedited hearing to contest the orders. *See Iowa Code Ann.* § 809A.14 4.

Notice of the judicial *in personam* forfeiture action must be served on the individual against whom the forfeiture judgment is directed. This generally is the defendant. Notice must also be given to parties with potential ownership interests in the property. This may include service of the complaint and a summons requiring the responding party to file an answer, thereby subjecting him or her to the *in personam* jurisdiction of the court. *See Ga. Code Ann.* § 16-13-49(p). Additionally notice of the forfeiture action should be given to all parties who have had property seized subject to any temporary restraining orders issued without prior notice. *See Hawaii Rev. Stat.* § 712A-13(4).

G. Application for Filing

When the application is submitted for filing it should be properly organized so the reviewer will be able to find the relevant information to make an informed decision in an expeditious manner. Given that forfeiture matters are civil actions, the reviewing authority will be looking for information that generally is not contained in regular criminal reports. Most federal and state agencies that process asset forfeiture cases have developed their own guidelines for information that should be included in the filing application. The following is a list of items that generally are part of an asset forfeiture application:

(1) A list of each item of property seized for which forfeiture is desired, including the date seized and the address or location of the seizure;

(2) An actual or appraised value for each seized item;

(3) Names and addresses of all potential interested parties of the seized property who should receive notice of the forfeiture action;

(4) A report listing all registered owners and lien holders of any seized airplanes, boats, or vehicles recorded in any federal or state databases;

(5) Complete copies of all investigative police reports and search warrants related to the seizure;

(6) Copies of all seizure orders or warrants served in the action;

(7) Copies of any forfeiture receipts or notices served by law enforcement during the seizure of the property;

(8) A statement of probable cause for each item of seized property and the theory of forfeiture.

It is also important to insure that the application be timely submitted so that any statutory filing deadlines will be met. For example, if a state agency in California desires to have a case filed under the state forfeiture procedures, it should submit the application to the local prosecutor within 15 days of the seizure. *See Cal. Health & Safety Code* § 11488.2. If the state agency elects instead to have the case adopted by a federal agency, it must submit the application to the federal law enforcement agency within 30 days of the seizure. *See Asset Forfeiture Policy Manual* (1996) Ch. 6, at 6-4. This is so that the federal agency may initiate the administrative forfeiture within 90 days of the seizure. *See* 18 U.S.C. § 983(a)(1)(A)(iv). The submitting agencies must keep the relevant federal and state statutory deadlines in mind when requesting filing of forfeiture actions. See Table 4-2.

H. The Filing Decision

The decision whether the case should be filed in the federal or state forfeiture system must be made by the seizing agency on a case-by-case basis with full consideration of such questions as:

(1) Was the property seized pursuant to federal or state seizure authority?
(2) Is the underlying criminal action being filed in the federal or state system?
(3) Does the property meet the criteria for federal forfeiture?
(4) Will the forfeiture be contested or uncontested?
(5) Which forfeiture program can process the forfeiture more quickly and expeditiously?
(6) Which forfeiture system offers the better procedures for ultimate success of the forfeiture action?

Note that any decision based on consideration of the amount of return to the law enforcement agency must comply with federal and state statutes and applicable ethical guidelines. See Chapter 13, Ethical Considerations.

The type of forfeiture action filed will depend upon the statutory authority provided within the filing jurisdiction and the relevant strengths and weaknesses of the method of forfeiture based upon the facts underlying the proposed forfeiture action. See Chapter 1 and Table 1-5, Comparison of Asset Forfeiture Laws.

I. Service of Process

One of the critical elements of a successful civil forfeiture action is adequate service of process. Unless all potential interested parties are given notice of the forfeiture action, the declaration or judgment of forfeiture will be set aside for violation of due process. *Games-Neeley ex rel. West Virginia State Police v. Real Property*, 211 W.Va. 236; 565 S.E.2d 358, 364 (W.Va. 2002); *In re Property Seized For Forfeiture From Williams*, 676 N.W.2d 607, 612 (Iowa 2004).

The service requirements on forfeiture actions generally are the same as other civil actions, *14.9 Grams of Methamphetamine v. State*, 28 S.W.3d 146, 147 (Tex. App. 2000), except that the specific requirements contained in the forfeiture statute prevail over the general rules of civil procedure. *State ex rel. Henry v. Seventeen Thousand Twenty-Three Dollars and Thirty-Six Cents ($17,023.36) in U.S. Currency*, 828 P.2d 448, 450-51 (Okla. App. 1992). Any person who reasonably appears to be a potential claimant should be given notice of the forfeiture action. Supplemental Rule G(4)(b)(i); *Redd v. Tennessee Dept. of Safety*, 895 S.W.2d 332, 334-35 (Tenn. 1995).

Adequate methods of service may include personal or substitute service, *Three Thousand Six Hundred Thirty Nine Dollars ($3,639.00) in U.S. Currency, v. State*, 133 S.W.3d 698, 701 (Tex. App. 2003), service on the attorney of a related criminal or civil action, Supplemental Rule G(4)(b)(iii), certified mail, *Com. v. One 1991 Cadillac Seville*, 853 A.2d 1093, 1095 (Pa. Cmwlth. 2004), publication, *People v. Mendocino County Assessor's Parcel No. 056-500-09*, 58 Cal. App. 4th 120, 125-26 (1997), or posting at the courthouse, *Brewer v. State*, 281 Ga. 283, 637 S.E.2d 677, 678 (Ga. 2006).

For more discussion on the constitutional issues raised by notice in forfeiture actions and the due process clause, see Chapter 12, Section D.3.

Notes

1. *See* Stefan D. Casella, *The Civil Asset Forfeiture Reform Act of 2000: Expanded Government Forfeiture Authority and Strict Deadlines Imposed on All Parties*, 27 J. Legis. 97, n.36 (2001).

2. These include the Internal Revenue Code of 1986, the Federal Food, Drug and Cosmetic Act, 21 U.S.C. § 301 *et seq.*, the Trading with the Enemy Act, 50 U.S.C. App. 1 *et seq.*, or International Emergency Economic Powers Act (IEEPA), 50 U.S.C. § 1701 *et seq.*, and section 1 of title VI of the Act of June 15, 1917, 40 Stat. 233; 22 U.S.C. § 401. *See* United States v. One TRW, Model M14, 7.62 Caliber Rifle, 441 F.3d 416, 418 (6th Cir. 2006) (Title 26 offenses exempt from CAFRA under 18 U.S.C. § 983(i)).

3. With the creation of the Office of Homeland Security in 2002, several federal agencies have been realigned among the Departments of Justice, Treasury, and Homeland Security; therefore, the "Customs Carve-out" is no longer limited to agencies assigned under the Treasury Department.

4. The Justice Department agency regulations for the FBI, DEA, and INS are found at 28 C.F.R. Part 9; U.S. Customs are 19 C.F.R. Chapter 1; IRS at 26 C.F.R. Chapter 1.

5. Note, however, that if the offense is part of the Customs carve-out provisions, the claim must be filed within 20 days. *See* 19 U.S.C. § 1608.

6. This may include returning the property pending the filing of the complaint, obtaining a court order extending the time for filing the complaint, or filing criminal forfeiture against the property. *See* 18 U.S.C. § 983(a)(3)(A)–(B).

7. On December 1, 2006, new Supplemental Rules were enacted for Forfeiture Actions In Rem under Rule G. Previously, Supplemental Rules C and E were applied to federal forfeiture actions. The prior filing requirements were referenced in Supplemental Rule C(6).

5 Civil Pretrial Motions

A. Overview

The strategy of both the prosecutor and defense attorney should be to conclude the litigation as quickly and inexpensively as possible. A pretrial motion brought early in the action could terminate the matter without the necessity of prolonged civil discovery or even a trial. Each side, therefore, should review potential motions that could be brought immediately after the action is filed. For ease of discussion, they will be categorized and discussed as potential prosecution and defense motions.

1. Prosecution Motions

Prosecution pretrial motions should be brought to attack any procedural defects in the defense's responsive documents or to challenge the claimant's standing to contest the forfeiture.

B. Standing

There are two types of standing required in asset forfeiture litigation. They are: (1) statutory standing; and (2) jurisdictional standing. In the federal system, jurisdictional standing is called case or controversy, Article III, or constitutional standing. *See United States v. $38,000 in U.S. Currency*, 816 F.2d 1538, 1543 (11th Cir. 1987); *United States v. $103,387.27*, 863 F.2d 555, 561, n.10 (7th Cir. 1988); *United States v. One-Sixth Share Lottery Ticket No. M246233*, 326 F.3d 36, 40 (1st Cir. 2003).

1. Statutory Standing

Current federal statutes set specific timelines within which the claim, *see* 18 U.S.C. § 983(a)(4)(A); Supplemental Rule G(4)(b)(ii)(B) (35 days); Supplemental Rule G(5)(a)(ii)(B) (30–60 days), and answer, *see* 18 U.S.C. § 983(a)(4)(B); Supplemental Rule G(5)(b) (20 days), must be filed. The states have similar filing requirements. See Table 4-2. Federal and state statutes also require that the responses be verified. *See* Supplemental Rule G(5)(a)(i)(C); *Ohio Rev. Code Ann.* §§ 2925.42(F)(3)(a), 2925.43(E)(3); *Ark. Code Ann.* § 5-64-505(g)(4).

These are statutory provisions, and once these procedural requirements have been met, the claimant has statutory standing to contest the forfeiture. *See $38,000 in U.S. Currency,* 816 F.2d at 1544; *United States v. $103,387.27,* 863 F.2d at 559.

Therefore, if the claim or answer are unverified, *see United States v. Commodity Account No. 54954930 at Saul Stone & Co.,* 219 F.3d 595, 597 (7th Cir. 2000); *Matter of $70,269.91 in U.S. Currency,* 172 Ariz. 15, 833 P.2d 32, 37 (Ariz. App. 1991), or untimely filed, *see United States v. One 1990 Mercedes Benz 300 CE,* 926 F. Supp. 1, 5 (D.D.C. 1996); *Stalvey v. State,* 210 Ga. App. 544; 436 S.E.2d 579, 580–81 (Ga. App. 1993), a motion to strike the pleadings should be brought for lack of statutory standing.

Federal and state courts generally have strictly enforced these filing requirements and stricken claims and answers that are not timely filed or properly verified. *See Mercado v. U.S. Customs Service,* 873 F.2d 641, 645 (2d Cir. 1989); *People v. $400,* 17 Cal. App. 4th 1615, 1620 (1993). Courts have discretion to waive these requirements, however, and occasionally exercise it. *See United States v. Yukon Delta Houseboat,* 774 F.2d 1432, 1436 (9th Cir. 1985); *United States v. Real Property at 2659 Roundhill Drive,* 194 F.3d 1020, 1024 (9th Cir. 1999); *United States v. $125,938.62,* 370 F.3d 1325, 1329 (11th Cir. 2004); *Games-Neeley ex rel. West Virginia State Police v. Real Property,* 211 W.Va. 236; 565 S.E.2d 358, 366 (W.Va. 2002). If the court does strike the claim and answer, the government should then proceed to obtain a default judgment.

2. Jurisdictional Standing

Federal Standing

Before a federal court can assert jurisdiction in a matter, it must assure that the litigant has an actual case or controversy as defined by Article III of the U.S. Constitution. This means that the litigant has alleged a personal stake in the outcome of the controversy as to warrant his or her invocation of federal court jurisdiction. *See Warth v. Seldin,* 422 U.S. 490, 499 (1975). Further, the plaintiff must have suffered some type of direct or indirect injury due to the act challenged in court. *See Vil. of Arlington Hts. v. Metro. Housing Dev.,* 429 U.S. 252, 261 (1977).

Federal case or controversy standing is difficult to describe because the federal courts have been remarkably imprecise in defining it. It is essentially a legal, possessory, or equitable interest in the property. *See United States v. 116 Emerson Street,* 942 F.2d 74, 78 (1st Cir. 1991); *United States v. Real Property at 221 Dana Avenue,* 261 F.3d 65, 71 n.5 (1st Cir. 2001). Some of the factors that the courts have considered in finding case or controversy standing include:

- Evidence of ownership, *see United States v. Coluccio,* 51 F.3d 337, 341 (2d Cir. 1995);
- Actual possession, *see United States v. $191,910.00 U.S. Currency,* 16 F.3d 1051, 1058 (9th Cir. 1994);
- Title owner, *see In re Seizure of $82,000,* 119 F. Supp. 2d 1013, 1017 (W.D. Mo. 2000); *United States v. One 1945 Douglas C-54 (DC-4) Aircraft,* 647 F.2d 864, 866 (8th Cir. 1981);
- Financial or personal stake, *see United States v. One Lincoln Navigator 1998,* 328 F.3d 1011, 1013 (8th Cir. 2003); *United States v. $120,751.00,* 102 F.3d 342, 343 n.2 (8th Cir. 1996); or
- Direct injury, *United States v. Cambio Exacto, S.A.,* 166 F.3d 522, 527 (2d Cir. 1999).

At a minimum, federal case or controversy standing requires a "facially colorable interest" in the property. *See United States v. $9,041,598.68,* 163 F.3d 238, 245 (5th Cir. 1998); *United States v. Premises Known as 7725 Unity Avenue,* 294 F.3d 954, 957 (8th Cir. 2002); *United States v. $38,570 U.S. Currency,* 950 F.2d 1108, 1112 (5th Cir. 1992); *United States v. U.S. Currency, $81,000,* 189 F.3d 28, 35 (1st Cir. 1999); *United States v. One-Sixth Share,* 326 F.3d 36, 41 (1st Cir. 2003).

A facially colorable interest should consist of at least an allegation of interest in addition to some supporting evidence. *See Mercado v. U.S. Customs Service,* 873 F.2d 641, 644–45 (2d Cir. 1989); *United States v. $38,570 U.S. Currency,* 950 F.2d 1108, 1111–13 (5th Cir. 1992); *United States v. One Parcel of Land Known as Lot 111-B,* 902 F.2d 1443, 1445 (9th Cir. 1990); *United States v. $9,041,598.68,* 976 F. Supp. 642, 648 n.10 (S.D. Tex. 1997); *United States v. $100,348,* 354 F.3d 1110, 1118 (9th Cir. 2004).

Even though a claimant may be able to demonstrate Article III or case or controversy standing to enter the lawsuit, he or she may not have sufficient evidence to establish the essential ownership interest to prevail on the affirmative defense issue of innocent owner once the case proceeds to trial. *See United States v. $9,041,598.68,* 163 F.3d 238, 245 (5th Cir. 1998); *United States v.*

One Lincoln Navigator 1998, 328 F.3d 1011, 1014–15 (8th Cir. 2003); *United States v. 5 S 351 Tuthill Road,* 233 F.3d 1017, 1026–27 (7th Cir. 2001); *United States v. 2001 Honda Accord EX,* 245 F. Supp. 2d 602, 607 n.4 (M.D. Pa 2003).[1] This is discussed more fully in Chapter 7, Section H.3.

Case or controversy standing is a pretrial legal question that should be determined by a court, not a jury. *See United States v. Cambio Exacto, S.A.,* 166 F.3d 522, 526 (2d Cir. 1999); *United States v. One Lincoln Navigator 1998,* 328 F.3d 1011, 1014 (8th Cir. 2003). The decision should not later be revisited based on evidence presented at trial or the facts found by the jury. *See United States v. $557,933.89 More or Less in U.S. Funds,* 287 F.3d 66, 78 (2d Cir. 2002).

State Standing

Under state law, a claimant must also assert an interest in the property to contest a forfeiture action. *See Cal. Health & Safety Code* § 11488.5(a)(1); *Ore. Rev. Stat.* § 475A.055(3)(c). It appears that in the state system, however, jurisdictional standing is higher than the case or controversy or Article III standard articulated by the federal courts.

For example, in California the word "interest" has been defined as a bona fide ownership, possessory, or security interest. *See People v. $28,500 U.S. Currency,* 51 Cal. App. 4th 447, 467 (1996); *People v. Fifteen Thousand Two Hundred Seventeen Dollars,* 218 Cal. App. 3d 720, 724–25 (1990). Therefore, standing in this state means a legally cognizable interest that must be established at the outset rather than the end of the forfeiture proceeding. *See People v. $28,500 U.S. Currency,* 51 Cal. App. 4th. at 467. This is based on the premise that a claimant must establish an interest or standing in the property before the expenditure of time and expense on the merits of the forfeiture. *See Jauregi v. Superior Court,* 72 Cal. App. 4th 931, 943 (1999). Other states have similar requirements of pretrial standing placing the burden on the claimant to prove by a preponderance of the evidence that he or she is an owner or interest holder in the property before other evidence is taken. *See Ariz. Rev. Stat. Ann.* § 13-4310.D; *In re Forfeiture of One 1988 Lincoln Town Car,* 826 So. 2d 342, 344 (Fla. App. 2002), rem'd, 857 So. 2d 341; *In re Forfeiture of $18,000,* 189 Mich. App. 1; 471 N.W.2d 628, 630 (Mich. App. 1991).

Many state statutes require that, when filing a claim or answer, the claimant must set forth very specific information concerning the legal basis of his or her claim to the property, including the nature and extent of his or her interest in the property, the date of acquisition, the identity of the transferor, the circumstances of the transferred interest, and the specific provisions of the statute relied upon in asserting that the property is not subject to forfeiture. *See Ariz. Rev. Stat. Ann.* § 13-4311.E; *Ga. Code Ann.* § 16-13-49(n)(4); *Hawaii Rev. Stat.* § 712A-12(5); 725 *Ill. Compiled Statutes* 150/9; *Iowa Code Ann.* § 809A.13 4; *Kan. Stat. Ann.* § 60-4113; *La. Rev. Stat. Ann.* § 40:2612.

The State of Colorado recently has revised its forfeiture statute to require that the claimant establish pretrial standing by demonstrating by a preponderance of the evidence that he or she is a "true owner of the property or a true owner with an interest in the property." *See Colo. Rev. Stat.* § 16-13-303(5)(a). The claimant is required to submit a verified statement describing his or her interest in the property supported by documentation.

Some of the factors that the courts may consider in determining this finding of standing include:

- Whether the person had primary use, benefit, or possession of the property;
- Whether the consideration paid was reasonable;
- Whether the property was acquired through a shell, alter-ego, nominee, or fictitious person;
- Whether there was a relationship between the claimant and the perpetrator of the illegal acts;
- Whether there was a failure to provide evidence or documentation of the interest; and
- Whether there was a failure to record the interest in the public records.

See Colo. Rev. Stat. § 16-13-303(5)(a)–(f).

Given that these state statutes require the claimant to produce detailed facts and documentary evidence concerning his or her legal interest in the property as well as specific information pertaining to any alleged affirmative defenses, it is clear that jurisdictional standing is more than the mere case or controversy standing used in the federal system. *See People v. Superior Court (Plascencia),* 103 Cal. App. 4th 409, 431 (2002).

Indicia of Standing

Whether a claimant will have jurisdictional standing will depend upon the type of property interest he or she is asserting in the property. The following section will review some general categories of property interests that have been determined by the courts to have standing or to lack standing.

The appellate courts have found that the following categories of property interests have standing:

- Lien holder or mortgagee, *see United States v. One Urban Lot Located at 1 Street A-1*, 865 F.2d 427, 429 (1st Cir. 1989); *United States v. Premises Known as 7725 Unity Avenue*, 294 F.3d 954, 957 (8th Cir. 2002);

- Record title holder, *see United States v. 5000 Palmetto Drive*, 928 F.2d 373, 375 (11th Cir. 1991); *United States v. One Lincoln Navigator 1998*, 328 F.3d 1011, 1013 (8th Cir. 2003); *State ex rel. Dept. of Public Safety v. 1988 Chevrolet Pickup*, 852 P.2d 786, 789 (Okla. App. 1993).

- Assignees, *see United States v. Thirteen Thousand Dollars in U.S. Currency*, 733 F.2d 581, 583 (8th Cir. 1984); *United States v. Three Hundred Sixty Four Thousand Nine Hundred Sixty Dollars*, 661 F.2d 319, 327 (5th Cir. 1981);

- Trust beneficiaries, *see United States v. Coluccio*, 51 F.3d 337, 340 (2d Cir. 1995); *United States v. 5 S 351 Tuthill Road*, 233 F.3d 1017, 1021 (7th Cir. 2000);

- Bankruptcy trustees, *see In re Ryan*, 15 Bankr. 514, 519–20 (D. Md. 1981);

- Executors, *In re Forfeiture of $234,200*, 217 Mich. App. 320; 551 N.W.2d 444, 446–47 (Mich. App. 1996); *City of Bellevue v. Cashier's Checks*, 70 Wash. App. 697, 855 P.2d 330, 333 (Wash. App.1993).

Courts have determined that the following individuals do *not* have standing:

- General unsecured creditors, *see United States v. 2930 Greenleaf St.*, 920 F. Supp. 639, 646 (E.D. Pa. 1996); *United States v. $3,000 in Cash*, 906 F. Supp. 1061, 1065 (E.D. Va. 1995); *United States v. One 1965 Cessna 320C Twin Engine Airplane*, 715 F. Supp. 808, 810 (E.D. Ky. 1989); *United States v. One 1951 Douglas DC-6 Aircraft*, 525 F. Supp. 13, 15–16 (W.D. Tenn. 1979); *United States v. Approximately $44,888.35 in U. S. Currency*, 385 F. Supp. 2d 1057, 1061 (E.D. Cal. 2005); *Crenshaw v. State*, 206 Ga. App. 271, 425 S.E.2d 660, 661 (Ga. App. 1992); *United States v. All Funds on Deposit*, 955 F. Supp. 23, 26–27 (E.D.N.Y. 1997);

- Bailee, unless the bailor is identified and shows a colorable legitimate interest in the property, *see United States v. $321,470 U.S. Currency*, 874 F.2d 298, 304 (5th Cir. 1989), and the claimant verifies under penalty of perjury he or she is authorized to make the claim on behalf of the bailor, *see* Supplemental Rule G(5)(a)(iii); *United States v.*

$260,242.00 U.S. Currency, 919 F.2d 686, 687 (11th Cir. 1990); and
- Nominee or straw owner who exercised no dominion or control over the property, *see United States v. One 1976 Lincoln Continental Mark IV,* 584 F.2d 266, 267 (8th Cir. 1978); *United States v. One 1990 Chevrolet Corvette,* 37 F.3d 421, 422 (8th Cir. 1994); *United States v. Real Property Located at 5208 Los Franciscos Way,* 252 F. Supp. 2d 1060, 1064 (E.D. Cal. 2003); *United States v. Nava,* 404 F.3d 1119, 1130 n.6 (9th Cir. 2005); *State ex rel. Dugger v. 1988 Buick,* 969 P.2d 373, 375 (Okla. Civ. App. 1988); *Com. v. One 1986 Volkswagen GTI,* 630 N.E.2d 270, 273–74 (Mass. 1994).

Other individuals that may lack standing include:

- Couriers in mere possession, *see United States v. Currency U.S. $42,500,* 283 F.3d 977, 984 (9th Cir. 2002); *Mercado v. U.S. Customs Service,* 873 F.2d 641, 645 (2d Cir. 1989); *United States v. $321,470.00 U.S. Currency,* 874 F.2d 298, 304 (5th Cir. 1989);
- Shareholders, *see United States v. The New Silver Palace Restaurant,* 810 F. Supp. 440, 442–43 (E.D.N.Y. 1992);
- Finders of property, *see United States v. $5,644,540 in U.S. Currency,* 799 F.2d 1357, 1365 (9th Cir. 1986), *but see United States v. $347,542.00 in U.S. Currency,* 2001 WL 335828 (S.D. Fla. 2001); *United States v. $746,198 in U. S. Currency,* 299 F. Supp. 2d 923, 929–30 (S.D. Iowa 2004);
- Judgment creditor, *see United States v. One-Sixth Share Lottery Ticket No. M246233,* 326 F.3d 36, 43–44 (1st Cir. 2003); and
- Marital interest, *see United States v. One Parcel of Property Located at 1512 Lark Drive,* 978 F. Supp. 935, 940 (D.S.D. 1997); *United States v. 47 West 644 Route 38,* 962 F. Supp. 1081, 1086 (N.D. Ill. 1997); *Matter of $5,662 U. S. Currency,* 714 A.2d 106, 110 (Del. Super. 1998).

The federal courts look to state law to define the nature of the property interest when litigating standing issues. *See United States v. 9844 South Titan Court,* 75 F.3d 1470, 1478 (10th Cir. 1996); *United States v. Ranch Located in Young, Arizona,* 50 F.3d 630, 632 (9th Cir. 1995); *United States v. $746,198 in U. S. Currency,* 299 F. Supp. 2d 923, 929 (S.D. Iowa 2004); *United States v. 392 Lexington Parkway South,* 386 F. Supp. 2d 1062, 1069 (D. Minn. 2005).

C. Standing Motion Procedures

There are three methods that standing motions may be brought by the prosecution. They are by filing a motion for judgment on the pleadings (motion to strike), summary judgment, or an evidentiary hearing.

1. Motion for Judgment on the Pleadings (Motion to Strike)

A claimant is required to allege his or her interest or right in the property when filing the verified claim opposing the forfeiture. See Supplemental Supplemental Rule G(5)(a)(i)(B). If the claim or answer fails to allege any interest in the property or state a cognizable interest in the property, a motion challenging the claimant's standing should be filed. See Supplemental Rule G(8)(c)(i)(A)–(B); *United States v. Three Parcels of Real Property*, 43 F.3d 388, 392 (8th Cir. 1994); *State v. $8,000.00 U.S. Currency*, 827 So. 2d 634, 639 (La. App. 2002). It may be titled as a motion to strike, *State v. $3,356,183.00 U.S. Currency*, 894 So. 2d 339, 342 (La. App. 2004), or a motion for judgment on the pleadings, *United States v. 328 Pounds of Wild American Ginseng*, 347 F. Supp. 2d 241, 248–49 (W.D.N.C. 2004). This is the same motion used to challenge an unverified or untimely filed claim or answer.

The grounds for the motion must appear on the face of the challenged pleading or matters that the court may receive by judicial notice. See *Cal. Code of Civil Procedure* § 437(a); *State v. $1,480.00 in U.S. Currency*, 637 So. 2d 1255 (La. App. 1994). At the hearing, the court will be limited to the four corners of the pleadings and documents on file with the court, and no extrinsic evidence will be permitted. See *United States v. Funds in the Amount of $29,266.00*, 96 F. Supp. 2d 806, 809 (N.D. Ill. 2000); *United States v. $244,320.00 in U.S. Currency*, 295 F. Supp. 2d 1050, 1055–56 (S.D. Iowa 2003).

Unless the lack of standing is clearly evident from the filed claim or answer, this motion probably will be unsuccessful. See *United States v. $347,542.00 in U.S. Currency*, 2001 WL 335828 (S.D. Fla. 2001).

2. Summary Judgment

The most common procedure used to challenge standing is the summary judgment motion. Supplemental Rule G(8)(c)(ii)((B). This will be discussed in more detail in Chapter 6. Summary judgment is appropriate when the record reveals that there is no genuine issue of material fact, and the moving party is entitled to judgment as a matter of law. *See Fed. R. Civ. Pro.* 56(c); *Celotex Corp. v. Catrett*, 477 U.S. 317, 323 (1986).

In the asset forfeiture context, this motion generally is not brought until after the completion of civil discovery when the factual issues relating to standing have been refined. The motion will include civil discovery responses as well as sworn witness declarations and affidavits, which the magistrate will evaluate to determine the merits of the motion. *See United States v. 1990 Chevrolet Silverado Pickup*, 804 F. Supp. 777, 780 (W.D.N.C. 1992); *People v. $28,500 U.S. Currency*, 51 Cal. App. 4th at 464.

If there are no material issues of fact in dispute, and it appears that the claimant does not have a legal basis to establish his standing, a summary judgment motion should be considered. *See United States v. Real Property Located at 5208 Los Franciscos Way*, 252 F. Supp. 2d 1060, 1065 (E.D. Cal. 2003); *United States v. $20,193.39 U. S. Currency*, 16 F.3d 344, 348 (9th Cir. 1994).

One advantage of challenging standing by summary judgment is that the claimant may be required to produce more than a "colorable interest" to defeat the motion. In discussing Article III standing in federal cases, the U.S. Supreme Court held in *Lujan v. Defenders of Wildlife*, 504 U.S. 555 (1992), that standing "must be supported in the same way as any other matter on which the plaintiff bears the burden of proof, i.e., with the manner and degree of evidence required at the successive stages of the litigation." *Id.* at 561. Therefore, in the federal system, where a "colorable interest" is sufficient to defeat a motion to dismiss, the court may require a higher burden of proof, such as preponderance of the evidence, when standing is challenged by summary judgment motion or at trial. *See United States v. $57,790.00 in U.S. Currency*, 263 F. Supp. 2d 1239, 1244–45 (S.D. Cal. 2003).

3. Evidentiary Hearing

There are times that the standing issue cannot be resolved by a summary judgment motion because the factual issues are in dispute. *People v. $241,600 U.S. Currency*, 67 Cal. App. 4th 1100, 1114 (1998). The federal rules and case law provide authority for a noticed evidentiary hearing. *See* Supplemental Rule G(8)(c)(ii)(B); *United States v. 1998 BMW "I" Convertible*, 235 F.3d 397, 400 (8th Cir. 2000). This permits the magistrate to evaluate the credibility of the witnesses and to resolve factual disputes before ruling on the legal merits of the motion. *See Bischoff v. Osceola County, Fla.*, 222 F.3d 874, 881 (11th Cir. 2000); *Munoz-Mendoza v. Pierce*, 711 F.2d 421, 425 (1st Cir. 1983).

D. Strategic Advantages of Standing Motion

There are several strategic advantages for challenging the claimant's jurisdictional standing. First, standing is a threshold issue; therefore, until a claimant establishes his or her standing, he or she has no right to put the government to its proof or even challenge the forfeiture. *See United States v. $321,470.00 U.S. Currency,* 874 F.2d 298, 303 (5th Cir. 1989); *United States v. $15,500 in U.S. Currency,* 558 F.2d 1359, 1361 (9th Cir. 1977); *People v. $28,500 U.S. Currency,* supra, 51 Cal. App. 4th at 467; *People v. $241,600 U.S. Currency,* 67 Cal. App. 4th 1100, 1107 (1998). Therefore, unless the claimant can establish standing, the government has no burden of producing evidence in the forfeiture action.

Further, the claimant may be required to prove standing to a civil burden of proof, such as preponderance of the evidence, *see People v. Nazem,* 51 Cal. App. 4th 1225, 1232, n.7 (1996); *Cal. Evidence Code* § 115; *People v. $497,590 U.S. Currency,* 58 Cal. App. 4th 145, 150 (1997), by admissible nonhearsay evidence, *see Jauregi v. Superior Court,* 72 Cal. App. 4th 931, 939 (1999). Placing this burden on the claimant "assures to some extent that such property will not be released to a person whose claim is spurious or contrived. A legitimate claimant can be expected to have access to the evidence necessary to establish his or her professed rights in the property...." *See Jauregi,* 72 Cal. App. 4th at 943.

The prosecutor may have three opportunities to challenge standing in a pretrial hearing. If it is apparent from the pleadings that the claimant lacks a "colorable interest" (federal) or "ownership interest" (state) in the property, then a motion to strike or dismiss should be brought immediately. If there are no materials issues of fact once discovery is completed, standing may be challenged by a summary judgment motion. Even in situations where discovery has disclosed contested issues of fact relating to standing, a noticed evidentiary hearing could be set and the issue of standing litigation pretrial. The type and timing of the motion will depend upon the specific facts of the case and the law of the jurisdiction.

Whether brought as a motion for judgment on the pleadings, summary judgment, or evidentiary hearing, the standing motion is a powerful opportunity to dispose of spurious claims early in the litigation and should be used vigorously by prosecutors.

E. Fugitive Disentitlement

Prior to 1996, the federal courts had developed a judicial doctrine called "fugitive disentitlement" to strike the claim of a party in the civil forfeiture action who had absconded on the criminal case. However, in *Degen v. United States*, 517 U.S. 820, 828 (1996), the U.S. Supreme Court ruled that a fugitive in a pending criminal action was not barred from filing a claim in a related civil asset forfeiture case against his or her property. The court did not preclude a legislative fix, and that is exactly what Congress did in the Civil Asset Forfeiture Reform Act of 2000 ("CAFRA"), Section 14, 106 Pub. L. No. 185, 114 Stat. 202, 219. Now found at 28 U.S.C. § 2466, the statute prohibits a person from using federal judicial resources when he or she knowingly leaves or evades the jurisdiction on account of a pending criminal action. *Collazos v. United States*, 368 F.3d 190, 198 (2d Cir. 2004). The motion may be brought either as a motion to dismiss or summary judgment motion. *United States v. $6,976,934.65 Plus Interest*, 478 F. Supp. 2d 30, 46 (D.D.C. 2007). Many states have similar statutory provisions. *See Cal. Health & Safety Code* § 11488.5(k); *Pa. Consol. Stat. Ann.* Title 42 § 6802(e); *Co. Rev. Stat.* § 16-13-505(1.5)(a). If a claimant has failed to appear in a pending criminal action, a motion to strike the claim should be brought under these provisions. *See United States v. $1,231,349.68 in Funds*, 227 F. Supp. 2d 130, 133 (D.D.C. 2003).

1. Defense Motions

The priorities for defense counsel on a forfeiture matter are:

(1) Obtain the release of the property;
(2) Contest the probable cause for the forfeiture;
(3) Move to set aside any defaults entered in the action;
(4) Challenge the sufficiency of the pleadings; and
(5) Suppress any evidence seized in violation of the Constitution.

F. Appointment of Counsel

If counsel is not retained in the matter, the first step is to attempt to be appointed to represent the claimant. This is an uphill battle because federal case law has held uniformly that there is no Sixth Amendment right to counsel in a civil asset forfeiture matter. *See United States v. $292,888.04 in U.S. Currency*, 54 F.3d 564, 569 (9th Cir. 1995); *United States v. 817 N.E. 29th Drive*,

Wilton Manors, 175 F.3d 1304, 1311 n.14 (11th Cir. 1999); *United States v. Deninno,* 103 F.3d 82, 86 (10th Cir. 1996); *United States v. 87 Blackheath Road,* 201 F.3d 98, 99 (2d Cir. 2000).

However, CAFRA Section 2, 106 Pub. L. No. 185, 114 Stat. 202, 205, now permits appointment of counsel in federal civil forfeiture actions in two limited circumstances.

First, if an attorney has been appointed to represent a party in a related criminal case, the attorney may petition the court to be appointed to represent the same person in a judicial civil forfeiture matter, provided the claimant demonstrates to the court that he or she has standing to contest the forfeiture, is financially unable to obtain retain counsel, and makes the claim in good faith. *See* 18 U.S.C. § 983(b)(1).

Second, if the property subject to forfeiture is real property, and the claimant is financially unable to obtain representation, he or she may request the court to appoint an attorney for the Legal Services Corporation to represent him concerning the claim, provided the claimant demonstrates that he or she has standing to contest the forfeiture, and the real property that is subject to forfeiture is the claimant's primary residence. *See* 18 U.S.C. § 983(b)(2).

State courts have likewise found no Fifth or Sixth Amendment right to appointed counsel in civil forfeiture cases. *People v. $30,000 U.S. Currency,* 35 Cal. App. 4th 936, 943 (1995); *$1,568.00 U.S. Currency v. State,* 612 So. 2d 497, 500 (Ala. Civ. App. 1992); *Resek v. State,* 706 P.2d 288, 293 (Alaska 1985); *Com. v. $9,847.00 U.S. Currency,* 550 Pa. 192; 704 A.2d 612, 617 (Pa. 1997); *State v. Cruz,* 122 P.3d 543, 555 (Utah 2005); *State ex rel. Lawson v. Wilkes,* 202 W.Va. 34; 501 S.E.2d 470, 476 (W.Va. 1998). In a recent case from South Dakota, however, the court found that an incarcerated claimant on a parole violation who was confronted with civil discovery from a related forfeiture action was entitled to appointed counsel under the due process clause of the Fourteenth Amendment. *State v. $1,010.00 in American Currency,* 722 N.W.2d 92, 99–100 (S.D. 2006).

Two states have provisions permitting appointment of counsel in forfeiture cases, although they are not as restrictive as the federal CAFRA statute. New Mexico permits public defenders to represent clients in civil forfeiture proceedings, *see N.M. Code Ann.* § 31-27-6c(3), and Utah provides for indigent representation for noncriminal defendants, *see Utah Code Ann.* § 24-1-9.

Under prevailing federal and state case law, unless the practitioner can find statutory authority for appointment of counsel, the request probably will be denied.

G. Motion for Return of Property

One of the first pretrial motions that should be considered is the motion for return of property. This generally is brought under the criminal law provisions of the federal or state statute. *See Fed. R. Crim. Pro.* 41(g);[2] *Cal. Penal Code* §§ 1536, 1538.5(e), 1539, 1540. It is used to test the seizure and continued retention of property by law enforcement before formal legal proceedings are instituted and requires the government to establish that the property is subject to forfeiture or is required as evidence. *See United States v. Clymore*, 245 F.3d 1195, 1201–02 (10th Cir. 2001).

Once the government initiates a forfeiture action, the court should not grant a motion for return of property because the claimant now has an adequate remedy at law by challenging the forfeiture action. *See United States v. One 1974 Learjet*, 191 F.3d 668, 673 (6th Cir. 1999); *$8,050.00 in U.S. Currency v. United States*, 307 F. Supp. 2d 922, 927 (N.D. Ohio 2004). Therefore, a motion for return of property may be defeated merely with proof that a civil forfeiture has been filed and is pending. *See United States v. Akers*, 215 F.3d 1089, 1106 (10th Cir. 2000).

Prior to the enactment of CAFRA, when there was no time constraint on the government to initiate the forfeiture action, a Rule 41(g) motion for return of property was used to force the government's hand to file the forfeiture case. *See Muhammed v. DEA*, 92 F.3d 648, 652 (8th Cir. 1996). Now that CAFRA has imposed deadlines for implementing federal administrative, *see* 18 U.S.C. § 983(a)(1)(A)(i), (iv) (60 or 90 days), and many judicial forfeiture actions, *see* 18 U.S.C. § 983(a)(3)(A) (90 days), the claimant can bring a motion for return under the CAFRA provisions if those time limits are exceeded.

Rule 41(g) motions are now limited to prefiling seizures or property unduly detained without initiation of a forfeiture action. *United States v. Sims*, 376 F.3d 705, 708 (7th Cir. 2004). The motion should be timely filed in the federal district court in which the seizure took place, *Polanco v. United States DEA*, 158 F.3d 647, 655 (2d Cir. 1998), and the federal government must have actual or constructive possession of the property. *United States v. Copeman*, 458 F.3d 1070, 1072 (10th Cir. 2006).

It should also be emphasized that filing a Rule 41(g) motion does not substitute for the requirement to file a timely claim and/or answer in the related administrative or judicial forfeiture actions as required by the governing statutes. *See United States v. Deninno*, 103 F.3d 82, 84 (10th Cir. 1996); *United States v. $70,000 in U.S. Currency*, 203 F.R.D. 308, 310 (S.D. Ohio 2000).

State litigation on motions to return property parallels the federal cases. Most states have specific deadlines for the filing of forfeiture actions (see Table 4-2), and failure to initiate the forfeiture action within that time frame may entitle the claimant to the return of the asset. *City of Hattiesburg v. Thirty-Five Thousand Three Hundred Seventy Dollars,* 872 So. 2d 701, 703 (Miss. App. 2004). Once the forfeiture action is filed, however, it is the exclusive means for return of the property. *District of Columbia v. Dunmore,* 749 A.2d 740, 745 (D.C. 2000); *City of Coral Gables v. Rodriguez,* 568 So. 2d 1302, 1303 (Fla. App. 1990); *City of Miami v. Barclay,* 563 So. 2d 203, 204 (Fla. App. 1990). Untimely requests, *Johnson v. Roberts,* 638 S.W.2d 401, 403 (Tenn. App. 1982), and failure to follow statutory requirements will preclude recovery. *State v. McGee,* 758 So. 2d 338, 339 (La. App. 2000).

H. Provisional Remedies

Federal and state statutes permit the use of provisional remedies to restrain property subject to forfeiture prior to or in conjunction with the filing of the forfeiture action. *See* 18 U.S.C. § 983(j); *Cal. Health & Safety Code* § 11492; see also Chapter 3. Many of these statutes provide for the issuance of temporary restraining orders that expire within a short time period after issuance. *See* 18 U.S.C. § 983(j)(3) (90 days with notice or 10 days without); *Ariz. Rev. Stat. Ann.* § 13-4312.D-E (10 days). This allows the owner to request an expedited hearing to contest the basis for the order and places the burden on the government to demonstrate that there is a substantial probability that it will prevail on the issue of forfeiture and that the need to preserve the property outweighs the hardship on the claimant. *See* 18 U.S.C. § 983(j)(1).

If provisional court orders are in effect that were issued ex-parte without notice, the claimant should challenge the legal basis for the order and continued detention of the property. This hearing must be heard at the earliest possible time and prior to the expiration of the temporary order. *See* 18 U.S.C. § 983(j)(3). This is an opportunity to get property released quickly or modify the terms to protect the property, yet permit reasonable use by the owner. *See Co. Rev. Stat.* § 16-13-308(1)(f).

Injunctive relief attacking the seizure and filing of a forfeiture action is not available to a claimant. *See Ewing v. Mytinger & Casselberry, Inc.,* 339 U.S. 594, 598–99 (1950). The only recourse is to file a claim contesting the forfeiture on the merits. *Genedo Pharmaceutical N.V. v. Thompson,* 308 F. Supp. 2d 881, 883 (N.D. Ill. 2003).

I. Hardship Provision

Another method of obtaining the immediate release of property is under the hardship provisions of CAFRA Section 2, 106 Pub. L. No. 185, 114 Stat. 202, 208. Found at 18 U.S.C. § 983(f), these provisions provide that the seized property may be returned to the claimant pending final judgment of forfeiture, provided the claimant can establish a possessory interest in the property, substantial ties to the community, and that continued possession of the property pending final judgment will cause the claimant substantial hardship that outweighs the risk the property may be destroyed, damaged, or lost. *United States v. $159,040 in U.S. Currency,* 517 F. Supp. 2d 437, 439 (D.D.C. 2007) (no substantial ties to community demonstrated). The request is first made to the seizing agency, 18 U.S.C. § 983(f)(2), which has 15 days to consider the demand, after which a petition may be filed with the court, *see* 18 U.S.C. § 983(f)(3), and a decision rendered within 30 days, *see* 18 U.S.C. § 983(f)(5). The court may set conditions before releasing the property, including procuring a bond, insurance, or lien to protect it. *See* 18 U.S.C. § 983(f)(7). This provision does not apply to contraband, currency, evidence of a crime, or property specifically designed for use in illegal activity or is likely to be used to commit other criminal acts if released. *See* 18 U.S.C. § 983(f)(8). In applying this provision, one court released two family-owned vehicles but declined to relinquish funds from a bank account. *See United States v. $1,231,349.68 in Funds,* 227 F. Supp. 2d 125, 129 (D.D.C. 2002). Under the terms of the statute, all of the conditions of 18 U.S.C. § 983(f)(1)(A) through (E) must be satisfied or the motion will be denied. *United States v. Undetermined Amount of U.S. Currency,* 376 F.3d 260, 264 (4th Cir. 2004).

A few states have comparable hardship provisions with minor variations. *See Ore. Rev. Stat.* §§ 131.573; 475A.060; *Utah Code Ann.* § 24-1-7. However, several states provide for an elective bond out provision that allows the owner to petition the seizing agency or the court to release the property to the claimant upon payment of an appropriate bond or security value that is then forfeited in place of the original seized property. *See Minn. Stat. Ann.* § 609.531 Subd. 5a; *Mo. Ann. Stat.* § 513.610.

This option certainly is worth exploring because it may allow the claimant to regain possession of the property and relieve the seizing agency the headache of property management.

J. Probable Cause Hearing

A fruitful area of attack may be to bring a motion challenging the probable cause for the seizure of the property. The theory of this motion is that, under the due process guarantees of the Constitution, the claimant is entitled to an early determination by the court that there is probable cause for the seizure and pending forfeiture action. The basis for such a motion is purely statutory; there is no constitutional requirement for a probable cause hearing in advance of the forfeiture trial. See United States v. Eight Thousand Eight Hundred & Fifty Dollars ($8,850) in United States Currency, 461 U.S. 555, 562 (1983); United States v. Von Neumann, 474 U.S. 242, 249 (1986); Gonzales v. Rivkind, 858 F.2d 657, 660 (11th Cir. 1988); United States v. Banco Cafetero Panama, 797 F.2d 1154, 1162 (2d Cir. 1986).

However, a recent federal appellate court has determined that a municipal ordinance forfeiting vehicles on an instrumentality theory violated due process by failing to provide for a prompt post-seizure, prejudgment hearing to test the probable cause for the seizure and the basis for continued retention of the property until trial. See Krimstock v. Kelly, 306 F.3d 40, 67 (2d Cir. 2002), cert. denied, 539 U.S. 969 (2003). Therefore, a forfeiture statute that does not contain sufficient protections and procedures for early release of property and the protection of innocent parties may be subject to constitutional challenge under the due process clause.

1. Federal Procedures

The government generally is not required to demonstrate probable cause until trial, unless the claimant challenges the validity of the seizure before trial. See United States v. Daccarett, 6 F.3d 37, 50 (2d Cir. 1993); Marine Midland Bank N.A. v. United States, 11 F.3d 1119, 1124 (2d Cir. 1993).

Strategies claimants have used to challenge a seizure prior to trial in the federal system include bringing a motion for return of property under Rule 41(g) (see Chapter 5, Section G) or as a separate civil motion based on equitable jurisdiction. See In Re McCorkle, 972 F. Supp. 1423, 1431 n.10 (M.D. Fla. 1997). Federal courts have entertained these motions in very limited circumstances. If the funds are necessary to retain counsel in the criminal matter and have been seized ex parte, an adversarial, post-restraint, pretrial probable cause hearing may be required. See United States v. Monsanto, 924 F.2d 1186, 1203 (2d Cir. 1991); United States v. Michelle's Lounge I, 39 F.3d 684, 701 (7th Cir. 1994); United States v. Michelle's Lounge II, 126 F.3d 1006, 1009 (7th Cir. 1997); United States v. Farmer, 274 F.3d 800, 805 (4th Cir. 2001). In addition, if the ex parte seizure seriously impacts an existing business, leaving it no other legal recourse to challenge the legal sufficiency of the property seizures, the courts have permitted an expedited pretrial probable cause hearing. *See In re Seizure of All Funds (Registry Publishing, Inc.),* 887 F. Supp. 435, 449 (E.D.N.Y. 1995); *In the Matter of the Seizure of One White Jeep Cherokee,* 991 F. Supp. 1077, 1081–82 (S.D. Iowa 1998).

Given that CAFRA contains statutory provisions for expedited filing of property seized for administrative forfeiture, *see* 18 U.S.C. § 983(a), hardship release, *see* 18 U.S.C. § 983(f), and a uniform innocent defense, *see* 18 U.S.C. § 983(d), federal challenges under *Krimstock v. Kelly* are unlikely to be successful. *United States v. All Funds on Deposit at Dime Savings Bank,* 255 F. Supp. 2d 56, 72 (E.D.N.Y. 2003).

2. State Procedures

Probable cause hearings are statutorily authorized in several states. See Table 5-1. Most statutes require that the claimant request the hearing within 10 days, *see Iowa Code Ann.* § 809A.12 3; *Kan. Stat. Ann.* § 60-4112, to 30 days,

Table 5-1
Summary of State Asset Forfeiture Statutes
Probable Cause Hearing

State	Statute
Arizona	Ariz. Rev. Stat. § 13-4310B
California	Cal. Health & Sat. Code § 11488,4(h)
Florida	Fla. Stat. Ann. § 932.703(2)(a)
Georgia	Ga. Code Ann. § 16-13-49(q)(4)
Hawaii	Hawaii Rev. Stat. § 712A-11(2)
Iowa	Iowa Code Ann. § 809A.12 3
Kansas	Kan. Stat. Ann. § 60-4112(c)
Louisiana	La. Rev. Stat. Ann. § 40:2611.C
Michigan	Mich. Comp. Laws § 600.4705
Missouri	Mo. Ann. Stat. § 513.645.4
Oregon	Ore. Rev. Stat. § 475A.045(8)
Tennessee	Tenn. Code Ann.§ 39-11-709(d)

see Ga. Code Ann. § 16-13-49(q)(4); *Tenn. Code Ann.* § 39-11-709(d), after receiving notice of the seizure or actual notice, whichever is earlier. Therefore, claimant and counsel must act quickly to preserve their right to this expedited hearing. *Wright v. Bryant,* 647 So. 2d 625, 626–27 (La. App. 1994). Notice of the motion is given to the prosecutor, and the hearing may be set as early as 21 days, *see Tenn. Code Ann.* § 39-11-709(d), or 30 days, *see Hawaii Rev. Stat.* § 712A-11(2). Failure to conduct the hearing within the statutory period may violate due process and result in the release of the property to the claimant. *Murphy v. Fortune,* 857 So. 2d 370, 371 (Fla. App. 2003).

There are three restrictions limiting the applicability of this motion in state courts. The first is that most states allow this hearing only if there has not been a prior judicial determination of probable cause. *See Ariz. Rev. Stat. Ann.* § 13-4310.B; *Ore. Rev. Stat.* § 475A.045(8). If the property was seized pursuant to a judicially reviewed seizure warrant or court order, this motion should not be available. However, there are a few jurisdictions that do not limit probable cause hearings to warrantless seizures. *See Cal. Health & Safety Code* § 11488.4(h); *Fla. Stat. Ann.* § 932.703(2)(a).

Next, before the motion can be brought, the claimant must establish standing to contest the forfeiture. This requires the claimant to prove that he or she is the owner or an interest holder of the property before any evidence is taken on the issue of probable cause, or the motion will be dismissed. *See Tenn. Code Ann.* § 39-11-709(d).

Finally, the motion is limited to the sole issue as to whether probable cause then exists for the forfeiture of the property. *See Ga. Code Ann.* § 16-13-49(q)(4); *La. Rev. Stat. Ann.* § 40:2611.C. This precludes any other issues, such as affirmative defenses, from being asserted until trial. *State v. 790 Cash,* 821 So. 2d 609, 613 (La. App. 2002).

At the probable cause hearing, state courts have relied on federal cases defining probable cause as less than prima facie proof, but more than a mere suspicion, based on the aggregate of facts. *See United States v. $129,727.00 U.S. Currency,* 129 F.3d 486, 489 (9th Cir. 1997). It is the same standard required to obtain a search warrant. *State v. Giles,* 697 So. 2d 699, 704 (La. App. 1997). The finding of probable cause may be based on circumstantial evidence, *Gillum v. One 1978 Kenworth Semi-Truck,* 543 So. 2d 462, 464 (Fla. App. 1989), including hearsay statements, *Com. v. Fourteen Thousand Two Hundred Dollars,* 653 N.E.2d 153, 155 (Mass. 1995); *State ex rel. Woods v. Filler,* 169 Ariz. 224, 818 P.2d 209, 213 (Ariz. App. 1991); *Banks v. State,* 277 Ga. 543, 592 S.E.2d 668, 670 (Ga. App. 2004), and is not limited to evidence at the time of the seizure or filing, but may include after-acquired evidence. *See People v.*

Ten $500 Barclays Bank Visa Traveler's Checks, 16 Cal. App. 4th 475, 479 (1993); *Beary v. Bruce,* 804 So. 2d 579, 581 (Fla. App. 2002). The hearing generally is conducted by the use of declarations, affidavits, and other documentary evidence, but the statute may also permit the use of oral testimony. *See Fla. Stat. Ann.* § 932.703(2)(c).

There are several strategic advantages to the probable cause motion. First, it allows the claimant to quickly set a hearing to contest the prosecutor's probable cause for the forfeiture action. If successful, the property is released and the litigation is terminated. Even if the claimant does not prevail, he or she has an early opportunity to evaluate the probable cause for the seizure and forfeiture action.

K. Motion to Set Aside Default

If any declarations or judgments have been obtained forfeiting the property in an administrative or uncontested judicial proceeding, the next step is to attempt to set aside those defaults. There are two procedures that can be used to set aside those actions. In an administrative action, is it called a Motion to Set Aside Forfeiture, *see* 18 U.S.C. § 983(e), and in a judicial case, it is called a Motion to Set Aside Judicial Default. *See Fed. R. Civ. Pro.* 60.

1. Motion to Set Aside Administrative Forfeiture

Prior to CAFRA, the appellate courts had determined that judicial review of completed administrative forfeiture actions was limited to whether all potential claimants had received adequate notice of the proceeding and had an opportunity to contest the action. *See United States v. Eubanks,* 169 F.3d 672, 674 (11th Cir. 1999); *Toure v. United States,* 24 F.3d 444, 446 (2d Cir. 1994). Attacks on the merits of the forfeiture were not permitted. *See United States v. Derenak,* 27 F. Supp. 2d 1300, 1304 (M.D. Fla. 1998); *Concepcion v. United States,* 938 F. Supp. 134, 138 (E.D.N.Y 1996); *United States v. Wade,* 230 F. Supp. 2d 1298, 1308 (M.D. Fla. 2002).

CAFRA Section 2, 106 Pub. L. No. 185, 114 Stat. 202, 207, codifies that position and permits a person to set aside a declaration of forfeiture if he or she were entitled to written notice of the nonjudicial proceeding but did not receive it. *See* 18 U.S.C. § 983(e)(1). If the evidence shows that the government knew or should have known of the person's potential interest and failed to take reasonable steps to provide notice, AND the party did not have reason to know of the forfeiture within sufficient time to file a timely claim, the motion should be granted. *See* 18 U.S.C. § 983(e)(1)(A)–(B). Failure to timely commence the administrative forfeiture also is reviewable by the court. *United States v. Robinson*, 434 F.3d 357, 364 (5th Cir. 2005); *United States v. Assorted Jewelry*, 386 F. Supp. 2d 9, 13 (D. P.R. 2005).

However, this victory may be short-lived because CAFRA then permits the prosecutor to initiate a nonjudicial forfeiture within 60 days and a judicial forfeiture within six months of the order granting the motion. *See* 18 U.S.C. § 983(e)(2)(B). The expiration of any applicable statute of limitations does not bar this new action. *See* 18 U.S.C. § 983(e)(2)(A).

There are a few factors to remember in bringing these motions. First, they only apply to completed administrative forfeiture actions. *See Upshaw v. U.S. Customs Service*, 153 F. Supp. 2d 46, 49 (D. Mass 2001). Second, the claimant must prove his or her standing to contest the forfeiture and demonstrate that he or she was entitled to written notice of the action. *See* 18 U.S.C. § 983(e)(1); *Munoz-Valencia v. United States*, 169 Fed. Appx. 150, 151 (3d Cir. 2006). Third, the claimant must bring this motion within five years after the date of final publication of the notice of forfeiture. *See* 18 U.S.C. § 983(e)(3). Finally, this motion is the exclusive remedy to set aside a completed administrative forfeiture. *See* 18 U.S.C. § 983(e)(5); *Turner v. Gonzales*, 2007 WL 1302126 (7th Cir. 2007).

State courts have also set aside administrative declarations of forfeiture where the claimant did not receive adequate notice of the hearing to file a timely claim opposing the forfeiture action. *See Nasir v. Sacramento County Off. of the Dist. Atty.*, 11 Cal. App. 4th 976, 990 (1992); *Baca v. Minier*, 229 Cal. App. 3d 1253, 1265 (1991); *People v. Smith*, 275 Ill.App.3d 844, 656 N.E.2d 797, 801–02 (Ill. App. 1995).

2. Motion to Set Aside Judicial Default

When a judicial default judgment or order has been entered, the correct procedure to set aside the default in the federal system is a motion for relief under Federal Rules of Civil Procedure Rule 60(b). *See United States v. Aponte-Vega*, 230 F.3d 522, 525 (2d Cir. 2000); *United States v. Madden*, 95 F.3d 38, 40 (10th Cir. 1996).

This section is the judicial equivalent to the administrative motion to set aside found at 18 U.S.C. § 983(e) with two important distinctions. First, Rule 60 relief may be sought wherever a default is entered by mistake, inadvertence, surprise, or excusable neglect. *United States v. One Star Class Sloop Sailboat*, 458 F.3d 16, 19 (1st Cir. 2006). An administrative motion to set aside is limited solely to lack of notice. *See* 18 U.S.C. § 983(e)(1). Therefore, the grounds for bringing a Rule 60(b) motion are broader, and relief may be granted even where the claimant had notice but, by some error, mistake, or omission on his part or counsel failed to timely file the claim or answer causing the default. *United States v. $100,348*, 354 F.3d 1110, 1117–19 (9th Cir. 2004). Second, the time period to bring the motion is one year from entry of judgment, *see Whiting v. United States*, 231 F.3d 70, 75 n.2 (1st Cir. 2000), rather than five years for administrative forfeitures. *See* 18 U.S.C. § 983(e)(3).

State civil procedure codes grant trial courts discretion to set aside judicial default judgments for mistake, inadvertence, surprise, or excusable neglect. *State, Dept. of Law Enforcement (Cade) v. One 1990 Geo Metro*, 126 Idaho 675, 889 P.2d 109, 114 (Idaho App. 1995); *Games-Neeley ex rel. West Virginia State Police v. Real Property*, 211 W.Va. 236; 565 S.E.2d 358, 367 (W.Va. 2002). However, the time to bring the motion may be as short as 90 days but not more than six months. *See Cal. Code of Civil Procedure* § 473. Defaults may also be set aside on equitable principles where the claimant demonstrates: (1) quick action to set aside the default; (2) good cause for the failure to file in a timely manner; and (3) a meritorious defense. *See People v. One Parcel of Land*, 235 Cal. App. 3d 579, 583 (1991). If there is any factual basis to set aside a default judgment, the motion should be brought as soon as possible to preserve the claimant's right to contest the order.

L. Motion to Dismiss/Demurrer

One method of attacking a forfeiture action in federal court is to file a motion to dismiss. Federal Rules of Civil Procedure Rule 12(b) lists several defenses that may be brought by motion, which include lack of jurisdiction, Rule 12(b)(1), improper venue, Rule 12(b)(3), and failure to state a claim upon which relief can be granted. Rule 12(b)(6). Prior to filing the motion, however, a claimant must establish his or her standing to contest the forfeiture. Supplemental Rule G(8)(b)(i). The motion may be set prior to the filing of a responsive pleading. *United States v. $8,221,877.16 in U.S. Currency*, 330 F.3d 141, 157 (3d Cir. 2003).

A forfeiture action may be brought in the district where any of the criminal acts or omissions occurred or anywhere for which venue is specifically provided. *See* 28 U.S.C. § 1355; *United States v. $633,021.67 in U.S. Currency*, 842 F. Supp. 528, 534 (N.D. Ga. 1993). Venue lies in the district where the property has been found or brought. *See* 28 U.S.C. § 1395; *United States v. $88,260.00 in U.S. Currency*, 925 F. Supp. 838, 840 (D.D.C. 1996). If there is any issue pertaining to jurisdiction or venue of the district court where the forfeiture action has been filed, it should be brought as a motion to dismiss.

The most common motion under this section is for failure to state a claim by challenging the sufficiency of the complaint or pleading. Previously, these motions were brought under Rule E(2), but the provision is now contained in Supplemental Rule G(8)(b). A complaint should be sufficient if it contains a detailed description of the property, the circumstances concerning the seizure, the statute under which the forfeiture is brought, and detailed facts to support a reasonable belief that the government can meet its burden of proof at trial. *See* Supplemental Rule G(2); *United States v. Mondragon,* 313 F.3d 862, 865 (4th Cir. 2002). A recent CAFRA amendment and supplemental rule clarify that a complaint may not be dismissed on the ground that the government did not have adequate evidence at the time the complaint was filed to establish the forfeitability of the property. *See* 18 U.S.C. § 983(a)(3)(D); Supplemental Rule G(8)(b)(ii); *United States v. Suffield Terrace,* 209 F. Supp. 2d 919, 923 (N.D. Ill. 2002).

Whether the complaint will be sufficient to defeat the motion will be driven by the specific facts of the litigation. Cases where the courts found the complaint sufficient include *United States v. All Funds on Deposit (Perusa, Inc.),* 935 F. Supp. 208, 213 (E.D.N.Y. 1996), and *United States v. A Certain Parcel of Land,* 781 F. Supp. 830, 833 (D.N.H. 1992). Cases where the court found a lack of specificity and granted the motion are *United States v. Certain Accounts,* 795 F. Supp. 391, 397 (S.D. Fla. 1992), *United States v. One Parcel of Real Property (6 Patricia Drive),* 705 F. Supp. 710, 720 (D.R.I. 1989), and *United States v. $40,000 U.S. Currency,* 999 F. Supp. 234, 239 (D.P.R. 1998).

A motion to dismiss is not the correct procedure to challenge the probable cause for the seizure of property or to suppress evidence. *United States v. $78,850.00 in U.S. Currency,* 444 F. Supp. 2d 630, 636 (D.S.C. 2006). That issue should be challenged by a motion to suppress. Supplemental Rule G(8)(a).

States may also have procedural equivalents to the federal motion to dismiss in their civil procedures statutes. For example, in California a claimant may either file a demurrer to the complaint, *see Cal. Code of Civil Procedure* § 430.10; *People v. Ten $500 Barclays Bank Visa Traveler's Checks,* 16 Cal. App. 4th 475, 478 (1993), or a motion for judgment on the pleadings. *See Cal. Code of Civil Procedure* § 438; *People v. $20,000,* 235 Cal. App. 3d 682, 692 (1991).

These motions are limited to specific challenges, such as lack of jurisdiction or failure to state facts sufficient to state a cause of action. These are defects that should be apparent from the face of the pleading so extrinsic evidence is not permitted. *See Cal. Code of Civil Procedure* § 438(d).

State jurisdiction and venue requirements parallel federal law in that the action may be brought in the county in which the property was seized or where the alleged conduct giving rise to the forfeiture occurred. *See Hawaii Rev. Stat.* § 712A-3. The sufficiency of the pleadings will be examined under the provisions of the particular state civil procedure code, and they may not be as stringent as the federal Supplemental Supplemental Rule G(2). For example, California requires merely that the pleading contain a "statement of the facts constituting the cause of action, in ordinary and concise language." *See Cal. Code of Civil Procedure* § 425.10(a)(1). However, it is unclear how specific or detailed those facts must be alleged in the pleading and even leaves open the prospect that notice pleading similar to Federal Rules of Civil Procedure Rule 8 may be sufficient. *See Witkin, California Procedure,* 4th Ed., § 340. However, even if the claimant were to prevail, leave to amend the complaint is routinely granted, so a motion brought on this ground rarely will result in complete dismissal of the action. *See People v. $20,000,* 235 Cal. App. 3d 682, 692 (1991).

M. Statute of Limitations

Failure to commence the civil proceedings within the applicable statute of limitations may be another avenue to attack forfeiture pleadings. Under CAFRA Section 11, 106 Pub. L. No. 185, 114 Stat. 202, 218, the federal statute of limitations was amended to require that the forfeiture be initiated within five years from the time of the discovery of the offense or two years from the date of the discovery of the involvement of the forfeitable property, whichever is later. *See* 18 U.S.C. § 1621; *United States v. Wright,* 361 F.3d 288, 290 (5th Cir. 2004). The statute is tolled while the claimant is a fugitive. *See United States v. 657 Acres of Land in Park County,* 978 F. Supp. 999, 1004 (D. Wyo. 1997). It is an affirmative defense that is waived if not asserted in a timely manner. *See United States v. Grover,* 119 F.3d 850, 852 (10th Cir. 1997); *United States v. One Parcel of Real Property (170 Westfield Dr.),* 34 F. Supp. 2d 107, 119 (D.R.I. 1999).

A timely filing also is a jurisdictional requirement in state *in rem* forfeiture actions. *State v. $1970,* 648 A.2d 917, 921 (Conn. Super. 1994). State statute of limitations provisions range from one year, *see Cal. Health & Safety Code* § 11488.4(a), to five years. *See Ga. Code Ann.* § 16-13-49(x)(5); *Iowa*

Code Ann. § 809A.20; *Kan. Stat. Ann.* § 60-4120; *Mo. Ann. Stat.* § 513.630). The statute begins to run from the date of the seizure of the property. *In re Forfeiture of one 1994 Honda Prelude,* 730 So. 2d 334, 336 (Fla. App. 1999); *People v. Ten $500 Barclays Bank Visa Traveler's Checks,* 16 Cal. App. 4th 475, 479 (1993).

Failure to file the forfeiture complaint within the applicable statute of limitations period divests the court of jurisdiction, resulting in dismissal of the action. *In re $3,636.24,* 198 Ariz. 504, 11 P.3d 1043, 1045 (Ariz. App. 2000); *Ziegler v. State,* 780 N.E.2d 1169, 1170 (Ind. App. 2003); *Prince George's County v. Vieira,* 340 Md. 651; 667 A.2d 898, 906 (Md. 1995); *Lewis v. State,* 481 So. 2d 842, 844 (Miss. 1985).

N. Suppression Motion

Another pretrial defense motion is the motion to suppress evidence. There is a divergence of opinion on the applicability of the exclusionary rule to civil forfeiture actions.

In *One 1958 Plymouth Sedan v. Pennsylvania,* 380 U.S. 693, 702 (1965), the U.S. Supreme Court applied the exclusionary rule, finding that the forfeiture action was, in reality, a quasi-criminal action. Several federal cases have applied the exclusionary rule to civil forfeiture actions based on this holding. *See United States v. Premises and Real Property (500 Delaware Street),* 113 F.3d 310, 313 n.3 (2d. Cir. 1997); *United States v. $57,443.00 in U.S. Currency,* 42 F. Supp. 2d 1293, 1297 (S.D. Fla. 1999); *United States v. Ford Pick-up,* 148 F. Supp. 2d 1258, 1259 n.1 (M.D. Ala. 2001); *United States v. $404,905.00 in U.S. Currency,* 182 F.3d 643, 646 (8th Cir. 1999). Supplemental Rule G(8)(a) specifically provides for suppression motions in federal forfeiture litigation.

However, in *United States v. Janis,* 428 U.S. 433, 446 (1976), the high court declined to apply the exclusionary rule because it is a remedial device and has never been applied in a civil proceeding, federal or state. *See I.N.S. v. Lopez-Mendoza,* 468 U.S. 1032, 1042 (1984). There are a few states that decline to exclude suppressed evidence from their forfeiture actions because their courts have found that their forfeiture statutes are civil and remedial or other statutory authority. However, the majority of the states do apply the exclusionary rule. See Table 5-2.

Table 5-2
State Constitutional Protections
Fourth Amendment Exclusionary Rule

State	Applicable	Not Applicable	Authority
Alabama		X	*McNeese v. State Ex Rel. Cramer*, 592 So.2d 615, 617 (Ala. Civ. App. 1992)
Arizona		X	*Ariz. Rev. Stat. Ann.* § 13-4310.E.3
California		X	*People v. $241,600 U.S. Currency*, 67 Cal.App.4th 1100, 1113 (1998)
Colorado	X		*People v. Taube*, 843 P.2d 79, 82 (Colo. App. 1992)
Florida	X		*In re ($48,900.00) U.S. Currency*, 432 So.2d 1382, 1385 (Fla. App. 1983)
Georgia		X	*Ga. Code Ann.* § 16-13-49(g)(3)
Idaho	X		*Richardson v. Four Thousand Five Hundred Forty-three Dollars U.S. Currency*, 120 Idaho 220, 814 P.2d 952, 957 (Idaho. App. 1991)
Indiana	X		*Caudill v. State*, 613 N.E.2d 433, 439 (Ind. App. 1993)
Maine	X		*State v. One Uzi Semi-Automatic 9mm Gun*, 589 A.2d 31, 33 (Me. 1991)
Maryland	X		*One 1995 Corvette v. Mayor and City Council of Baltimore*, 353 Md. 114; 724 A.2d 680, 692 (Md. 1999)

Table 5-2 (continued)
State Constitutional Protections
Fourth Amendment Exclusionary Rule

State	Applicable	Not Applicable	Authority
Massachusetts	X		*Com v. Nine Hundred and Ninety-Two Dollars*, 422 N.E.2d 767, 769 n. 2 (Mass. 1981)
Michigan	X		*In re Forfeiture of U.S. Currency*, 172 Mich.App. 200; 431 N.W.2d 437, 440 (Mich. App. 1988); *In re Forfeiture of U.S. Currency*, 166 Mich.App. 81; 420 N.W.2d 131, (Mich. App. 1988)
Minnesota		X	*Rife v. One 1987 Chevrolet Cavalier*, 485 N.W.2d 318, 322 (Minn. App. 1992)
Missouri	X		*State v. Washington*, 902 S.W.2d 893, 894 (Mo. App. E.D. 1995)
Nevada	X		*One 1970 Chevrolet Motor Vehicle v. Nye County*, 90 Nev. 31; 518 P.2d 38, 39 (Nev. 1973)
New Jersey	X		*State v. Jones*, 181 N.J.Super. 549, 438 A.2d 581, 583 (N.J. Super.L. 1981)
New Mexico	X		*In re Forfeiture of $28,000.00 in U.S. Currency et al.*, 124 N.M. 661, 954 P.2d 93, 96 (N.M. App. 1997); *In re One 1967 Peterbilt Tractor*, 84 N.M. 652, 506 P.2d 1199 , 1201 (N.M. 1973)

Table 5-2 (continued)
State Constitutional Protections
Fourth Amendment Exclusionary Rule

State	Applicable	Not Applicable	Authority
Oklahoma	X		*State ex rel. Edmondson v. Two Hundred Thousand Four Hundred Ninety Dollars ($200,490.00) in U.S. Currency,* 39 P.3d 160, 164 (Okla. Civ. App. 2001)
Pennsylvania	X		*Com. v. $26,556.00 Seized from Polidoro,* 672 A.2d 389, 392 (Pa. Cmwlth. 1996)
Tennessee	X		*Fell v. Armour,* 355 F.Supp. 1319, 1325 (D.C.Tenn. 1972)
Texas*	X		*State v. $217,590.00 in U.S. Currency,* 18 S.W.3d 631, 632 n. 1 (Tex. 2000)
Washington	X		*Deeter v. Smith,* 106 Wash.2d 376, 721 P.2d 519, 521 (Wash. 1986); *Barlindal v. City of Bonney Lake,* 84 Wash.App. 135, 925 P.2d 1289, 1292 (Wash App. 1996)
Wyoming	X		*State v. Eleven Thousand Three Hundred Forty-Six Dollars & No Cents.* 777 P.2d 65, 69 (Wyo. 1989)

*   Texas Supreme Court did not actually rule on this issue as all parties assumed that the exclusionary rule applied.

In bringing a motion to suppress, the claimant must establish his or her standing to contest the search. Supplemental Rule G(8)(a). Standing in this area consists of a two-fold privacy interest. First, the party must have a personal privacy interest in the area searched, and, second, the party must have a privacy interest in the particular items seized. *See United States v. Salvucci*, 448 U.S. 83, 92 (1980); *United States v. $1,790,021 in U.S. Currency*, 261 F. Supp. 2d 310 (M.D. Pa. 2003); *In re Forfeiture of $44,010.00*, 668 So. 2d 1000, 1001 (Fla. App. 1996). This is separate and distinct from the standing required to contest the forfeiture that is centered more on a legal or possessory interest. See Section B. Given that many state jurisdictions require a showing of legal standing before a forfeiture action may be contested, it appears in these jurisdictions that the claimant must show a legal or possessory interest in the property subject to forfeiture *and* a privacy interest in the area searched and property seized pursuant to the alleged illegal search before the motion may proceed. *State v. $3,356,183.00 U.S. Currency*, 894 So. 2d 339, 348 (La. App. 2004). One state resolves that issue by requiring the claimant to allege and prove at the hearing that the property was unlawfully seized and that the claimant is entitled to lawful possession of the seized property by a preponderance of the evidence. *See Ohio Rev. Code Ann.* § 2925.45(C)(1).

If the motion is granted, all evidence derived from the illegal search will be suppressed as "fruit of the poisonous tree." *See United States v. Real Property Known as 22249 Dolorosa Street*, 167 F.3d 509, 513 (9th Cir. 1999). However, this does not automatically require dismissal of the forfeiture action because other independent evidence may be used to prove that the property is subject to forfeiture. *See* Supplemental Rule G(8)(a); *United States v. 155 Bemis Road*, 760 F. Supp. 245, 251 (D.N.H. 1991); *Ore. Rev. Stat.* § 475A.035(6); *United States v. Real Property Known as 415 East Mitchell Ave.*, 149 F.3d 472, 476 (6th Cir. 1998) (state criminal plea); *United States v. 47 West 644 Route 38*, 962 F. Supp. 1081, 1090 (N.D. Ill. 1997) (discovery responses); *United States v. One 1978 Mercedes Benz*, 711 F.2d 1297, 1302–03 (5th Cir.1983); *In re $48,900 U.S. Currency*, 432 So. 2d 1382, 1386 (Fla. App. 1983).

Finally, a claimant is precluded from relitigating a suppression motion in the forfeiture action that has already been heard as part of a corresponding criminal case, even if it was not in the same jurisdiction. *See United States v. Real Property Located in El Dorado County*, 59 F.3d 974, 979–80 (9th Cir. 1995); *United States v. Real Property Known as 415 East Mitchell Ave.*, 149 F.3d 472, 476 (6th Cir. 1998); *Cannon v. State*, 918 So. 2d. 734, 746 (Miss. App. 2005).

O. Preemption

The final method of challenging a municipal forfeiture action is on the basis of preemption. Under the law of preemption, cities and counties cannot enact or enforce ordinances that conflict with a state's general laws. A conflict exists if the local ordinance duplicates, contradicts, or enters an area fully occupied by state law. *Sherwin-Williams Co. v. City of Los Angeles*, 4 Cal. 4th 893, 897, 16 Cal. Rptr. 2d 215, 844 P.2d 534 (1993).

Whether a local ordinance conflicts with state law requires judicial review. A New York City municipal ordinance forfeiting the vehicles of repeat-offender, driving-under-the-influence defendants was found not preempted by state law, *Grinberg v. Safir*, 181 Misc. 2d 444, 694 N.Y.S.2d 316, 321 (N.Y. Sup. 1999), but similar city and county ordinances for drug and prostitution offenses were found to be preempted by state law. *City of Miami v. Wellman*, 875 So. 2d 635, 640 (Fla. App. 2004); *Mulligan v. City of Hollywood*, 871 So. 2d 249, 256 (Fla. App. 2003); *O'Connell v. City of Stockton*, 41 Cal. 4th 1061, 1067 (2007). Municipal forfeiture ordinances are particularly vulnerable to constitutional attack when the due process requirements for the municipal forfeiture provision are lower than the state requirements. *City of Springfield v. Gee*, 149 S.W.3d 609, 617 (Mo. App 2004) (state law required criminal conviction).

P. Motion Strategy

The motions that could be filed and litigated will depend upon the merits of each action. In every case, however, the prosecutor should keep in mind the following strategic questions:

(1) Are there any procedural defects in the responsive pleadings?

(2) Does the claimant have standing to contest the forfeiture?

Conversely, defense counsel should ask the following:

(1) Can I get the property released to my client?

(2) Is there probable cause for the initiation of the forfeiture action?

(3) Are there any pretrial procedures to test probable cause in court?

(4) Do I need to set aside any administrative or judicial defaults?

(5) Are there any defects in the pleadings?

(6) Is there a search or seizure issue that needs to be litigated?

(7) Does the municipal ordinance conflict with state law?

Notes

1.   For an excellent discussion of the difference between federal case and controversy or Article III standing and the ownership interest required to prevail on the uniform innocent owner defense enacted by CAFRA at 18 U.S.C. § 983(d), *see* Stefan D. Cassella, *The Uniform Innocent Owner Defense to Civil Asset Forfeiture,* 89 KY. L.J. 653 (2001).

2.   Prior to December 2002, motions for return of property were authorized under Federal Rules of Criminal Procedure Rule 41(e). In December 2002, the rule was revised and renumbered as Rule 41(g). The case law prior to December 2002 refers to these actions as 41(e) motions.

6 Civil Discovery

A. Introduction

One of the alluring aspects of a civil forfeiture action is the availability of civil discovery. *Com. v. Nine-Hundred and Ninety-Two Dollars*, 422 N.E.2d 767, 775–76 (Mass. 1981); *State v. Rodriguez*, 130 N.J. Super. 57, 324 A.2d 911, 914 (N.J. Super. A.D. 1974); *State v. One 1973 Cadillac*, 95 Wis. 2d 641; 291 N.W.2d 626, 644 (Wis. App. 1980); *State v. $19,238.00 in U.S. Currency*, 157 Ariz. 178; 755 P.2d 1166, 1169 (Ariz. App. 1987). It may also be the most dangerous because many criminal prosecutors and defense attorneys generally are not well acquainted with civil discovery and motion practice. That conundrum was articulated by a California appellate court with this counsel:

> "Like the thorns that accompany the rose, however, the application of civil procedure rules to forfeiture proceedings carries with it the specter of discovery battles, depositions, and demurrers. . . . [P]rosecutors' offices should be aware that the forfeiture statutes open up a veritable Pandora's box of discovery, in which their Investigators, their confidential informants, and their very files may be fair game."

See People v. 25651 Minoa Drive, 2 Cal. App. 4th 787, 791 (1992).

With that judicial advisory, we will now review civil discovery as it relates to civil asset forfeiture actions.

B. Civil Discovery Overview

The purpose of civil discovery is to determine all legal and factual issues that are part of the litigation, including:

(1) Standing of the claimant to contest the forfeiture;
(2) Identifying all affirmative defenses;

(3) Evaluating probable cause for the seizure;

(4) Determining legal theories for the initiation of the forfeiture proceedings; and

(5) Reviewing all evidence that the proponent contends establishes the necessary burden of proof on any issue he or she is required to meet to either prevail or defeat the forfeiture action.

If the parties fail to comply with the discovery demands, sanctions may be imposed for noncompliance, including the dismissal of the action. Once civil discovery is complete, the parties will be in a position to bring a summary judgment motion, enter settlement discussions, or set the matter for trial.

In federal and state forfeiture practice, the general rules of civil procedure apply unless they are inconsistent with the forfeiture statute. *Jauregi v. Superior Court,* 72 Cal. App. 4th 931, 938 (1999); *People v. Cory,* 514 P.2d 310, 311 (Colo. App. 1973); *Com. v. $8006.00 U.S. Currency Seized from Carter,* 166 Pa. Cmwlth. 251; 646 A.2d 621, 624 (Pa. Cmwlth. 1994). For ease of discussion we will utilize the statutory references in the Federal Rules of Civil Procedure.

Any matter that is relevant and not privileged that appears reasonably calculated to lead to the discovery of admissible evidence is discoverable. *See Fed. R. Civ. Pro.* 26(b)(1). There are various methods of discovery found in the federal civil code (*see* Rules 26 through 37), but the tools that are most helpful in the civil forfeiture context are interrogatories, request for production of documents, depositions, and request for admissions. Each will be examined and discussed separately.

C. Interrogatories

Interrogatories are written questions directed to a party that must be answered in writing under oath within a prescribed period of time. *See Fed. R. Civ. Pro.* 33. To avoid discovery abuse, most codes limit the number of interrogatories that may be propounded, *see Fed. R. Civ. Pro.* 33(a) (not exceeding 25); *Cal. Code of Civil Procedure* § 2030.030(a)(1) (limit of 35), but that number may be increased with leave of court. *See Fed. R. Civ. Pro.* 33(a). Some states also provide for official form interrogatories that request basic civil case background information, which are not counted in the special interrogatory limit. *See Cal. Code of Civil Procedure* §§ 2033.710; 2030.030(a)(2). In these jurisdictions, litigators will want to use the form interrogatories to obtain general case information and draft specially prepared interrogatories for specific information pertaining to the forfeiture action.

Some state jurisdictions permit the interrogatories to be served along with the complaint for forfeiture, requiring the claimant to file an answer to the complaint and responses to the interrogatories at the same time. *See Ariz. Rev. Stat. Ann.* § 13-4311.G. This is especially helpful in those jurisdictions that permit expedited probable cause hearings so the prosecutor will have relevant discovery information prior to the hearing. See Chapter 5, Section J.

Federal practice used to permit the service of interrogatories with the complaint, *see* Supplemental Rule C(6)(c), but that provision was eliminated with the enactment of Supplemental Rule G, effective December 1, 2006. However, the new rules created a discovery tool called Special Interrogatories. Supplemental Rule G(6). After a claim is filed, the government may serve special interrogatories limited to the claimant's identity and relationship to the defendant property. Supplemental Rule G(6)(a). Answers or objections to these interrogatories must be filed within 20 days of service. Supplemental Rule G(6)(b).

The special interrogatories serve two important purposes. First, they are designed to garner evidence concerning the claimant's standing to contest the forfeiture. Depending upon the responses received, the government may file a motion contesting the claimant's standing. See Chapter 5, Section C. Second, if a claimant files a motion to dismiss under Federal Rules of Civil Procedure 12(b) (see Chapter 5, Section L), the government may serve special interrogatories within 20 days of service of the motion, Supplemental Rule G(6)(a), and defer responding to the motion until 20 days after the claimant has answered the interrogatories. Supplemental Rule G(6)(c). The Special Interrogatories under Supplemental Rule G(6) are available only to the government.

Responses must be signed by the party making the responses, and if there are any objections to the interrogatories, by the attorney making them. *See Fed. R. Civ. Pro.* 33(b). When interrogatories are served on the government, they must be signed and verified by an officer or agent for the agency. *See Fed. R. Civ. Pro.* 33(a). This generally will be an agent for the law enforcement agency that conducted the underlying criminal and forfeiture investigation.

Failure to respond timely may have deleterious consequences, such as waiver of any objections to the interrogatories or of privileges, *see Cal. Code of Civil Procedure* § 2030.290(a), and failure to comply with court orders mandating compliance may lead to the imposition of monetary and other types of sanctions. *See Cal. Code of Civil Procedure* § 2023.030.

If the response to an interrogatory requires a compilation, abstract, or summary of business records in possession of the agency, the code may provide for the responding party to permit the requesting party to inspect and make copies of the records. *See Fed. R. Civ. Pro.* 33(d). This is useful where law enforcement agencies would prefer to provide the official agency police reports that are responsive to the interrogatory request in lieu of preparing summaries of the reports. *See Cal. Code of Civil Procedure* § 2030.230.

The pleadings in the case should guide the questions that are contained in the interrogatories. Prosecutors should carefully examine the filed claim and formulate questions relating to the interest of the party in the claimed property, where and when it was acquired, from whom it was obtained, the nature of the transaction, and the identification of any documents that verify the transaction. This may lead to a subsequent discovery request for production of these documents. Questions pertaining to claims of innocent ownership should also be included in the first set of interrogatories. A prosecutor should have a pre-designed set of interrogatories to serve in civil asset forfeiture cases to cover basic information to evaluate the validity of the claim. Subsequent interrogatory request may then be drafted for specific cases with unique factual issues not covered in the initial set of interrogatories.

Claimants should carefully review the complaint or petition and focus their questions on such issues as when and where the property was seized, the circumstances and probable cause for the seizure, and the theory of the government for the forfeiture of the property. Names and addresses of potential witnesses also should be obtained.

Although the utility of interrogatories is limited because all responses are carefully prepared and crafted by counsel, they are helpful in laying out the framework of the case and formulating subsequent discovery strategies.

D. Request for Production of Documents

The Request for Production of Documents is used to obtain documents that are in the possession or control of a party to the litigation. *See Fed. R. Civ. Pro.* 34(a). The request sets out by item or category the requested documents and the date and place of production. *See Fed. R. Civ. Pro.* 34(b). The receiving party must serve a written response indicating whether he or she objects or will comply to each requested item within a specific time period—usually 30 days. *See Fed. R. Civ. Pro.* 34(b); *Cal. Code of Civil Procedure* § 2031.260.

This discovery device is useful in obtaining records and documents in the possession of a party. For prosecutors in cases where standing or innocent ownership are at issue, all documents relating to the claimant's ownership interest should be requested. If the forfeiture is based on a proceeds theory, all documents of the claimant's income and expenses for a specified time period should be produced, along with any other legitimate income that could account for the funds. Where a financial institution account is subject to forfeiture, the documentary records in the possession of the claimant should be obtained in order to trace the origin of the funds in the account.

Claimants should obtain all law enforcement reports that are the basis for the forfeiture action and any other written documents or other physical evidence seized during the investigation and relevant to the forfeiture action. This may include photographs or audiotapes of any interviews conducted. If the prosecutor does not elect to produce law enforcement reports in response to interrogatories, *see Fed. R. Civ. Pro.* 33(d), the reports should be requested under this section.

A request for production of documents is limited to parties to the forfeiture action; however, there are other methods to obtain records from nonparties. A deposition subpoena may be obtained that requires business records to be produced with or without the necessity of having the custodian of records attend the deposition. *See Fed. R. Civ. Pro.* 45; *Cal. Code of Civil Procedure* §§ 2020.410 through 2020.440. In addition, for certain federal offenses, a subpoena duces tecum may be issued to a financial institution to produce books or other records at a place designated by the requesting party. *See* 18 U.S.C. § 986(a).

The request for production of documents can be an important tool in analyzing the strength of a forfeiture case. Failure to produce documents that substantiate affirmative defenses significantly casts doubt on the veracity of the claimant, prolongs the litigation, and weakens the defense position at settlement and trial.

E. Deposition

A deposition is an oral or written examination of a person under oath. *See Fed. R. Civ. Pro.* 30, 31. Oral examination also includes a deposition by telephone or other electronic means. *See Fed. R. Civ. Pro.* 30(b)(7); *United States v. Currency U.S. $42,500*, 283 F.3d 977, 980 (9th Cir. 2002). It is the most useful discovery tool because it allows the attorney to question the deponent before a court reporter under penalty of perjury, and the testimony is transcribed and preserved for future hearings. It is not limited to the parties in the case, and is therefore the only discovery tool that permits the questioning of nonparties. Attendance is compelled by subpoena, and failure to appear may subject the deponent to sanctions. The deponent may also be ordered to produce documents that are listed on the deposition subpoena, making the deposition another method of obtaining documentary evidence relevant to the case.

Depositions are expensive and time consuming, however, and therefore are not routinely conducted in asset forfeiture litigation. Nevertheless, there are a few factors that weigh in favor of holding depositions, such as whether the case has significant monetary value, whether the credibility of the witness must be evaluated under direct and cross-examination, or whether there is a need to preserve the testimony of a potential witness who may not be available at trial.

Individuals who should be considered for depositions in asset forfeiture litigation include the claimant and any other nonparty who may have material testimony relating to the forfeiture. Witnesses from any related criminal offense usually are not deposed because transcripts should be available from those proceedings. However, if there is no pending criminal case, a claimant's attorney may want to depose a law enforcement witness to evaluate whether a motion to suppress or other pre-trial motion may be appropriate.

Deposing attorneys should prepare an outline of areas of inquiry prior to the scheduled deposition and review all prior discovery responses received, including interrogatories and documents, to determine the areas that will require follow-up during the deposition. Most of the basic personal data concerning the deponent should already have been acquired with the earlier discovery responses; therefore, detailed questioning in this area generally is not productive.

An asset forfeiture deposition might follow the following outline:

(1) Review all property listed on the filed claim and the standing of the party to contest the forfeiture of those items;

(2) Examine the theory of forfeiture and all facts and statements from the witness that either substantiate or refuse it;

(3) Determine the relationship of the witness to parties, criminal defendants, or other individuals connected to the criminal activity;

(4) Identify all affirmative defenses and the witnesses' knowledge of facts relating to those defenses;

(5) In proceeds theory cases, examine all documents pertaining to income and expenses for the relevant time period corresponding to the alleged criminal activity; and

(6) Focus on any areas where there are inconsistent statements or documentary evidence for future impeachment purposes.

In determining whether to take a deposition in an asset forfeiture case, the practitioner must balance the time and cost involved versus the potential testimony, documents, and impeachment evidence that may be gained from the proceeding.

F. Protective Order

Although civil discovery is a powerful tool, it can also be abused and used in a manner to annoy, harass, or burden the opposing party. This is especially true in civil asset forfeiture cases because there are often criminal charges pending against the same parties. The interplay of criminal charges and civil asset forfeiture cases is called parallel proceedings and will be discussed at length in Chapter 9. In the civil discovery context, there is a concern that the claimant may use civil discovery in an attempt to gain confidential information concerning the criminal case, *see United States v. Certain Real Property Located at 5137/5139 Central Avenue,* 776 F. Supp. 1090, 1092 (W.D.N.C. 1991), or that the prosecutor would place a claimant in a position to choose between defending the criminal case or foregoing the Fifth Amendment right against self-incrimination to contest the civil forfeiture action. *See United States v. A Certain Parcel of Land,* 781 F. Supp. 830, 833 (D.N.H. 1992). There are two ways of resolving this dilemma.

The first option is to obtain a protective order. Federal and state codes of civil procedure provide for protective orders to prevent discovery abuse. *See Fed. R. Civ. Pro.* 26(c); *Cal. Code of Civil Procedure* § 2019.030. The court may enter orders to protect a party from annoyance, oppression, or undue burden or expense by precluding the conduct of any discovery or limiting the scope of discovery. *See Fed. R. Civ. Pro.* 26(c); *In re Forfeiture of $1,159,420,* 194 Mich. App. 134; 486 N.W.2d 326, 332 (Mich. App. 1992). This permits the court to balance the competing rights and interests of the government and the claimant and still allow the civil forfeiture case to proceed. *See United States v. U.S. Currency,* 626 F.2d 11, 15 (6th Cir. 1980), *cert. denied,* 449 U.S. 993. Several states also permit the stay of discovery pending the resolution of the criminal action. *See Kan. Stat. Ann.* § 60-4112(p); *Tenn. Code Ann.* § 39-11-710(g).

The second alternative is to obtain a stay of the civil case pending the conclusion of the criminal action. One of the modifications of CAFRA Section 8, 106 Pub. L. No. 185, 114 Stat. 202, 215–216, was to make the stay provisions of 18 U.S.C. § 981(g) available to both the government and the claimant. A prosecutor may obtain a stay of the civil forfeiture proceeding if the court finds that civil discovery will adversely impact a related criminal investigation or prosecution. *See* 18 U.S.C. § 981(g)(1); *United States v. All Funds Deposited in Account No. 200008524845*, 162 F. Supp. 2d 1325, 1328 (D. Wyo. 2001).

A claimant may also obtain a stay of the civil forfeiture case if the court finds that the claimant is the subject of a related criminal investigation, has standing to assert a claim in the civil forfeiture action, and continuation of the forfeiture matter will burden the claimant's right against self-incrimination. *See* 18 U.S.C. § 981(g)(2).

The court still has the option of (1) limiting the scope of discovery with a protective order if doing so would be sufficient to protect the respective interests of the parties, *see* 18 U.S.C. § 981(g)(3); (2) receive government evidence ex parte to protect confidential information, *see* 18 U.S.C. § 981(g)(5); and (3) issue orders to preserve the value of the property pending the stay, *see* 18 U.S.C. § 981(g)(6). Additionally, a finding of standing under this provision does not preclude the government from challenging a claimant's standing in another pretrial motion or at trial. *See* 18 U.S.C. § 981(g)(7).

Many states also provide for the stay of a civil forfeiture case pending the resolution of the criminal matter. *See Mo. Ann. Stat.* § 513.617.1; *Cal. Health & Safety Code* § 11488.5(e); *Ariz. Rev. Stat. Ann.* § 13-4310.I.

For more information on this topic, see Chapter 9, Parallel Proceedings Sections D–E.

G. Motion to Compel

Failing to respond to discovery requests can lead to serious consequences in civil asset forfeiture cases. If a claimant does not file responses to interrogatories or request for production of documents or fails to appear for a scheduled deposition, sanctions may be imposed against the offending party. *See Fed. R. Civ. Pro.* 37(d). Sanctions may also be assessed when a party obtains a court order compelling responses to evasive or incomplete responses, and the responding party fails to comply. *See Fed. R. Civ. Pro.* 37(a). The court has many options in imposing sanctions, ranging from evidence preclusion, *People v. 1515 Coolidge Ave.*, 308 Ill. App. 3d 805; 721 N.E.2d 205, 211 (Ill. App. 1999), to striking the pleadings, dismissing the action, and entering default judgment, *see Fed. R. Civ. Pro.* 37(b)(2)(A)–(C). States also have similar civil procedure sanctions for discovery noncompliance, providing for monetary, issue admission, evidence preclusion, and terminating sanctions. *See Cal. Code of Civil Procedure* § 2023.030.

Federal and state courts have not been reticent to apply terminating sanctions to civil asset forfeiture actions for failure to answer interrogatories, *see United States v. U.S. Currency in the Amount of $24,170.00,* 147 F.R.D. 18, 22 (E.D.N.Y. 1993), respond to production of documents, *see United States v. $49,000 U.S. Currency,* 330 F.3d 371, 378–79 (5th Cir. 2003), or appear for a deposition, *see United States v. U.S. Currency in the Amount of $600,343.00,* 240 F.R.D. 59, 63 (E.D.N.Y. 2007); *United States v. One 1999 Forty-Seven Foot Fountain Motor Vehicle,* 240 F.R.D. 695, 698 (S.D. Fla. 2007); *People v. $4,503 U.S. Currency,* 49 Cal. App. 4th 1743, 1745 (1996).

Thus, one of the side benefits of conducting civil discovery is that the pleadings may be stricken and default judgment entered for noncompliance. *See Degen v. United States,* 517 U.S. 820, 827 (1996).

H. Request for Admissions

A request for admission is a written demand from one party to another party to admit or deny the truth of specific facts, opinions, or genuineness of documents. *See Fed. R. Civ. Pro.* 36(a). Upon service of the requests, the responding party has a specific time period during which to respond or object. *See Fed. R. Civ. Pro.* 36(a) (30 days); *Cal. Code of Civil Procedure* § 2033.250(a) (30 days).

If a party fails to timely respond to the requests, the matters are deemed admitted in most jurisdictions, *see Fed. R. Civ. Pro.* 36(a), and a summary judgment may be obtained based upon the unanswered requests for admissions. *See United States v. 204 Barbara Lane,* 960 F.2d 126, 129–30 (11th Cir. 1992). However, there are some states that require a noticed motion and court order before the requests will be deemed true. *See Cal. Code of Civil Procedure* § 2033.280.

In jurisdictions where failure to respond results in automatic admission of the requests, some practitioners place requests for admissions at the top of their discovery plan with the hope that the responding party will fail to respond, resulting in early conclusion of the matter. Although this strategy may occasionally succeed, more often it results in a useless list of denials.

In civil asset forfeiture litigation, the request for admission is most useful to narrow the issues before trial and prepare for a summary judgment motion. Skillfully prepared requests for admissions will contain, in one discovery device, all of the essential facts, opinions, and case documents that will lead to a successful summary judgment motion. A request for the genuineness of documents should be propounded for each document that may be introduced into evidence at the hearing to overcome foundational and hearsay objections.

Although some states permit serving requests for admissions very early in the discovery plan with the complaint, *see Ariz. Rev. Stat. Ann.* § 13-4311G, it generally is a better strategy to preserve the request for admissions until after interrogatories, requests for documents, and any depositions have been conducted. Doing so will permit counsel to review all previous discovery responses and formulate requests that are tailored to the issues of the case.

I.   Summary Judgment

A motion for summary judgment is an excellent method to resolve cases prior to trial. Authorized under federal, *see Fed. R. Civ. Pro.* 56, and state civil procedure statutes, *see Cal. Code of Civil Procedure* § 437c, a motion for summary judgment permits a court to find that there is no genuine issue of material fact to be resolved, and the moving party is entitled to judgment as matter of law. *See Celotex Corp. v. Catrett,* 477 U.S. 317, 323 (1986). Even if an entire case is incapable of resolution by summary judgment, the court is empowered to enter a summary adjudication as to those issues that are not in controversy, and the trial will proceed as to only the unresolved issues. *See Fed. R. Civ. Pro.* 56(d); *Cal. Code of Civil Procedure* § 437c(f); *United States v. Route 2, Box 472, 136 Acres More or Less,* 60 F.3d 1523, 1526 (11th Cir. 1995).

The motion is based on declarations or affidavits of witnesses with personal knowledge of the facts and other admissible evidence, including civil discovery responses to interrogatories, depositions, and request for admissions. *See Fed. R. Civ. Pro.* 56(e). A responding party must vigorously defend the motion and go beyond merely denying the allegations in the pleadings by presenting affidavits or other evidence demonstrating a genuine issue for trial, or judgment will be entered against him or her. *See Fed. R. Civ. Pro.* 56(e). Conclusory assertions and mere denials do not raise genuine issues of fact and a party opposing summary judgment "must present affirmative evidence." *See Anderson v. Liberty Lobby, Inc.,* 477 U.S. 242, 257 (1986).

In ruling on a summary judgment motion, the judge must view the evidence through "the prism of the substantive evidentiary burden" of proof that will be required at trial. *See id.* at 255; *United States v. One Parcel of Property Located at 15 Black Ledge Drive, Marlboro, Connecticut,* 897 F.2d 97, 101 (2d Cir. 1990). To be considered "material," a genuine issue must relate to facts that, if proved, would enable the party opposing summary judgment to prevail on the merits of the case as a matter of law. *See United States v. Real Property in Mecklenburg County,* 814 F. Supp. 468, 473 (W.D.N.C. 1993).

1. Federal Summary Judgment Motion

There are three basic areas where summary judgments motions have been utilized in federal asset forfeiture actions. They are: (1) standing; (2) forfeitability of the property; and (3) affirmative defenses. Standing already has been discussed as a pre-trial motion in Chapter 5; therefore, the balance of this section will discuss forfeitability of the property and affirmative defenses.

2. Forfeitability of the Property

Prior to the enactment of CAFRA, the federal burden of proof for summary judgment in a forfeiture case was probable cause; the burden then shifted to the claimant to prove that the property was not subject to forfeiture, or any other defense to forfeiture, by a preponderance of the evidence. *See United States v. Miscellaneous Jewelry,* 667 F. Supp. 232, 237–41 (D. Md. 1987); 19 U.S.C. § 1615. "Probable cause" was defined as requiring the same evidence as that for establishing the basis for a search warrant—namely, reasonable grounds to believe that the property was involved in the alleged offense, supported by less than prima facie proof, but more than a mere suspicion. *See United States v. One 56-Foot Motor Yacht Named Tahuna,* 702 F.2d 1276, 1281–83 (9th Cir. 1983). Hearsay evidence also was admissible to support the probable cause showing. *See United States v. $250,000 in U.S. Currency,* 808 F.2d 895, 899 (1st Cir. 1987); *United States v. Yukon Delta Houseboat,* 774 F.2d 1432, 1434 (9th Cir. 1985).

Under this standard, the government generally was easily able to prevail on the issue of forfeitability of the property. *See United States v. Property at 4492 S. Livonia Road,* 889 F.2d 1258, 1269 (2d Cir. 1989); *United States v. All Monies ($477,048.62),* 754 F. Supp. 1467, 1476 (D. Haw. 1991).

CAFRA Section 2, 106 Pub. L. No. 185, 114 Stat. 202, 205–206, has raised the burden of proof in most forfeiture cases to preponderance of the evidence, *see* 18 U.S.C. § 983(c)(1), and also provides that all evidence gathered after the filing of the complaint may be used to establish this standard. *See* 18 U.S.C. § 983(c)(2). This significantly impacts the government's burden of proof in summary judgment motions in federal forfeiture practice because it now places the burden of proving that the property is subject to forfeiture solely on the government, at a higher burden of proof, and without the use of hearsay evidence. *See United States v. One Parcel (2526 Faxon Avenue),* 145 F. Supp. 2d 942, 950 (W.D. Tenn. 2001); *United States v. $21,510 in U.S. Currency,* 292 F.

Supp. 2d 318, 320–21 (D.P.R. 2003). Thus, care must now be exercised in relying on pre-CAFRA cases while preparing federal summary judgment motions because of the new burden of proof.

Summary judgment motions brought on facilitation theory forfeitures require a substantial connection between the property and the illegal activity. *United States v. Real Property in Section 9*, 308 F. Supp. 2d 791, 808 (E.D. Mich. 2004); *United States v. 3402 53rd Street West*, 178 Fed. Appx. 946, 948 (11th Cir. 2006). Summary judgment may be granted on proceeds theory forfeitures on a showing that the claimant lacked legitimate income to purchase the asset. *United States v. $174,206.00 in U.S. Currency*, 320 F.3d 658, 662 (6th Cir. 2003); *United States v. 6 Fox Street*, 480 F.3d 38, 42 (1st Cir. 2007).

3. Affirmative Defenses

Prior to CAFRA, the claimant bore the burden of proof for any affirmative defense by a preponderance of the evidence. *See United States v. One Parcel of Property Located at 755 Forest Road, Northford, Connecticut*, 985 F.2d 70, 72 (2d Cir. 1993); *United States v. Land, Property Currently Recorded in the Name of Neff*, 960 F.2d 561, 563 (5th Cir. 1992).

The passage of CAFRA did not change that rule, and the claimant still must establish affirmative defenses by a preponderance of the evidence. *See United States v. One Parcel (2526 Faxon Avenue)*, 145 F. Supp. 2d at 951. General denials are insufficient, and admissible evidence is required supporting the affirmative defense. *See United States v. Two Parcels of Real Property*, 92 F.3d 1123, 1129 (11th Cir. 1996); *United States v. Parcel of Land (18 Oakwood Street)*, 958 F.2d 1, 4–5 (1st Cir. 1992); *United States v. $4,629,00 in U.S. Currency*, 359 F. Supp. 2d 504, 509–10 (W.D. Va. 2005).

Summary judgment should be denied where there is a material issue of fact, *United States v. $21,000 in US Postal Money Orders*, 298 F. Supp. 2d 597, 605 (E.D. Mich. 2003), or the testimony or the credibility of witnesses is challenged, *United States v. 3234 Washington Avenue North*, 480 F.3d 841, 845–46 (8th Cir. 2007).

Where an innocent ownership defense is asserted, courts may be reluctant to grant summary judgment where the issue of knowledge of the claimant is raised because that is a question of fact and requires a determination of the credibility of the witness. *See United States v. Dollar Bank Money Market Account*, 980 F.2d 233, 240–41 (3d Cir. 1992); *United States v. Leak*, 123 F.3d 787, 794 (4th Cir. 1997); *United States v. $200,000*, 805 F. Supp. 585, 591 (N.D. Ill. 1992); *United States v. Three Tracts of Property (Beaver Creek)*, 994 F.2d 287, 290 (6th Cir. 1993). However, summary judgment may be still granted if the denial of knowledge is totally inconsistent with the other uncontested evidence proffered in the motion. *See United States v. One Parcel of Property Located at 755 Forest Road, Northford, Connecticut,* 985 F.2d 70, 72 (2d Cir. 1993); *United States v. One 1992 Lexus SC400,* 167 F. Supp 2d 977, 986–88 (N.D. Ill. 2001).

4. State Summary Judgment Motion

Summary judgment also is available in state forfeiture actions and is similar to the federal practice. The motion must be supported with declarations containing admissible evidence to establish the forfeitability of the property. *People v. Hernandez & Associates, Inc.,* 736 P.2d 1238, 1239–40 (Colo. App. 1986). However, in preparing points and authorities in support of the motion on the issue of forfeitability of the property, state practitioners should be careful in relying on any federal case finding summary judgment based on the pre-CAFRA probable cause standard if the state burden of proof is higher. State prosecutors should determine the requisite burden of proof in the state action and the party who carries that burden of proof before bringing a state summary judgment motion because the federal and state evidentiary burdens may not be the same. For a full discussion of this topic, see Chapter 7 and Table 7-2.

Examples of issues that have been litigated in state courts as summary judgment motions include standing, *see People v. $28,500 U.S. Currency,* 51 Cal. App. 4th 447, 470–71 (1996), probable cause for forfeiture, *see People v. $48,715 U.S. Currency,* 58 Cal. App. 4th 1507, 1519 (1997), and innocent owner defenses. *See People v. $241,600 U.S. Currency,* 67 Cal. App. 4th 1100, 1114–15 (1998).

State summary judgment motions have been denied in forfeiture actions where there is a material issue of fact, including the connection of the property to the illegal activity, *Matter of One 1987 Toyota,* 621 A.2d 796, 798 (Del. Super. 1992); *State ex rel. Macy v. Thirty Thousand Seven Hundred Eighty-one Dollars,* 865 P.2d 1262, 1264–65 (Okla. App. 1993), the credibility of the witnesses, *State v. Giles,* 697 So. 2d 699, 705 (La. App. 1997), and the knowledge of the claimant of the illegal use. *In re Forfeiture of $19,050.00,* 519 So. 2d 1134, 1135 (Fla. App. 1988).

J. Settlement

Once civil discovery and motions are completed, it is time to either settle the case or set it for trial. This is the opportunity for the litigator to critically review the case and determine the relative merits of the action. A fair and reasonable offer will depend upon the strength of the evidence establishing the forfeiture, balanced against the merits of any affirmative defenses that have been raised. The credibility of witnesses and the desires of the investigative agency and the claimant will also factor into the settlement equation.

Given that there are numerous ethical issues that arise whenever a joint settlement of a criminal and civil forfeiture cases is proposed, each office must establish sound policies that weigh the public interest in crime prevention and punishment along with the remedial goal of stripping criminals of their illicit proceeds. The ethical issues relating to settlement are discussed in Chapter 13, Ethical Issues.

7 Civil Trial Proceedings

A. Trial Setting

Because asset forfeiture cases are civil matters, trial setting usually is governed by the federal or state civil rules of civil procedure. *See Fed. R. Civ. Pro.* 16; *Cal. Health & Safety Code* § 11488.5(c)(3). This means that a trial date will not be set until it is requested or assigned by the court pursuant to the applicable civil procedure rules.

However, on account of the quasi-criminal nature of forfeiture proceedings, *see Boyd v. United States,* 116 U.S. 616, 634–35 (1886), and the potential link to a pending criminal case, some state jurisdictions have set unique rules that conflict with the general civil rules of procedure.

These jurisdictions emphasize that, although the civil procedure rules apply, priority is to be given to forfeiture actions over other civil actions. *See Nev. Rev. Stat.* § 179.1173; *Cal. Health & Safety Code* § 11488.5(c)(1). This reminds court staff that forfeiture actions should be placed on an expedited hearing calendar.

A few states set a specific time within which the forfeiture case is to be set or heard. *See Hawaii Rev. Stat.* § 712A-12(6). This could range from as short as 14 days, *see Vt. Stat. Ann.* Title 18 § 4244, to 90 days, *see N.H. Rev. Stat. Ann.* § 318-B:17-b IV(c). In certain states, those time periods are merely directory, *State v. Residential Unit & Real Estate,* 26 K.A.2d 260; 983 P.2d 865, 867 (Kan. 1999); *Howard County v. Connolley,* 137 Md. App. 99; 767 A.2d 926; 932 (Md. App. 2001), but others consider them mandatory, and failure to comply may result in the court losing jurisdiction. *See In re Property Seized from Williams,* 676 N.W.2d 607, 612 (Iowa 2004); *State v. Rosen,* 72 Wis. 2d 200; 240 N.W. 2d 168, 171–72 (Wisc. 1976).

A few jurisdictions provide that the civil forfeiture trial shall be heard in conjunction with any related criminal action as a bifurcated matter before the same trier of fact, with the criminal procedure rules applying to the criminal trial, and the civil procedure rules to the civil forfeiture. *See Cal. Health &*

Safety Code §§ 11488.4(i)(3), (5); *Ore. Rev. Stat.* § 475A.075(6); *N.M. Code Ann.* § 31-27-6C(1)-(2).* To facilitate the trial setting of these matters, the civil file generally is assigned to the trial department hearing the criminal case, and the forfeiture matter is assigned to trail it.

If an incarcerated claimant desires to attend the trial, he or she should seek a motion to be transported for the trial because neither the state nor the court is obligated to transfer an inmate to testify in a civil hearing. *State v. Scott,* 933 S.W.2d 884, 887 (Mo. App. 1996); *State v One 1980 Cadillac,* 21 P.3d 212, 216 (Utah 2001); *State v. Property Located at No. 70 Oakland Street,* 727 So. 2d 1240, 1244–45 (La. App. 1999).

The practitioner must become familiar with the relevant statutes and trial setting procedures for the jurisdiction in which he or she is practicing. The practitioner must also bear in mind that, in those states with specific deadlines for the trial setting or requirements that it be heard in conjunction with a pending criminal action, it may be difficult to conduct any meaningful civil discovery prior to the forfeiture hearing, unless the dates set for discovery compliance are substantially shortened by court order.

B. Right to Jury Trial

Because asset forfeiture cases are civil actions, the right to a jury trial will depend upon the law of the specific jurisdiction. In most federal civil forfeiture actions, the right to a jury trial is guaranteed by the Seventh Amendment, *United States v. One Lincoln Navigator 1998,* 328 F.3d 1011, 1014 n.2 (8th Cir. 2003); however, that right may be waived unless the claimant makes a timely demand. *See* Supplemental Rule G(9); *United States v. 110 Bars of Silver,* 508 F.2d 799, 801 (5th Cir. 1975). Under federal rules, the demand for a jury trial is made at the commencement of the action and not later than 10 days after the service of the last pleading. *See Fed. R. Civ. Pro.* 38(b), (d). Federal practitioners must remember to make this demand early in the proceeding.

In the state system, the right to a jury trial varies among the states. See Table 7-1. Several states specifically grant a statutory right to a jury trial, *see Fla. Stat. Ann.* § 932.704(3); *Mo. Ann. Stat.* § 513.612; *R.I. Gen. Laws* § 21-28-5.04.2(j); *Utah Code Ann.* § 24-1-4(6)(d); *Va. Code Ann.* § 19.2-386.10, and a few hold that the right to a jury trial is guaranteed under the state constitution. *See People v. One 1941 Chevrolet Coupe,* 37 Cal.2d 283, 300; 231 P.2d 832 (1951); *Idaho Dep't of Law Enforcement Ex Rel. Cade v. Real Property Located in Minidoka County,* 126 Idaho 422, 426; 885 P.2d 381 (Idaho 1994).

Table 7-1
Summary of State Asset Forfeiture Statutes
State Trial Procedures

State	Jury Trial	Court Trial
Alaska		Alaska Stat. § 17.30.116(c)
Arkansas		Ark. Code Ann. § 5-64-505(h)
California	Cal. Health & Saf. § 11488.4(i)(5)	
Colorado		Colo. Rev. Stat §§ 16-13-307(7); 16-13-505(6)
Delaware	*Brown v. State,* 721 A.2d 1263, 1266 (Del. S. Ct. 1998)	
Florida	Fla. Stat. Ann. § 932.704	
Georgia		Ga. Code Ann. § 16-13-49(o)(5)
Idaho	*Idaho Dept of Law Enforcement ex rel Cade v. Real Property Located in Minidoka County,* 126 Idaho 422; 885 P.2d 381, 386 (Idaho 1994)	
Illinois	*People ex. Rel. O'Malley v. 6323 North LaCrosse Ave.,* 158 Ill. 2d 453; 634 N.E.2d 743, 746 (Ill. 1994)	
Iowa		Iowa Code Ann. § 809A.13
Kansas		Kansas Code Ann. § 60-4113(g)

Table 7-1 (continued)
Summary of State Asset Forfeiture Statutes
State Trial Procedures

State	Jury Trial	Court Trial
Louisiana		La. Stat. Ann § 40:2612G; *State v. Clark,* 670 So. 2d 493, 510 (La. App. 1996)
Maine	*State v. One 1981 Chevrolet Monte Carlo,* 728 A.2d 1259, 1261 (Me. 1999)	
Massachusetts	*Com. v. One 1972 Chevrolet Van,* 431 N.E.2d 209, 211 (Mass. 1982)	
Michigan		*In re Forfeiture of 301 Cass Street,* 194 Mich. App. 381; 487 N.W.2d 795, 798 (Mich. App. 1992)
Mississippi		Miss. Op. Atty.Gen. No. 94-0352
Missouri	Mo. Ann. Stat. § 513.612	
Montana		Mont. Code Ann. § 44-12-203(3)
New Jersey	*State v. One 1990 Honda Accord,* 154 N.J. 373; 712 A.2d 1148, 1157 (N.J. 1998)	
New Mexico	N.M. Stat. Ann. § 31-27-6.C	
New York	*Matter of Vergari v. Marcus,* 26 N.Y.2d 764; 309 N.Y.S. 2d 204; 257 N.E.2d 652, 653 (N.Y. 1970); N.Y.C.P.L.R. § 1311(2)	

Table 7-1 (continued)
Summary of State Asset Forfeiture Statutes
State Trial Procedures

State	Jury Trial	Court Trial
North Dakota		*State v. $17,515.00 in Cash Money,* 2003 ND 168; 670 N.W.2d 826, 828 (N.D. 2003)
Pennsylvania	*Com. v. One Thousand Four Hundred Dollars ($1,400) in U.S. Currency,* 667 A.2d 452 , 454 (Pa. Cmwlth. 1995); *Com. v. One (1) 1984 Z-28 Camaro Coupe,* 530 Pa. 523; 610 A.2d 36, 41 (Pa. 1992);	*Com. v. One 1986 Ford Mustang EXP,* 397 Pa. Super. 116; 579 A.2d 958, 960 (Pa. Super. 1990)
Rhode Island	R.I. Gen. Laws § 21-28-5.04.2(j)(1)	
South Carolina	*Medlock v. 1985 Ford F-150 Pick Up,* 308 S.C. 68; 417 S.E.2d 85, 86 (S.C. 1992)	S.C. Code Ann. § 44-53-530(a)
South Dakota		S.D. Codified Laws Ann. § 19-03.1-36.6
Tennessee	Tenn. Code Ann. § 53-11-452(b)(4)	*Helms v. Tennessee Dept. of Safety,* 987 S.W.2d 545, 548 (Tenn. 1999)
Utah	Utah Code Ann. § 24-1-4 (6)(d)	
Virginia	Va. Code Ann. § 19.2-386.10(A)	
Washington	*State v. Clark,* 68 Wash. App. 592; 844 P.2d 1029,1037 (Wash. App. 1993) affirmed 124 Wash.2d 90; 875 P.2d 613	

However, a claimant may impliedly waive that right by failing to assert it. *People v. $17,522.08 U.S. Currency*, 142 Cal. App. 4th 1076, 1084 (2006); *Brown v. State*, 721 A.2d 1263, 1266 (Del. Supr. 1998).

Other states opt for a trial by court. *See La. Rev. Stat. Ann.* § 40:2612.G; *Mont. Code Ann.* § 44-12-203; *S.C. Code Ann.* § 44-53-530(a); *S.D. Codified Laws, Ann.* § 19-03.1-36.6. Even in those states that provide for a jury trial, it is not uncommon for the parties to waive it and stipulate to a bench trial. *See People v. $497,590 U.S. Currency*, 58 Cal. App. 4th 145, 150 (1997).

C. Criminal Conviction

Under the federal system, there is no requirement of a criminal conviction for a civil forfeiture action. *The Palymra*, 25 U.S. 1, 15 (1827). Acquittal on the underlying criminal action, *United States v. One Assortment of 89 Firearms*, 465 U.S. 354, 366 (1984); *One Lot of Emerald Cut Stones v. United States*, 409 U.S. 232 (1972), or subsequent reversal of the criminal conviction on appeal has no effect on the civil forfeiture. *United States v. One "Piper" Aztec "F" Deluxe Model 250 PA 23 Aircraft*, 321 F.3d 355, 360 (3d Cir. 2003); *United States v. Real Property (Parcel 03179-005R)*, 287 F. Supp. 2d 45, 62 (D.D.C. 2003).

A criminal conviction is not required in most state civil forfeiture actions. *State v. One 1994 Ford Thunderbird*, 349 N.J. Super. 352; 793 A.2d 792, 803 (N.J. Super. A.D. 2002); *People v. $52,204.00 U.S. Currency*, 252 Ill.App.3d 778; 623 N.E.2d 959, 961 (Ill. App. 1993); *Bozman v. Office of Finance of Baltimore County*, 52 Md. App. 1; 445 A.2d 1073, 1077 (Md. App. 1982); *In re Forfeiture of $53.00*, 178 Mich. App. 480; 444 N.W.2d 182, 189 (Mich. App. 1989); *Jackson v. State ex rel. Mississippi Bureau of Narcotics*, 591 So. 2d 820, 822 (Miss. 1991); *Com. v. $11,600.00 Cash*, 858 A.2d 160, 167 (Pa. Cmwlth. 2004); *State v. One 1966 Pontiac Auto*, 270 N.W.2d 362, 364 (S.D. 1978); *Tex. Code Crim. Proc.* § 59.05(d); *Va. Code Ann.* § 19.2-386.10B; *State v. Hooper*, 122 Wis.2d 748; 364 N.W.2d 175, 177 (Wis. App. 1985); *Katner v. State*, 655 N.E.2d 345, 348 (Ind. 1995); *Ga. Code Ann.* § 16-13-49 (v); *Osborne v. Com.*, 839 S.W.2d 281, 283 (Ky. 1992).

However, there are a few states that may require a criminal conviction as part of the civil forfeiture procedure. *See Cal. Health & Safety Code* § 11488.4(i)(3); *Co. Rev. Stat.* § 16-13-307; *Ky. Rev. Stat. Ann.* § 218A.460; *N.M. Code Ann.* § 31-27-6E(2); *Mo. State v. Eicholz*, 999 S.W.2d 738, 742 (Mo. App. 1999); *State v. Residence Located at 5708 Paseo, Kansas City, Mo.*, 896

S.W.2d 532, 537 (Mo. App. 1995); *N.Y. C.P.L.R.* § 1311 1(a); *Ore. Constitution* Article XV Sec. 10(3); *Utah Code Ann.* § 24-1-8(1); *Vt. Stat. Ann.* Title 18 § 4244.

A plea to a substantially related federal criminal conviction, *Ware v. State*, 128 S.W.3d 529, 531–32 (Mo. App. 2003); *State v. Woods*, 146 N.C. App. 686; 554 S.E.2d 383, 385 (N.C. App. 2001); *Hendley v. Clark*, 147 A.D.2d 347; 543 N.Y.S.2d 554, 556 (N.Y. A.D. 1989), or juvenile adjudication, *City of Sparks, Police Dept., Washoe County Nev. v. Nason*, 107 Nev. 202; 807 P.2d 1389, 1390 (Nev. 1991); *In re Property Seized from Terrell*, 639 N.W.2d 18, 20 (Iowa 2002), may be sufficient to satisfy this requirement.

A few state statutes also require that minimum quantity thresholds of controlled substances be proven as part of the civil forfeiture on a facilitation theory. *See Ca. Health & Saf. Code* § 11470(d) (57 grams of Sch I or II substances or 10 lbs. of marijuana); *Vt. Stat. Ann.* tit. 18 § 4241(b) (at least two ounces of marijuana); *Ga. Code Ann.* § 16-13-49(e)(2) (at least one gram of cocaine or four ounces of marijuana); *S.D. Codified Laws* § 34-20B-73 (½ lb. of marijuana). These provisions are based upon the premise that civil forfeitures are not intended for personal-use amounts of drugs or misdemeanor offenses. *State v. One 1972 Pontiac Grand Prix*, 90 S.D. 455; 242 N.W.2d 660, 662 (S.D. 1976); *State v. One 1972 Lincoln Continental*, 295 N.W.2d 343, 345 (S.D. 1980). In these state jurisdictions, the trial court will require the prosecutor to offer proof of the criminal conviction and minimum-quantity threshold.

D. Proof at Trial

The federal and state burdens of proof at trial differ depending upon the type of case.

1. Federal Burden of Proof

Prior to CAFRA, most federal asset forfeiture statutes incorporated the customs law provisions that required the government to establish only the forfeiture by probable cause and permitted the introduction of reliable hearsay evidence. *See United States v. $200,000*, 805 F. Supp. 585, 589 (N.D. Ill. 1992); *United States v. One 1986 Chevrolet Van*, 927 F.2d 39, 42 (1st Cir. 1991). Once probable cause was established, the burden of proof shifted to the claimant to present his or her defense by a preponderance of the evidence, which could then be rebutted by the government. *See* 19 U.S.C. § 1615; *Boas v. Smith*, 786 F.2d 605, 609 (4th Cir. 1986).

This shifting burden of proof resulted in many courts bifurcating the trial proceeding into a "probable cause stage," followed by a "merits stage," *see United States v. $189,825.00 in U.S. Currency,* 8 F. Supp. 2d 1300, 1303 (N.D. Okla. 1998), to insulate the jury from the hearsay evidence introduced during the probable cause portion of the trial. *See United States v. One Parcel of Real Estate (1012 Germantown Road),* 963 F.2d 1496, 1503 (11th Cir. 1992).

With the passage of CAFRA Section 2, 106 Pub. L. No. 185, 114 Stat. 202, 205–06, the burden of proof is now squarely on the government to establish that the property is subject to forfeiture by a preponderance of the evidence, *see* 18 U.S.C. § 983(c)(1); *United States v. Dodge Caravan Grand SE,* 387 F.3d 758, 761 (8th Cir. 2004), unless the case is exempted under the customs carve out provision, *see* 18 U.S.C. § 983(i), or other exemption, *see Pub. L.* 107-56, 115 Stat. § 316. Hence, there is no more probable cause finding or burden shifting, and the government must now establish that the property is subject to forfeiture without using any hearsay evidence. *See United States v. One Parcel (2526 Faxon Avenue),* 145 F. Supp. 2d 942, 950 (W.D. Tenn. 2001). This should obviate the need for the bifurcated trial hearing in the federal system.

2. State Burden of Proof

Table 7-2 is a summary of the states listing the trial burden of proof in forfeiture actions. All of these trial burdens of proof are on the prosecution. Table 7-2 reveals that there are four different burdens of proof that may apply in contested state forfeiture actions.

Table 7-2
Summary of State Asset Forfeiture Statutes
Civil Forfeiture Burden of Proof

State	Burden of Proof	Statute
Alabama	Prima facie evidence	*Miller v. State*, 567 So.2d 331 (Ala. Civ. App. 1990); *Grant v. State*, 668 So. 2d 20 (Ala. Civ. App. 1995)
Alaska	Probable cause	*Resek v. State*, 706 P.2d 288, 290 (Alaska 1985)
Arizona	Preponderance of the evidence	Ariz. Rev. Stat. Ann. § 13-4311 M
Arkansas	Preponderance of the evidence	Ark. Code Ann. § 5-64-505 (g) (5) (B)
California	Beyond a reasonable doubt Clear and convincing evidence	Cal. Health & Safety Code § 11488.4 (i) (2); Cal. Health & Safety Code § 11488.4 (i) (4)
Colorado	Clear and convincing evidence	Co. Rev. Stat. § 16-13-303 (5.1)(a); 16-13-504 (2.1)(a)
Connecticut	Clear and convincing evidence	Con. Gen. Stat. Ann. § 54-36h (b)
Delaware	Probable cause	*Brown v. State*, 721 A.2d 1263, 1265 (Del. S. Ct. 1998)
District of Columbia	Probable cause	D.C. Code Ann. § 48-905.02 (d)(3)(G)
Florida	Clear and convincing evidence	Fla. Stat. Ann. § 932.704 (8)
Georgia	Probable cause Preponderance of the evidence	Ga. Code Ann. § 16-13-49 (s) *See, Bettis v. State*, 228 Ga.App. 120, 121; 491 S.E.2d 155 (Ga. App. 1997)

Table 7-2 (continued)
Summary of State Asset Forfeiture Statutes
Civil Forfeiture Burden of Proof

State	Burden of Proof	Statute
Hawaii	Preponderance of the evidence	Hawaii Rev. Stat.§ 712A-10 (10) & § 712A-12 (8)
Idaho	Preponderance of the evidence	Idaho Code § 37-2744 (d)
Illinois	Probable cause	725 ILCS 150/9 (G)
Indiana	Preponderance of the evidence	Ind. Code Ann. § 34-24-1-4 (a)
Iowa	Preponderance of the evidence	Iowa Code Ann. § 809A.13 7
Kansas	Preponderance of the evidence	Kan. Stat. Ann. § 60-4113 (g)
Kentucky	Clear and convincing evidence Preponderance of the evidence	Ky. Rev. Stat. Ann. § 218A.410 (1)(j); *Hinckle v. Com.*, 104 S.W.2d 778 (Ky. App. 2002)
Louisiana	Preponderance of the evidence	La. Rev. Stat. Ann. § 40:2612 G
Maine	Preponderance of the evidence	Me. Rev. Stat. Ann. Title 15 Ch. 517 § 5822 3
Maryland	Preponderance of the evidence	*1986 Mercedes Benz 560 CE v. State*, 334 Md. 264, 638 A.2d 1164 (Md. 1994)
Massachusetts	Probable cause	Mass. Ann. Laws Ch. 94C:47(d)
Michigan	Preponderance of the evidence	Mich. Comp. Laws § 600.4707 (6)
Minnesota	Clear and convincing evidence	Minn. Stat. Ann. § 609.531 6a

Table 7-2 (continued)
Summary of State Asset Forfeiture Statutes
Civil Forfeiture Burden of Proof

State	Burden of Proof	Statute
Mississippi	Preponderance of the evidence	Miss. Code Ann. § 41-29-179 (2)
Missouri	Preponderance of the evidence	Mo. Ann. Stat. § 513.607.2; *State v. Residence Located at 5708 Paseo*, 896 S.W.2d 532, 536 (Mo. App. 1995)
Montana	Probable cause	Mont. Code Ann. § 44-12-103 (1)
Nevada	Clear and convincing evidence	Nev. Rev. Stat. § 179.1173 3
New Hampshire	Preponderance of the evidence	N.H. Rev. Stat. Ann. § 318-B:17-b IV (b)
New Jersey	Preponderance of the evidence	*State v. Seven Thousand Dollars*, 136 N.J. 223, 238; 642 A.2d 967 (S. Ct. 1994)
New Mexico	Clear and convincing evidence	N.M. Stat. Ann. 31-27-6D
New York	Clear and convincing evidence Preponderance of the evidence	N.Y. Civil Practice Law § 1311 3 (a)-(b)
North Dakota	Probable Cause Preponderance of the evidence	N.D. Cent. Code § 19.03.1-36.6; § 19-03.1-36.2
Ohio	Clear and convincing evidence	Ohio Rev. Code Ann. § 2925.43 (E) (4)
Oklahoma	Preponderance of the evidence	Okla. Stat. Ann. § 63-2-506 G
Oregon	Preponderance of the evidence Clear and convincing evidence	Or. Rev. Stat. § 475A.080(3) Ore. Constitution Article XV Sec. 10(3)

Table 7-2 (continued)
Summary of State Asset Forfeiture Statutes
Civil Forfeiture Burden of Proof

State	Burden of Proof	Statute
Pennsylvania	Preponderance of the evidence	*Commonwealth v. Fidelity Bank Accts.,* 158 Pa. Commw. 109, 120; 631 A.2d 710 (Pa. Cmwlth. 1993)
Rhode Island	Probable cause	R.I. Gen. Laws § 21-28-5.04.2 (p)
South Carolina	Probable cause	*Medlock v. One 1985 Jeep Cherokee,* 322 S.C. 127, 131; 470 S.E. 2d 373 (S. Ct. 1996)
South Dakota	Probable Cause Preponderance of the evidence	S.D. Codified Laws Ann. § 34-20B-88; 34-20B-80
Tennessee	Beyond a reasonable doubt Preponderance of the evidence	Tenn. Code Ann. § 53-11-452 (d)(E); Tenn. Code Ann. § 40-33-107 (4) § 39-11-708 (c)
Texas	Preponderance of the evidence	Tx. Code of Crim. Procedure § 59.05 (b)
Utah	Clear and convincing evidence	Utah Code Ann. § 24-1-4 (6) (c)
Vermont	Clear and convincing evidence	Vt. Stat. Ann. Title 18: § 4244 (c)
Virginia	Preponderance of the evidence	Va. Code Ann. § 19.2-386.10 A
Washington	Probable Cause Preponderance of the evidence	*Escamilla v. Tri City Metro,* 100 Wash.App. 742; 999 P.2d 625 (Wash. App. 2000); Wash. Rev. Code Ann. § 69.50.505 (5)
West Virginia	Preponderance of the evidence	W. Va. Code § 60A-7-705 (e)
Wisconsin	Reasonable certainty	Wis. Stat. Ann. § 961.555(3)
Wyoming	Probable cause	Wyo. Stat. Ann. § 35-7-1049(b); *State v. Eleven Thousand Three Hundred Forty-Six Dollars & No Cents,* 777 P.2d 65, 81 (Wyo. (1989)

Several states and the District of Columbia allow forfeiture by probable cause, the standard used in the federal system prior to CAFRA. *See D.C. Code Ann.* § 48-905.02(d)(3)(G); *725 Ill. Comp. Stat.* 150/9(G); *Mass. Ann. Laws* Ch. 94C § 47(d); *Mont. Code Ann.* § 44-12-103(1); *R.I. Gen. Laws* § 21-28-5.04.2(p).

The majority of states set the trial burden of proof at preponderance of the evidence. *See Idaho Code* § 37-2744(d); *Me. Rev. Stat. Ann.* Title 15 Ch. 517 § 5822.3; *Miss. Code Ann.* § 41-29-179(2); *Tex. Code of Crim. Proc.* § 59.05(b). This is the current burden of proof established by CAFRA for federal cases.

Some states have set their trial burden of proof at clear and convincing evidence, a standard higher than the federal burden. *See Fla. Stat. Ann.* § 932.704(8); *Ky. Rev. Stat. Ann.* § 218A.410(1)(j); *Minn. Stat. Ann.* § 609.531 Subd. 6a; *Ohio Rev. Code Ann.* § 2925.43(E)(4). A recent trend among states has been to raise the burden of proof to the clear and convincing standard as a result of legislative action, *see Co. Rev. Stat.* § 16-13-303 (5.1); 16-13-504 (2.1)(a); *Nev. Rev. Stat.* § 179.1173 3; *N.M. Code Ann.* § 31-27-6), and voter initiatives, *see Ore. Const. Art.* XV Sec. 10(3); *Utah Code Ann.* § 24-1-4(6)(c).

A few states have dual burdens of proof depending upon various factors. For example, in Tennessee, the burden of proof for most property is preponderance of the evidence, *see Tenn. Code Ann.* § 40-33-107(4), but real property must be proven beyond a reasonable doubt, *see Tenn. Code Ann.* § 53-11-452(d)(1)(E). California has a higher burden of proof for currency instruments valued under $25,000, *see Cal. Health & Safety Code* § 11488.4(i)(2) (beyond a reasonable doubt), and a lower burden of proof for those worth $25,000 or more, *see Cal. Health & Safety Code* § 11488.4(i)(4) (clear and convincing evidence). New York has various burdens of proof depending upon the status of the claimant (criminal defendant—preponderance of the evidence; noncriminal defendant—clear and convincing evidence) and the status of any related criminal case (preconviction versus post-conviction). *See N.Y. Civil Practice Law* § 1311.3.

Thus, prior to trial, the litigants should review the applicable statute to be certain of the burden of proof the prosecution must attain.

E. Nexus

1. Federal Procedure

To prevail on the forfeiture action, the government must establish a nexus between the criminal activity and the seized property. The strength of that nexus depends on the theory of forfeiture.

For proceeds forfeitures, the prosecutor must show that the property was derived from or traceable to criminal activity by demonstrating a connection between the seized property and illegal activity. *See United States v. Thomas,* 913 F.2d 1111, 1117 (4th Cir. 1990); *United States v. $364,960 in U.S. Currency,* 661 F.2d 319, 324 (5th Cir. 1981); *United States v. $93,685.61 U.S. Currency,* 730 F.2d 571, 572 (9th Cir. 1984).) However, it is not necessary to demonstrate a substantial connection as articulated in 18 U.S.C. § 983(c)(3) because that section is limited to facilitation forfeitures. *United States v. $21,000 in US Postal Money Orders,* 298 F. Supp. 2d 597, 601–02 (E.D. Mich. 2003); *United States v. $118,170.00 in U.S. Currency,* 69 Fed. Appx. 714, 717 n.1 (6th Cir. 2003).

There is no requirement that the government tie the asset to a specific illicit transaction; it is sufficient to connect the item to the criminal activity in general. *See United States v. Four Million Two Hundred Fifty-Five Thousand,* 762 F.2d 895, 904 (11th Cir. 1985); *United States v. One 1987 Mercedes 560 SEL,* 919 F.2d 327, 331 (5th Cir. 1990); *United States v. $242,484.00,* 389 F.3d 1149, 1160 (11th Cir. 2004).

Because the proceeds theory includes any asset indirectly exchanged for criminal profits in one or more "intervening legitimate transactions or otherwise changed in form," *see United States v. Banco Cafetero Panama,* 797 F.2d 1154, 1158 (2d Cir. 1986), the burden is on the government to trace the seized asset to the underlying criminal activity. *See United States v. Gonzalez,* 240 F.3d 14, 17 (1st Cir. 2001). If illegitimate funds are commingled with legitimate funds, the government is entitled to the share traceable to the illegal activity. *See United States v. Pole No. 3172 (Hopkinton),* 852 F.2d 636, 639–40 (1st Cir. 1988); *United States v. 1980 Rolls Royce,* 905 F.2d 89, 90 (5th Cir. 1990).

Under federal law, if property is traced into a financial institution account, it is not a defense that the property involved in the offense has been removed and replaced with identical funds. Under the fungible funds statute (18 U.S.C. § 984), identical property found in the same account as the property involved in the offense is subject to forfeiture, provided the action is commenced within one year from the date of offense. *See United States v. U.S. Currency Deposited in Account No. 1115000763247,* 176 F.3d 941, 946 (7th Cir. 1999). This relieves the government of the strict tracing requirement in civil forfeitures involving money-laundering offenses. *See Marine Midland Bank N.A. v. United States,* 11 F.3d 1119, 1126 (2d Cir. 1993); *United States v. One Parcel of Real Property (170 Westfield Drive),* 34 F. Supp. 2d 107, 118 (D.R.I. 1999). This provision applies only if relied upon by the government in its pleadings. *United States v. Contents in Account No. 059-644190-69,* 253 F. Supp. 2d 789, 794 (D. Vt. 2003).

In federal cases that are prosecuted on a facilitation or instrumentality theory, CAFRA Section 2, 106 Pub. L. No. 185, 114 Stat. 202, 206, now requires that the government establish a substantial connection between the seized property and the offense, 18 U.S.C. § 983(c)(3), by a preponderance of the evidence. *United States v. Real Property in Section 9*, 308 F. Supp. 2d 791, 806 (E.D. Mich. 2004).

Defining the term "substantial connection" is difficult because "it is a question of degree which is in turn a question of fact not susceptible to generalization." *See United States v. One 1974 Cadillac Eldorado*, 407 F. Supp. 1115, 1116, n.3 (S.D.N.Y. 1975). However, a substantial connection has been found where the seized property was used to further the criminal activity, *see United States v. One Parcel (2526 Faxon Avenue)*, 145 F. Supp. 2d 942, 951 (W.D. Tenn. 2001); *United States v. Real Property (40 Clark Road)*, 52 F. Supp. 2d 254, 261 (D. Mass. 1999); *United States v. Dodge Caravan Grand SE*, 387 F.3d 758, 761–62 (8th Cir. 2004), or was the location of the criminal offense. *See United States v. Two Parcels of Real Property (101 North Liberty Street)*, 80 F. Supp. 2d 1298, 1308 (M.D. Ala. 2000); *United States v. .30 Acre Tract of Land (524 Cheek Road)*, 425 F. Supp. 2d 704, 708–09 (M.D.N.C. 2006).

2. State Procedures

States also require that a causal relationship or nexus be established between the seized asset and criminal activity. *State v. One 1988 Honda Prelude*, 252 N.J. Super. 312; 599 A.2d 932, 934 (N.J. Super. A.D. 1991).

As in federal practice, several state courts have determined that there is no requirement that the asset be tied to a specific transaction; tracing to criminal activity in general, such as drug sales, is sufficient. *Com v. Brown*, 688 N.E.2d 1356, 1360 (Mass. 1998); *In re Forfeiture of $1,159,420*, 194 Mich. App. 134; 486 N.W.2d 326, 333–34 (Mich. App. 1992); *In re $207,523.46 in U.S. Currency*, 130 N.H. 202; 536 A.2d 1270, 1273 (N.H. 1987); *Lettner v. Plummer*, 559 S.W.2d 785, 787 (Tenn. App. 1977). A few states also specify this in their statutes. *See Hawaii Rev. Stat.* § 712A-11(4); *Iowa Code Ann.* § 809A.12 11; *Kan. Stat. Ann.* § 60-4112(l).

In proceeds cases, tracing may be accomplished by circumstantial evidence. *Com. v. $6,425.00 Seized from Esquilin*, 583 Pa. 544; 880 A.2d 523, 530 (Pa. 2005). One state court found there was sufficient tracing to sustain the forfeiture of assets obtained two years prior to the filing of the forfeiture petition. *In re Forfeiture of $1,159,420*, 194 Mich. App. 134; 486 N.W.2d 326, 334–35 (Mich. App. 1992).

If funds are commingled, the state is entitled to the portion of the funds traceable to illegal activity. *People v. $9,632.50 U.S. Currency*, 64 Cal. App. 4th 163, 174 (1998); *State v. One House*, 346 N.J. Super. 247; 787 A.2d 905, 908 (N.J. Super. A.D. 2001).

On facilitation forfeiture cases, state courts also require a connection between the asset and the underlying criminal activity. Although a few courts articulate that the nexus must be "more than incidental or fortuitous," *Katner v. State*, 655 N.E.2d 345, 349 (Ind. 1995), or "some" nexus, *People v. $1,124,905 U.S. Currency*, 177 Ill.2d 314; 685 N.E.2d 1370, 1381 (Ill. 1997), the vast majority require a substantial connection for forfeiture. *Matter of H.E.W., Inc.*, 530 N.W.2d 460, 463 (Iowa App. 1995); *In re Forfeiture of 301 Cass Street*, 194 Mich. App. 381; 487 N.W.2d 795, 797 (Mich. App. 1992); *Strand v. Chester Police Dept.*, 687 A.2d 872, 876 (Pa. Cmwlth. 1997); *$9,050.00 in U.S. Currency v. State*, 874 S.W.2d 158, 161 (Tex. App. 1994); *Lee v. Com.*, 253 Va. 222; 482 S.E.2d 802, 804 (Va. 1997). A few states have also enacted the substantial connection standard into their statutes, similar to the federal CAFRA standard. *See Co. Rev. Stat.* § 16-13-502(1.7); *Fla. Stat. Ann.* § 932.703(8); *N.H. Rev. Stat. Ann.* § 318-B:17-b IV(e)(1).

Examples of state facilitation forfeitures include real property that served as the base of the drug operations, *Brewer v. Com.*, 206 S.W.3d 313, 325 (Ky. 2006), and vehicles that provided transportation, shelter, and privacy for the drug sales. *Matter of One 1985 Mercedes Benz*, 644 A.2d 423, 429 (Del. Super. 1992).

F. Trial Evidence

Forfeitures may be established by both direct and circumstantial evidence, and neither is entitled to any greater weight as a form of proof. *See United States v. Register*, 182 F.3d 820, 830 (11th Cir. 1999). Hearsay evidence is inadmissible in the civil trial unless it is limited to the issue of probable cause or other exception under the rules of evidence. *See United States v. 1987 Mercedes Benz 300E*, 820 F. Supp. 248, 251 (E.D. Va. 1993); *City of Coral Springs v. Forfeiture of 1997 Ford Ranger*, 803 So. 2d 847, 850 (Fla. App. 2002).

Direct evidence may consist of the surveillance or observations of officers, and civilian witnesses and admissions made by the claimant during the investigation. *See United States v. Leak*, 123 F.3d 787, 790 (4th Cir. 1997). This usually is the primary evidence in cases where the theory of forfeiture is that the property was exchanged for, furnished, or facilitated the underlying criminal activity. *See United States v. $88,500*, 671 F.2d 293, 296 (8th Cir. 1982). Responses to civil discovery including admissions, relevant documentary evidence, and prior criminal convictions may also be utilized to demonstrate the nexus between the seized asset and the underlying criminal activity. *See United States v. One 1975 Mercury Monarch,* 423 F. Supp. 1026, 1028 (S.D.N.Y. 1976).

Circumstantial evidence has been used extensively in federal civil asset forfeiture actions to establish probable cause that the property is subject to forfeiture. *See United States v. One Lot of U.S. Currency ($36,674),* 103 F.3d 1048, 1055–56 (1st Cir. 1997); *United States v. One Parcel Known as 352 Northrup St.,* 40 F. Supp. 2d 74, 81–82 (D.R.I. 1999). Although CAFRA has increased the federal burden of proof to preponderance of the evidence, the government has still been able to reach this higher standard by using circumstantial evidence. *See United States v. $22,991.00,* 227 F. Supp. 2d 1220, 1236 (S.D. Ala. 2002); *United States v. $345,510.00 in U.S. Currency,* 2002 WL 22040 (D. Minn. 2002); *United States v. Currency U.S. $42,500,* 283 F.3d 977, 984 n.1 (9th Cir. 2002); *United States v. $30,670 in U.S. Funds,* 2002 WL 31093587 (N.D. Ill. 2002); *United States v. $181,087.14,* 2002 WL 31951270 (S.D. Ohio 2002). State courts have likewise upheld the forfeiture of assets relying on circumstantial evidence. *In re Parcel of Land Located in Effingham,* 561 A.2d 1061, 1063 (N.H. 1989); *$162,950 in U.S. Currency v. State,* 911 S.W.2d 528, 529 (Tex. App. 1995).

In evaluating whether the circumstantial evidence is sufficient to demonstrate the forfeitability of the property, the courts look at "the totality of the circumstances . . . judged not with clinical detachment but with a common sense view to the realities of normal life." *See United States v. Four Million Two Hundred Fifty-Five Thousand,* 762 F.2d 895, 904 (11th Cir. 1985); *United States v. One 1987 Mercedes 560 SEL,* 919 F.2d 327, 332 (5th Cir. 1990); *People v. $1,124,905.00 U.S. Currency,* 269 Ill.App.3d 952; 647 N.E.2d 1028, 1032 (Ill. App. 1995); *State v. Isaac,* 722 So. 2d 353, 355 (La. App. 1998); *One (1) 1979 Ford 15V v. State ex rel. Mississippi Bureau of Narcotics,* 721 So. 2d 631, 637 (Miss. 1998).

Some of the factors that the courts have considered in sustaining the forfeitability of the property include:

- Large amounts of currency, *United States v. $121,100.00 in U.S. Currency,* 999 F.2d 1503, 1507 (11th Cir. 1993); *United States v. One Lot of U.S. Currency ($36,674),* 103 F.3d 1048, 1055 (1st Cir. 1997); *United States v. $124,700 in U.S. Currency,* 458 F.3d 822, 825 (8th Cir. 2006); *People v. $48,715 U.S. Currency,* 58 Cal. App. 4th 1507, 1518 (1997); *Matter of Property Seized from DeCamp,* 511 N.W.2d 616, 620 (Iowa 1994); *In re Forfeiture of $19,250,* 209 Mich. App. 20; 530 N.W.2d 759, 765 (Mich. App. 1995); *Com. v. Nine-Thousand Three Hundred Ten Dol-*

lars U. S. Currency, 162 Pa. Cmwlth. 315; 638 A.2d 480, 483 (Pa. Cmwlth. 1994).

- Quantity and packaging of the currency, *United States v. $141,770.00 in U.S. Currency*, 157 F.3d 600, 608 (8th Cir. 1998); *United States v. $129,727.00 U.S. Currency*, 129 F.3d 486, 490 (9th Cir. 1997); *United States v. $99,990 in U.S. Currency*, 69 Fed. Appx. 757, 763 (6th Cir. 2003) (heat-sealed plastic wrapped in tape); *United States v. $252,300.00 in U. S. Currency*, 484 F.3d 1271, 1275 (10th Cir. 2007) (rubber bands and wrapped in cellophane); *People v. $497,590 U.S. Currency*, 58 Cal.App.4th 145, 155 (1997) (in trash bags bundled by denomination); *Jennings v. State*, 553 N.E.2d 191, 193 (Ind. App. 1990) (large roll of $100 and $50 bills); *United States v. One Hundred Three Thousand Twenty-Five Dollars ($103,025.00) in U.S. Currency*, 741 F. Supp. 903, 905 (M.D. Ga. 1990) (small denominations; rubber bands); *State v. $10,000 Seized from Mary Patrick*, 562 N.W.2d 192, 193 (Iowa App. 1997) ($10,000 in $20 bills).

- Drug residue on seized currency, *In re Com., $803 Cash, U.S. Currency*, 403 Pa. Super. 526; 589 A.2d 735, 737 (Pa. Super. 1991); *$165,524.78 v. State*, 47 S.W.3d 632, 637 (Tex. App. 2001).

- Canine alert, *United States v. $22,474 in U.S. Currency*, 246 F.3d 1212, 1216 (9th Cir. 2001); *United States v. One Lot of U.S. Currency ($36,674)*, 103 F.3d 1048, 1054–55 (1st Cir. 1997); *United States v. $84,615 in U.S. Currency*, 379 F.3d 496, 501 (8th Cir. 2004); *United States v. Gaskin*, 364 F.3d 438, 462 (2d Cir. 2004); *United States v. $30,670 in U.S. Funds*, 403 F.3d 448, 462 (7th Cir. 2005); *United States v. $433,980 in U.S. Currency*, 473 F. Supp. 2d 685, 690 (E.D.N.C. 2007); *United States v. $78,850.00 in U.S. Currency*, 517 F. Supp. 2d 792, 798 (D.S.C. 2007); *People v. Superior Court (Moraza)*, 210 Cal. App. 3d 592, 600 (1989); *Young v. State, Dept. of Safety*, 911 S.W.2d 729, 732 (Tenn. 1995); *Antrim v. State*, 868 S.W.2d 809, 814 (Tex. App. 1993);

- Large quantity of drug contraband, *Brewer v. Com.*, 206 S.W.3d 313, 326 (Ky. 2006) (several pounds of marijuana);

- Drug contraband and paraphernalia, *United States v. $39,873.00*, 80 F.3d 317, 319 (8th Cir. 1996) (rolling papers); *United States v. 6 Fox Street*, 480 F.3d 38, 41 (1st Cir. 2007) (scales, ziplock baggies, rolling paper); *State v. $10,000 Seized from Mary Patrick*, 562 N.W.2d 192, 195 (Iowa App. 1997) (plastic baggies, duct tape and plastic containers); *Osborne v. Com.*, 839 S.W.2d 281, 282 (Ky. 1992) (scales);

- Drug contraband and weapons, *State ex rel. Callahan v. Collins*, 978 S.W.2d 471, 475 (Mo. App. 1998) (handgun); *$136,205.00 (Johnson) v.*

State, 848 S.W.2d 888, 890 (Tex. App. 1993) (several handguns); *United States v. $206,323.56 in U.S. Currency,* 998 F. Supp. 693, 699 (S.D.W. Va. 1998) (two loaded semi- automatic firearms);

- Drug courier profile, *United States v. $189,825.00 in U.S. Currency*, 8 F. Supp. 2d 1300, 1313–14 (N.D. Okla. 1998); *United States v. $86,020.00 in U.S. Currency,* 1 F. Supp. 2d 1034, 1037–38 (D. Ariz. 1997); *United States v. $30,670 in U.S. Funds,* 2002 WL 31093587 (N.D. Ill. 2002); *United States v. $124,700 in U.S. Currency*, 458 F.3d 822, 826 (8th Cir. 2006); *Idaho DLE Richardson v. $34,000 U.S. Currency,* 121 Idaho 211; 824 P.2d 142, 151 (Idaho App. 1991); *State v. $8,000 U.S. Currency,* 827 So. 2d 634, 641 (La. App. 2002); *State v. Eleven Thousand Five Hundred Sixty-Six ($11,566.00) Dollars,* 919 P.2d 34, 35 (Okla. App. 1996);

- Drug records, *Matter of Rush*, 448 N.W.2d 472, 478 (Iowa App. 1989) (drug account books); *In re $207,523.46 in U.S. Currency*, 130 N.H. 202; 536 A.2d 1270, 1273 (N.H. 1987) (drug records); *United States v. 6 Fox Street*, 480 F.3d 38, 43 (1st Cir. 2007) (drug records documenting 20 years of drug transactions);

- Criminal conviction on underlying offense, *United States v. United States Currency Amounting to the Sum of Thirty Thousand Eight Hundred Dollars*, 555 F. Supp. 280, 282; (E.D.N.Y. 1983); *United States v. All Right, Title & Interest in Real Property Known as 303 West 116th Street,* 901 F.2d 288, 290–92 (2d Cir. 1990); *United States v. One Hundred Three Thousand Twenty-Five Dollars ($103,025.00) in U.S. Currency*, 741 F. Supp. 903, 905 (M.D. Ga 1990);

- Prior criminal history, *United States v. $8,880*, 945 F. Supp. 521, 525 (W.D.N.Y. 1996); *United States v. 228 Acres of Land*, 916 F.2d 808, 812 (2d Cir. 1990); *United States v. Sixty-Eight Thousand Five Hundred Eighty Dollars $68,580) in U.S. Currency*, 815 F. Supp. 1479, 1483 (M.D. Ga. 1993); *United States v. One Hundred Three Thousand Twenty-Five Dollars ($103,025.00) in U.S. Currency*, 741 F. Supp. 903, 904 (M.D. Ga. 1990) (history of drug offenses); *State v. $7379.54 U.S. Currency*, 844 A.2d 220, 224 (Conn. App. 2003) ("career drug purveyor"); *State ex rel. Gibson v. 1997 Dodge*, 35 P.3d 1009, 1015 (Okla. Civ. App. 2001) (previously used business as front for drugs); *$9,050.00 in U.S. Currency v. State*, 874 S.W.2d 158, 162 (Tex. App. 1994) (prior drug sale conviction from same location);

- Admissions of drug trafficking, *United States v. U.S. Currency in the Sum of $185,000*, 455 F. Supp. 2d 145, 155 (E.D.N.Y. 2006) (admitted money courier); *Matter of Rush*, 448 N.W.2d 472, 477 (Iowa 1989) (admissions to probation officer); *People ex rel. Birkett v. 1995 Pontiac Trans Am*, 358 Ill.App.3d 184; 830 N.E.2d 876, 881 (Ill. App. 2005); *People v. $1,124,905.00 U.S. Currency*, 269 Ill.App.3d 952; 647 N.E.2d 1028, 1032–33 (Ill. App. 1995) (admitted money courier); *Carter v. State*, 254 Ga. App. 187; 561 S.E.2d 856, 857–58 (Ga. App. 2002) (admitted obtaining marijuana three to four times per month from source); *Salmon v. State*, 249 Ga. App. 591; 549 S.E.2d 421, 422 (Ga. App. 2001) (admitted intent to sell); *State v. 1984 Monte Carlo SS*, 521 N.W.2d 723, 725 (Iowa 1994) (admitted purchasing car with drug proceeds); *State v. Six Hundred Seventy Six Dollars $676 U.S. Currency Seized from Branch*, 719 So. 2d 154, 156 (La. App. 1998) (admitted money was drug proceeds); *Jones v. State ex rel. Mississippi Dept. of Public Safety*, 607 So. 2d 23, 29 (Miss. 1991) (admitted growing marijuana); *Lee v. Com.*, 253 Va. 222; 482 S.E.2d 802, 804–05 (Va. 1997) (admitted selling eight to nine ounces of cocaine per week);

- Witness/accomplice testimony of drug trafficking, *Matter of Property Seized from Chiodo*, 555 N.W.2d 412, 416 (Iowa 1996) (written statement of drug dealing by former girlfriend); *In re Forfeiture of U.S. Currency*, 164 Mich. App. 171; 416 N.W.2d 700, 703 (Mich. App. 1987) (testimony from former workers who sold drugs for claimant);

- False statements, *United States v. $8,880*, 945 F. Supp. 521, 524 (W.D.N.Y. 1996); *United States v. $215,300*, 882 F.2d 417, 419 (9th Cir. 1989); *United States v. $345,510.00 U.S. Currency*, 2002 WL 22040 (D. Minn. 2002); *United States v. $84,615 in U.S. Currency*, 379 F.3d 496, 502 (8th Cir. 2004); *United States v. Gaskin*, 364 F.3d 438, 462 (2d Cir. 2004);

- Inconsistent statements, *United States v. $252,300.00 in U.S. Currency*, 484 F.3d 1271, 1274 (10th Cir. 2007) (multiple changes in story); *State v. Albritton*, 610 So. 2d 209, 214 (La. App. 1992) (conflicting stories regarding travel); *Com. v. Nineteen Hundred and Twenty Dollars U.S. Currency*, 149 Pa. Cmwlth. 132; 612 A.2d 614, 620 (Pa. Cmwlth. 1992) (conflicting stories regarding source of money); *Antrim v. State*, 868 S.W.2d 809, 814 (Tex. App. 1993) (inconsistent statements regarding travel and source of money);

- Sale to undercover officer, *A 1983 Volkswagen v. Washoe County Sheriff's Dept.*, 101 Nev. 222; 699 P.2d 108, 110 (Nev. 1985); *Lee v. Com.*, 253 Va. 222; 482 S.E.2d 802, 804 (Va. 1997);

- Confidential source information, *Com. v. McJett*, 811 A.2d 104, 109 (Pa. Cmwlth. 2002);

- Surveillance, *United States v. One Parcel of Property (Bryan County)*,

801 F. Supp. 737, 739 (S.D. Ga. 1992); *People v. $497,590 U.S. Currency*, 58 Cal. App. 4th 145, 148 (1997);

- Wiretapped conversations, *Com. v. $126,730.50*, 399 Pa. Super. 118; 581 A.2d 953, 955 (Pa. Super. 1990);
- Expert testimony of agents, *Marine Midland Bank N.A. v. United States*, 11 F.3d 1119, 1126 (2d Cir. 1993); *United States v. $149,442.43 in U.S. Currency*, 965 F.2d 868, 873–74 (10th Cir. 1992); *United States v. $242,484.00*, 389 F.3d 1149, 1162–63 (11th Cir. 2004) (drug courier profile, packaging of money); *Hickman v. State ex rel. Mississippi Dept of Public Safety*, 592 So. 2d 44, 47–48 (Miss. 1991) (drug courier profile);
- Lack of legitimate income, *United States v. Funds in the Amount of $29,266*, 96 F. Supp. 2d 806, 811–12 (N.D. Ill. 2000); *United States v. Thomas*, 913 F.2d 1111, 1115 (4th Cir. 1990); *United States v. $22,991.00*, 227 F. Supp. 2d 1220, 1234–35 (S.D. Ala. 2002); *United States v. $174,206.00 in U.S. Currency*, 320 F.3d 658, 662 (6th Cir. 2003) (income not verified by tax returns); *United States v. $118,170.00 in U.S. Currency*, 69 Fed. Appx. 714, 717 (6th Cir. 2003) (same); *United States v. $30,670 in U.S. Funds*, 403 F.3d 448, 468 (7th Cir. 2005) (bankruptcy filing and federal income tax returns); *United States v. U.S. Currency in the Sum of $185,000*, 455 F. Supp. 2d 145, 148–49 (E.D.N.Y. 2006) (minimal income established at claimant's deposition); *In re Young*, 670 N.W.2d 430 (Table) n.1 (Iowa App. 2003) (unemployed for eight years); *Com. v. Nine-Thousand Three Hundred Ten Dollars U.S. Currency*, 162 Pa. Cmwlth. 315; 638 A.2d 480, 483 (Pa. Cmwlth. 1994) (no legitimate source of income); *Jones v. Greene*, 946 S.W.2d 817, 828 (Tenn. App. 1996) (no proof that money was "life savings");
- Unexplained source of income, *In re Forfeiture of $1,159,420*, 194 Mich. App. 134; 486 N.W.2d 326, 333 (Mich. App. 1992) (retired factory worker); *In re Forfeiture of U.S. Currency*, 181 Mich. App. 761; 450 N.W.2d 93, 95 (Mich. App. 1989) (proof that money was loans rejected); *Forty-Seven Thousand Two Hundred Dollars U.S. Currency v. State*, 883 S.W.2d 302, 309 (Tex. App. 1994) (proof that money came from workers compensation award or personal loan rejected); *$165,524.78 v. State*, 47 S.W.3d 632, 637 (Tex. App. 2001) (proof that money came from inheritance, sale of rental property and legitimate businesses rejected);
- Large cash expenditures, *United States v. Certain Real Property Located on Hanson Brook*, 770 F. Supp. 722, 725 (D. Me. 1991) (numerous real property purchases with no mortgages); *United States v. A*

Parcel of Land (92 Buena Vista), 937 F.2d 98, 104 (3d Cir. 1991) (large cash deposit for real property); *United States v. Carrell,* 252 F.3d 1193, 1201 (11th Cir. 2001) (cash purchase of real property); *State v. 1984 Monte Carlo SS,* 521 N.W.2d 723, 725 (Iowa 1994) ($3,000 cash down payment);

- Expenses exceed legitimate income, *Com. v. Fidelity Bank Accounts,* 158 Pa. Cmwlth 109; 631 A.2d 710, 716–17 (Pa. Cmwlth. 1993); *McEwen v. Tennessee Dept. of Safety,* 173 S.W.3d 815, 826 (Tenn. Ct. App. 2005); *Escamilla v. Tri-City Metro Drug Task Force,* 100 Wash. App. 742, 999 P.2d 625, 631 (Wash. App. 2000);

- Asset obtained during same time period as criminal activity, *State v. 1984 Monte Carlo SS,* 521 N.W.2d 723, 725 (Iowa 1994); *State v. Forty Three Thousand Dollars ($43,000.00) in Cashier's Checks,* 214 W.Va. 650; 591 S.E.2d 208, 213–14 (W.Va. 2003*); In re Three Pieces of Property Located in Monticello,* 81 Ark. App. 235; 100 S.W.3d 76, 81–82 (Ark. App. 2003);

- Lack of corroboration, *McEwen v. Tennessee Dept. of Safety,* 173 S.W.3d 815, 827 (Tenn. Ct. App. 2005) (no proof that jewelry was gift or inheritance); *$19,070.00 v. State,* 869 S.W.2d 608, 612 (Tex. App. 1994) (claim was inconsistent with records).

The court should make a practical, common-sense decision whether, given all of the circumstances, there is a fair probability that the property is subject to forfeiture, *see United States v. One 1987 Mercedes Benz 300E,* 820 F. Supp. 248, 251 (E.D. Va. 1993), and base its finding on the overall "aggregate of facts," *see United States v. $93,685.61 U.S.* Currency, 730 F.2d 571, 572 (9th Cir. 1984), and avoid "parsing [the] evidence in isolation." *See United States v. Thomas,* 913 F.2d 1111, 1117 (4th Cir. 1990).

G. Trial Presumptions

Realizing the circumstantial nature of most asset forfeiture cases, many jurisdictions have enacted rebuttable presumptions to assist in making the nexus between the criminal activity and the seized property. If the prosecutor is able to establish certain facts, the trier of fact is permitted to infer that the property is either used to facilitate or constitutes proceeds of the illegal activity. The burden is then placed on the claimant to rebut the presumption.

Table 7-3 is a list of presumptions found in state civil forfeiture statutes.

Table 7-3
Summary of State Asset Forfeiture Statutes
State Evidentiary Presumptions

State	Statute	Presumption
Arkansas	Ark. Code Ann. § 5-64-505(a)(7)	Close proximity
Arizona	Ariz. Rev. Stat. Ann. § 13-4305 E	Property acquired during period of conduct giving rise to forfeiture; no other likely source.
	Ariz. Rev. Stat. Ann. § 13-4305 F	Close proximity
Colorado	Colo. Rev. Stat. §§ 16-13-303; 16-13-509	Cash over $1,000; Canine Alert
Delaware	Del. Code Ann. tit 16, § 4784(a)(7)(a)	Close proximity
	Del. Code Ann. tit. 16 § 4784(a)(7)(b)	Trace amount of controlled substances
District of Columbia	D.C. Code Ann. § 48-905.02(a)(7)(B)	Close proximity
Georgia	Ga. Code Ann § 16-13-49(d)(6)	Close proximity
	Ga. Code Ann. § 16-13-49(s)(3	Property acquired during period of conduct giving rise to forfeiture; no other likely source
Hawaii	Haw. Rev. Stat. § 712A-6 Haw. Rev. Stat. § 712A-11(3)((a)-(c)	Close proximity Property acquired during time period of criminal conduct or within reasonable time thereafter; no other likely source
Idaho	Idaho Code § 37-2744(a)(6)(A)	Close proximity
Illinois	725 ILCS 150/7	Close proximity Property acquired between dates of commission of controlled substance offenses.
Indiana	Ind. Code Ann. § 34-24-1-1(d)	Property found near or on the person committing or attempting to commit the offense

Table 7-3 (continued)
Summary of State Asset Forfeiture Statutes
State Evidentiary Presumptions

State	Statute	Presumption
Iowa	Iowa Code Ann. § 809A.12 9-10	Close proximity Property acquired during time period of conduct giving rise to forfeiture or reasonable time thereafter; no other likely source
Kansas	Kan. Stat. Ann. § 60-4112 (j)-(k)	Close proximity Property acquired during time period of conduct giving rise to forfeiture or reasonable time thereafter; no other likely source
Kentucky	Ky. Rev. Stat. Ann. § 218A.410(1)(j)	Close proximity
Louisiana	La. Rev. Stat. Ann. § 40:2611(G)-(H)	Close proximity Property acquired during time period of conduct giving rise to forfeiture or reasonable time thereafter; no other likely source
Maryland	Md. Code Ann., Crim. Proc. § 12-102(b); Md. Code Ann., Crim. Proc. § 12-312	Close proximity Person has violated or attempted to violate criminal laws; property acquired during time of violation or reasonable time thereafter and no other likely source.
Michigan	Mich. Comp. Laws § 333.7521(1)(f)	Close Proximity
Minnesota	Minn. Stat. Ann. § 609.5314 sub. 1	Money & firearms in Close Proximity; Conveyances containing controlled substances with retail value over $100 chargeable as a felony
Mississippi	Miss. Code Ann. § 41-29-153	Close Proximity

Table 7-3 (continued)
Summary of State Asset Forfeiture Statutes
State Evidentiary Presumptions

State	Statute	Presumption
Missouri	Mo. Ann. Stat. § 195.140.2(2)	Close Proximity
Montana	Mont. Code Ann. § 44-12-203(1)	Rebuttable presumption that all property listed in § 44-12-102, except real property, is forfeited.
Nevada	Nev. Rev. Stat. § 453.301.9	Cash exceeding $300 in possession of person arrested for drug trafficking offense was exchanged for controlled substances
New Hampshire	N.H. Rev. Stat. § 318-B:17-b I (c)	Close proximity
New Jersey	N. J. Stat. Ann. § 2C:64-3.j	Related criminal conviction establishes rebuttable presumption that property was used in furtherance of illegal activity
New York	N.Y.C.P.L.R. § 1311(d) N.Y.C.P.L.R. § 1311(c)	For cases involving a criminal defendant 1) Close proximity A non-criminal defendant is presumed to have knowledge if: 1) He did not pay fair consideration for the property; or 2) Had knowledge of a provisional order when he obtained the property or; 3) Has criminal liability and possess an interest in the proceeds.

Table 7-3 (continued)
Summary of State Asset Forfeiture Statutes
State Evidentiary Presumptions

State	Statute	Presumption
North Dakota	N.D. Cent. Code § 19-03.1-23.3	1. Close proximity a. Over $10,000 currency b. Transported through airport, highway or port of entry c. Concealed in unusual manner d. False information provided e. Close proximity to measurable amount of drugs f. Positive canine alert 2. Acquired during period of time of criminal offense or reasonable time thereafter AND no other likely source. 3. Transported or transferred from major drug-transit country 4. Person convicted of drug offense or is fugitive from prosecution.
Ohio	Ohio Rev. Code Ann. § 2925.42(C)	Property acquired during time period of conduct giving rise to forfeiture or reasonable time thereafter; no other likely source
Oklahoma	Okla. Stat. Ann § 63-2-503A.7 Okla. Stat. Ann § 63-2-503.B	Close Proximity Property acquired during time period of conduct giving rise to forfeiture or reasonable time thereafter; no other likely source.
Pennsylvania	Pa. Cons. Stat. Ann. tit. 42 § 6801(a)(6)(ii)	Close Proximity
Rhode Island	R.I. Gen. Laws § 21-28-5.04(a)	Close Proximity

Table 7-3 (continued)
Summary of State Asset Forfeiture Statutes
State Evidentiary Presumptions

State	Statute	Presumption
South Carolina	S.C. Code Ann. § 44-53-520(a)(8)	Close Proximity
Tennessee	Tenn. Code Ann. § 39-11-708(e)	Property acquired during period of conduct giving rise to forfeiture or reasonable time thereafter; no other likely source
Texas	Tex. Code Crim. Proc. § 59.05(d)	Acquittal of underlying offense raises presumption that property is nonforfeitable.
Utah	Utah Code Ann. § 24-1-6 (6)	Engaged in conduct giving rise to forfeiture; Property acquired during period of conduct giving rise to forfeiture or reasonable time thereafter; no other likely source

These presumptions generally fall into two categories: the "close proximity" and "no likely source" presumptions.

Any property found in close proximity to controlled substances or other indicia of sales, manufacturing, or distribution of controlled substance is presumed to be forfeitable as proceeds of the conduct or was used or intended to be used to facilitate the criminal activity. *City of Hoisington v. $2,044 in U.S. Currency*, 27 K.A.2d 825; 8 P.3d 58, 62 (Kan. App. 2000); *In re Return of Property Confiscated October 30, 1999 from 411 East Mac Dade Blvd.*, 856 A.2d 238, 248 (Pa. Cmwlth. 2004); *Carlisle v. Ten Thousand Four Hundred Forty-seven Dollars in U.S. Currency*, 104 Haw. 323; 89 P.3d 823, 833 (Hawaii 2004). The term "close proximity" is not defined in terms of distance and is determined on a case-by-case basis. *City of Meridian v. Hodge*, 632 So. 2d 1309, 1312 (Miss. 1994); *Bozman v. Office of Finance of Baltimore County*, 52 Md. App. 1; 445 A.2d 1073, 1075 (Md. App. 1982). Generally, the presumption does not apply to simple possession charges. *State v. Eighteen Thousand Six Hundred Sixty-Three Dollars and Twenty-Five Cents ($18,663.25) Cash*, 11 P.3d 1253, 1255 (Okla. Civ. App. 2000). It does not substitute for the prosecutor's burden to show a nexus between the seized property and illegal activity. *Matter of U.S. Currency in Amount of $315,900.00*, 183 Ariz. 208, 902 P.2d 351, 357 (Ariz. App. 1995).

The presumption may be rebutted by a preponderance of the evidence, *In re Seizure of $23,691.00*, 273 M 474; 905 P.2d 148, 154 (Mont. 1995); *People v. $5,970 U.S. Currency*, 279 Ill.App.3d 583; 664 N.E.2d 1115, 1119 (Ill. App. 1996), and placing this burden on the claimant does not violate due process. *Matter of Ten Thousand Ninety-Eight Dollars ($10,098.00) in U.S. Currency*, 175 Ariz. 237, 854 P.2d 1223, 1229 (Ariz. App. 1993); *Ewachiw v. Director of Finance of Baltimore City*, 70 Md. App. 58, 519 A.2d 1327, 1331 (Md. App. 1987).

The federal civil forfeiture statutes do not contain a comparable presumption.

In the second category, property is presumed forfeitable if a person has engaged in criminal activity and the property subject to forfeiture was acquired during the period of time of the illegal conduct or shortly thereafter, and there is no other likely source for the property other than the criminal activity giving rise to the forfeiture.

This presumption also requires the prosecutor to prove the criminal nexus before it applies. *State v. Eighteen Thousand Six Hundred Sixty-Three Dollars and Twenty-Five Cents ($18,663.25) Cash*, 11 P.3d 1253, 1255 (Okla. Civ. App. 2000). It is designed to assist prosecutors in meeting the burden of proof in cases litigated on the proceeds theory.

The federal civil forfeiture statutes do not contain this presumption, but a similar provision is found in the federal criminal forfeiture statutes. *See* 21 U.S.C. § 853(b).

Other factors that may be considered in statutory rebuttable presumptions include the amount of currency seized, *Nev. Rev. Stat.* § 453.301.9 (over $300); *Colo. Rev. Stat.* § 16-13-303 (over $1,000); *N.D. Stat.* § 19.03.1-23.3 (over $10,000); canine alert, *Colo. Rev. Stat.* § 16-13-509; *N.D. Stat.* 19-03.1-23.3; trace amounts of controlled substances, *Del. C.* § 4784(7)(b); and related criminal convictions. *N.J. Stat. Ann.* § 2C:64-3j; *N.Y.C.P.L.R.* § 1311(c); *N.D. Stat.* § 19.03.1-23.3.

State prosecutors should carefully review their state statutes for additional presumptions that may assist them in meeting their burden of proof at trial.

H. Trial Defenses

If the prosecution establishes the forfeitability of the property, the defense must present any affirmative defenses by a preponderance of the evidence. *See United States v. One 56-foot Motor Yacht Named Tahuna*, 702 F.2d 1276, 1281

(9th Cir. 1983); *Iowa Code Ann.* § 809A.13 7; *Kan. Stat. Ann.* § 60-4113(g); *Del. Code Ann.* Title 16 § 4785(a). Trial defenses fall into three areas: (1) insufficient nexus; (2) legitimate source; and (3) innocent owner.

1. Insufficient Nexus

One method of defeating a forfeiture action is by demonstrating that there is insufficient evidence to prove that the property was involved in criminal activity. *See United States v. $557,933.89 More or Less in U.S Funds,* 287 F.3d 66, 77 (2d Cir. 2002). Unless there is a nexus between the seized property and the alleged criminal activity, the forfeiture will fail. *See United States v. $30,060.00,* 39 F.3d 1039, 1044 (9th Cir. 1994); *People v. $47,050,* 17 Cal. App. 4th 1319, 1323 (1993).

Because the factors in support of forfeiture are circumstantial, the totality of the circumstances must be sufficiently persuasive to demonstrate the required nexus between the specific assets and detailed criminal activity. *See United States v. $405,089.23 U.S. Currency,* 122 F.3d 1285, 1290–91 (9th Cir. 1997).

Courts that have found an insufficient nexus generally remark on the following factors:

- Absence of prior criminal arrests, convictions, or criminal charges filed, *see United States v. One Lot of U.S. Currency Totaling $14,665,* 33 F. Supp. 2d 47, 58–59 (D. Mass. 1998); *Com. v. One Thousand Two Hundred and Twenty Dollars ($1,220.00) Cash,* 749 A.2d 1013, 1017 (Pa. Cmwlth. 2000) (no current charges); *State v. $107,156 U.S. Currency,* 935 So. 2d 827, 836 (La. App. 2006);
- No contraband, paraphernalia, or weapons seized, *see United States v. $10,700.00 in U.S. Currency,* 258 F.3d 215, 219 (3d Cir. 2001); *United States v. Sixty-Eight Thousand Five Hundred Eighty Dollars ($68,580) in U.S. Currency,* 815 F. Supp. 1479, 1484 (M.D. Ga 1993); *Com. v. Marshall,* 548 Pa. 495; 698 A.2d 576, 579 (Pa. 1997);
- Controlled substance amounts seized are consistent with personal use, *One 1978 Lincoln Versailles v. State,* 388 So. 2d 1383, 1385 (Fla. App. 1980) (marijuana "sweepings"); *Com v. One 1969 Mercedes-Benz Auto,* 378 N.E.2d 65, 68 (Mass. 1978) (small quantities); *Howard County v. One 1994 Chevrolet Corvette,* 119 Md. App. 93; 704 A.2d 455, 463 (Md. App. 1998) (miniscule value); *State ex rel. Dept. of Public Safety v. 1985 GMC Pickup,* 898 P.2d 1280, 1281 (Okla. 1995) (misdemeanor possession of marijuana); *Burnett v. State,* 51 Ark. App. 144; 912 S.W.2d 441, 442 (Ark. App. 1995) (marijuana roach; .9 gram of methamphet-

amine); *One (1) 1992 Isuzu Rodeo v. Grenada Police Dept.*, 743 So. 2d 1062, 1063 (Miss. App. 1999) (marijuana seeds);

- Insufficient connection to criminal activity, *State v. Giles*, 697 So. 2d 699, 706 (La. App. 1997) (insufficient connection to drugs); *State v. Cash Totalling $15,156.00*, 623 So. 2d 114, 121 (La. App. 1993) (same); *State v. $77,014.00 Dollars*, 607 So. 2d 576, 577–78 (La. App. 1992) (same); *Jackson v. State ex rel. Mississippi Bureau of Narcotics*, 591 So. 2d 820, 823 (Miss. 1991) (vehicle not used in transaction); *In re Forfeiture of $11,250 in U.S. Currency*, 121 Ohio Misc.2d 111; 782 N.E.2d 1251, 1254 (Ohio Com.Pl. 2002) (suspended license offense only—no connection to drugs); *State ex rel. Means v. One Million, Three Hundred Fifty-Four Thousand, Four Hundred Fifty Dollars and Fifty Cents ($1,354,450.50) in U.S. Currency*, 841 P.2d 616, 618 (Okla. App. 1992) (no connection to drugs); *Schoka v. Sheriff, Washoe County*, 108 Nev. 89; 824 P.2d 290, 292 (Nev. 1992) (no nexus between vehicle and investment account and fraud);

- Lack of a connection between the claimant and any known criminal suspect or organization, *see United States v. $40,000 in U.S. Currency*, 999 F. Supp. 234, 239 (D.P.R. 1998);

- Canine alert unreliable, *see United States v. $30,060.00*, 39 F.3d 1039, 1042 (9th Cir. 1994); *United States v. $49,576.00 U.S. Currency*, 116 F.3d 425, 427 (9th Cir. 1997); *People ex rel. Devine v. $30,700.00 U.S. Currency*, 316 Ill.App.3d 464; 736 N.E.2d 137, 144 (Ill. App. 2000);

- Large amount of currency is insufficient, *United States v. $58,920 in U.S. Currency*, 385 F.Supp.2d 144, 151 (D.P.R. 2005); *State v. Property Seized from Jorge L. Rios*, 478 N.W.2d 870, 873 (Iowa App. 1991);

- Insufficient tracing of proceeds to criminal activity, *Tri-City Metro Drug Task Force v. Contreras*, 119 P.3d 862, 864 (Wash. App. 2005) (consistent with legitimate income); *State v. Burgraff*, 208 W.Va. 746; 542 S.E.2d 909, 911 (W.Va. 2000) (house); *People v. Cerrone*, 780 P.2d 562, 564 (Colo. App. 1989) (motorhome); *In re Forfeiture of $25,505*, 220 Mich. App. 572; 560 N.W.2d 341, 344 (Mich. App. 1996) (furniture); *State ex rel. Dept. of Public Safety v. 1983 Ford Bronco*, 877 P.2d 53, 54–55 (Okla. App. 1994) (jewelry); *One (1) 1979 Ford 15V v. State ex rel. Mississippi Bureau of Narcotics*, 721 So. 2d 631, 637 (Miss. 1998) (bank account); *State ex rel. MacLaughlin v. Treon*, 926 S.W.2d 13, 17 (Mo. App. 1996) (bank account and securities); *Com. v. Funds in Merrill Lynch Account Owned by Peart*, 777 A.2d 519, 526–27 (Pa. Cmwlth. 2001) (bank funds deposited prior to criminal activity).

2. Legitimate Source Defense

Another common defense is that the seized funds had an independent innocent source and are not traceable to criminal activity. *See United States v. $215,300 United States Currency*, 882 F.2d 417, 420 (9th Cir. 1989).

Examples of evidence that may be proffered as independent innocent sources for a defense to a proceeds theory forfeiture case include:

- Employment income, *see United States v. 6 Patricia Drive*, 705 F. Supp. 710, 719 (D.R.I. 1989); *United States v. Property at 2323 Charms Road*, 726 F. Supp. 164, 169 (E.D. Mich. 1989); *Castelon v. Hudson County Treasurer*, 145 N.J. Super. 134; 366 A.2d 1358, 1359 (N.J. Super. A.D. 1976);

- Business income, *United States v. 228 Acres of Land*, 916 F.2d 808, 812–13 (2d Cir. 1990); *United States v. Miscellaneous Jewelry*, 667 F. Supp. 232, 240–41 (D. Md. 1987); *United States v. $22,991.00*, 227 F. Supp. 2d 1220, 1228 (S.D. Ala. 2002); *Neely v. State ex rel. Mississippi Dept. of Public Safety*, 607 So. 2d 23, 26 (Miss. 1991); *State v. $107,156 U.S. Currency*, 935 So. 2d 827, 835 (La. App. 2006);

- Gambling proceeds, *United States v. Thomas*, 913 F.2d 1111, 1118 (4th Cir. 1990); *United States v. 11348 Wyoming*, 705 F. Supp. 352, 354 (E.D. Mich. 1989); *United States v. $557,933.89*, 287 F.3d 66, 75 (2d Cir. 2002);

- Loans, *United States v. Yukon Delta*, 774 F.2d 1432, 1435 (9th Cir. 1985); *United States v. One 1980 Chevrolet Blazer*, 572 F. Supp. 994, 997 (E.D.N.Y. 1983); *United States v. 1990 Chevrolet Silverado Pickup Truck*, 804 F. Supp. 777, 780 (W.D.N.C. 1992); *State v. $29,177 U.S. Currency*, 638 So. 2d 653, 655 (La. App. 1994);

- Inheritance, *United States v. 1998 BMW "I" Convertible*, 235 F.3d 397, 399 (8th Cir. 2000);

- Savings, *United States v. $28,000*, 727 F. Supp. 520, 522 (E.D. Mo. 1989); *People v. $47,050*, 17 Cal. App. 4th 1319, 1322 (1993); *United States v. $30,670 in U.S. Funds*, 2002 WL 31093587 (N.D. Ill. 2002); *State v. $29,177 U.S. Currency*, 638 So. 2d 653, 655 (La. App. 1994);

- Gift, *United States v. A Parcel of Land (92 Buena Vista Ave.)*, 507 U.S. 111, 124 (1993); *United States v. One 1986 Nissan Maxima*, 895 F.2d 1063, 1064 (5th Cir. 1990); *Magone v. Aul*, 269 M 281; 887 P.2d 1235, 1236 (Mont. 1994);

- Personal injury/workers compensation award, *United States v. $95,945.18*, 727 F. Supp. 242, 245 (W.D.N.C. 1989); *United States v. $25,055*, 728 F. Supp. 1406, 1407 (E.D. Mo. 1990);

- Disability/SSI payment, *$3,417.46 US Money v. Kinnamon*, 326 Md. 141; 604 A.2d 64, 66 (Md. 1992); *Com. v. Giffin*, 407 Pa. Super. 15; 595 A.2d 101, 105–06 (Pa. Super. 1991);
- Cash hoard, *United States v. One Parcel of Real Property*, 648 F. Supp. 436, 437 (D. Mass. 1986);
- Insurance settlement, *In re Forfeiture of $18,000*, 189 Mich.App.1; 471 N.W.2d 628, 630 (Mich. App. 1991) (wrongful death); *Harbin v. Com.*, 121 S.W.3d 191, 197 (Ky. 2003) (car accident); *State v. Gauthier*, 854 So. 2d 910, 912 (La. App. 2003) (car accident);
- Welfare payment, *Com. v. Giffin*, 407 Pa. Super. 15; 595 A.2d 101, 105–06 (Pa. Super. 1991);
- Sale of property, *State v. $2,434.00 Cash*, 461 N.W.2d 346, 347 (Iowa App. 1990) (vehicle); *Com. v. One 1973 Mercedes Benz Sedan*, 9 Pa. D. & C.4th 332, 334 (Pa. Com. Pl. 1990) (vehicle); *Frail v. $24,900.00 in U.S. Currency*, 192 W.Va. 473; 453 S.E.2d 307, 316 (W.Va. 994) (real property);
- Tax refund, *Harbin v. Com.*, 121 S.W.3d 191, 197 (Ky. 2003);
- Bank account withdrawal not traceable to criminal activity, *State v. $2,200.00 in U.S. Currency*, 851 P.2d 1081, 1082–83 (Okla. App. 1993); *Pope v. Gordon*, 359 S.C. 572; 598 S.E.2d 288, 295 (S.C. App. 2004).

Because this is an affirmative defense, the burden is on the claimant to demonstrate that the seized property is not illegitimate proceeds, *see United States v. 1990 Chevrolet Silverado Pickup Truck*, 804 F. Supp at 782, with credible evidence, including records documenting the legitimate source. *See United States v. $149,442.43 in U.S. Currency*, 965 F.2d 868, 877–78 (10th Cir. 1992); *United States v. $87,118.00 in U.S. Currency*, 95 F.3d 511, 519 (7th Cir. 1996).

To defeat the legitimate source defense, the prosecutor may offer rebuttal evidence to show that the seized funds are not from legal sources. In three post-CAFRA federal cases, prosecutors offered evidence gathered during the discovery process and subsequent investigation including tax returns, bankruptcy filings, outstanding debts and collection notices, and other personal financial documents to successfully show that the claimants' expenses exceeded their known income, and the courts determined that the seized funds were not from legitimate sources. *See United States v. $30,670 in U.S. Funds*, 2002 WL 31093587 (N.D. Ill. 2002); *United States v. $22,991.00*, 227 F. Supp. 2d 1220, 1227–28 (S.D. Ala. 2002); *United States v. $181,087.14*, 2002 WL 31951270 (S.D. Ohio 2002).

A claimant who asserts a legitimate source defense may also maintain an innocent owner exemption, as the two defenses are not mutually exclusive. *See United States v. Real Property Located at 20832 Big Rock Drive,* 51 F.3d 1402, 1409 (9th Cir. 1995).

3. Innocent Owner Defense

Although there is no constitutional requirement that a forfeiture statute contain an innocent owner defense, *see Bennis v. Michigan,* 516 U.S. 442, 446 (1996); see also Chapter 12, Constitutional Protections, the federal and most state statutes contain an exemption for innocent parties.

Federal Innocent Owner Exemption

Prior to CAFRA, there was much confusion and inconsistency in the application of the innocent owner statutes in the federal system.[1] Although some statutes contained innocent owner exemptions, others did not. *See* 18 U.S.C. § 545; *United States v. An Antique Platter of Gold,* 184 F.3d 131, 139 (2d Cir. 1999) (smuggling); 18 U.S.C. § 1955(d); *United States v. $734,578.82 in U.S. Currency,* 286 F.3d 641, 649 n.7 (3d Cir. 2002) (gambling). Even within the same statute there were different definitions of when the innocent owner exemption applied. *Compare* 21 U.S.C. § 881(a)(4) (drug conveyance facilitation statute exemption for knowledge, consent, or willful blindness) *with* 21 U.S.C. § 881(a)(6) (drug proceed statute—willful blindness omitted). This resulted in conflicting case law and disparate application of the same innocent owner statute within the federal circuits. *Compare United States v. 10936 Oak Run Circle,* 9 F.3d 74, 76 (9th Cir. 1993) *with United States v. One 1973 Rolls Royce,* 43 F.3d 794, 801–02 (3d Cir. 1994).

One of the most significant provisions of CAFRA Section 2, 106 Pub. L. No. 185, 114 Stat. 202, 206, was the enactment of a uniform innocent owner defense for most civil forfeiture actions.[2] *See* 18 U.S.C. § 983(d). The statute is clear that this is an affirmative defense, and the burden of proof is on the claimant by a preponderance of the evidence. *See* 18 U.S.C. § 983(d)(1).

The key distinction in the definition is between pre-existing and after-acquired interests. Pre-existing owners are governed by 18 U.S.C. § 983(d)(2), and parties who acquired their ownership interest after the commission of the conduct giving rise to the forfeiture are covered under 18 U.S.C. § 983(d)(3).

Where a party has a pre-existing interest in the property to prevail, he or she must establish two elements.

First, the party must show that he or she is an owner of the property. *See United States v. $100,348 U.S. Currency,* 157 F. Supp. 2d 1110, 1117 (C.D.

Cal. 2001). An owner is a person with an ownership interest in the specific property, including leaseholds, liens, mortgages, recorded security interest, or valid assignments, *see* 18 U.S.C. § 983(d)(6)(A), as defined by state law. *See United States v. U.S. Currency, $81,000.00,* 189 F.3d 28, 33 (1st Cir. 1999); *United States v. 1980 Lear Jet,* 38 F.3d 398, 402 (9th Cir. 1994); *United States v. One Parcel of Property Located at 1512 Lark Drive,* 978 F. Supp. 935, 940 (D.S.D. 1997).

Ownership does not include general unsecured creditors, bailees, unless the bailor is identified, and the bailee shows a colorable legitimate interest in the property or nominees who exercise no dominion and control over the property. *See* 18 U.S.C. § 983(d)(6)(B).

Even where the court initially found that the claimant had standing to contest the forfeiture, if the claimant cannot demonstrate a legally recognizable ownership interest in the property, he or she cannot prevail on an innocent owner defense. *See United States v. $9,041,598.68,* 163 F.3d 238, 245 (5th Cir. 1998); *United States v. $100,348 U.S. Currency,* 157 F. Supp. 2d 1110, 1118 (C.D. Cal. 2001); *Sanchez v. United States,* 781 F. Supp, 835, 839 (D.P.R. 1991); *United States v. 2001 Honda Accord EX,* 245 F. Supp. 2d 602, 607 n.4 (M.D. Pa 2003).

Therefore, a person must demonstrate that he or she exercised dominion and control over the property to show that he or she was more than a nominee or straw owner of the property. *See United States v. Premises and Real Property (500 Delaware Street),* 113 F.3d 310, 312 (2d Cir. 1997); *United States v. One 1990 Chevrolet Corvette,* 37 F.3d 421, 422 (8th Cir. 1994); *United States v. 2930 Greenleaf St.,* 920 F. Supp. 639, 646–47 (E.D. Pa. 1996); *United States v. One 1988 Prevost Liberty Motor Home,* 952 F. Supp. 1180, 1203 (S.D. Tex. 1996).

If the claimant establishes that he or she is an owner of the property, the claimant must next show that he or she is innocent as defined by the statute. *See* 18 U.S.C. § 983(d)(2). This is demonstrated by proof that the claimant did not know of the conduct giving rise to the forfeiture, *see* 18 U.S.C. § 983(d)(2)(A)(i), OR, upon learning of the conduct, took all reasonable steps to terminate the illegal use. *See* 18 U.S.C. § 983(d)(2)(A)(ii); *United States v. One Parcel (2526 Faxon Avenue),* 145 F. Supp. 2d 942, 950 (W.D. Tenn. 2001). Note that this prong of the defense is in the disjunctive. The claimant may prove either lack of knowledge or that all reasonable steps were taken. Some of the factors that may be considered in determining whether the party took all reasonable steps include timely notice to law enforcement and a good-faith attempt to revoke permission to use the property. *See* 18 U.S.C. § 983(d)(2)(B).

Where a party did not acquire his or her ownership interest until after the conduct giving rise to the forfeiture, the party must prove that he or she was a bona fide purchaser or seller for value AND that he or he did not know, AND was reasonably without cause to believe, that the property was subject to forfeiture. *See* 18 U.S.C. § 983(d)(3). Note that these provisions are in the conjunctive. They all must be established to successfully prevail on this defense. *United States v. 392 Lexington Parkway South*, 386 F. Supp. 2d 1062, 1069 n.9 (D. Minn. 2005).

A bona fide purchaser is one who gives something of value in exchange for the property. *See United States v. Infelise*, 938 F. Supp. 1352, 1368 (N.D. Ill. 1996). By limiting after-acquired innocent owner exemptions to bona fide purchasers, CAFRA has totally eliminated the innocent owner defense for anyone that did not pay value for the property, including donees, heirs, spouses, or anyone else that did not have a pre-existing ownership interest in the property prior to the illicit conduct. *See United States v. Hooper*, 229 F.3d 818, 822 (9th Cir. 2000) (spouse); *United States v. Real Property at 221 Dana Avenue*, 261 F.3d 65, 73 n.7 (1st Cir. 2001) (spouse); *United States v. One Single Family Residence at 2200 SW 28th Ave.*, 204 F. Supp. 2d 1361, 1365 (S.D. Fla. 2002) (heir). (There is a limited exemption for real property that is the primary residence of the claimant that will be discussed in Chapter 11, Real Property Forfeitures.)

Thus, in preparing for an innocent owner defense in the federal system, defense counsel must ask these questions:

(1) Does my client have a legal ownership interest in the property as defined by state law?

(2) Can my client demonstrate dominion and control over the property?

(3) Did my client acquire that ownership interest prior to the illegal conduct giving rise to the forfeiture?

(4) Can my client show lack of knowledge or that all reasonable steps to terminate the unlawful use were taken?

(5) If my client acquired an ownership interest after the illegal conduct giving rise to the forfeiture, is he or she a bona fide purchaser?

State Innocent Owner Exemption

Table 7-4 is a selected summary of innocent owner exemptions from the states listing the burden of proof and the party who must carry that burden. Most states follow the federal system, where it is considered an affirmative defense, placing the burden on the claimant by a preponderance of the evidence. *State v. One 1984 Toyota Truck*, 311 Md. 171, 533 A.2d 659, 665 (Md. 1987); *Blanche v. 1995 Pontiac Grand Prix*, 599 N.W.2d 161, 167 (Minn. 1999); *State ex rel. McGehee v. 1987 Oldsmobile Cutlass*, 867 P.2d 1354, 1356 (Okla. App. 1993).

Table 7-4
Summary of State Asset Forfeiture Statutes
Civil Forfeiture Innocent Owner Exemptions

State	Statute	Innocent Owner Exemption	Burden of Proof	Party
Alabama	Ala. Code § 20-2-93 (h)	Knowledge or consent		Plaintiff for real property; Claimant for all other property
Alaska	Ak. Stat. § 17.30.110 (4)(A)-(B)	Consent nor privy to violation	Preponderance of the evidence	Claimant
Arizona	Ariz. Rev. Stat. Ann. § 13-4310 D; 13-4304.4(c)	Knowledge or consent	Preponderance of the evidence	Claimant
Arkansas	Ark. Code Ann. § 5-64-505 (a)(4), (6), (7)	Knowledge or consent	Preponderance of the evidence	Claimant
California	Cal. Health & Safety Code § 11488.5 (d)(1)	Knowledge and consent	Reasonable doubt Clear and convincing evidence	Plaintiff
Colorado	Co. Rev. Stat. § 16-13-303 (5.1)(b)(II); 16-13-504 (2.1)(b)(II)(A)	Knowledge or consent	Clear and convincing evidence	Plaintiff
Connecticut	Con. Gen. Stat. Ann. § 54-36h (c)	Knowledge		Claimant

Table 7-4 (continued)
Summary of State Asset Forfeiture Statutes
Civil Forfeiture Innocent Owner Exemptions

State	Statute	Innocent Owner Exemption	Burden of Proof	Party
Delaware	Del. Code Ann. title 16 § 4784 (a)(4); (7); (8)	Knowledge or consent		Claimant
District of Columbia	D.C. Code Ann. § 48-905.02 (a)(4)(B); (a)(7)(A); (a)(8)(A)	Knowledge or consent Knowledge and consent (real property)		Claimant
Florida	Fla. Stat. Ann. § 932.703 (6)(a)	Knowledge	Preponderance of the evidence	Plaintiff
Georgia	Ga. Code Ann. § 16-13-49 (e)	Knowledge and consent		Claimant
Hawaii	Hawaii Rev. Stat. § 712A-5(2)(b)-(e)	Knowledge or consent (conveyances) Knowledge or consent (other property)	Preponderance of the evidence	Claimant
Idaho	Idaho Code § 37-2744 (d)(3)(D); 37-2744A(d)	Knowledge	Preponderance of the evidence	Claimant

Table 7-4 (continued)
Summary of State Asset Forfeiture Statutes
Civil Forfeiture Innocent Owner Exemptions

State	Statute	Innocent Owner Exemption	Burden of Proof	Party
Illinois	725 Ill. Compiled Stat. 150/8	Knowledge and consent	Preponderance of the evidence	Claimant
Indiana	Ind. Code Ann. § 34-24-1-4 (a); (e)	Knowledge	Preponderance of the evidence	Plaintiff for vehicles Claimant for other property
Iowa	Iowa Code Ann. § 809A.5.1	Knowledge or consent	Preponderance of the evidence	Claimant
Kansas	Kan. Stat. Ann. § 60-4106(a)	Knowledge or consent	Preponderance of the evidence	Plaintiff
Kentucky	Ky. Rev. Stat. Ann. § 218A.410 (1)(h) 2; (j); (k); 218A.460(4)	Knowledge or consent	Clear & Convincing Evidence Preponderance of the Evidence	Plaintiff for real property Claimant for all other property
Louisiana	La. Rev. Stat. Ann. § 40:2605	Knowledge and consent	Preponderance of the evidence	Claimant
Maine	Me. Rev. Stat. Ann. Title 15 Ch.517 § 5821 4, 6, 7	Knowledge or consent	Preponderance of the evidence	Plaintiff for real property primary residence; Claimant all other property

Table 7-4 (continued)
Summary of State Asset Forfeiture Statutes
Civil Forfeiture Innocent Owner Exemptions

State	Statute	Innocent Owner Exemption	Burden of Proof	Party
Maryland	Md. Ann. Code Art. 27 § 12-103 (a)	Actual knowledge	Preponderance of the evidence	Claimant
Massachusetts	Mass. Ann. Laws ch. 94C § 47 (c)-(d)	Knowledge		Claimant
Michigan	Mich. Comp. Laws) § 600.4702(2); § 600.4707 (6	Knowledge or consent	Preponderance of the evidence	Plaintiff
Minnesota	Minn. Stat. Ann. § 609.5311 3 (d), (e)	Knowledge or consent	Clear and convincing evidence	Claimant
Mississippi	Miss. Code Ann. § 41-29-153 (a)(4) B; § 41-29-153(a)(7)A	Knowledge or consent		Claimant
Missouri	Mo. Ann. Stat. § 195.140 2 (1); § 513.615	Knowledge or consent Actual knowledge		Claimant
Montana	Mont. Ann. Stat. § 44-12-204	Knowledge or consent		Claimant

Table 7-4 (continued)
Summary of State Asset Forfeiture Statutes
Civil Forfeiture Innocent Owner Exemptions

State	Statute	Innocent Owner Exemption	Burden of Proof	Party
Nevada	Nev. Rev. Stat. § 179.1164 2	Knowledge, consent or willful blindness		Claimant
New Hampshire	N.H. Rev. Stat. Ann. § 318-B:17-b III(a)	Knowledge and consent	Preponderance of the evidence	Claimant
New Jersey	N.J. Stat. Ann. § 2C:64-5 b	Knowledge and consent	Preponderance of the evidence	Claimant
New Mexico	N.M. Code Ann. § 30-31-34G	Knowledge or consent	Clear and convincing evidence	Plaintiff
New York	N.Y. Civil Practice Law § 1311 3 (b)(ii); § 1311 3(b)(v)	Knowledge / Knowledge or consent	Preponderance of the evidence / Clear & convincing evidence	Plaintiff / Plaintiff
North Dakota	N.D. Cent. Code § 19-03.1-36.1e(2),(4); 19.03.01-36.7	Knowledge or consent	Preponderance of the evidence	Claimant
Ohio	Ohio Rev. Code Ann. § 2925.42 (F)(5)(b)	Actual knowledge	Preponderance of the evidence	Plaintiff

Table 7-4 (continued)
Summary of State Asset Forfeiture Statutes
Civil Forfeiture Innocent Owner Exemptions

State	Statute	Innocent Owner Exemption	Burden of Proof	Party
Oklahoma	Okla. Stat. Ann. § 63-2-503A.4, 8	Knowledge or consent		Claimant
Oregon	Ore. Rev. Stat. § 475A.080(2)	Intent to defeat the forfeiture	Clear and convincing evidence	Plaintiff
Pennsylvania	Pa. Consol. Stat. Ann. Title 42 § 6801 (a) 4, 6	Knowledge or consent		Claimant
Rhode Island	R.I. Gen. Laws § 21-28-5.04.2 (a), (3),(p)	Knowledge or consent	Preponderance of the evidence	Claimant
South Carolina	S.C. Code Ann. § 44-53-586	Knowledge or consent	Preponderance of the evidence	Claimant
South Dakota	S.D. Codified Laws Ann. § 34-20B-70.1; § 34-20B-73	Actual knowledge Knew or should have known	Preponderance of the evidence	Claimant
Tennessee	Tenn. Code Ann. § 53-11-451 (a)(4)(B); (6)(B)	Knowledge or consent		Claimant

Table 7-4 (continued)
Summary of State Asset Forfeiture Statutes
Civil Forfeiture Innocent Owner Exemptions

State	Statute	Innocent Owner Exemption	Burden of Proof	Party
Texas	Tx. Code of Crim. Proc. § 59.02 (c)	Knowledge	Preponderance of the evidence	Claimant
Utah	Utah Code Ann. § 24-1-6	Knowledge or consent	Clear and convincing evidence	Plaintiff
Vermont	Vt. Stat. Ann. Title 18 § 4241 (a)(5); § 4241 (6); § 4244 (c)	Knowledge or consent	Clear and convincing evidence	Plaintiff
Virginia	Va. Code Ann. § 19.2-386.8	Knowledge or consent	Preponderance of the evidence	Claimant
Washington	Wash. Rev. Code Ann. § 69.50.505 (1)(d)(ii); (g); (h); 69.50.506	Knowledge or consent	Preponderance of the evidence	Claimant
West Virginia	W. Va. Code § 60A-7-703(a)(4)(ii); (7); (8)	Knowledge or consent		Claimant

Table 7-4 (continued)
Summary of State Asset Forfeiture Statutes
Civil Forfeiture Innocent Owner Exemptions

State	Statute	Innocent Owner Exemption	Burden of Proof	Party
Wisconsin	Wis. Stat. Ann. § 961.55(1)(d)2; § 961.55 (1)(d)4; § 961.56	Knowledge or consent		Claimant
Wyoming	Wyo. Stat. § 35-7-1049 (a)(v)(B); § (D) 35-7-1049 (a)(viii); § 35-7-1050 (a)	Knowledge or consent		Claimant

To prevail on the state innocent owner defense, the claimant must first demonstrate that he or she has a valid ownership interest in the property. *State v. 1973 Fleetwood Mobile Home*, 802 S.W.2d 582, 584 (Mo. App. 1991). In evaluating ownership, state courts look at such factors as title, possession, control, and financial stake in the property. *State v. Kirch*, 222 Wis.2d 598; 587 N.W.2d 919, 922 (Wis. App. 1998); *State v. 1984 Monte Carlo SS*, 521 N.W.2d 723, 725 (Iowa 1994) (title and car loan in claimant's name; made all car loan and insurance payments). The ownership interest must exist prior to the filing of the forfeiture action. *Matter of Forfeiture of a 1977 Chevrolet Pickup*, 734 P.2d 857, 859 (Okla. App. 1987) (post-seizure lien invalid).

A lien holder should perfect his or her security interest by recording the title documents with the appropriate governmental agency, *In re Forfeiture of One 1946 Lockheed*, 493 So. 2d 10, 11 (Fla. App. 1986) (unrecorded aircraft title); *In re Forfeiture one 1979 Chevrolet C10 Van*, 490 So. 2d 240, 241 (Fla. App. 1986) (unrecorded vehicle title), or the lien will become subordinate to the forfeiture action. *Bay Co. Sheriffs Office v. Tyndall FCU*, 738 So. 2d 456, 459 (Fla. App. 1999); *In re Forfeiture of 1977 Kenworth Tractor*, 566 So. 2d 70, 71 (Fla. App. 1990); *State ex rel. Rooney v. One 1974 Green Targa Porsche*, 112 Idaho 432, 732 P.2d 670, 675 (Idaho 1986). A parent who loans money to a child to purchase a car is not a secured creditor. *City of Pendleton v. One 1998 Dodge Stratus*, 180 Or. App. 72; 42 P.3d 339, 343 n.11 (Or. App. 2002).

A person who exercises no dominion or control over the property is a mere straw owner or nominee and will not qualify for an innocent owner exemption. *Matter of One Residence Located at 4030 W. Avocado, Cortaro Ridge*, 184 Ariz. 219; 908 P.2d 33, 35 (Ariz. App. 1995) (title owner was 18-year-old, never-employed student); *Matter of One 1985 Mercedes Benz*, 644 A.2d 423, 431–32 (Del. Super. 1992) (title in her name but vehicle purchased and controlled by defendant); *In re Forfeiture of U.S. Currency*, 164 Mich. App. 171; 416 N.W.2d 700, 703–04 (Mich. App. 1987) (title in girlfriend's name; lived together with defendant); *Shannon v. North Mississippi Narcotics Unit*, 815 So. 2d 1255, 1260 (Miss. App. 2002) (car receipts in defendant's name; prior owner said he sold car to defendant); *One Ford Mustang v. State ex rel. Clay County Sheriff Dept.*, 676 So. 2d 905, 906 (Miss. 1996) (drug dealer paid for and controlled vehicle; no evidence title owner ever in possession of car); *In re One 1988 Toyota Corolla*, 675 A.2d 1290, 1296 (Pa. Cmwlth. 1996) (drug dealer had control over car although title in another name); *State v. Michael*, 55 Wash. App. 841; 781 P.2d 496, 497–98 (Wash. App. 1989) (title holder unaware of color, make or purchase price of car); *One Ford Motor Vehicle v. State*, 104 Md. App. 744; 657 A.2d 825, 829 (Md. App. 1995) (defendant had exclusive use since day of purchase, parked at his residence and had both sets of keys).

The second element of the state innocent owner exemption is knowledge or consent. The requirements under this provision vary widely among the states. Some focus only on the element of knowledge requiring actual knowledge, *Ducworth v. Neely*, 319 S.C. 158; 459 S.E.2d 896, 899 (S.C. App. 1995), and others on constructive knowledge. *See Fla. Stat. Ann.* § 932.703(6)(a) ("should have known"); *City of Daytona Beach v. Bush*, 742 So. 2d 335, 338 (Fla. App. 1999) (actual knowledge not required); *State v. Tucker*, 242 Ga. App. 3; 528 S.E. 2d 523, 528 (Ga. App. 2000) (same).

A few states look solely at the element of consent, *see Md. Ann. Code Crim. Proc.* § 12-130(a) ("without consent"); *Co. Rev. Stat.* § 16-13-303(5.2) ("all reasonable steps"), and others an alternative of the elements of knowledge or consent. *Parcel Real Property Located at 335 West Ash Street, Jackson MS v. City of Jackson*, 664 So. 2d 194, 195 (Miss. 1995) (knowledge or consent); *One 1978 Chevrolet Van v. Churchill County ex rel. Banovich*, 97 Nev. 510; 634 P.2d 1208, 1209 (Nev. 1981) (same).

Some of the factors that state prosecutors should consider when evaluating the issue of knowledge and consent are the relationship between the parties, the manner that the property was transferred to the wrongful user, the nature of the property transferred, and the ability of the owner to dictate the use of the property to the user. *State v. U.S. Currency*, 239 N.J. Super. 241; 570 A.2d 1304, 1307–08 (N.J. Super. L. 1990).

State prosecutors are also reminded that there are several states that place the burden of proof on the plaintiff to prove that the claimant is not an innocent owner and at a higher civil burden of proof. See Table 7-4; *see also Fla. Stat. Ann.* § 932.703(6)(a); *Mich. Comp. Laws* § 600.4707(6)(c) (clear and convincing evidence). Before trial, practitioners should carefully review the relevant forfeiture statutes, assess what the burden of proof is, and who carries that burden in respect to an innocent owner claim.

4. Establishing the Innocent Owner Defense

In the federal system, the claimant is not required to prove the innocent owner defense until after the government establishes that the property is forfeitable. *United States v. Real Property in Section 9*, 308 F. Supp. 2d 791, 811 (E.D. Mich. 2004). Because it is an affirmative defense, the claimant must produce some evidence because a silent record will be resolved against him or her. *See United States v. Certain Real Property 566 Hendrickson Boulevard*, 986 F.2d 990, 995 (6th Cir. 1993). Generally, this consists of direct evidence with the claimant taking the stand to deny any knowledge or consent, or to explain the steps he or she took in response to the illegal use. Circumstantial evidence, including lack of involvement in the underlying criminal activity, may also be introduced to bolster the credibility of the claimants. *See United States v. 15 Bosworth Street*, 236 F.3d 50, 56 (1st Cir. 2001).

Claimants have prevailed with innocent owner exemptions in the following situations:

- Evidence showed no knowledge of illegal activity, *In re 1975 Pontiac Grand Prix*, 374 So. 2d 1119, 1121 (Fla. App. 1979); *One 1988 Jeep Cherokee v. City of Salisbury*, 98 Md. App. 676, 635 A.2d 21, 25 (Md. App. 1994) (no actual knowledge of illegal use of vehicle);
- Title owner with no knowledge of illegal activity, *In re One 1983 Toyota Silver Four-Door Sedan*, 169 Ariz. 399, 814 P.2d 356, 360–61 (Ariz. App. 1991); *State v. Beaird*, 914 S.W.2d 374, 378 (Mo. App. 1996); *State v. Gauthier*, 854 So. 2d 910, 912–13 (La. App. 2003);
- Co-owner with no knowledge of illegal activity, *In re Forfeiture of $53.00*, 178 Mich. App. 480; 444 N.W.2d 182, 188 (Mich. App. 1989); *One 1978 Chevrolet Van v. Churchill County ex rel. Banovich*, 97 Nev. 510; 634 P.2d 1208, 1209 (Nev. 1981);
- Spouse with no knowledge of illegal activity, *Galloway v. City of New Albany*, 735 So. 2d 407, 412 (Miss. 1999); *In re Forfeiture of Certain Real Property*, 112 Ohio App.3d 249; 678 N.E.2d 595, 597 (Ohio App. 1996).

The prosecutor may attempt to rebut this evidence by demonstrating that the claimant knew about the illegal conduct through statements he or she made to agents, third parties, or in response to civil discovery, *see United States v. 15 Bosworth Street, Ibid.* p. 56), inconsistent statements, *Matter of Scott*, 508 N.W.2d 653, 657 (Iowa 1993) (owner impeached by statements made during search), or his or her involvement in ancillary matters that supported the illegal conduct. *One 1985 Cadillac Auto (Munro) v. State*, 805 S.W.2d 944, 945 (Tex. App. 1991) (present at drug sales).

There are two additional arguments that may be used to rebut the innocent owner defense. The first is that the claimant was "willfully blind" to the illegal use. Willful blindness is defined as an owner who deliberately closes his or her eyes to the illegal conduct and whose acts of omission demonstrate a conscious purpose to avoid knowing the truth. *See United States v. 1989 Jeep Wagoneer*, 976 F.2d 1172, 1175 (8th Cir. 1992); *United States v. All Monies ($477,048.62)*, 754 F. Supp. 1467, 1477 (D. Haw. 1991); *United States v. 1988 Checolet 410 Turbo Property Aircraft*, 282 F. Supp. 2d 1379, 1383 (S.D. Fla. 2003). If a person is willfully blind to the illegal use, he or she does not qualify as an innocent owner, as ignorance is equated with knowledge. *See United States v. 3814 N.W. Thurman Street*, 164 F.3d 1191, 1197 (9th Cir. 1999); *United States v. $705,270.00 in U.S. Currency*, 820 F. Supp. 1398, 1403 (S.D. Fla. 1993); *United States v. Collado*, 348 F.3d 323, 327 (2d Cir. 2003); *Parcel Real Property Located at 335 West Ash Street, Jackson MS v. City of Jackson*, 664 So. 2d 194, 197 n.2 (Miss. 1995).

The second attack is that the claimant failed to take all reasonable steps to prevent the illegal use. *See* 18 U.S.C. § 983(d)(2)(A)(ii). Failure to take such action is evidence of consent to the unlawful use. *See United States v. Certain Real Property (418 57ᵗʰ Street)*, 922 F.2d 129, 132 (2d Cir. 1990); *United States v. One Parcel of Real Estate (1012 Germantown Road)*, 963 F.2d 1496, 1504 (11th Cir. 1992); *People ex rel. Birkett v. 1998 Chevrolet Corvette*, 331 Ill.App.3d 453; 772 N.E.2d 331, 339 (Ill. App. 2002) (loaned car to daughter who had prior drug arrests using same vehicle); *Little v. State*, 279 Ga. App. 329; 630 S.E.2d 903, 904 (Ga. App. 2006) (parents aware of son's prior drug arrest and placed no limit on use of car); *State v. 1984 Monte Carlo SS*, 521 N.W.2d 723, 725 (Iowa 1994) (parents aware of son's prior drug dealings and gave him exclusive use of car); *Com. v. $2,523.48 U.S. Currency*, 538 Pa. 551; 649 A.2d 658, 660 (Pa. 1994) (failed to take affirmative steps to stop illegal use). Merely taking a few steps is insufficient; every reasonable action to eliminate the conduct must be taken. *See United States v. Property Identified as 1813 15th Street, N.W.*, 956 F. Supp. 1029, 1037 (D.D.C. 1997); *United States v. 5.382 Acres*, 871 F. Supp. 880, 884 (W.D. Va. 1994). However, what is considered reasonable must be measured in light of the circumstances faced by the claimant. *See United States v. One Parcel (7079 Chilton County Road)*, 123 F. Supp. 2d 602, 609–10 (M.D. Ala. 2000); *United States v. Lot Numbered One of the Lavaland Complex*, 256 F.3d 949, 955–56 (10th Cir. 2001).

In some state jurisdictions, the burden is on the government to overcome the innocent owner exemption as part of its case in chief. *See N.Y. C.P.L.R.* § 1311 3(b)(ii); *Ore. Const.* Art. XV Sec.10(4). This forces the prosecutor to prove that the claimant had knowledge or consented to the illegal activity. These are difficult elements for the prosecution to prove because the claimant is in the better position to have this evidence. However, the government may meet this burden by introducing direct evidence of the admissions or inconsistent statements of the claimant garnered from interviews or civil discovery, and interviews with third-party witnesses demonstrating his or her knowledge or consent. However, heavy reliance usually is placed on circumstantial evidence, such as a connection with the underlying criminal activity, prior criminal record, relationship to other known criminal suspects, manner and circumstances under which the property was purchased, efforts to hide or conceal an ownership interest in the property, and any documentary evidence.

There are two standards for determining whether a person had knowledge or consented to the illegal use. The first is an objective test. Under this standard, the trier of fact compares the conduct of the claimant to what a reasonable man should have known or done under the circumstances. If the claimant failed to measure up to what a reasonable person would have done under the same facts, he or she would fail the objective standard. *See United States v. Cuartes,* 155 F. Supp. 2d 1338, 1343 (S.D. Fla. 2001); *In Re: Moffitt, Zwerling & Kemler, PC,* 846 F. Supp. 463, 475 (E.D. Va. 1994). The second test is a subjective standard. Here the question is whether the claimant had either actual knowledge of the illegal use of the property or if the steps that the claimant personally took to terminate the illegal use were reasonable under the circumstances. *See United States v. Four Million Two Hundred Fifty-Five Thousand,* 762 F.2d 895, 906 (11th Cir. 1985). The specific statute and relevant case law must be examined to determine which standard should apply.

I. Judgment

After all of the evidence, affirmative defenses, and rebuttal testimony have been presented at the trial, a verdict is rendered. The court receives the decision from the jury when one is requested or renders the decision itself on any bench trial. *See United States v. $22,991.00,* 227 F. Supp. 2d 1220, 1222 (S.D. Ala. 2002). Because this is a civil action, it does not require a unanimous verdict. Even in states that require the criminal and civil forfeiture to be heard by the same jury, it does not need to reach a unanimous verdict because the forfeiture portion of the trial is a civil action. This is true even if the burden of proof in the civil forfeiture trial is beyond a reasonable doubt. *See People v. Washington,* 220 Cal.App.3d 912, 917 (1990).

If the verdict is for the prosecution, the property is ordered forfeited and a judgment of forfeiture is entered. *See Cal. Health & Safety Code* § 11488.5(f). The court has discretion to order forfeiture in whole or in part. *City of Worthington Police Dept. v. One 1988 Chevrolet Berretta,* 516 N.W.2d 581, 583 (Minn. App. 1994).

Under CAFRA Section 2, 106 Pub. L. No. 185, 114 Stat. 202, 210, if the government prevails and the court finds that the claim was frivolous, a civil fine may be imposed of 10% of the value of the property, to be not less than $250 or greater than $5,000. *See* 18 U.S.C. § 983(h). A few states assess costs against a losing claimant who fails to establish an exemption from forfeiture. *See Ga. Code Ann.* § 16-13-49(t)(3); *Twenty-four Thousand One Hundred and Eighty ($24,180.00) Dollars in U.S. Currency v. State,* 865 S.W.2d 181, 188 (Tex. App. 1993).

If the decision is for the defense, the property is ordered returned. *See Cal. Health & Safety Code* § 11488.5(e). This raises the question whether a successful claimant is entitled to attorney fees and interest in forfeiture actions.

J. Attorney Fees

Prior to CAFRA, attorney fees were not available in civil *in rem* actions because the general rule in American civil jurisprudence requires each party to pay its own costs in the absence of a statutory provision to the contrary. *See United States v. One 1989 Harley Davidson Motorcycle,* 743 F. Supp. 589, 592 (C.D. Ill. 1990). However, there are two circumstances in federal law where attorney fees may be awarded to successful claimants.

The first is under the federal Equal Access to Justice Act (EAJA), 28 U.S.C. § 2412, which authorizes a party to receive attorney fees if he or she prevails in the forfeiture action, and the government's position was not substantially justified or reasonable under the circumstances. *See United States v. $515,060.42 in U.S. Currency,* 152 F.3d 491, 506–07 (6th Cir. 1998). A determination of whether the government's position was substantially justified will be a factual determination by the court.

Courts have found the government's position not substantially justified in situations where there was a lack of nexus between the property and the crime, *see United States v. Real Property Known as 22249 Dolorosa Street,* 190 F.3d 977, 982 (9th Cir. 1999), the government's legal position was in contravention of established case law, *see United States v. Real Property at 2659 Roundhill Drive,* 283 F.3d 1146, 1153 (9th Cir. 2002), or the case was settled for substantially less than sought in the complaint, *see United States v. One 1997 Toyota Land Cruiser,* 248 F.3d 899, 906 (9th Cir. 2001), or the amount seized was not great in comparison to the claimant's cost in litigating the matter, *see United States v. $16,500 in U.S. Currency,* 48 F. Supp. 2d 1268, 1275 (D. Ore. 1999).

CAFRA Section 4,106 Pub. L. No. 185, 114 Stat. 202, 211–212, now specifically provides for reasonable attorney fees in federal forfeiture actions where the claimant substantially prevails in the action. *See* 28 U.S.C. § 2465(b). This eliminates the element of EAJA that the position of the government was "substantially justified" and focuses solely on whether the claimant "substantially prevailed."

The federal courts have just commenced to define the contours of the term "substantially prevailed." A claimant who successfully brings a motion to suppress evidence preventing the prosecution from proceeding with the forfeiture action is entitled to CAFRA fees, *United States v. $100,120.00 in U.S. Currency*, 494 F. Supp. 2d 960, 970 (N.D. Ill. 2007), but claimants who settle their forfeiture cases are not. *United States v. U.S. Currency in the Sum of Six Hundred Sixty Thousand, Two Hundred Dollars ($660,200.00)*, 438 F. Supp. 2d 67, 73 (E.D.N.Y. 2006).

Additionally, CAFRA excludes the award of attorney fees for convicted defendants or where there are multiple claims to the property and the government:

(1) promptly recognizes such claim;

(2) promptly returns the interest of the claimant in the property to the claimant, if the property can be divided without difficulty and there are no competing claims to that portion of the property;

(3) does not cause the claimant to incur additional, reasonable costs or fees; and

(4) prevails in obtaining forfeiture with respect to one or more of the other claims.

See 28 U.S.C. § 2465(b)(2)(C); *United States v. Khan*, 497 F.3d 204, 209 (2d Cir. 2007).

CAFRA attorney fees are not limited to the EAJA caps but are paid at the prevailing market rate. *United States v. $60,201.00 U.S. Currency*, 291 F. Supp. 2d 1126, 1130 (C.D. Cal. 2003); *United States v. 4,432 Mastercases of Cigarettes*, 322 F. Supp. 2d 1075, 1078 (C.D. Cal. 2004).

State courts decline to award attorney fees absent specific statutory authority. *In re Forfeiture of U.S. Currency*, 181 Mich. App. 761; 450 N.W.2d 93, 96 (Mich. App. 1989) (prosecutor); *Howell v. Com.*, 163 S.W.3d 442, 450–51 (Ky. 2005) (public defender fees); *Mitchell v. State*, 982 P.2d 717, 724–25 (Wyo. 1999) (same); *State v. Gauthier*, 854 So. 2d 910, 913 (La. App. 2003) (pro se claimant). However, a few states contain provisions in their forfeiture statutes for the awarding of attorney fees to prevailing claimants. *See Fla. Stat. Ann. §* 932.704(10); *Minn. Stat. Ann.* § 609.5314 Subd. 3(d); *Tenn. Code Ann.* § 40-33-215; *Utah Code Ann.* § 24-1-11; *Wash. Rev. Code Ann.* § 69.50.505(6). In addition, courts have upheld the payment of attorney fees under these statutes. *Wolf Motor Co., Inc. v. One 2000 Ford F 350*, 658 N.W.2d 900, 904 (Minn. App. 2003); *State v. One Lot of Personal Property*, 90 P.3d 639, 643 (Utah 2004) (claimant prevailed when state dismissed claim before court ruling);

Moen v. Spokane City Police Dept., 110 Wash. App. 714; 42 P.3d 456, 460 (Wash. App. 2002).

K. Pre-judgment Interest and Costs

Before CAFRA, the payment of interest generally was denied in forfeiture actions on the basis of sovereign immunity. *See Library of Congress v. Shaw,* 478 U.S. 310, 314 (1986). However, there were a few courts that permitted the payment of prejudgment interest holding that the government must disgorge any interest actually earned. *See United States v. $277,000,* 69 F.3d 1491, 1493 (9th Cir. 1995); *United States v. $515,060.42 in U.S. Currency,* 152 F.3d 491, 504 (6th Cir. 1998).

This conflict was resolved with CAFRA Section 4, 106 Pub. L. No. 185, 114 Stat. 202, 212, and the federal statute now provides for the payment of pre-judgment interest if the claimant prevails. *See* 28 U.S.C. § 2465(b); *United States v. $30,006.25 in U.S. Currency,* 236 F.3d 610, 615 (10th Cir. 2000).

A few states also permit payment of interest and costs to prevailing claimants. *Espinoza v. City of Everett,* 87 Wash. App. 857; 943 P.2d 387, 395 (Wash. App. 1997) (costs); *Wolf Motor Co., Inc. v. One 2000 Ford F 350,* 658 N.W.2d 900, 903–04 (Minn. App. 2003) (prejudgment interest); *State v. Rodriguez,* 138 N.J. Super. 575; 351 A.2d 784, 786 (N.J. Super. A.D. 1976) (post-judgment interest only); *Utah Code Ann.* § 24-1-10 (prejudgment and post-judgment interest); *Spota v. Astra Motors,* 28 A.D.2d 471; 813 N.Y.S.2d 194, 195 (N.Y.A.D. 2006) (predecision interest).

Also, under CAFRA Section 3, Pub. L. No. 106-185, 114 Stat, 202, 211, Congress added 18 U.S.C. § 2680(c) to make the government liable for damage or loss to the property if it was not forfeited, and the claimant was not subsequently convicted of the related criminal offense. *Adeleke v. United States,* 355 F.3d 144, 154 (2d Cir. 2004). This includes liability for negligence of the agents in the seizure, release, or sale of the property, *see Cervantes v. United States,* 330 F.3d 1186, 1189–90 (9th Cir. 2003), but excludes compensatory or consequential damages. *United States v. Plunk,* 511 F.3d 918, 923 (9th Cir. 2007). If seized property has been sold and subsequently not forfeited, the claimant is entitled to the value of the property at the time of the sale, rather than the date of return. *United States v. Plunk, Id.* p. 923; *United States v. Marshall,* 338 F.3d 990, 993 (9th Cir. 2003).

States also have provisions for compensation for damaged property. *Utah Code Ann.* § 24-1-12; *People v. Taube,* 843 P.2d 79, 83 (Colo. App. 1992).

No storage fees may be charged on returned property. *Genes-Perez v. Kelly,* 333 F.3d 313, 317 (1st Cir. 2003); *Utah Code Ann.* § 24-1-13; *People v. 6344 Skyway, Paradise, CA,* 71 Cal.App.4th 1026, 1034–35 (1999); *In re Forfeiture of 1987 Mercury,* 252 Mich. App. 533; 652 N.W.2d 675, 682 (Mich. App. 2002).

L. Judicial *In Personam* Trial Procedures

Certain states provide for forfeiture as a judicial *in personam* matter. See Chapter 2, Section G.4. Although several statutes have specific provisions regulating the procedures in conducting these matters, *see Ariz. Rev. Stat. Ann.* § 12-4312; *Iowa Code Ann.* § 809A.14, others merely reference the state code of civil practice. *See Ga. Code Ann.* § 16-13-49(p); *Mo. Ann. Stat.* § 513.607.5; *N.Y. Civil Practice Law* § 1350.

Once a civil *in personam* action is filed, provisional remedies such as attachment orders, receiverships, or injunctive relief may be obtained to preserve the property. *Kuriansky v. Bed-Stuy Health Care Corp,* 135 A.D.2d 160; 525 N.Y.S.2d 225, 227–28 (N.Y.A.D. 1988); *Spota v. Conti,* 9 Misc.3d 349, 799 N.Y.S.2d 693, 696 (N.Y. Sup. 2005).

In those states with specific statutory procedures, the litigation generally follows the same path as a judicial civil *in rem* forfeiture case up to the point where the defendant is either found guilty, or a finding of liability is determined. At this juncture, the court enters a judgment for forfeiture against the property listed in the complaint or indictment and authorizes the seizure of any other property not already in the possession of the state. *See Ark. Code Ann.* § 5-64-505(j)(4); *State v. 790 Cash,* 821 So. 2d 609, 614 (La. App. 2002). A money judgment may also be issued. N.Y. C.P.L.R. § 1311 subd 1. This may include substitute assets up to the value of the defendant or claimant's property found by the court to be forfeitable. *See Hawaii Rev. Stat.* § 712A-14; *State ex rel. Riley County Police Dept. v. $1,489 U.S. Currency,* 31 K.A.2d 54, 59; 59 P.3d 1045, 1049 (Kan. App. 2002).

The statutes next require that either the court or the prosecutor notify potential owners and interest holders who may have a legal interest in the forfeited property and have not previously been given notice so that they may have an opportunity to contest the forfeiture judgment. *See Ariz. Rev. Stat. Ann.* § 13-4312.H.1. Most statutes require a claim to be filed within 30 days from receipt of the notice. *See Kan. Stat. Ann.* § 60-4114(f); *La. Rev. Stat. Ann.* § 40:2613.F. If a claim is filed, a few jurisdictions provide for a hearing within 60 days. *See Ariz. Rev. Stat. Ann.* § 13-4312.H.4; *Hawaii Rev. Stat.* §

712A-13(7)(c). Others provide that, if the state contests the interest, the matter must be litigated using the judicial *in rem* procedures. *See Iowa Code Ann.* § 809A.14 7.; *Kan. Stat. Ann.* § 60-4114(f); *La. Rev. Stat. Ann.* § 40:2613 F.

There is no right to a jury in the ancillary hearing, *see La. Rev. Stat. Ann.* § 40:2613 F), and the burden is on the claimant to prove his or her legal interest and exemption from forfeiture by a preponderance of the evidence. *See Kan. Stat. Ann.* § 60-4114(g). Generally, this will require a showing that the claimant is an owner or interest holder in the property, and that he or she qualifies as an innocent party as defined under the applicable statute. *See Ariz. Rev. Stat. Ann.* § 13-4312 .H 5.

If the court makes a finding that the claimant has maintained his or her burden of proof and established the necessary elements of ownership and innocence, the court may amend the order of forfeiture to recognize the interest. *See Hawaii Rev. Stat.* § 712A-13(8).

M. Summary

Civil *in rem* forfeiture cases have a long history in American forfeiture jurisprudence, and trial procedures generally are well established by reference to the related federal or state statute or civil code of procedure.

Civil *in personam* forfeiture actions are relatively new and trial proceedings are a hybrid of criminal and civil procedural rules. Although some state statutes have well-defined trial procedures, *see Hawaii Rev. Stat.* § 712A-13, others do not, *see Ga. Code Ann.* § 16-13-49(p), and await further definition either by legislation or judicial decision.

There are many similarities in procedures litigating state civil *in personam* and state criminal actions. The reader is directed to Chapter 8, Section K to contrast the two systems.

Notes

1.   An excellent review of the history of the federal innocent owner defense and the major changes effective with the passage of CAFRA is found at, Stefan D. Cassella, *The Uniform Innocent Owner Defense to Forfeiture,* 89 KY. L.J. 653 (2001). The reader is encouraged to read this article in its entirety.

2.   The CAFRA innocent owner exemption does not apply to forfeitures filed under the "Customs Carve-Out" sections (See Chapter 4, n.2), United States v. One Lucite Ball, 252 F. Supp. 2d 1367 (S.D. Fla. 2003), or forfeitures litigated on a contraband theory. *See* United States v. 144,774 Pounds of Blue King Crab, 410 F.3d 1131 (9th Cir. 2005).

8 Criminal Forfeiture Proceedings

A. Introduction

After 15 years as a spy for the former Soviet Union, veteran FBI agent Robert Hanssen pled guilty to 15 counts of espionage and conspiracy and received a life term in federal prison. Federal prosecutors alleged that Hanssen made $1.4 million dollars from his espionage activity, $600,000 of which was in cash and jewelry.[1] However, investigators were unable to find more than a small portion of those illicit profits. As part of his criminal plea, therefore, Hanssen stipulated to a criminal forfeiture money judgment of $1.4 million dollars.[2] This plea demonstrates the growing importance of criminal forfeiture as a weapon in recouping the profits of illegal activity.

There are three basic rules to remember when litigating a criminal forfeiture action—namely:

(1) A criminal conviction is required, *see United States v. Aramony*, 88 F.3d 1369, 1387 n.11 (4th Cir. 1996);
(2) It is limited to the defendant's interest in the property, *see United States v. Harris*, 246 F.3d 566, 575 (6th Cir. 2001); and
(3) There must be a nexus between the property and the criminal activity, *see Fed. R. Crim. Pro.* 32.2(b)(1).

This chapter will review the federal and state procedures commonly utilized in criminal forfeiture actions.

B. Federal Criminal Forfeiture

The most common federal criminal forfeiture procedure statutes are found in the racketeering (RICO), *see* 18 U.S.C. § 1963, and drug forfeiture statutes, *see* 21 U.S.C. § 853. Because most federal statutes adopt the drug forfeiture

statute provisions, *see* 18 U.S.C. § 982(b)(1), and Congress specifically provides that the provisions of 21 U.S.C. § 853 apply to all stages of a criminal
proceeding filed under 28 U.S.C. § 2461, we will refer to those procedures.[3]

C. Initiation

A federal criminal forfeiture action is initiated with notice in the indictment or information that the government seeks forfeiture as part of the criminal sentence. *See Fed. R. Crim. Pro.* 32.2(a); *United States v. Grammatikos,*
633 F.2d 1013, 1024 (2d Cir. 1980). General language tracking the forfeiture
statute followed up with a bill of particulars listing specific forfeitable property prior to trial is sufficient. *See Fed. R. Crim. Pro.* 7(c)(2); *United States v.
Davis,* 177 F. Supp. 2d 470, 484 (E.D. Va. 2001). However, substitute assets are
not required to be listed in the indictment or elsewhere. *United States v. Hatcher,*
323 F.3d 666, 673 (8th Cir. 2003); *United States v. Misla-Aldarondo,* 478 F.3d
52, 75 (1st Cir. 2007). If property has been seized for civil forfeiture, the Civil
Asset Forfeiture Reform Act ("CAFRA") Section 2, 106 Pub. L. No. 185, 114
Stat. 202, 204, gives the prosecutor the option of listing the property in a
criminal indictment in lieu of proceeding on the civil forfeiture. *See* 18 U.S.C.
§ 983(a)(3)(B)(ii)(I).

D. Seizure of Property

There is no specific warrantless seizure authority in federal criminal forfeiture procedure similar to that authorized under the civil forfeiture process.
See 18 U.S.C. § 981(b)(2). However, many criminal forfeitures commence as
administrative or civil forfeitures, or the property is seized pursuant to a lawful
search or arrest warrant; therefore, 18 U.S.C. § 981(b)(2) does have practical
application to criminal forfeitures. Seizing property under the civil forfeiture
procedures and filing a parallel criminal case or converting the civil action to
a criminal forfeiture is specifically acknowledged and approved in CAFRA
Section 2. *See* 18 U.S.C. § 983(a)(3)(B)–(C).

To preserve and maintain custody of property for criminal forfeiture, prosecutors may obtain two types of preindictment restraining orders. An ex parte
10-day temporary restraining order is available without notice to the opposing
side, provided there is a showing of probable cause, and notice would jeopardize the availability of the asset for forfeiture. *In re Restraint of Bowman
Gaskins Financial Group Accounts,* 345 F. Supp. 2d 613, 619 (E.D. Va. 2004).

A hearing must be held at the earliest time possible and prior to the expiration of the order, *see* 21 U.S.C. § 853(e)(2), where the government must show:

(1) A substantial probability of prevailing on the forfeiture;

(2) A threat that the property may be destroyed or unavailable for trial; and

(3) The need to preserve outweighs the hardship against the owner.

At that hearing, the court could then convert the 10-day TRO into a preindictment restraining order for up to 90 days and, if an indictment or information is filed, it may remain in effect through trial. *See United States v. Kirschenbaum*, 156 F.3d 784, 792 (7th Cir. 1998).

In lieu of seeking a 10-day temporary restraining order, the prosecutor may elect to apply directly for a 90-day restraining order by giving notice to the opposing side and providing an opportunity for a hearing. *See* 21 U.S.C. § 853(e)(1)(B). Because many prosecutors are concerned that notice would cause the property to be concealed, they usually opt for the 10-day restraining order provision.

Post-indictment restraining orders also are available ex parte by alleging that the property would be subject to forfeiture upon conviction. *See* 21 U.S.C. § 853(e)(1)(A); *United States v. Acord*, 47 F. Supp. 2d 1339, 1341 (M.D. Ala. 1999); *United States v. Jamieson*, 427 F.3d 394, 405–06 (6th Cir. 2005).

Does a claimant have a right to an adversarial hearing to contest criminal restraining orders? The general rule is that there is no right to a prerestraint hearing when an order is issued either preindictment or post-indictment. *See United States v. Monsanto*, 924 F.2d 1186, 1192 (2d Cir. 1991); *United States v. Bissell*, 866 F.2d 1343, 1352 (11th Cir. 1989); *United States v. St. Pierre*, 950 F. Supp. 334, 338 (M.D. Fla. 1996); *United States v. Musson*, 802 F.2d 384, 387 (10th Cir. 1986).

However, when a claimant's Sixth Amendment right to counsel may be infringed, and he or she has no other funds to retain counsel, a hearing may be required to determine whether the restrained funds should be released to hire counsel in the criminal case. *See United States v. Jones*, 160 F.3d 641, 647 (10th Cir. 1998); *United States v. Farmer*, 274 F.3d 800, 805 (4th Cir. 2001); *United States v. Moya-Gomez*, 860 F.2d 706, 729 (7th Cir. 1988). The claimant is required to show a lack of funds to retain counsel and that there is no probable cause for the forfeiture of the funds. *United States v. St. George*, 241 F. Supp. 2d 875, 878–80 (E.D. Tenn. 2003). If the court finds probable cause that the assets are forfeitable, the temporary restraining order remains in place, even if the funds are needed to pay for attorney fees. *United States v. Melrose East Subdivision*, 357 F.3d 493, 507 (5th Cir. 2004). However, if no probable cause is established, the funds are released. *United States v. Wittig*, 333 F. Supp. 2d 1048, 1052 (D. Kan. 2004).

May the government restrain the assets of third parties if it alleges that the property is subject to criminal forfeiture? The majority view is that property held by third parties may be restrained to preserve the government's interest, *see United States v. Regan*, 858 F.2d 115, 120 (2d Cir. 1988); *United States v. Jenkins*, 974 F.2d 32, 36 (5th Cir. 1992); however, a few courts have declined to permit restraining orders of property held by third parties, reasoning that the orders are limited to the defendant and his or her agents. *See United States v. Kirschenbaum*, 156 F.3d 784, 794 (7th Cir. 1998); *United States v. Lugo*, 63 F. Supp. 2d 896, 897 (N.D. Ill. 1999). If restraining orders are issued against property held by third parties, they are entitled to a post-restraint hearing to challenge the scope of the order. *See United States v. Real Property in Waterboro*, 64 F.3d 752, 755–56 (1st Cir. 1995); *United States v. Siegal*, 974 F. Supp. 55, 58 (D. Mass 1997); *In re Restraint of Bowman Gaskins Financial Group Accounts*, 345 F. Supp. 2d 613, 628 (E.D. Va. 2004). The third party may assert a superior interest in the property or challenge the nexus between the property and the charged criminal offense, but may not attack the underlying indictment. *United States v. Siegal*, 974 F. Supp. 55, 59 (D. Mass. 1997); *Roberts v. United States*, 141 F.3d 1468, 1471 n.6 (11th Cir. 1998).

Are substitute assets subject to restraint by pretrial orders? Although a few federal courts have allowed pretrial restraint of substitute assets, *see United States v. Bollin*, 264 F.3d 391, 421, (4th Cir. 2001); *In Re Billman*, 915 F.2d 916, 920–21 (4th Cir. 1990), the vast majority does not permit it. *See United States v. Gotti*, 155 F.3d 144, 149 (2d Cir. 1998); *United States v. Floyd*, 992 F.2d 498, 502 (5th Cir. 1993); *In Re Assets of Martin*, 1 F.3d 1351, 1359 (3d Cir. 1993); *United States v. Field*, 62 F.3d 246, 249 (8th Cir. 1995); *United States v. Ripinsky*, 20 F.3d 359, 364 (9th Cir. 1994).

If a court does allow a post-restraint hearing to be conducted, the government is required to establish probable cause that the restrained property is traceable to the underlying offense, *see United States v. Jones*, 160 F.3d 641, 648 (10th Cir. 1998); *United States v. Bollin*, 264 F.3d 391, 421 (4th Cir. 2001), and the issues are limited to the forfeitability of the property. *See United States v. Moya-Gomez*, 860 F.2d 706, 730 (7th Cir. 1988); *United States v. St. Pierre*, 950 F. Supp. 334, 338 (M.D. Fla. 1996).

Two additional provisional remedies that may be utilized to preserve assets for criminal forfeiture include performance bonds and lis pendens. Performance bonds are specifically authorized under the criminal forfeiture statute, *see* 21 U.S.C. § 853(e)(1), and the government may accept a cash bond and release the property to the defendant pending the trial. *See United States v. Lugo*, 63 F. Supp. 2d 896, 897 n.2 (N.D. Ill. 1999).

A lis pendens is an ex parte notice commonly filed in real property forfeitures actions to restrict the transfer of title to property that is subject to litigation. Although it is not specifically listed in the criminal forfeiture procedure statute as an authorized order, it would fall under the provision that the government may "take any other action to preserve the availability of [the] property." *See* 21 U.S.C. § 853(e)(1). Lis pendens have been used successfully in criminal forfeiture actions and upheld against due process attacks. *See Aronson v. City of Akron*, 116 F.3d 804, 812 (6th Cir. 1997); *United States v. Register*, 182 F.3d 820, 837 (11th Cir. 1999); *United States v. Miller*, 26 F. Supp. 2d 415, 432 n.15 (N.D.N.Y. 1998). However, a few courts have held that a lis pendens cannot be filed to restrain substitute assets in anticipation of a money judgment. *See United States v. Jarvis*, 499 F.3d 1196, 1203 (10th Cir. 2007) (New Mexico statute); *United States v. Kramer*, 2006 WL 3545026 at 10–11 (E.D.N.Y. 2006) (New York statute).

Another technique that may be used to seize property for criminal forfeiture is a criminal seizure warrant. *See* 21 U.S.C. § 853(f). It is similar to the seizure warrant authorized for civil forfeiture, *see* 18 U.S.C. § 981(b)(2), with the exception that the court must find probable cause for forfeiture upon conviction *and* that a protective order under 21 U.S.C. § 853(e) is not sufficient or available. *See United States v. Walker*, 943 F. Supp. 1326, 1331 (D. Colo. 1996).

This raises an interesting issue under CAFRA pertaining to property that has been seized for civil forfeiture but has been included in a criminal forfeiture indictment in lieu of civil forfeiture. *See* 18 U.S.C. § 983(a)(3)(B)(ii)(I). CAFRA Section 2, 106 Pub. L. No. 185, 114 Stat. 202, 204, states that the government must take steps necessary to preserve the property and maintain custody as provided under the applicable criminal forfeiture statute. *See* 18 U.S.C. § 983(a)(3)(B)(ii)(II). Is the government required to reseize the property for criminal forfeiture once it is already in its custody? Courts have determined that the government must file some form of process to comply with the criminal seizure provision contained in 21 U.S.C. § 853(f). *In Re 2000 White Mercedes ML320*, 220 F. Supp. 2d 1322, 1326 n.5 (M.D. Fla. 2001) (court order); *United States v. Martin*, 460 F. Supp 2d 669, 677 (D. Md. 2006) (criminal seizure warrant).

Whenever the government initiates a criminal forfeiture action, it must take steps to protect the property and insure that it will be available upon conviction for forfeiture. The tools the prosecutor will use include temporary restraining orders and injunctions, bonds, lis pendens, and criminal seizure warrants. The defense strategy will be to challenge any orders issued and attempt to have the court conduct a post-seizure hearing on the ultimate forfeitability of the property. Such should always be pursued when the property belongs to third parties or constitutes substitute assets.

E. Remission/Mitigation

A third-party claimant has no right to intervene in the criminal action, *see* 21 U.S.C. § 853(k)(1); *United States v. Messino,* 122 F.3d 427, 428 (7th Cir. 1997), nor can a third-party claimant commence a separate civil action contesting the seizure or forfeiture. *See* 21 U.S.C. § 853(k)(2); *United States v. McCorkle,* 143 F. Supp. 2d 1311, 1319 (M.D. Fla. 2000). An option that the third party may next pursue is to file a petition for remission or mitigation of his or her interest in the property.

The Attorney General is authorized to grant petitions for remission or mitigation on criminal matters under 21 U.S.C. § 853(i)(1), and the enabling provisions are contained in 28 C.F.R. § 9.4(e). The petition is filed directly with the U.S. Attorney who forwards the investigation and his or her recommendation to the Chief of the Asset Forfeiture and Money Laundering Section in Washington D.C. for ruling. For more detail on the remission/mitigation process, see Chapter 4.

To succeed on a petition for remission or mitigation in a criminal forfeiture, the petitioner must demonstrate:

(1) A legally cognizable interest in the property; AND
(2) The petitioner held that legal interest at the time of the violation OR was a bona fide purchaser for value without cause to believe the property was subject to forfeiture. *See* 28 C.F.R. § 9.5(a)(1)(ii).

This is the same as the innocent owner exemption contained in 21 U.S.C. § 853(n)(6).

The remission process is also available to victims of criminal activity or other innocent parties, provided it is not inconsistent with the other provisions of the criminal forfeiture statute. *See* 21 U.S.C. § 853(i)(1); *United States v. BCCI Holdings (Luxembourg) S.A. (Final Order of Forfeiture and Disbursement),* 69 F. Supp. 2d 36, 41–42 (D.D.C. 1999).

Thus, if it appears that the claimant has grounds to prevail in the ancillary hearing, it is in his or her best interest to file a petition for mitigation or remission to expedite the decision rather than wait until the ancillary hearing, which will not be held until after the resolution of the criminal case.

F. Plea Agreement

Many criminal forfeiture cases are resolved by a plea to the criminal action and stipulating to the forfeiture. For example, former CIA agent Aldrich Ames, who was paid $1.88 million dollars by the KGB during the four years that he worked for them, received a life sentence in prison on the espionage charges and agreed to forfeit his assets to the United States, with $547,000 transferred into the Justice Department's Victim Assistance Fund.[4]

There are a few basic rules to remember when obtaining a plea on a criminal forfeiture. The first is that, because forfeiture is part of the criminal sentence, there is no requirement that the court find a factual basis in support of the forfeiture order. See Libretti v. United States, 516 U.S. 29, 39 (1995); United States v. Boatner, 966 F.2d 1575, 1581 (11th Cir. 1992). Second, the government is authorized to settle a criminal forfeiture case along with the underlying criminal action. In re WR Huff Asset Management Co., LLC, 409 F.3d 555, 564 (2d Cir. 2005). If a joint settlement cannot be reached, a defendant may plead guilty to the criminal offense and still contest the forfeiture order. See United States v. Cunningham, 201 F.3d 20, 24 (1st Cir. 2000); United States v. Iacaboni, 363 F.3d 1, 2–3 (1st Cir. 2004). Thus, any plea agreement to a criminal offense should also include an express stipulation to the forfeiture, including substitute assets. United States v. Alamoudi, 452 F.3d 310, 312–13 (4th Cir. 2006). Finally, if a criminal defendant withdraws his or her criminal plea, the defendant also sets aside the agreement to the criminal forfeiture. See United States v. Caldwell, 88 F.3d 522, 526 (8th Cir. 1996).

G. Trial Procedure

The general procedures for federal criminal forfeiture trials are contained in the Federal Rules of Criminal Procedure 32.2.

A party is entitled to a bifurcated trial determining the guilt and forfeiture actions, and the forfeiture hearing should be heard as soon as practicable after the guilty verdict. See Fed. R. Crim. Pro. 32.2(b)(1).

Does a criminal defendant have a right to a jury trial in the bifurcated forfeiture hearing and, if so, what is the burden of proof?

The U.S. Supreme Court addressed this question in *United States v. Libretti*, 516 U.S. 29 (1995). In that case, the court made four important findings pertaining to criminal forfeitures.

(1) Forfeiture is an element of the sentence following conviction and is not a separate substantive offense. *Libretti*, 516 U.S. at 30.
(2) The right to a jury determination of the forfeiture is a statutory provision, not a constitutional right guaranteed under the Sixth Amendment. *Id.* at 49.
(3) The court is not required to give a specific advisal concerning the waiver of the right to a jury determination of the forfeitability of the assets. *Id.* at 50.
(4) Finally, the court is not obligated to inquire into the factual basis for the forfeiture of assets. *Id.* at 51.

Following *Libretti*, the federal courts consistently have found that criminal forfeiture is part of the criminal sentence and can be established by preponderance of the evidence. *See United States v. Dicter*, 198 F.3d 1284, 1289 (11th Cir. 1999); *United States v. Garcia-Guizar*, 160 F.3d 511, 517–18 (9th Cir. 1998); *United States v. DeFries*, 129 F.3d 1293, 1312 (D.C. Cir. 1997); *United States v. Bellomo*, 176 F.3d 580, 595 (2d Cir. 1999); *United States v. Ortiz-Cintron*, 461 F.3d 78, 82 (1st Cir. 2006).

In 2000, the U.S. Supreme court determined that any fact that increases a penalty beyond a prescribed statutory maximum must be submitted to a jury and proven beyond a reasonable doubt. *See Apprendi v. New Jersey*, 530 U.S. 466, 490 (2000). Arguments were raised that this decision raised the burden of proof in criminal forfeitures, but federal appellate courts have determined that, under criminal forfeiture, all property representing proceeds is forfeitable, and because there is no prescribed statutory maximum, *Apprendi* is inapplicable. Hence, the preponderance of the evidence standard still applies. *See United States v. Corrado*, 227 F.3d 543, 550–51 (6th Cir. 2000); *United States v. Keene*, 341 F.3d 78, 85–86 (1st Cir. 2003); *United States v. Vera*, 278 F.3d 672, 673 (7th Cir. 2002); *United States v. Najjar*, 300 F.3d 466, 485 (4th Cir. 2002); *United States v. Cabeza*, 258 F.3d 1256, 1257–58 (11th Cir. 2001); *United States v. Gasanova*, 332 F.3d 297, 300–01 (5th Cir. 2003); *United States v. Shryock*, 342 F.3d 948, 991 (9th Cir. 2003); *United States v. Ida*, 207 F. Supp. 2d 171, 189–90 (S.D.N.Y. 2002); *United States v. Davis*, 177 F. Supp. 2d 470, 483 (E.D. Va. 2001).

In *Blakely v. Washington*, 542 U.S. 296 (2004), the U.S. Supreme Court further refined *Apprendi,* stating that the "'statutory maximum' for *Apprendi* purposes is the maximum sentence a judge may impose solely on the basis of the facts reflected in the jury verdict or admitted by the defendant." *Blakely,* 542 U.S. at 303. This was immediately followed by *United States v. Booker,* 543 U.S. 220 (2005), where a divided court found that the federal sentencing guidelines were subject to the Sixth Amendment and were advisory, not mandatory. Of particular note in the section of the opinion discussing the portions of the sentencing statute that the court found "perfectly valid" is the fact that the court cites 18 U.S.C. § 3554 (forfeiture). One appellate court already has commented, "*Booker* itself expressly states that 18 U.S.C. § 3554 is still valid.... In other words, *Booker* itself suggests that a district court determination [of criminal forfeiture] does not offend the Sixth Amendment." *United States v. Fruchter,* 411 F.3d 377, 382 (2d Cir. 2005); *United States v. Alamoudi,* 452 F.3d 310, 314–15 (4th Cir. 2006).

In the aftermath of *Blakely* and *Booker,* renewed attempts to attack the burden of proof in criminal forfeiture under the preponderance of the evidence standard have continued to meet defeat. *See United States v. Melendez,* 401 F.3d 851, 856 (7th Cir. 2005); *United States v. Hall,* 411 F.3d 651, 654 (6th Cir. 2005); *United States v. Fruchter,* 411 F.3d 377, 382–83 (2d Cir. 2005).

Thus, it appears that, in spite of *Apprendi, Blakely,* and *Booker, Libretti* is still good law, and federal criminal forfeitures are considered part of the sentencing and may be established by preponderance of the evidence. However, there are a few federal criminal forfeiture offenses that are required to be established beyond a reasonable doubt, pursuant to the terms of the statutes. *See* 18 U.S.C. § 1467(e)(1) (obscenity); 18 U.S.C. § 2253(e) (child exploitation).

Either party has a right to a jury trial, *see Fed. R. Crim. Pro.* 32.2(b)(4), which may be waived by the parties. *United States v. Schlesinger,* 396 F. Supp. 2d 267, 270 (E.D.N.Y. 2005). This is a statutory, rather than a constitutional, right, *see Libretti v. United States,* 516 U.S. 29, 49 (1995), which may be waived if not timely asserted. *See United States v. Davis,* 177 F. Supp. 2d 470, 483 (E.D. Va. 2001); *United States v. Hively,* 437 F.3d 752, 763 (8th Cir. 2006); *United States v. Leahy,* 438 F.3d 328, 331 (3d Cir. 2006). The special verdict of the jury is limited to the issue of whether there is a nexus between the property and the offense committed by the defendant. *See Fed. R. Crim. Pro.* 32.2(b)(4); *United States v. Derman,* 211 F.3d 175, 184 (1st Cir. 2000). This should include all property used to facilitate the offense and gross proceeds of the operation. *United States v. Boulware,* 384 F.3d 794, 813 (9th Cir. 2004).

There is no Sixth Amendment right to have the jury determine what property is forfeitable or the amount of any money judgment. *United States v. Tedder*, 403 F.3d 836, 841 (7th Cir. 2005); *United States v. McAuliffe*, 490 F.3d 526, 540 (6th Cir. 2007); *United States v. Reiner*, 393 F. Supp. 2d 52, 55 (D. Me. 2005) (no right to jury if money judgment only). The forfeiture order cannot be based on criminal offenses that were not charged or counts that were dismissed or acquitted. *United States v. Hasson*, 333 F.3d 1264, 1279 n.19 (11th Cir. 2003); *United States v. Cherry*, 330 F.3d 658, 670 (4th Cir. 2003).

To assist in proving the nexus to criminal proceeds in narcotic offenses, the government has the benefit of a rebuttable presumption that property is subject to forfeiture if it was acquired during the period of time of the offense and there is no other likely source for the property. *See* 21 U.S.C. § 853(d); *United States v. Wingerter*, 369 F. Supp. 2d 799, 805 n.8 (E.D. Va. 2005). The fungible property presumption under 18 U.S.C. § 984 has no application to criminal forfeiture and is limited to federal civil *in rem* forfeitures. *United States v. Jennings*, 487 F.3d 564, 586 (8th Cir. 2007). When a jury is unable to arrive at a verdict on the forfeiture issue, the court should impanel a new jury. *United States v. Messino*, 382 F.3d 704, 714 (7th Cir. 2004).

If a jury is waived, a bench trial is held, and the court makes the determination whether a nexus exists between the specific forfeitable property and the offense. *See Fed. R. Crim. Pro.* 32.2(b)(1); *United States v. Singh*, 390 F.3d 168, 190–91 (2d Cir. 2004). In making its decision, the court may rely on evidence already in the record from the guilt phase of the trial as well as testimony introduced during the forfeiture hearing, which may include reliable hearsay evidence. *See United States v. Gaskin*, 2002 WL 459005 (W.D.N.Y. 2002).) If a money judgment is sought, the court determines the amount of the order. *United States v. Conner*, 752 F.2d 566, 576 (11th Cir. 1985).

H. Preliminary Order of Forfeiture

Upon finding that property is subject to forfeiture, the court must promptly enter a preliminary order of forfeiture stating the amount of the money judgment or the specific assets ordered forfeited. The order is entered irrespective of any third-party claims, as those will be resolved at the ancillary hearing. *See Fed. R. Crim. Pro.* 32.2(b)(2); *United States v. Faulk*, 340 F. Supp. 2d 1312, 1315 (M.D. Ala. 2004). The order will not become final as to the defendant until sentencing, and as to the third-party claimant until after the ancillary hearing. *United States v. Bennett*, 423 F.3d 271, 275 n.1 (3d Cir. 2005).

Once the preliminary order has been issued, the government may obtain an order seizing any specific property not already in the custody of law enforcement that is subject to the forfeiture order. *See Fed. R. Crim. Pro.* 32.2(b)(3). Discovery may also be conducted and court orders obtained to locate hidden assets. *See United States v. Saccoccia,* 898 F. Supp. 53, 60 (D.R.I. 1995); *United States v. Barnette,* 129 F.3d 1179, 1182 (11th Cir. 1997); *United States v. Saccoccia,* 344 F.3d 31, 34 (1st Cir. 2003). The preliminary order subsequently may be amended to include the newly found property. *See Fed. R. Crim. Pro.* 32.2(e)(1)(A); *United States v. BCCI Holdings (Luxembourg) S.A. (Petition of Bank of California International),* 980 F. Supp. 522, 524 (D. D.C. 1997); *United States v. Ferrario-Pozzi,* 368 F.3d 5, 9 (1st Cir. 2004). The order may include specific assets as well as a money judgment equal to the value of the profits that the defendant obtained from the offense. *United States v. Hall,* 434 F.3d 42, 60 n.8 (1st Cir. 2006); *United States v. Vampire Nation,* 451 F.3d 189, 203 (3d Cir. 2006); *United States v. Huber,* 404 F.3d 1047, 1056 (8th Cir. 2005).

The government also is authorized to forfeit substitute assets of the defendant if the specific property ordered forfeited:

(1) Cannot be located;
(2) Has been transferred to a third party;
(3) Is beyond the jurisdiction of the court;
(4) Has been substantially diminished in value; or
(5) Has been commingled with other property and cannot easily be divided.

See 21 U.S.C. § 853(p); *United States v. Alamoudi,* 452 F.3d 310, 315–16 (4th Cir. 2006); *United States v. Faulk,* 340 F. Supp. 2d 1312, 1313–14 (M.D. Ala. 2004).

Substitute assets also may be used to satisfy any money judgment that has been obtained. *See United States v. Baker,* 227 F.3d 955, 970 (7th Cir. 2000); *United States v. Candelaria-Silva,* 166 F.3d 19, 42 (1st Cir. 1999); *United States v. Bermudez,* 413 F.3d 304, 306–07 (2d Cir. 2005). The preliminary order of forfeiture can be amended at any time to include the substitute property. *See Fed. R. Crim. Pro.* 32.2(e)(1)(B). The forfeiture of substitute assets is solely within the determination of the court, as there is no right to a jury trial on this issue. *See* 21 U.S.C. § 853(p)(2); *Fed. R. Crim. Pro.* 32.2(e)(3); *United States v. Thompson,* 837 F. Supp. 585, 586 (S.D.N.Y. 1993).

I.   Ancillary Hearing

The ancillary hearing provides third parties with the opportunity to challenge the preliminary forfeiture order by establishing their legitimate right to the property.[5] *See United States v. Gilbert,* 244 F.3d 888, 911 (11th Cir. 2001); *United States v. Padilla-Galarza,* 351 F.3d 594, 600 (1st Cir. 2003). The procedures are contained in 21 U.S.C. § 853(n) and Federal Rules of Criminal Procedure 32.2(c). It is the exclusive method for a third party to challenge a criminal forfeiture action, as the statute specifically forbids the filing of any legal or equitable action to litigate an interest in the property subsequent to the criminal forfeiture filing. *See* 21 U.S.C. § 853(k); *DSI Associates LLC v. United States,* 496 F.3d 175, 185 (2d Cir. 2007); *De Almeida v. United States,* 459 F.3d 377, 381 (S.D.N.Y. 2006); *United States v. Nava,* 404 F.3d 1119, 1125 (9th Cir. 2005); *United States v. Puig,* 419 F.3d 700, 703 (8th Cir. 2005); *In re American Basketball League, Inc,* 317 B.R. 121, 129 (Bankr. N.D. Cal. 2004) (bankruptcy petition). Requiring the third party to wait until the ancillary hearing does not violate due process. *United States v. Lazarenko,* 469 F.3d 815, 824–25 (9th Cir. 2006). The ancillary procedures should be followed whenever specific assets of the defendant have been ordered forfeited, either as directly related to the criminal offense or as substitute assets, and a third party may have a legal interest in the property. No ancillary hearing is required if the forfeiture consists merely of a money judgment. *See Fed. R. Crim. Pro.* 32.2(c)(1). It essentially is a civil proceeding that permits civil discovery, law, and motion and uses civil appellate rules. *See United States v. Lavin,* 942 F.2d 177, 178 (3d Cir. 1991); *United States v. BCCI Holdings (Luxembourg) S.A. (Final Order of Forfeiture and Disbursement),* 69 F. Supp. 2d 36, 57 (D.D.C. 1999).

Notice of the order of forfeiture is given to known interested parties either in writing or by publication, *see* 21 U.S.C. § 853(n)(1); *United States v. Carmichael,* 440 F. Supp. 2d 1280, 1282 (M.D. Ala. 2006), and potential claimants have 30 days after receipt of written notice or publication of forfeiture to petition the court for a hearing. *See* 21 U.S.C. § 853(n)(2). If no claims are filed during the notice period, the preliminary order becomes the final order. *See Fed. R. Crim. Pro.* 32.2(c)(2); *United States v. Puig,* 419 F.3d 700, 704 (8th Cir. 2005).

The petition must be personally verified, *United States v. Speed Joyeros, S.A.,* 410 F. Supp. 2d 121, 124 (E.D.N.Y. 2006), state specific facts alleging the nature and extent of the interest in the property, *United States v, Perkins,* 382 F. Supp. 2d 146, 149 (D. Me. 2005); *United States v. Soreide,* 461 F.3d 1351, 1355 (11th Cir. 2006), and be timely filed. *See* 21 U.S.C. § 853(n)(3); *United States v. Carmichael,* 440 F. Supp. 2d 1280, 1281 (M.D. Ala. 2006).

Although the statute provides for a hearing within 30 days of the filing of the petition "to the extent practical and consistent with the interests of justice," *see* 21 U.S.C. § 853(n)(4), that is not always feasible, especially where there are multiple claims. *See United States v. BCCI Holdings (Luxembourg) S.A. (Final Order of Forfeiture and Disbursement),* 69 F. Supp. 2d 36, 54 (D.D.C. 1999). Doing so would also preclude any authorized civil discovery or law and motion to be litigated prior to the hearing.

The government may bring a prehearing motion to dismiss the petition for lack of standing, *see Fed. R. Crim. Pro.* 32.2(c)(1)(A); *United States v. Weiss,* 467 F.3d 1300, 1307–08 (11th Cir. 2006), and the claimant must demonstrate a colorable legal interest in the property to establish standing to contest the forfeiture action. *See United States v. Salam,* 191 F. Supp. 2d 725, 729 (E.D. La. 2001). Failure to make a prima facie showing of standing may result in dismissal of the petition without an ancillary hearing. *See United States v. Campos,* 859 F.2d 1233, 1240 (6th Cir. 1988); *United States v. Dempsey,* 55 F. Supp. 2d 990, 992 (E.D. Mo 1998).

Categories of petitioners that generally will have standing in the criminal ancillary hearing include:

- Spouses, *see United States v. Henry,* 850 F. Supp. 681, 684–85 (M.D. Tenn. 1994); *United States v. Hooper,* 229 F.3d 818, 819 n.4 (9th Cir. 2000);
- Lien holders, *see United States v. Harris,* 246 F.3d 566, 574 (6th Cir. 2001);
- Secured creditors, *see United States v. BCCI Holdings (Luxembourg) S.A. (Final Order of Forfeiture and Disbursement),* 69 F. Supp. 2d 36, 58 (D.D.C. 1999);
- Title owners, *see United States v. Ida,* 14 F. Supp. 2d 454, 460 (S.D.N.Y. 1998);
- Bailee, *United States v Alcaraz-Garcia,* 79 F.3d 769, 775 (9th Cir. 1996) (when bailor identified);
- Judgment creditors, *see United States v. Douglas,* 55 F.3d 584, 586 (11th Cir. 1995).

Parties who lack standing to file a petition in the ancillary hearing include:

- Defendants, *see* 21 U.S.C. § 853(n)(2); *United States v. Houghton,* 132 Fed. Appx. 130, 132 (9th Cir. 2005);

- Co-Defendants, *see Fed. R. Crim. Pro.* 32.2(c)(2);
- General creditors, *see United States v. Schwimmer,* 968 F.2d 1570, 1581 (2d Cir. 1992); *United States v. Campos,* 859 F.2d 1233, 1239–40 (6th Cir. 1988); *United States v. BCCI Holdings (Luxembourg) S.A. (Petition of Chawla),* 46 F.3d 1185, 1191 (D.C. Cir. 1995);
- Stockholders, *see United States v. East Carroll Correctional Systems, Inc.,* 14 F. Supp. 2d 851, 853–54 (W.D. La. 1998); *United States v. Wyly,* 193 F.3d 289, 304 (5th Cir. 1999); *United States v. Brown,* 86 Fed. Appx. 749 (5th Cir. 2004);
- Tort victims, *see United States v. BCCI Holdings (Luxembourg) S.A. (Petition of BCCI Campaign Committee),* 980 F. Supp. 16, 21 (D. D.C. 1997); *United States v. BCCI Holdings (Luxembourg) S.A. (Petition of Republic of Panama),* 833 F. Supp. 29, 31 (D. D.C. 1993); and
- Title owners without dominion and control, *United States v. Nava,* 404 F.3d 1119, 1130 n.6 (9th Cir. 2005); *In re Bryson,* 406 F.3d 284, 291 (4th Cir. 2005).

Although a party may have standing to contest the forfeiture in the ancillary hearing, that is no guarantee that he or she will qualify for an exemption from forfeiture because there are additional elements that might not be established. *See United States v. Alcaraz-Garcia,* 79 F.3d 769, 774 n.10 (9th Cir. 1996); *United States v. BCCI Holdings (Luxembourg) S.A. (Final Order of Forfeiture and Disbursement),* 69 F. Supp. 2d 36, 60 (D.D.C. 1999). For example, although a claimant may be able to demonstrate a colorable interest in the property to establish standing in the ancillary hearing, he or she may yet fail to prove an ownership interest by a preponderance of the evidence. *See United States v. Salam,* 191 F. Supp. 2d 725, 729 (E.D. La. 2001).

The prosecutor may also move to dismiss the petition on the basis that it fails to contain sufficient facts to specify the petitioner's right, title, or interest in the property, *see* 21 U.S.C. § 853(n)(3); *Fed. R. Crim. Pro.* 32.2(c)(1)(A); *United States v. BCCI Holdings (Luxembourg) S.A. (Petition of Richard Eline),* 916 F. Supp. 1286, 1289 (D.D.C. 1996); *United States v. BCCI Holdings (Luxembourg), S.A. (Fourth Round Petitions of General Creditors),* 956 F. Supp. 1, 5 (D.D.C. 1996), or was not timely filed. *See Fed. R. Crim. Pro.* 32.2(c)(1)(A); *United States v. BCCI Holdings (Luxembourg) S.A. (Petitions of B. Gray Gibbs et al.),* 916 F. Supp. 1270, 1275 (D.D.C. 1996); *United States v. McCorkle,* 143 F. Supp. 2d 1311, 1322 (M.D. Fla. 2000).

The court may authorize civil discovery as part of the ancillary proceeding, *see Fed. R. Crim. Pro.* 32.2(c)(1)(B); *United States v. BCCI Holdings (Lux-*

embourg) S.A. (Final Order of Forfeiture and Disbursement), 69 F. Supp. 2d 36, 57 (D.D.C. 1999), and even strike the petition as a sanction if the third party fails to comply with court-ordered discovery. *See United States v. Reyes,* 307 F.3d 451, 458 (6th Cir. 2002).

An ancillary hearing may be disposed of by summary judgment motion if the court finds that the claim lacks basis as a matter of law. *See Fed. R. Crim. Pro.* 32.2(c)(1)(B); *United States v. Martinez,* 228 F.3d 587, 588 n.2 (5th Cir. 2000); *United States v. BCCI Holdings (Luxembourg) S.A. (Petitions of People's Republic of Bangladesh and Bangladesh Bank),* 977 F. Supp. 1, 6 (D.D.C. 1997).

The ancillary hearing is held by the court because there is no right to a jury on this issue. *See Fed. R. Crim. Pro.* 32.2(c)(1); 21 U.S.C. § 853(n)(2); *United States v. McHan,* 345 F.3d 262, 276 (4th Cir. 2003). The burden is on the petitioner to prove by a preponderance of the evidence, *see United States v. Gilbert,* 244 F.3d 888, 901 n.30 (11th Cir. 2001); *Pacheco v. Serendensky,* 393 F.3d 348, 351 (2d Cir. 2004), that he or she held an ownership interest in the property at the time of the offense that was superior to that held by the defendant, *see* 21 U.S.C. § 853(n)(6)(A), OR that he or she was a bona fide purchaser for value without knowledge that the property was subject to forfeiture. *See* 21 U.S.C. § 853(n)(6)(B); *United States v. Schecter,* 251 F.3d 490, 494 (4th Cir. 2001).

Legal ownership in the property is determined by reference to state law, *United States v. McCollum,* 443 F. Supp. 2d 1154, 1165 (D. Neb. 2006); *United States v. Nektalov,* 440 F. Supp. 2d 287, 297 (S.D.N.Y. 2006), but whether that legal interest qualifies for an exemption is evaluated by the terms of the federal statute. *See United States v. Lester,* 85 F.3d 1409, 1412 (9th Cir. 1996); *United States v. Kennedy,* 201 F.3d 1324, 1334 (11th Cir. 2000); *United States v. Bollin,* 264 F.3d 391, 423–24 (4th Cir. 2001).

A petitioner cannot challenge the forfeitability of the property or the underlying criminal offense, *see United States v. Strube,* 58 F. Supp. 2d 576, 587 (M.D. Pa. 1999), but if the government's theory of forfeiture is that the property constitutes proceeds of the underlying offense, the petitioner is allowed to contest that finding. *See United States v. Farley,* 919 F. Supp. 276, 278–79 (S.D. Ohio 1996); *United States v. Santiago,* 227 F.3d 902, 907–08 (7th Cir. 2000); *United States v. Brooks,* 112 F. Supp. 2d 1035, 1040 (D. Haw. 2000).

There are two ways to qualify for an exemption under the statute. The first is for pre-existing interests that arose prior to the offense. In this situation, the petitioner may demonstrate that legal interest vested in him or her, in whole or in part, rather than the defendant or was superior to that held by the defendant.

See 21 U.S.C. § 853(n)(6)(A). This is consistent with the relation-back doctrine found at 21 U.S.C. § 853(c), which states that all property interest vests in the government upon the commission of the offense, *see United States v. McClung,* 6 F. Supp. 2d 548, 550 (W.D. Va. 1998); *United States v. Nava,* 404 F.3d 1119, 1124 (9th Cir. 2005), and is designed to prevent subsequent transfers of the property after the offense to circumvent forfeiture.

To merit an exemption under this provision, the petitioner must prove a legal interest in the property at the time of the offense. Thus, if the seized property is proceeds of criminal activity, the claim must fail because no one can have a legal interest in proceeds of criminal offenses, especially prior to the commission of the offense. *See United States v. Hooper,* 229 F.3d 818, 822 (9th Cir. 2000); *United States v. Martinez,* 228 F.3d 587, 590 (5th Cir. 2000); *United States v. Wahlen,* 459 F. Supp. 2d 800, 813–14 (E.D. Wis. 2006); *United States v. Timley,* 507 F.3d 1125, 1130 (8th Cir. 2007).

Although the first part of the criminal forfeiture owner exemption is similar to the first prong of the civil innocent owner exemption enacted by CAFRA, *see* 18 U.S.C. § 983(d)(2)(A), there is one important distinction. There is no requirement under the criminal statute to demonstrate innocence or lack of knowledge—it requires only a showing of superior ownership. *See United States v. Lester,* 85 F.3d 1409, 1413 (9th Cir. 1996); *United States v. Kennedy,* 201 F.3d 1324, 1332 n.14 (11th Cir. 2000); *United States v. Totaro,* 345 F.3d 989, 995 (8th Cir. 2003); *United States v. Soreide,* 461 F.3d 1351, 1355 (11th Cir. 2006). Therefore, the success of proving an exemption under this prong of the criminal forfeiture statute depends entirely upon whether the petitioner has a valid legal interest in the property prior to the offense.

Areas in which courts have recognized valid legal interests under the criminal forfeiture statute include:

- Marital interest, *see United States v. Lester,* 85 F.3d 1409, 1412 (9th Cir. 1996) (community property);
- Bailor, *see United States v. Alcaraz-Garcia,* 79 F.3d 769, 775 (9th Cir. 1996); and
- Lien holder/secured creditors, *United States v. Schecter,* 251 F.3d 490, 494–95 (4th Cir. 1990).

Alleged ownership interests that have not qualified as legal interests under the criminal forfeiture statute include:

- Criminal proceeds, *United States v. Brooks,* 112 F. Supp. 2d 1035, 1040 (D. Haw. 2000);

- Nominee/straw owner, *United States v. Morgan*, 224 F.3d 339, 343 (4th Cir. 2000); *United States v. Ida*, 14 F. Supp. 2d 454, 460–61 (S.D.N.Y. 1998);
- Unsecured creditors, *United States v. Ribadeneira*, 105 F.3d 833, 836 (2d Cir. 1997);
- Judgment creditor, *United States v. McClung*, 6 F. Supp. 2d 548, 552 (W.D. Va. 1998);
- Gift/loan, *United States v. Kennedy*, 201 F.3d 1324, 1335 (11th Cir. 2000); *In re Bryson*, 406 F.3d 284, 291 (4th Cir. 2005); and
- Tort victims, *United States v. Mageean*, 649 F. Supp. 820, 826 (D. Nev. 1986).

If a claimant obtained an interest after the commission of the underlying criminal offense, he or she may still qualify for an exemption from forfeiture if the claimant can demonstrate that he or she obtained a legal interest: (1) as a bona fide purchaser for value; and (2) without cause to believe that the property was subject to forfeiture. *See* 21 U.S.C. § 853(n)(6)(B).

The definition of bona fide purchaser comes from commercial law, *see United States v. Lavin*, 942 F.2d 177, 185 (3d Cir. 1991); *United States v. McCorkle*, 143 F. Supp. 2d 1311, 1325 (M.D. Fla. 2000), and is essentially: (1) a purchaser; (2) who pays valuable consideration; (3) without knowledge of the underlying criminal activity. *United States v. Frykholm*, 362 F.3d 413, 416 (7th Cir. 2004) (must pay value).

Under this definition, the petitioner must be a purchaser who paid value for the property. This would include:

- Mortgagee, *United States v. Schoenauer*, 237 F. Supp. 2d 1094, 1096–97 (S.D. Iowa 2002); and
- Lien holders, *In Re Metmor Fin. Inc.*, 819 F.2d 446, 448 (4th Cir. 1987).

It excludes the following:

- Spouse, *United States v. Infelise*, 938 F. Supp. 1352, 1368 (N.D. Ill. 1996);
- Family members, *United States v. Hentz*, 1996 WL 355327 (E.D. Pa. 1996);
- Donees, *see United States v. McCorkle*, 143 F. Supp. 2d 1311, 1321 (M.D. Fla. 2000);
- General creditors, *see United States v. BCCI Holdings (Luxembourg) S.A. (Petition of Chawla)*, 46 F.3d 1185, 1191 (D.C. Cir. 1995); *United States v. Watkins*, 320 F.3d 1279, 1282 (11th Cir. 2003); and

- Victims, *see United States v. Lavin*, 942 F.2d 177, 185–87 (3d Cir. 1991).

In addition to proof that the petitioner is a bona fide purchaser for value, he or she must show that the property was purchased without cause to believe it was subject to forfeiture. *See* 21 U.S.C. § 853(n)(6)(B); *Federal Trade Commission v. Assail, Inc.*, 410 F.3d 256, 265 (5th Cir. 2005) (attorney had notice because assets listed in indictment). The test is one of objective reasonableness as to what the claimant knew or should have known under the circumstances. *See United States v. Cuartes*, 155 F. Supp. 2d 1338, 1343 (S.D. Fla. 2001); *United States v. BCCI Holdings (Luxembourg) S.A. (Petition of American Express Bank II)*, 961 F. Supp. 287, 296 (D.D.C. 1997). The criminal forfeiture bona fide purchaser exemption statute basically is the same as the civil CAFRA post-offense innocent owner statute, *see* 18 U.S.C. § 983(d)(3)(A), so case law interpreting the two sections could be equally applied.[6]

A petitioner may testify at the ancillary hearing, and both sides may call and cross-examine additional witnesses in support or rebuttal of the claim. *See* 21 U.S.C. § 853(n)(5). Additionally, the court may consider the evidence and verdicts entered in the criminal trial in rendering its decision on the petition. *See United States v. Morgan*, 224 F.3d 339, 345 (4th Cir. 2000); *United States v. Messino*, 917 F. Supp. 1303, 1307 (N.D. Ill. 1996).

J. Final Order

The preliminary order of forfeiture does not become final automatically. It must be included in the sentence and judgment imposed on the defendant. *United States v. Bennett*, 423 F.3d 271, 275 (3d Cir. 2005). The court may amend the preliminary order of forfeiture to recognize any third-party rights established in the ancillary hearing. *See Fed. R. Crim. Pro.* 32.2(c)(2), (6). A final order of forfeiture entered gives the government clear title to sell or transfer the property. *See* 21 U.S.C. § 853(n)(7); *United States v. BCCI Holdings (Luxembourg) S.A. (Final Order of Forfeiture and Disbursement)*, 69 F. Supp. 2d 36, 37 (D.D.C. 1999). However, the criminal forfeiture judgment abates if the claimant dies before the appeal is final. *United States v. Oberlin*, 718 F.2d 894, 895 (9th Cir. 1983); *United States v. Lay*, 456 F. Supp. 2d 869, 874 (S.D. Tex. 2006).

A court may issue a forfeiture judgment and an order for restitution because they serve different functions. The forfeiture judgment separates the offender from the instrumentalities of the crime and serves as a disincentive to commit the crime, whereas the restitution order compensates victims. *United States v. O'Connor*, 321 F. Supp. 2d 722, 729 (E.D. Va. 2004).

If a claimant prevails in the criminal ancillary proceeding, he or she may be entitled to Equal Access to Justice Act fees, *see* 28 U.S.C. § 2412; *United States v. Bachner*, 877 F. Supp. 625, 627 (S.D. Fla. 1995); *United States v. Douglas*, 55 F.3d 584, 587 (11th Cir. 1995), but not CAFRA fees under 28 U.S.C. § 2465(b). *United States v. Gardiner*, 512 F. Supp. 2d 1270, 1272 (S.D. Fla. 2007).

K. State Criminal Forfeiture Procedure

Because many state criminal statutes are patterned after the federal criminal racketeering, *see* 18 U.S.C. § 1963, or narcotic forfeiture statutes, *see* 21 U.S.C. § 853, the state and federal criminal forfeiture procedures are very similar.

The property subject to forfeiture is charged in the criminal indictment, information, or complaint and may be supplemented by subsequent amended filings. *See Ariz. Rev. Stat. Ann.* § 13-4312.A; *Me. Rev. Stat. Ann.* Title 15 Ch. 517 § 5826.2. Some state statutes provide for a separate petition for forfeiture, which is filed in conjunction with the criminal case. *See Neb. Rev. Stat.* § 28-431(4); *Cal. Penal Code* § 186.4(a). Protective orders, including temporary restraining orders, injunctions, receivers, bonds, or other actions to preserve the property are available both preindictment and post-filing. *See Ga. Code Ann.* § 16-13-49(q); *Nev. Rev. Stat.* § 207.440; *Idaho Code* § 37-2805). Two states provide for court-issued seizure warrants. *See Neb. Rev. Stat.* § 28-431(2); *N.C. Gen. Stat.* § 90-112(b).

Upon service of the criminal forfeiture petition, a claimant must file a responsive pleading (claim and/or answer) within the deadlines specified by the statute. *See Neb. Rev. Stat.* § 28-431(4) (30 days to file answer); *Cal. Penal Code* § 186.5(a) (30 days to file verified claim). A few states allow for remission or mitigation of the forfeiture action to give third-party interests an early opportunity to prove their ownership interest and resolve the matter. *See N.C. Gen. Stat.* § 90-112.1; *Ore. Rev. Stat.* § 475A.090; *N.Y. Penal Code Law* § 480.10.9; *Ohio Rev. Code Ann.* § 2925.42(E)(2)(a).

The trial may be either before the court, *see Idaho Code* § 37-2801(2), or by the same jury that heard the criminal case, *see Cal. Penal Code* § 186.5(c)(1). A jury trial is bifurcated between the guilt and forfeiture phases. *See Me. Rev. Stat. Ann.* Title 15 Ch. 517 § 5826.4.C; *Ohio Rev. Code Ann.* § 2925.42(B)(4).

The defendant must be convicted of a criminal offense subject to forfeiture. *State v. Johnson,* 124 N.C. App. 462; 478 S.E.2d 16, 25 (N.C. App. 1996) (mere possession conviction not subject to forfeiture); *State v. Jones,* 158 N.C. App. 465; 581 S.E.2d 107, 110 (N.C. App. 2003) (not convicted of controlled substance offenses). The prosecutor must then prove a nexus between the criminal conviction and the seized property, *State v. Stevens,* 139 Idaho 670; 84 P.3d 1038, 1043 (Idaho App. 2004); *State v. Fink,* 92 N.C. App. 523; 375 S.E.2d 303, 309 (N.C. App. 1989), either beyond a reasonable doubt, *see Utah Code Ann.* § 24-1-8(4)(b); *Neb. Rev. Stat.* § 28-431(4); *State v. 1987 Jeep Wagoneer,* 241 Neb. 397; 488 N.W.2d 546, 548 (Neb. 1992), or by a preponderance of the evidence. *See Me. Rev. Stat. Ann.* Title 15 Ch. 517 § 5826.4.A; *Ohio Rev. Code Ann.* § 2925.42(B)(1)(a)(3)(a); *R.I. Gen. Laws* § 21-28-5.04.1(f)(6); *Tenn. Code Ann.* § 39-11-708(d); *People v. Arman,* 215 Ill.App.3d 687; 576 N.E.2d 11, 15 (Ill. App. 1991).

Rebuttable presumptions, such as money found in close proximity to controlled substances, *see N.Y. Penal Code Law* § 480.35, or property acquired during the period of time of the criminal offense is criminal proceeds may be available to prove the nexus to criminal activity. *See Tenn. Code Ann.* § 39-11-708(d).

State criminal forfeiture statutes also contain innocent owner exemptions, but the elements differ among the states. For example, in Nebraska the claimant must prove that he or she had no knowledge of the illegal activity by a preponderance of the evidence, *see Neb. Rev. Stat.* § 28-431(4), but in North Carolina the claimant may demonstrate either lack of knowledge or consent. *See N.C. Gen. Stat.* §§ 90-112(a)(4) b & d; *N.C. Gen. Stat.* § 90-113.1; *State v. Meyers,* 45 N.C. App. 672; 263 S.E.2d 835, 837 (N.C. App. 1980).

If the court finds that the property is subject to forfeiture, it enters a judgment of forfeiture and issues orders to seize all property not previously seized or in the possession of law enforcement. *See Ariz. Rev. Stat. Ann.* § 13-4312.G.

Ancillary hearing procedures for third-party interests also are similar to the federal system. Actual or published notice is given to potential third-party interest holders, and they may petition the court for a hearing on their legal interest. *See Ariz. Rev. Stat. Ann.* § 13-4312.H.1; *Ohio Rev. Code Ann.* § 2925.42(F)(2). Most states require third-party petitions to be filed within 30 days from the date of service, *see Ohio Rev. Code Ann.* § 2923.32(E)(2); *Utah Code Ann.* § 24-1-8(10)(b), although one state allows petitions to be filed as late as 180 days after service. *See R.I. Gen. Laws* § 21-28-5.04.1(f)(2). The ancillary hearing may be heard from 30 days, *see Ohio Rev. Code Ann.* § 2923.32; *R.I. Gen. Laws* § 21-28-5.04.1(f)(4), to 60 days after the petition is filed. *See Ariz. Rev. Stat. Ann.* § 13-4312.H.3; *Hawaii Rev. Stat.* § 712A-13(7)(c). At the hearing, the petitioner bears the burden of proof by a preponderance of the evidence that he or she qualifies for an exemption from forfeiture under the state statute. Several state statutes have adopted the federal criminal forfeiture exemption statute under 21 U.S.C. § 853(n)(6) or 18 U.S.C. § 1963(l)(6), which require that the petitioner have a vested or superior legal title or be a bona fide purchaser without knowledge that the property was forfeitable. *See Ohio Rev. Code Ann.* § 2925.42(F)(5)(a); *Utah Code Ann.* § 24-1-8(10)(f). There is no right to a jury determination of the issues in the ancillary hearing except in Utah. *See Utah Code Ann.* § 24-1-8(10)(b).

If the court determines that the third party has established his or her legal interest in the property and qualifies for an exemption under the statute, the order of forfeiture is amended.

A few states have discovery procedures comparable to those contained in the federal criminal statutes that provide for post-judgment discovery to locate property subject to the forfeiture order. *See Ariz. Rev. Stat. Ann.* § 13-4312.I; *Hawaii Rev. Stat.* § 712A-13(9).

Substitute assets also are available in many states to satisfy the forfeiture order on the same basis as under the federal statutes, *see* 21 U.S.C. § 853(p), when the property cannot be located or has been transferred to third parties, placed beyond the jurisdiction of the court, substantially diminished in value, or commingled with other property. *See Ga. Code Ann.* § 16-13-49(x)(1); *Idaho Code* § 37-2814; *Minn. Stat. Ann.* § 609.905 Subd. 2; *Nev. Rev. Stat.* § 207.420.

Although criminal forfeiture is a relatively new form of procedure, it is gaining widespread acceptance in both the federal and state systems, and with its provisions for money judgments and substitute assets, it is becoming especially helpful as a companion to civil *in rem* forfeiture.

Notes

1. *See "Alleged Spy Crimes, 'the most traitorous actions imaginable',"* *available at* www.cnn.com/SPECIALS/2001/hanssen/overview.html.

2. United States v. Robert Philip Hanssen Criminal No. 01-188-A, E.D. Va.

3. A question whether the pre-indictment restraining order provisions of 21 U.S.C. § 853(e) were incorporated with the addition of 28 U.S.C. § 2461(c) of CAFRA in 2001 to all civil forfeitures, *See* United States v. Razmilovic, 419 F.3d 134 (2d Cir. 2005), was resolved in 2006 with an amendment to the statute clarifying that the procedures of 21 U.S.C. § 853 apply to *all* stages of a criminal forfeiture proceeding. *See* 120 Stat. 192, 246.

4. *See* www.fbi.gov/libref/historic/famcases/ames/ames.htm.

5. A detailed review of the ancillary hearing and the federal exemption for third-party interests in criminal forfeiture actions is discussed in Stefan D. Cassella, *Third Party Rights in Criminal Forfeiture Cases,* 32 CRIM. L. BULL. 499 (Nov./Dec. 1996).

6. *See* Stefan D. Cassella, *The Uniform Innocent Owner Defense in Forfeiture,* 89 KY. L.J. 653, 692 (2001).

9 Parallel Proceedings

A. Background: "Tale of Two Cases"

1. Criminal Forfeiture

In June 1991, a federal criminal indictment was issued against Charles Arlt and several other defendants for conspiracy to manufacture methamphetamine and for money laundering. Arlt was convicted of those charges, but the conviction subsequently was reversed for failure to allow the defendant to represent himself at trial. *See United States v. Arlt*, 41 F.3d 516, 524 (9th Cir. 1994). In May 1995, a second indictment was returned, adding a criminal forfeiture allegation for all criminal proceeds related to the conspiracy. Arlt was convicted in April 1997 and received a life term in prison. *See United States v. Arlt*, 15 Fed. Appx. 431, 438 (9th Cir. 2001). In August 1998, after denying any third-party petitions, final orders of forfeiture were issued granting forfeiture of the criminal proceeds. *See United States v. Arlt*, 2000 U.S. App. LEXIS 21492 (9th Cir. 2000).

2. Civil Forfeiture

Five days after the criminal indictment was returned in June 1991, the government filed a civil *in rem* forfeiture action against over $537,000 U.S. Currency, an airplane, boat, helicopter, and several vehicles, alleging that they were used to facilitate or represented proceeds of the underlying criminal activity of the methamphetamine manufacturing conspiracy. The parties agreed to stay the civil proceedings until the parallel criminal action was completed. Upon conviction, summary judgment was entered in April 1993 based on the criminal conviction. That judgment was reversed in September 1994 when the appellate court determined that the forfeiture violated the double jeopardy clause. *See United States v. $405,089.23 U.S. Currency*, 33 F.3d 1210, 1222 (9th Cir. 1994). After the U.S. Supreme Court reversed the decision, holding that the double jeopardy clause was not violated, *see United States v. Ursery*, 518 U.S. 267, 275 (1996), the Ninth Circuit reversed the civil forfeiture judgment in September 1997 on the basis that there was an insufficient nexus between the property and the criminal activity. *See United States v. $405,089.23 U.S. Currency,* 122 F.3d 1285, 1290–91 (9th Cir. 1997).[1] In June 1998, the trial court found probable cause and granted summary judgment, *see United States v. $405,089.23 U.S. Currency,* 1998 U.S. Dist. LEXIS 8692, and the Ninth Circuit once again reversed, finding no probable cause for the nexus. *See United States v. $405,089.23 U.S. Currency,* 191 F.3d 461 (9th Cir. 1999). Finally, in May 2001 the government dismissed the civil *in rem* forfeiture case and defeated a request for EAJA fees. *See United States v. $405,089.23 U.S. Currency,* 9 Fed. Appx. 709, 711 (9th Cir. 2001).

This tale demonstrates the hazards and complications that may arise when attempting to litigate contemporaneous criminal and civil actions arising from the same offense and how legal strategy may change during the proceeding. For example, in the Arlt case, it was obvious that the government initially intended to forfeit the property civilly, reasoning that they would have a lower burden of proof, but due to court decisions restricting the evidence available in making the probable cause determination in the civil action, they were able to procedurally side step that problem by resorting to criminal forfeiture to include a review of all of the evidence introduced during the trial.

A review of the various rules, strategies, and pitfalls of parallel criminal and civil cases is the topic of this chapter.

B. Introduction

Parallel proceedings are defined as criminal and civil actions arising from the same transaction that involve a person who may be a party to both actions. There is no constitutional prohibition against parallel criminal and civil cases or investigations because the government has the right to vindicate several interests simultaneously in different forums. *See United States v. Kordel,* 397 U.S. 1, 11 (1970); *Securities & Exchange Commission v. Dresser,* 628 F.2d 1368, 1374–75 (D.C. Cir. 1980); *Securities & Exchange Commission v. First Financial Group of Texas,* 659 F.2d 660, 666–67 (5th Cir. 1981); *Cassell v. United States,* 348 F. Supp. 2d 602, 606 (M.D.N.C. 2004).

Thus, the government may file a civil forfeiture action while a criminal action is pending, *see United States v. One Parcel (Lot 41, Berryhill Farm),* 128 F.3d 1386, 1390 (10th Cir. 1997), seize property with a civil seizure order or initiate an administrative forfeiture and, when contested, proceed with criminal forfeiture, *see United States v. Candelaria-Silva,* 166 F.3d 19, 43 (1st Cir.

1999); *United States v. Lugo*, 63 F. Supp. 2d 896, 897 n.2 (N.D. Ill. 1999), or obtain a criminal forfeiture judgment and then revive a parallel civil forfeiture action. *See United States v. One 1978 Piper Cherokee Aircraft*, 91 F.3d 1204, 1206 (9th Cir. 1996). Even in the Arlt litigation, it was not vindictive for the government to amend the criminal indictment to add a criminal forfeiture allegation after receiving an adverse appellate decision on the parallel civil *in rem* action. *See United States v. Arlt*, 15 Fed. Appx. 431, 437 (9th Cir. 2001).

The issues that are raised by parallel proceedings include:

(1) Use of grand jury information;
(2) Civil discovery and the Fifth Amendment privilege against self-incrimination;
(3) Stay of the civil case;
(4) Application of the Fifth Amendment double jeopardy clause; and
(5) Res judicata and collateral estoppel.

C. Grand Jury Information

Under Federal Rules of Criminal Procedure 6(e)(3)(C)(i), a court order is required before grand jury information may be disclosed to another party, including government attorneys. *See United States v. Sells Engineering*, 463 U.S. 418, 420 (1983); *Illinois v. Abbott & Associates, Inc.* 460 U.S. 557, 568 (1983). Thus, a civil forfeiture order that was based on grand jury information obtained without a disclosure order could be reversed. *See United States v. Coughlan*, 842 F.2d 737, 740 (4th Cir. 1988).

This dilemma was resolved with CAFRA Section 10, 106 Pub. L. No. 185, 114 Stat. 202, 217, by amending 18 U.S.C. § 3322(a) to allow that any grand jury information received as a government attorney may be disclosed to another government attorney for use in connection with any civil forfeiture provision of federal law.

D. Civil Discovery and the Fifth Amendment Privilege Against Self-Incrimination

Because civil discovery rules are very broad, there is a concern that they may be used in the criminal trial to give an unfair advantage to either the defense or prosecution. Thus, the government may not act in bad faith and bring a civil case solely to obtain evidence for a criminal prosecution, *see United States v. Kordel*, 397 U.S. 1, 11–12 (1970), and the defense should not be allowed to make use of the liberal civil discovery procedures to avoid the restrictions on criminal discovery. *See Campbell v. Eastland*, 307 F.2d 478, 487 (5th Cir. 1962); *Founding Church of Scientology v. Kelley*, 77 F.R.D. 378, 380 (D.D.C. 1977).

There is an inherent tension between the purposes of civil discovery and the Fifth Amendment privilege against self-incrimination. The Fifth Amendment privilege covers responses that furnish a link in the chain of evidence needed to prosecute the claimant, *see Hoffman v. United States*, 341 U.S. 479, 486 (1951), and may be asserted in "any proceeding civil or criminal, administrative or judicial, investigatory or adjudicatory. . . ." *See Kastigar v. United States*, 406 U.S. 441, 444 (1972).

There are, however, limitations to invoking the Fifth Amendment in forfeiture actions. First, it does not prevent the government from requiring a claimant to establish standing by asserting a valid property interest in the seized items. *See Baker v. United States*, 722 F.2d 517, 519 (9th Cir. 1983). Second, it may not be used as a substitute for a burden of proof that belongs to the claimant. *See United States v. Certain Real Property 566 Hendrickson Boulevard*, 986 F.2d 990, 996 (6th Cir. 1993); *Arango v. United States Department of the Treasury*, 115 F.3d 922, 926 (11th Cir. 1997); *People v. Delatorre*, 279 Ill. App. 3d 1014; 666 N.E.2d 33, 35 (Ill. App. 1996) (standing); *State v. $8,000.00 U.S. Currency*, 827 So. 2d 634, 639 (La. App. 2002) (same). Third, a blanket refusal to answer all questions is an improper invocation of the Fifth Amendment and is not a defense to a forfeiture proceeding. *See United States v. $250,000 in United States Currency*, 808 F.2d 895, 901 (1st Cir. 1987); *United States v. Lot 5, Fox Grove*, 23 F.3d 359, 364 (11th Cir. 1994); *United States v. $148,840.00 in U.S. Currency*, 485 F. Supp. 2d 1254, 1259 (D.N.M. 2007). Finally, the privilege is not self-executing and may be affirmatively waived or lost by not asserting it in a timely fashion. *See Maness v. Myers*, 419 U.S. 449, 466 (1975). In sum, a claimant cannot use the privilege as a sword and a shield. *See United States v. Rylander*, 460 U.S. 752, 758 (1983).

An additional consequence for asserting the privilege is that it may lead to an adverse inference against the claimant at trial. The U.S. Supreme Court has held that the "Fifth Amendment does not forbid an adverse inference against parties to civil actions when they refuse to testify in response to probative evidence offered against them . . .," *see Baxter v. Palmigiano*, 425 U.S. 308, 318 (1976), and there is no violation of due process where a party is faced with the choice of testifying or invoking the Fifth Amendment. *See United States v. Kordel*, 397 U.S. 1, 7–8 (1970).

Several federal and state courts have allowed adverse inferences to be drawn against a claimant in civil forfeiture actions, *see United States v. Thomas*, 913 F.2d 1111, 1115 (4th Cir. 1990); *United States v. A Single Family Residence*, 803 F.2d 625, 630 n.4 (11th Cir. 1986); *United States v. $75,040.00 in U.S. Currency*, 785 F. Supp. 1423, 1429 (D. Or. 1991); *United States v. Two Parcels of Real Property*, 92 F.3d 1123, 1129–30 (11th Cir. 1996); *United States v. Two Parcels (2730 Highway 31)*, 909 F. Supp. 1450, 1457 (M.D. Ala. 1995); *United States v. $433,980 in U.S. Currency*, 473 F. Supp. 2d 685, 692 (E.D.N.C. 2007); *People v. $1,124,905 U.S. Currency*, 177 Ill.2d 314; 685 N.E.2d 1370, 1379 (Ill. 1997), but a few have ruled against it, reasoning that they are more closely related to criminal sanctions. *See United States v. Real Property Known & Numbered as Rural Route 1, Box 137-B*, 24 F.3d 845, 851 (6th Cir. 1994).

There is an evidentiary burden or restriction assumed by the claimant when asserting a Fifth Amendment privilege. For example, a claimant cannot invoke the Fifth Amendment during discovery and then attempt to produce the same testimony to defeat summary judgment or at trial. *See United States v. Parcels of Land*, 903 F.2d 36, 42–43 (1st Cir. 1990); *In Re Edmond*, 934 F.2d 1304, 1306 (4th Cir. 1991); *United States v. Certain Real Property 4003–4005 Fifth Avenue*, 840 F. Supp. 6, 7 (E.D.N.Y. 1993); *United States v. One 1991 Chevrolet Corvette*, 390 F. Supp. 2d 1059, 1063–64 (S.D. Ala. 2005); *United States v. U.S. Currency in the Sum of $185,000*, 455 F. Supp. 2d 145, 150 (E.D.N.Y. 2006). Further, if the claimant elects to produce evidence, the Fifth Amendment does not immunize that testimony from cross-examination, *see Brown v. United States*, 356 U.S. 148, 156 (1958), and if a witness testifies on direct and then asserts the Fifth Amendment to avoid cross-examination, the court may strike the testimony. *See Lawson v. Murray*, 837 F.2d 653, 656 (4th Cir. 1988).

Options to consider when the Fifth Amendment is invoked during discovery include staying the civil case, seeking sanctions to prevent the claimant from testifying, or striking the answer and entering default judgment. *See Whippany Paper Board Co. v. Alfano*, 176 N.J. Super. 363; 423 A.2d 648, 653 (N.J. Super. A.D. 1980).

E. Stay of the Civil Case

At times the government desires to stay the civil case to prevent discovery of its criminal case or the claimant wants a stay to avoid a waiver of his or her Fifth Amendment rights while the criminal case is pending. The courts have discretionary power to stay discovery in the interests of justice when special circumstances demonstrate that the proceedings may prejudice substantial rights of either the claimant or the government. *See Securities & Exchange Commission v. Dresser Industries,* 628 F.2d 1368, 1375 (D.C. Cir. 1980).

Additionally, there is statutory authority found in the forfeiture codes for stay of the civil proceedings.

In federal forfeiture, CAFRA Section 8, 106 Pub. L. No. 185, 114 Stat. 202, 216, amended 18 U.S.C. § 981(g) to provide for a stay of the civil forfeiture case for both the government and the claimant. The criteria for granting the stay differ, however.

The government may request a stay if the court makes a finding that civil discovery will adversely affect a related criminal investigation or prosecution. *See* 18 U.S.C. § 983(g)(1); *United States v. All Funds on Deposit in Business Marketing Account,* 319 F. Supp. 2d 290, 294 (E.D.N.Y. 2004) (compromise confidential informant); *United States v. All Funds on Deposit in Suntrust Account Number XXXXXXXXXXX8359,* 456 F. Supp. 2d 64, 65–66 (D.D.C. 2006) (same). The government may submit evidence in an ex-parte hearing to avoid disclosure that would adversely affect the ongoing investigation or trial. *See* 18 U.S.C. § 983(g)(5); *United States v. GAF Financial Services,* 335 F. Supp. 2d 1371, 1373 n.2 (S.D. Fla. 2004).

A claimant may request a stay if: (1) her or she is the subject of a related criminal investigation or case; (2) he or she has standing to assert a claim in the civil forfeiture action; and (3) failure to grant the stay will burden the right of the claimant against self-incrimination in the related investigation or criminal case. *See* 18 U.S.C. § 981(g)(2). A finding of standing for this motion does not preclude the government from challenging it in a subsequent motion. *See* 18 U.S.C. § 981(g)(7).

A stay should be granted anytime that issuance of a protective order would allow one party to proceed with discovery while the opposing party would be essentially precluded from doing so. *United States v. One Assortment of 73 Firearms,* 352 F. Supp. 2d 2, 4 (D. Me 2005). The parties should be placed on equal footing during the discovery process. However, the stay may be denied if the criminal and civil cases are not related and it is not timely pursued. *United States v. U.S. Currency in the Sum of $185,000,* 455 F. Supp. 2d 145, 151 (E.D.N.Y. 2006).

Many states have similar provisions that allow for the stay of civil discovery, *see Kan. Stat. Ann.* § 60-4112(p); *Tenn. Code Ann.* § 39-11-710(g); *Money of U.S. in Amount of $8,500.00 v. State,* 774 S.W.2d 788, 793 (Tex. App. 1989), or the civil proceeding pending the resolution of the criminal case. *See Mass. Ann. Laws* Ch. 94C § 47(d); *Hawaii Rev. Stat.* § 712A-11(8); *Ore. Rev. Stat.* § 475A.075(5); *Va. Code Ann.* § 19.2-386.10B; *In re Forfeiture of $2,367.00 U.S. Currency,* 91 Ohio App.3d 384, 632 N.E.2d 943, 946 (Ohio App. 1993). However, conclusory statements alleging that civil discovery would compromise the criminal case may be insufficient. *Christopher v. State,* 185 Ga. App. 532; 364 S.E.2d 905, 906 (Ga. App. 1988).

At times, continuing the civil forfeiture case may not be the best option because it will delay resolution of the matter, and the seized asset may depreciate or incur substantial storage and maintenance costs. There are alternatives that the court may consider to control discovery in lieu of a complete stay of the civil proceeding including:

- Issuing protective orders, *see* 18 U.S.C. § 981(g)(3); *Fed. R. Civ. Pro.* 26(c); *Degen v. United States,* 517 U.S. 820, 826 (1996);
- Quashing or modifying subpoenas, *see Fed. R. Civ. Pro.* 45(c);
- Limiting examinations, *see Fed. R. Civ. Pro.* 26(c); *Degen,* 517 U.S. at 826;
- Sealing confidential material, *see United States v. $9,041,598.68,* 163 F.3d 238, 251 (5th Cir. 1998);
- Limiting attendance and sealing the deposition, *see D'Ippolito v. American Oil Co.,* 272 F. Supp. 310, 312 (S.D.N.Y. 1967); and
- Granting use immunity or certification of nonprosecution, *see United States v. U.S. Currency,* 626 F.2d 11, 16 (6th Cir. 1980).

F. Fifth Amendment Double Jeopardy Clause

The double jeopardy clause protects against multiple punishments for the same offense. *See North Carolina v. Pearce,* 395 U.S. 711, 717 (1969). The issue has been raised whether transactionally related criminal and civil cases are subject to the double jeopardy clause.

Although the U.S. Supreme Court previously had held that the double jeopardy clause was inapplicable to a civil forfeiture that followed an acquittal in a prior criminal proceeding, *see United States v. One Assortment of 89 Firearms,* 465 U.S. 354, 359 (1984), two federal appellate courts later determined that parallel criminal and civil forfeiture actions constitute punishment and were barred under the double jeopardy clause. *See United States v. $405,089.23 U.S. Currency,* 33 F.3d 1210, 1216 (9th Cir. 1994); *United States v. Ursery,* 59

F.3d 568, 573 (6th Cir. 1995). After a spate of considerable federal and state appellate litigation on this issue, the U.S. Supreme Court reviewed both cases in a consolidated appeal and reversed the lower court's holding that civil forfeitures do not constitute "punishment" for purposes of the double jeopardy clause. *See United States v. Ursery,* 518 U.S. 267, 289 (1996).

Although the *Ursery* decision would seem to end the debate, there are two states that do apply the double jeopardy clause to certain state forfeiture statutes and prohibit parallel criminal and civil actions, finding that they are either criminal statutes, *see Nebraska v. Juan Franco, Jr.,* 257 Neb. 15; 594 N.W.2d 633, 639 (Neb. 1999), or barred under the protection of the state double jeopardy clause. *See State v. Nunez,* 129 N.M. 63; 2 P.3d 264, 281 (1999); see also Chapter 12, Section C. Therefore, when analyzing double jeopardy issues there are five questions that should be addressed.

1. Did the defendant contest the civil case?

An uncontested civil forfeiture does not violate the double jeopardy clause because a default judgment does not constitute punishment as defined by the Fifth Amendment. *See United States v. Renato Torres,* 28 F.3d 1463, 1465 (7th Cir. 1994: *United States v. Kemmish,* 869 F. Supp. 803, 805 (S.D. Cal. 1994); *United States v. Amiel,* 995 F.2d 367, 370 (2d Cir. 1993); *State v. Guenzel,* 140 N.H. 685; 671 A.2d 545, 547 (N.H. 1996) (claimant waived forfeiture).

2. Are the cases being litigated by the same governmental power?

Separate criminal and civil actions by state and federal authorities do not violate the Fifth Amendment if each is acting as an independent governmental entity under the principle of dual sovereignty recognized in American federalism. *See Department of Revenue of Montana v. Kurth Ranch,* 511 U.S. 767, 782 n.22 (1994); *United States v. Certain Real Property (38 Whaler's Cove Drive),* 954 F.2d 29, 38 (2d Cir. 1992); *United States v. Branum,* 872 F. Supp. 801, 803 (S.D. Cal. 1994); *United States v. Alverez,* 235 F.3d 1086, 1090 (8th Cir. 2000).

3. Are the criminal and civil cases being litigated in the same proceeding?

Separate criminal and civil actions litigated in the same proceeding do not raise double jeopardy protections. *See United States v. Halper,* 490 U.S. 435, 450 (1989); *Department of Revenue of Montana,* 511 U.S. at 778. A few states do provide for consolidation of the civil forfeiture with the criminal case for trial. *See Cal. Health & Safety Code* § 11488.4(i)(3); *N.M. Code Ann.* § 31-27-6C; *Ore. Rev. Stat.* § 475A.075(6).

4. Is the civil penalty punitive or remedial?

Remedial civil actions are not prohibited from parallel proceedings under the Fifth Amendment, *see Halper,* 490 U.S. at 448–449, *Austin v. United States,* 509 U.S. 602, 608 n.4 (1993), and civil *in rem* forfeiture actions are remedial under the double jeopardy clause. *See Ursery,* 518 U.S. at 278; *United States v. One Lot of $17,220 in U.S. Currency,* 183 F.R.D. 54, 56 (D. R.I. 1998).

5. Do the criminal and civil cases pass the "same elements" test?

If the criminal and civil actions are based on different offenses or independent elements, they do not violate the double jeopardy clause. *See United States v. Dixon,* 509 U.S. 688, 696–97 (1993).

In jurisdictions where there may be a concern about potential double jeopardy challenges, there are a few strategies that may be followed to circumvent problems:

- Use criminal forfeiture procedures or consolidate with the pending criminal action;
- Have federal and state entities separately pursue criminal and civil actions under the dual sovereign rule;
- Global settlement of criminal and civil actions in one proceeding;
- Stipulated waiver of double jeopardy challenge as part of any criminal or civil settlement.

G. Res Judicata and Collateral Estoppel

Res Judicata is a bar to any subsequent litigation when:

(1) The prior judgment was a final judgment on the merits;
(2) The same parties are involved in both lawsuits;
(3) The two actions are based on the same issues and material facts; and
(4) The two proceedings present the same cause of action.

See Commissioner v. Sunnen, 333 U.S. 591, 597 (1948); *United States v. Mumford,* 630 F.2d 1023, 1027 (4th Cir. 1980).

Generally, res judicata should not be an issue in civil forfeitures because the criminal prosecution and civil forfeiture represent different parties, issues, and causes of action. *See United States v. Tilley,* 1998 WL 812395 (N.D. Tex 1998); *United States v. Wade,* 230 F. Supp. 2d 1298, 1308 n.9 (M.D. Fla. 2002).

Collateral estoppel prevents relitigation of an issue of ultimate fact that has been determined by a valid judgment on the merits in any future lawsuit between the same parties. *See United States v. One 1975 Chevrolet,* 495 F. Supp. 737, 741 (W.D. Mich. 1980); *Concepcion v. United States,* 298 F. Supp. 2d 351, 357 (E.D.N.Y. 2004) (jury found that money was drug proceeds). A criminal conviction works as an estoppel in subsequent civil proceedings as to those matters determined by the criminal judgment. *See Kennedy v. Mendoza-Martinez,* 372 U.S. 144, 157 (1963); *United States v. Beaty,* 245 F.3d 617, 624 (6th Cir. 2001); *United States v. Real Property (Parcel 03179-005R),* 287 F. Supp. 2d 54, 63 (D.D.C. 2003).

Before collateral estoppel applies, there must be a showing that:

(1) The issue determined is identical to that involved in the subsequent action, *see United States v. 16 Sequoia, Hawthorne Woods, Ill.,* 764 F. Supp. 1285, 1289 (N.D. Ill. 1991);

(2) The issue was actually litigated in the earlier action, *see United States (DEA) v. One 1987 Jeep,* 972 F.2d 472, 477 (2d Cir. 1992); *Matter of $5,662 U.S. Currency,* 714 A.2d 106, 111 (Del. Super. 1998) (lawful search); and

(3) The party against whom estoppel is asserted is a party or was in privity with a party in the prior case, *see United States v. One Single Family Residence 18755 North Bay Road,* 13 F.3d 1493, 1496 (11th Cir. 1994).

If a defendant is convicted in a criminal case, he or she is estopped in the civil proceeding from denying facts that established the criminal conviction. *See 16 Sequoia,* 764 F. Supp. at 1287–88; *United States v. One 1987 Mercedes Benz 300E,* 820 F. Supp. 248, 253 (E.D. Va. 1993). However, an acquittal in a criminal case does not bar a subsequent civil case because there is no identity of issues, and the civil case has a lower burden of proof. *See United States v. One Assortment of 89 Firearms,* 465 U.S. 354, 366 (1984); *One Lot of Emerald Cut Stones v. United States,* 409 U.S. 232, 234–35 (1972); *United States v. Dunn,* 802 F.2d 646, 647 (2d Cir. 1986). However, the state is precluded from relitigating issues that were resolved against it in the criminal case. *State v. Rodriguez,* 130 N.J. Super. 57; 324 A.2d 911, 913 (N.J. Super. A.D. 1974); *State ex rel. Edmondson v. Two Hundred Thousand Four Hundred Ninety Dol-*

lars ($200,490.00) in U.S. Currency, 39 P.3d 160, 163 (Okla. Civ. App. 2001) (no violation of state drug statute).

If the government litigates and loses a civil case, collateral estoppel may apply in any subsequent criminal prosecution. *See United States v. Mumford,* 630 F.2d 1023, 1027 (4th Cir. 1980); *People v. One 1979 Chevrolet C-20 Van,* 248 Ill. App. 3d 640; 618 N.E.2d 1290, 1293 (Ill. App. 1993). However, if the government merely acquiesces to a finding in a criminal sentencing, it is not precluded from contesting that fact in a subsequent civil action. *See United States v. U.S. Currency in the Amount of $119,984,* 304 F.3d 165, 171 (2d Cir. 2002).

H. Tactical Considerations and Options

There are three options when filing parallel criminal and civil actions. The first option is to file and complete the criminal case prior to any civil proceedings, as a delay in filing a civil action because of a criminal parallel proceeding does not violate the claimant's due process rights. *See United States v. Eight Thousand Eight Hundred & Fifty Dollars ($8,850) in U.S. Currency,* 461 U.S. 555, 564 (1983). Advantages of this procedure are:

- Grand Jury issues are resolved;
- Discovery issues are determined;
- The defendant will not benefit from civil discovery in the criminal case;
- The defendant will not be able to assert the Fifth Amendment privilege against self-incrimination on evidence already disclosed in the criminal trial;
- No necessity to move for a stay of the civil case to protect confidential information;
- Issues determined in the criminal conviction will have collateral estoppel effect on similar issues in the civil proceeding;
- If the defendant is convicted, it encourages settlement of the civil matters.

Disadvantages are:

- If property has been seized for civil forfeiture any delay initiating the forfeiture action could violate CAFRA and state filing deadlines. *See* 18 U.S.C. § 983(a)(1) and Table 4-2.

- Criminal discovery is limited and is generally not reciprocal.
- Discourages settlement of civil case if no criminal conviction.
- Delays obtaining civil remedies until criminal case is resolved.

The second option would be to file the civil proceeding before the criminal prosecution. The advantages to doing this are:

- The lower burden of proof in the civil case;
- Civil discovery is broader and reciprocal;
- It forces the defendant to assert the Fifth Amendment privilege against self-incrimination to maintain standing in the civil case;
- Defendant may waive Fifth Amendment rights, and testimony may be used in subsequent criminal prosecution.

Disadvantages are:

- Defendant may obtain a stay and thwart discovery; and
- Collateral estoppel may bar religitation of issues determined adverse to the government in the subsequent criminal case. See *United States v. Eight Thousand Eight Hundred & Fifty Dollars in U.S. Currency Id.* p. 567.

The third option is simultaneous criminal prosecution and civil proceeding. Advantages include:

- Obtain concurrent criminal penalties and civil sanctions;
- Coordination will allow successful preseizure planning to occur;
- The subject of the investigation will not learn that he or she is the target of an investigation if civil and criminal investigations are planned jointly;
- May use civil discovery in the pending criminal case;
- No adverse collateral estoppel issues; and
- Encourages global settlement of criminal and civil cases.

Disadvantages include:

- Difficulty in coordinating concurrent criminal and civil cases, *see United States v. Millan-Colon*, 836 F. Supp. 994, 1003 (S.D.N.Y. 1993);

- Defendant may obtain a stay of the civil case until the conclusion of the criminal case, *see United States v. All Assets of Statewide Auto Parts, Inc.,* 971 F.2d 896, 905 (2d Cir. 1992);
- Government must avoid conflicts in the application of the Fifth Amendment privilege against self-incrimination to the criminal and civil actions; and
- Ethical considerations involved in global settlement. See Chapter 13 Section I.

I. Summary

Most federal and state jurisdictions choose to file and litigate separately filed criminal and civil actions as outlined in option 3 above. Careful coordination of the criminal and civil actions is essential to circumvent adverse consequences of a plea or dismissal of either of the related cases. Ethical issues relating to global settlement of criminal and civil actions is discussed in Chapter 13, Ethical Considerations.

Note

1. This decision was based on the rule in the Ninth Circuit in effect at the time that the government was required to establish probable cause for forfeiture as of the date of filing the complaint for forfeiture. *See* United States v. $191,910.00 U.S. Currency, 16 F.3d 1051, 1071 (9th Cir. 1994). This prevented the government from relying on the defendant's conviction or any evidence acquired after the filing of the complaint in the probable cause determination. This anomaly was corrected in 2000 by CAFRA Sec. 2, 106 Pub. L. No. 185, 14 Stat. 202, 206, (18 U.S.C. § 983(c) (2)), which now permits evidence gathered after the filing to establish the forfeitability of the property.

10 Disposition of Forfeited Property

A. Introduction

One of the goals of asset forfeiture is to "rededicate the money from the illegal activity to the public good."[1] In fiscal year 2007, the federal government seized almost $1.6 billion.[2] This chapter will review the disposition of property after it has been forfeited and how those proceeds are spent by the federal and state agencies.

B. Federal Distribution

The principle statutory provisions for distribution of civilly forfeited property are found at 21 U.S.C. § 881(e) and 18 U.S.C. § 981(e) and for criminally forfeited property at 21 U.S.C. § 853(h)(1); 18 U.S.C. § 982(b)(1); and 18 U.S.C. § 1963(g).) For ease of reference, we will utilize the civil drug forfeiture procedures contained in 21 U.S.C. § 881(e).

The federal government has established two separate funds for the deposit of forfeited proceeds. The Department of Justice Assets Forfeiture Fund is authorized under 28 U.S.C. § 524(c), and the Department of the Treasury Forfeiture Fund at 31 U.S.C. § 9703(a). Federal Treasury investigative agencies (i.e., U.S. Immigration and Customs Enforcement (ICE), Internal Revenue Service, and U.S. Secret Service) participate in the Treasury forfeiture program, and all other federal agencies are part of the Department of Justice program (i.e., Federal Bureau of Investigation (FBI), Drug Enforcement Administration (DEA), and Bureau of Alcohol, Tobacco and Firearms (ATF). In this section we will follow the guidelines for the Justice Asset Forfeiture Fund.

When cash is ordered forfeited, it is transferred into the Assets Forfeiture Fund. *See* 28 U.S.C. § 524(c)(4). Personal property is sold at public sale[3] and, after deducting the cost of sales, *see* 28 U.S.C. § 524(e)(2)(A), the net proceeds are deposited into the fund. *See* 28 U.S.C. § 524(e)(2)(B).

In lieu of selling personal property, the federal investigative agency also has the option of retaining the property for law enforcement use, *see* 21 U.S.C. § 881(e)(1)(A); 18 U.S.C. § 981(e); 19 U.S.C. § 1616a(c)(1)(A); 31 U.S.C. § 9703(h)(1)(A), or transferring it to another federal agency that directly participated in the forfeiture. *See* 21 U.S.C. § 881(e)(1)(A); 18 U.S.C. § 981(e)(1); 19 U.S.C. § 1616a(c)(1)(B)(i); 31 U.S.C. § 9703(h)(1)(B)(i).

Expenditures from the fund are authorized for costs related to property management, *see* 28 U.S.C. § 524(c)(1)(A), informant awards, *see* 28 U.S.C. § 524(c)(1)(B)–(C), payoffs to lien holders and mortgagees, *see* 28 U.S.C. § 524(c)(1)(D), claims of remission and mitigation, *see* 28 U.S.C. § 524(c)(1)(E), and investigative expenses. *See* 28 U.S.C. § 524(c)(1)(I). Courts cannot order disbursement of forfeiture funds not authorized under the statute. *United States v. Wilkinson*, 628 F. Supp. 29, 31 (D. Colo. 1985) (federal income tax liability).

C. Federal Equitable Sharing

Equitable sharing is an important component of the federal forfeiture program and is authorized in numerous federal statutes, including drug forfeiture, *see* 21 U.S.C. §§ 881(e)(1)(A), (e)(3), money laundering and fraud offenses, *see* 18 U.S.C. § 981(e)(2), racketeering, *see* 18 U.S.C. § 1963(g), and customs offenses. *See* 19 U.S.C. § 1616a; 31 U.S.C. §§ 9703(a)(1)(G), (b)(4).

The importance of federal equitable sharing to state and local law enforcement agencies cannot be overstated. From 2003 through 2007, federal payments were made to 8,000 agencies amounting to $1.4 billion, and in fiscal year 2007 it totaled $417 million.[4]

The general rules for federal equitable sharing are contained in the U.S. Department of Justice publication, *A Guide to Equitable Sharing of Federally Forfeited Property for State and Local Law Enforcement Agencies* or Department of Treasury publication, *Guide to Equitable Sharing for Foreign Countries and Federal, State, Local Law Enforcement Agencies.* For this section, reference will be restricted to the Department of Justice Guidebook.

A state or local law enforcement agency may request participation in the sharing of a federal forfeiture by filing either a Justice Department DAG-71 or Treasury Department TD F 92-22.46 form with the appropriate federal law enforcement agency within 60 days from the date of the seizure. *See Guide to Equitable Sharing,* at 6. The amount shared will depend upon the type of forfeiture. On joint investigations, the share will be based on the degree of direct participation of the agency resulting in the forfeiture. This generally is determined by the hours contributed by the agents involved in the case, but may include additional factors such as (1) whether the agency originated the information that led to the seizure; (2) provided unique or indispensable assistance or; (3) converted a state investigation into a multi-jurisdictional action by joining forces with federal agencies. *See Guide to Equitable Sharing*, at 7.

On adoptive forfeitures where all of the preseizure activity was conducted by the state or local agency, the federal share is a flat 20% of the net proceeds. *See Guide to Equitable Sharing*, at 7. See also Chapter 4, Section B for more detail on joint investigation versus adoptive forfeiture.

Additionally, the state or local law enforcement agency may request that personal or real property be transferred to it for law enforcement use. *See* 21 U.S.C. § 881(e)(1)(A); 18 U.S.C. § 981(e)(2); 19 U.S.C. § 1616a(c)(1)(B)(ii); 31 U.S.C. § 9703(h)(1)(B)(ii); *Guide to Equitable Sharing*, at 14–15.

The decision maker who determines the equitable share for each requesting agency depends on the type of forfeiture case and dollar value. The head of the federal investigative agency makes the decision for administrative forfeitures under $1 million. Likewise, for judicial criminal or civil forfeitures under $1 million, the local U.S. Attorney determines the equitable share. For all cases involving property valued at $1 million or more, the Office of the Deputy Attorney General approves the sharing percentages. *See Guide to Equitable Sharing*, at 9.

D. Use of Equitably Shared Federal Funds

Equitably shared property is designed to enhance and supplement law enforcement resources. Property awarded must be used in accordance with federal policy guidelines. Failure to comply with the provisions could result in sanctions being imposed against the agency, including disbarment from participation in future sharing, offsets from future sharing to compensate for the impermissible use, civil enforcement, or criminal prosecution. *See Guide to Equitable Sharing*, at 19; *United States v. Kranovich*, 244 F. Supp. 2d 1109, 1112 (D. Nev. 2003).

Permissible uses of shared property include activities designed to enhance future investigations, such as payment of overtime, provide law enforcement training, purchase equipment, improve law enforcement facilities, upgrade detention facilities, and conduct drug education awareness programs. *See Guide to Equitable Sharing*, at 10. Impermissible expenditures include payment of salaries for existing positions, nonlaw enforcement expenses, or extravagant expenditures. *See Guide to Equitable Sharing*, at 12.

It is a firm rule in the federal program that the sharing is to increase or supplement the resources of the agency and not supplant existing budgetary resources. *See Guide to Equitable Sharing*, at 14. To insure compliance, the federal Justice and Treasury forfeiture programs require an equitable sharing agreement to be completed by the state or local law enforcement agency and an annual certification report to be filed at the conclusion of the agency fiscal year. *See Guide to Equitable Sharing*, at 19.

Most state statutes provide that federally shared funds are exempt from state distribution requirements. *Colo. Rev. Stat.* § 16-13-601; 16-13-702; *Cal. Health & Saf. Code* § 11489(c). In some states, if the amount in the federal fund exceeds a certain monetary threshold, the balance is transferred to the state forfeiture fund. *Ark. Code Ann.* § 5-64-503(i)(4)(B); *Utah Code Ann.* § 24-1-15(8)(b).

A challenge to limit the use of federally shared funds received by state law enforcement agencies was recently waged in Oregon and Utah. By voter referendum, these two states mandated that federally shared proceeds were restricted to the distribution provisions mandated by state law. *See Ore. Const.* Art. XV Sec. 10(8); *Utah Code Ann.* § 24-1-15(3).[5] Under the state distribution formulas, the majority of the funds were ordered spent for substance abuse programs or the state school fund. As these provisions conflicted with the Justice and Treasury equitable sharing guidelines, legal challenges were filed.

In Utah, the court determined that the state restriction on federally shared funds did not violate the supremacy clause of the U.S. Constitution because the program was voluntary, and the state could elect not to participate. *Kennard v. Leavitt*, 246 F. Supp. 2d 1177, 1183 (D. Utah. 2002). This restriction was later modified by state legislative action. *Utah Code Ann.* § 24-1-15(8)(a); Utah Laws 2004, c. 296, § 11, eff. May 3, 2004.

The restrictions on civil forfeiture imposed by Oregon Measure 3 led most police agencies to significantly reduce use of this statute. Seizures by police agencies dropped 75% between 2000 and 2001.[6] A state drug task force challenged the constitutionality of Oregon Measure 3 and its limits on the use of federal equitable sharing funds. After extensive litigation, the measure was upheld by the Oregon Supreme Court in *Lincoln Interagency Narcotics Team (LINT) v. Kitzhaber*, 341 Or. 496; 145 P.3d 151 (2006). Consequently, forfeiture activity using this statute essentially has ceased.[7]

E. State Distribution

State forfeiture actions also generate significant resources to state and local agencies. A small sampling of four recent state annual forfeiture reports shows combined forfeiture distributions of $51.3 million.[8]

Table 10-1 is a summary of state forfeiture distribution statutes. A review of these statutes indicates the following patterns concerning state forfeiture distributions.

Table 10-1
Summary of State Asset Forfeiture Statutes
Distribution Procedures

State	Distribution	Statute
Alabama	Retain for official use. Percentage determined by the court depending on agency contribution.	Ala. Code § 20-2-93 (e)
Alaska	Retain for official use if property is worth $5,000 or less. 75% of property to law enforcement agency for money or if property is worth more than $5,000. Forfeited property is disposed by Commissioner of Administration who may destroy, sell, transfer for law enforcement use or forward to DEA	Ak. Stat. § 17.30.112; 17.30.122
Arizona	Retain for official use. Property sold. Money to reimburse law enforcement agencies for investigative costs and expenses or prosecution. Excess funds deposited into anti-racketeering fund of state or county.	Ariz. Rev. Stat. Ann. § 13-4315
Arkansas	Retain for official use not to exceed 2 years unless approved by court on annual basis. When property sold 80% to retaining agency and 20% to state treasury for crime lab equipment fund. Asset Forfeiture fund maintained by county prosecuting attorney. If fund exceeds $20,000 during calendar year 20% of the subsequent sale or proceeds are deposited in state asset forfeiture fund for drug intervention, education, crime lab and drug court.	Ark. Code Ann. § 5-64-505 (h) & (i)
California	65% to law enforcement agency of which 15% is set aside for drug education and gang prevention; 10% to prosecutor; 24% to state general fund and 1% for statewide asset forfeiture training.	Cal. Health & Safety Code § 11489

Table 10-1 (continued)
Summary of State Asset Forfeiture Statutes
Distribution Procedures

State	Distribution	Statute
Colorado	Retain for law enforcement use. Up to 10% to District Attorney for litigation costs and 1% for court costs. 50% to the general fund of governing board for the law enforcement agency. Balance for alcohol detox and substance abuse treatment	Co. Rev. Stat. § 16-13-311; § 16-13-506
Connecticut	Deposited in drug assets forfeiture revolving account. 70% to Department of Public Safety & local police departments with 15% used for drug education; 20% to Department of Mental Health; 10% to Division of Criminal Justice for prosecution	Conn. Gen. Stat. § 54-36i
Delaware	Retain for official use. After payment of law enforcement expenses, balance of proceeds deposited in Special Law Enforcement Assistance Fund.	Del. Code Ann. Title 16 § 4784 (f)
District of Columbia	Retain for official use. Proceeds to finance law enforcement activities and any remaining balance to finance programs to rehabilitate drug addicts, educate citizens or prevent drug addiction.	D.C. Code Ann. § 48-905.02 (d) (4)
Florida	Retain for law enforcement use. County & municipal agency proceeds deposited into special law enforcement trust fund. Every fiscal year local law enforcement agencies that receive over $15,000 must donate no less than 15% for drug education and crime prevention programs. State agency funds are deposited into general or other designated state revenue funds.	Fla. Stat. Ann. § 932.7055

Table 10-1 (continued)
Summary of State Asset Forfeiture Statutes
Distribution Procedures

State	Distribution	Statute
Georgia	Retain for law enforcement use. Divided pro rata between state and local governments according to role played. State amount not to exceed 25%. County District Attorneys entitled to 10%. Agency receipts not to exceed 33 1/3% of agency budget during that fiscal year. Excess amount to be used for drug prevention, education.	Ga. Code Ann. § 16-13-49 (u) (4)
Hawaii	Retain for law enforcement use. 25% to state or local law enforcement agency; 25% to prosecuting attorney; 50% to state criminal forfeiture fund.	Hawaii Rev. Stat. § 712A-16 (2)
Idaho	Retain for official use. Proceeds deposited into state or county drug enforcement donation account.	Idaho Code § 37-2744 (e)
Illinois	65% to law enforcement agency; 12.5% to county states attorney; 12.5% to state attorney general; 10% to Department of State Police.	720 ILCS 550/12 (g)
Indiana	Deposited in state general fund or unit that employed the law enforcement officers that seized the property for reimbursement of costs; the excess deposited in state treasury for common school fund.	Ind. Code Ann § 34-24-1-4(d)
Iowa	Transfer for law enforcement use. To state Department of Justice or local law enforcement agency upon approval of state attorney general.	Iowa Code Ann. § 809A.17
Kansas	Retain for law enforcement use. 15% to county DA for uncontested forfeitures and 20% for contested cases. Remaining funds deposited in state or county special law enforcement trust fund.	Kan. Stat. Ann. § 60-4117

Table 10-1 (continued)
Summary of State Asset Forfeiture Statutes
Distribution Procedures

State	Distribution	Statute
Kentucky	Retain for law enforcement use. 85% to law enforcement agency and 15% to prosecutor.	Ky. Rev. Stat. Ann § 218A.420
Louisiana	Money deposited in district attorney asset forfeiture trust fund. 60% to law enforcement agency; 20% to criminal court fund; 20% to district attorneys office. Vehicle retained for law enforcement use.	La. Rev. Stat. Ann. § 40:2616
Maine	Retain for government use. To state general fund or any state, county, municipal agency or district attorney that made a substantial contribution to the criminal investigation or prosecution.	Me. Rev. Stat. Ann. Title 15 ch. 517 § 5822
Maryland	Retain for law enforcement use. Proceeds to state or local general fund.	Md. Code Ann. Crim. Proc. § 12-403
Massachusetts	Divided equally between prosecuting attorney & law enforcement agency. Funds deposited in special trust fund & allocated for investigations, federal grants. Up to 10% of prosecutor funds may be for drug rehabilitation programs.	Mass. Ann. Laws Ch. 94C § 47 (d)
Michigan	Retain for law enforcement use. Proceeds to treasury of governing board of law enforcement agency. 75% to enhance enforcement of criminal laws, 25% for crime victim's rights act.	Mich. Comp. Laws § 333.7524 Mich. Comp. Laws § 600.4708(F)
Minnesota	Retain for official use. 70% to law enforcement agency; 20% to prosecuting attorney; 10% to state general fund.	Minn. Stat. Ann. § 609.5315

Table 10-1 (continued)
Summary of State Asset Forfeiture Statutes
Distribution Procedures

State	Distribution	Statute
Mississippi	Retain for law enforcement use. 20% to state treasurer & 80% to law enforcement agency. For multi law enforcement cases 80% to agency that originated the criminal case & 20% divided between other agencies.	Miss. Code Ann. § 41-29-181
Missouri	Proceeds disbursed to county schools pursuant to Article IX section 7 of the state constitution.	Mo. Ann. Stat. § 513.623
Montana	Retain for law enforcement use. Funds deposited into drug forfeiture account maintained by governmental entity for law enforcement agency seizing the property.	Mont. Code Ann. § 44-12-206
Nebraska	Retain for law enforcement use not to exceed 2 years. Funds to county treasurer of seizing county. 50% disbursed under state constitution for fines, penalties and the remaining 50% to county drug law enforcement & education fund.	Neb. Rev. Stat. § 28-1439.02
Nevada	Retain for official use. Funds to special account of seizing agency maintained by governing board. 70% of funds in excess of $100,000 in account at end of fiscal year disbursed to the local schools.	Nev. Rev. Stat. §§ 179.118; 179.1187
New Hampshire	45% to law enforcement governing board; 10% to state department of health & human services; 45% to drug forfeiture fund administered by department of justice	N.H. Rev. Stat. Ann. § 318-B:17-b (V)(a)

Table 10-1 (continued)
Summary of State Asset Forfeiture Statutes
Distribution Procedures

State	Distribution	Statute
New Jersey	Divided by prosecuting agency. Amount shared with participating law enforcement agencies depending on contribution.	N.J. Stat. Ann. § 2C:64-6
New Mexico	Proceeds to general fund of governing board of seizing agency.	N.M. Code Ann. § 31-27-7A
New York	Reimbursement for case investigation, litigation & property management. After costs 40% to substance abuse fund. Of remaining balance 75% to state or local general fund law enforcement sub-account & 25% to state or local general fund for prosecution services sub-account.	N.Y. Civil Practice Law § 1349 (2) (e-h)
North Carolina	Retain for official use. Money paid to county treasurer for school fund of county where property seized.	N.C. Gen. Stat. § 90-112 (d)
North Dakota	Retain for official use. Proceeds deposited in state, county or city general fund.	N.D. Cent. Code Ann. § 19-03.1-36 5
Ohio	Retain for official use. 10% of juvenile court forfeitures awarded to alcohol or drug addiction program. 90% of juvenile court forfeitures and 100% of other court forfeitures to law enforcement trust fund of governing board for prosecutor & seizing agency. At least 10% of the first $100,000 and 20% of the amount exceeding $100,000 shall be used for community preventive education programs.	Ohio Rev. Code Ann. §§ 2925.44; 2933.43(D)

Table 10-1 (continued)
Summary of State Asset Forfeiture Statutes
Distribution Procedures

State	Distribution	Statute
Oklahoma	Retain for law enforcement use. To revolving fund of county where property seized. District Attorney may enter into agreements to return percentage of proceeds with other agencies similar to guidelines for federal sharing. State agency proceeds deposited into state agency revolving fund.	Okla. Stat. Ann. § 63-2-506L-M
Oregon	Retain for law enforcement use. 5% to Illegal Drug Cleanup Fund 2.5% to Asset Forfeiture Oversight Acct. 20% to Drug Court. 10% to State Commission on Children & Families Acct. 62.5% to law enforcement agency	Ore. Stat. Ann. § 475A.120
Pennsylvania	Retain for official use. Funds maintained by district attorney or attorney general to enforce controlled substances offenses	Pa. Consol. Stat. Ann. Title 35 § 6801 (e)-(h)
Rhode Island	Retain for law enforcement use. 20% to attorney general; 70% to law enforcement agency & 10% for state substance abuse programs.	R.I. Gen. Laws § 21-28-5.04 ((b)(3)(i)(A))
South Carolina	Retain for official use. 75% to law enforcement agency; 20% to prosecuting agency; 5% to state general fund.	S.C. Code Ann. § 44-53-530 (e)
South Dakota	Retain for official use. Proceeds paid into drug control fund or bureau of narcotics & dangerous drugs	S.D. Codified Laws Ann. § 34-20B-89

Table 10-1 (continued)
Summary of State Asset Forfeiture Statutes
Distribution Procedures

State	Distribution	Statute
Tennessee	Proceeds deposited in special revenue fund of arresting agency. Monies may be used only for local drug enforcement, education, or treatment program and nonrecurring general law enforcement expenditures.	Tenn. Code Ann. § 39-17-420
Texas	Retain for official use. Deposited to state general fund unless there is a local agreement between the state and local law enforcement agencies. Local agreement permits funds to be deposited into treasury for governing board for law enforcement purposes. 10% may be used for drug prevention & education programs	Tx. Code of Crim. Proc. § 59.06
Utah	(a) Deduct seizing agencies direct cost & expenses; (b) Pay legal costs to prosecuting agency; (c) Balance deposited into State Criminal Forfeiture Restricted Account	Utah Code Ann. § 24-1-17 (4)
Vermont	Delivered to state treasurer. All property sold at public sale.	Vt. Stat. Ann. Title 18 § 4247
Virginia	Retain for law enforcement use. Paid to state treasury special fund. 10% for asset sharing administrative fund for administrative costs. Law enforcement agencies entitled to request an equitable share of net proceeds depending on contribution.	Va. Code Ann. § 19.2-386.14

State	Distribution	Statute
Washington	Retain for law enforcement use. 10% to state violence reduction & drug enforcement account. Balance retained by law enforcement agencies.	Wash. Rev. Code Ann. § 69-50-505 (7)-(10)
West Virginia	10% to prosecutor. The balance in law enforcement investigation fund. Retain for law enforcement use.	W.Va. Code § 60A-7-706; 60A-7-707
Wisconsin	Retain for law enforcement use. 50% for administrative costs. The balance to the school fund. For currency, 70% of amount under $2,000 and 50% of amount over $2,000 for administrative costs and the balance to school fund.	Wis. Stat. Ann. § 961.55 (5)
Wyoming	Retain for law enforcement use. Proceeds to law enforcement agency.	Wyo. Stat. § 35-7-1049 (e)

Many states provide for specific percentages to be paid directly to the law enforcement agencies. The statutory shares range from 25%, *see Hawaii Rev. Stat.* § 712A-16(2), to 90%. *See Wash. Rev. Code Ann.* § 69-50-505(7)-(10); *W. Va. Code* § 60A-7-706(a). Some state law enforcement shares are flexible depending on agency contribution, *see Ala. Code* § 20-2-93(e); *In re Forfeiture of Certain Personal Property*, 441 Mich. 77; 490 N.W.2d 322, 325 (Mich. 1992), role played, *see Ga. Code Ann.* § 16-13-49(u)(4), or local agreement. *See Tex. Code of Crim. Proc.* § 59.06(a).

In other jurisdictions, the funds are not paid directly to the law enforcement agency but rather to a law enforcement trust fund maintained by the state or county. *See Ariz. Rev. Stat. Ann.* § 13-4315.A.2; *Fla. Stat. Ann.* § 932.7055(4)(a)-(c); *Tenn. Code Ann.* § 39-17-420.

Many prosecutor offices also receive a portion of the distribution, ranging from 10%, *see Co. Rev. Stat.* § 16-13-311(3)(a)(V); *Cal. Health & Safety Code* § 11489(b)(2)(B), to 25%. *See Hawaii Rev. Stat,* § 712A-16(2). In Pennsylvania, all of the funds are paid to and disbursed by the prosecutor to enforce the state controlled substances statute, *see Pa. Consol. Stat. Ann.* Title 42 § 6801(f); *Com. v. 6969 Foreset Ave.*, 713 A.2d 701, 705 (Pa. Cmwlth. 1998), and in Massachusetts the funds are divided equally between law enforcement and the prosecutor. *See Mass. Ann. Laws* Ch. 94C § 47(d).

In some states, all of the funds are paid into the state or county general fund. *See Md. Ann. Code Crim. Proc.* § 12-403(c)–(e); *Vt. Stat. Ann.* Title 18 § 4247. Others require a payment to be made into the general fund ranging from 10%, *see Minn. Stat. Ann.* § 609.5315 Subd. 5(3), to 60%. *See N.Y. Civil Practice Law* § 1349.2(e)–(h).

Payments to substance abuse programs are mandatory in many state jurisdictions, and the amount paid varies from 10%, *see R.I. Gen. Laws* § 21-28-5.04(b)(3)(A), to 75%. *See Ore. Constitution,* Article XV Sec.10(7).

Provisions for funding drug education and gang prevention programs are also statutorily authorized in two states. *See Cal. Health & Safety Code* § 11489(b)(2)(A)(i); *Fla. Stat. Ann.* § 932.7055(4)(c)(3).

Miscellaneous uses are approved in a handful of other states, consisting of court funding ranging from 1%, *see Co. Rev. Stat.* § 16-13-311(3)(a)(VI), to 20%, *see La. Rev. Stat. Ann.* § 40:2616.B(3)(b); *State v. Clark,* 670 So. 2d 493, 501 (La. App. 1996), indigent counsel representation, *see Ga. Code Ann.* § 16-13-49(u)(4)(D)(ii), and crime laboratories. *See Ark. Code Ann.* § 5-64-505(h), (i). However, criminal fines and penalties cannot be paid with the proceeds of forfeited property. *State ex rel. Macy v. Freeman,* 814 P.2d 147, 153 (Okla. 1991).

Use of forfeiture funds for general education has become more prevalent in the past few years. Three states have constitutional provisions or state statutes that require all of the money be paid into the state or county school fund. *See Ind. Code Ann.* § 34-24-1-6; *Mo. Ann. Stat.* § 513.623; *Reorganized School Dist. No. 7 Lafayette County v. Douthit,* 799 S.W.2d 591, 594 (Mo. 1990); *N.C. Gen. Stat.* § 90-112(d)(4). Payments of 50% and 70% after expenses are authorized in two other states. *See Wis. Stat. Ann.* § 961.55(5)(b); *Nev. Rev. Stat.* § 179.1187 1(d).

Although most states permit forfeited property to be awarded and retained for law enforcement use by the seizing agencies, *Com. v. One 1988 Camaro,* 7 Pa. D. & C.4th 105, 1990 WL 303072 (Pa. Com.Pl. 1990), a few states have restrictions on this procedure. Some states limit the time that the agency can retain property for official use from two, *see Ark. Code Ann.* § 5-64-505(i), to three years, *see Ind. Code Ann.* § 34-24-1-4(c), and then require that the property be sold.[9] California specifically prohibits the retention of any forfeited personal property for law enforcement use, and New Mexico also requires that forfeited personal property be sold. *See Cal. Health & Safety Code* § 11469(g); *N.M. Code Ann.* § 31-27-7A.[10]

State forfeiture funds, like federal equitable sharing funds, are intended to supplement, not supplant, existing law enforcement resources. Attempts by local governing boards to reduce law enforcement budgets on account of asset forfeiture funds received are strictly prohibited in most jurisdictions. *See Cal. Health & Safety Code* § 11489(d); *Colo. Rev. Stat.* § 16-13-314(3); *Ga. Code Ann.* § 16-13-49(u)(4)(D)(i); *Miss. Code Ann.* § 41-29-185; *Tenn. Code Ann.* § 39-11-713(d); *Tex. Code of Crim. Proc.* § 59.06(d); *Wyo. Stat.* § 35-7-1049(j).

To ensure that state forfeiture funds are properly accounted and expended, several states have enacted mandatory reporting and auditing requirements. *Cal. Health & Safety Code* § 11495; *Colo. Rev. Stat.* § 16-13-701; *La. Rev. Stat. Ann.* § 40:2616D; *Utah Code Ann.* § 24-1-19(11). Law enforcement agencies may be disqualified from receiving future distributions of the state funds if they fail to comply with the reporting provisions. *Ark. Code Ann.* § 5-64-505(f)(5)(A).

State forfeiture funds awarded to state law enforcement agencies are used in various ways to supplement their law enforcement mission. State statutes, case law, and audits report that law enforcement funds are being expended in six basic categories:

1. Personnel Costs—Fund community-oriented policing and pay over-time for specific drug raids and street sweeps. *See also Mont. Code Ann.* § 44-13-103.
2. Equipment—Update safety and surveillance equipment.
3. Federal Grant Match—Provide matching funds for federal grant pro-grams for drug and crime enforcement, especially for multi-jurisdic-tional task forces.
4. Informant Fees—Obtain information for complex cases. *See also Williams v. State*, 463 So. 2d 1064, 1069 (Miss. 1985).
5. Buy Money—Provide money for undercover agents to make drug pur-chases.
6. Other—Officer and prosecutor training and operation of community-based drug programs, such as D.A.R.E. See *Michigan Department of Community Health, 2002 Asset Forfeiture Report*, at 13.

F. Summary

In determining where funds from forfeited federal and state forfeiture ac-tions should be disbursed, the preamble from the National District Attorneys Association Guidelines for Civil Asset Forfeiture contains this advisal:

The National District Attorneys Association strongly believes that law en-forcement agencies and prosecutors should aggressively pursue forfeiture actions to eliminate the instrumentalities of crime and to confiscate the proceeds from criminal acts. To encourage such efforts it is important that forfeiture laws continue to allow most of the proceeds from forfeitures to be returned to the law enforcement community responsible for initiating these actions to be used to further their law enforcement efforts.[11]

Notes

1. Resolution of the Board of Directors National District Attorneys Association, *President's Commission on Model State Drug Laws Economic Remedies*, Dec. 1993, at A-75.

2. U.S. Dept. of Justice 2007 Asset Forfeiture Fund Reports at http://www.usdoj.gov/jmd/afp/02fundreport/2007affr/report1.htm

3. One of the most interesting forfeiture auctions was the sale of a Nevada brothel along with its service mark names "Mustang Ranch," "World Famous Mustang Ranch," and "World Famous Mustang Ranch Brothel" by the federal government on e-Bay. Burgess v. Gilman, 475 F. Supp. 2d 1051 (D. Nev. 2007).

4. According to U.S. Department of Justice 2007 Asset Forfeiture Fund Reports, the fund paid $207 million in 2003, $270 million in 2004, $257 million in 2005, $298 million in 2006, and $417 million in 2007. All reports are available on-line at http://www.usdoj.gov/jmd/afp/.

5. The section was added by Initiative B adopted November 7, 2000, effective March 1, 2001. It has been modified by subsequent legislative amendments. The current section approving the use of federal equitable sharing funds is found at UTAH CODE ANN. § 24-1-15(8)(c).

6. State of Oregon Annual Report of the Asset Forfeiture Oversight Advisory Committee Summarizing Forfeiture Activity During Calendar Year 2004, March 31, 2005, at 3, *available at* http://www.ocjc.state.or.us/CJC/Forfeiture/docs/2005AFOACReport.pdf.

7. *Id.* at 3.

8. The states are: Arkansas—$3.4 million, *see Uniform Controlled Substances Act—Asset Forfeiture Special Report,* Arkansas Division of Legislative Audit, July 12, 2002, at 8, *available at* www.legaudit.state.ar.us/auditmain.html; California—$25.7 million, *see* State of California, *Asset Forfeiture Report 2001,* at 4; Oregon—$1.9 million, *see 2000 Annual Report of the Asset Forfeiture Oversight Advisory Committee,* at 11, *available at* www.ocjc.state.or.us/Forfeiture/AFReport00.htm; and Michigan—$20.3 million, *see* Michigan Department of Community Health, *2002 Asset Forfeiture Report,* at 6, at 222, *available at* www.mdch.state.mi.us/pha/osr/index.asp.

9. Louisiana state law previously limited vehicles retained for law enforcement use to six months use, *see* LA. REV. STAT. ANN. § 40:2616.A(2), but that restriction was repealed in 2003 by enactment of Act. No. 356.

10.   Colorado amended its forfeiture statute in 2002 and deleted the prior provision, 16-13-311(3)(b), which permitted the official use of forfeiture property under this statute. *See* 2002 CO H.B. 1404. However, retention of vehicles or personal property is authorized for property forfeited under 16-13-506(4.5).

11.   Resolution of the Board of Directors National District Attorneys Association, *President's Commission on Model State Drug Laws Economic Remedies*, Dec. 1993, at A-77.

11 Real Property Forfeitures

A. Introduction

It is a well-acknowledged principle of American law that, "Individual freedom finds tangible expression in property rights," *see United States v. James Daniel Good Real Property et al.*, 510 U.S. 43, 61 (1993), and "[r]espect for the sanctity of the home . . . has been embedded in our traditions since the origins of the Republic." *See Payton v. New York*, 445 U.S. 573, 601 (1980). Because many federal and state statutes authorize the forfeiture of all real property from a "hobo's hovel to the Empire State Building," some jurists have expressed reservations concerning the breadth of such governmental power. *See James Daniel Good*, 510 U.S. at 81–82 (J. Thomas dissenting); *United States v. One Parcel of Property*, 964 F.2d 814, 818 (8th Cir. 1992). In response, Congress and state legislatures have established higher burdens of proof and procedures to protect against government overreaching.

This section will review some of the constitutional and statutory procedures and issues unique to the litigation of real property forfeitures.

B. Theories of Forfeiture

Federal and most state forfeiture statutes provide for the forfeiture of real property on the theory that it was used or was intended to be used to facilitate the commission of the offense. *See* 21 U.S.C. § 881(a)(7). Table 11-1 is a list of state statutes that authorize real property forfeiture on a facilitation theory. There are five states—Alaska, Nebraska, New Mexico, North Carolina, and Vermont—that do not contain any statutory authority for the forfeiture of real property used to facilitate criminal activity. *See Ak. Stat.* § 17.30.112; *Neb. Rev. Stat.* § 28-431; *N.M. Code Ann.* § 30-31-34; *N.C. Gen. Stat.* § 90-112; *Vt. Stat. Ann.* Title 18 § 4241.

Table 11-1
Summary of State Asset Forfeiture Statutes*
Civil Forfeiture—Real Property

State	Statute	Burden of Proof
Alabama	Ala. Code § 20-2-93 (a)(8)	Prima Facie Evidence
Arizona	Ariz. Rev. Stat. Ann. § 13-4304	Preponderance of the Evidence
Arkansas	Ark. Code Ann. § 5-64-505(j)(7)	Preponderance of the Evidence
California	Cal. Health & Safety Code § 11470 (g)	Beyond a Reasonable Doubt
Colorado	Co. Rev. Stat. § 16-13-303 (1)	Clear & Convincing Evidence
Connecticut	Con. Gen. Stat. Ann. § 54-36h (a)(2)-(5)	Clear & Convincing Evidence
Delaware	Del. Code Ann. title 16 § 4784 (a)(8)	Probable Cause
District of Columbia	D.C. Code Ann. § 48-905.02 (a)(8)	Probable Cause
Florida	Fla. Stat. Ann. § 932.701 (2)(a) 6	Clear & Convincing Evidence
Georgia	Ga. Code Ann. § 16-13-49 (d)(2)-(3)	Probable Cause
Hawaii	Hawaii. Rev. Stat. § 712A-5 (2)(a)	Preponderance of the Evidence
Idaho	Idaho Code § 37-2744A	Preponderance of the Evidence
Illinois	720 Ill. Compiled Statutes 550/12(a)(4)-(5)	Probable Cause
Indiana	Ind. Code Ann. § 34-24-1-1(a)(5)	Preponderance of the Evidence
Iowa	Iowa Code Ann. § 809A.4 2	Preponderance of the Evidence

*   Several states define their burden of proof by case law. See Table 7-2.

Table 11-1 (continued)
Summary of State Asset Forfeiture Statutes
Civil Forfeiture—Real Property

State	Statute	Burden of Proof
Kansas	Kan. Stat. Ann. §§ 60-4105 (b), (f)	Preponderance of the Evidence
Kentucky	Ky. Rev. Stat. Ann. § 218A.410 (1)(j), (k)	Clear & Convincing Evidence
Louisiana	La. Rev. Stat. Ann. § 40:2604 (2), (3)	Preponderance of the Evidence
Maine	Me. Rev. Stat. Ann. Title 15 Ch. 517 § 5821 7	Preponderance of the Evidence
Maryland	Md. Ann. Code Art. 27 § 12-102 (a) (10)	Preponderance of the Evidence
Massachusetts	Mass. Ann. Laws. Ch. 94C § 47 (a)(7)	Probable Cause
Michigan	Mich. Comp. Laws § 600.4702 (1)(b)	Preponderance of the Evidence
Minnesota	Minn. Stat. Ann. § 609.5311 Subd. 2	Clear & Convincing Evidence
Mississippi	Miss. Code Ann. § 41-29-153 (a)(7)	Preponderance of the Evidence
Missouri	Mo. Ann. Stat. §§ 513.605(7); 195.140 2	Preponderance of the Evidence
Montana	Mont. Code Ann. § 44-12-102 (1)(i)	Probable Cause
Nevada	Nev. Rev. Stat. § 453.301 8	Clear & Convincing Evidence
New Hampshire	N.H. Rev. Stat. Ann. § 318-B:17-b I (e)	Preponderance of the Evidence
New Jersey	N.J. Stat. Ann. § 2C:64-1 a (2)	Preponderance of the Evidence
New York	N.Y. Civil Practice Law § 1310.1	Clear & Convincing Evidence
North Dakota	N.D. Cent. Code § 19-03.1-36 h	Preponderance of the Evidence

Table 11-1 (continued)
Summary of State Asset Forfeiture Statutes
Civil Forfeiture—Real Property

State	Statute	Burden of Proof
Ohio	Ohio Rev. Code Ann. § 2925.43(A)(1)-(2)	Clear & Convincing Evidence
Oklahoma	Okla. Stat. Ann. § 63-2-503 8	Preponderance of the Evidence
Oregon	Ore. Rev. Stat. § 475A.020 (7)	Clear & Convincing Evidence
Pennsylvania	Pa. Consol. Stat. Ann. Title 42 § 6801 (a)(6)(i)(C)	Preponderance of the Evidence
Rhode Island	R.I. Gen. Laws § 21-28-5.04 (a)	Probable Cause
South Carolina	S.C. Code Ann. § 44-53-520 (a)(4), (7)	Probable Cause
South Dakota	S.D. Codified Laws Ann. § 34-20B-70.1	Preponderance of the Evidence
Tennessee	Tenn. Code Ann. § 53-11-452(d)(1)(E)	Beyond a Reasonable Doubt
Texas	Tx. Code of Crim. Proc. § 59.01 (2)	Preponderance of the Evidence
Utah	Utah Code Ann. § 58-37-13 (2)(i)	Clear & Convincing Evidence
Vermont	Vt. Stat. Ann. title 18 § 4241(a)(5)	Clear & Convincing Evidence
Virginia	Va. Code Ann. § 18.2-386.22.A(iii)	Preponderance of the Evidence
Washington	Wash. Rev. Code Ann. § 69.50.505 (1)(h)	Preponderance of the Evidence
West Virginia	W. Va. Code § 60A-7-703 (a)(8)	Preponderance of the Evidence
Wisconsin	Wis. Stat. Ann. § 961.55 (1)(f)	Reasonable Certainty
Wyoming	Wyo. Stat. § 35-7-1049 (a)(vii)	Probable Cause

Real property has been forfeited as facilitating property when it was used to sell or store drugs. *People v. 25651 Minoa Dr.*, 2 Cal. App. 4th 787, 791 (1992) (selling drugs on premises); *In re Forfeiture of 45649 Maben Road*, 173 Mich. App. 764; 434 N.W.2d 238, 242 (Mich. App. 1988) (storing drugs on property); *Levingston v. Washoe County By and Through Sheriff of Washoe County*, 112 Nev. 479; 916 P.2d 163, 165 (Nev. 1996) (crack house); *In re Forfeiture of $5,264*, 432 Mich. 242; 439 N.W.2d 246, 261 (Mich. 1989) (building site of drug deals, or cultivating marijuana); *United States v. All Tract 686.64 Acres of Property*, 820 F. Supp. 1433, 1434 (M.D. Ga. 1993); *In re Forfeiture of 30800 Grandview*, 178 Mich. App. 434; 444 N.W.2d 547, 548 (Mich. App. 1989). The facilitation theory applies because the real property is being used to hide, conceal, or shelter drug trafficking. *State v. Hill*, 70 Ohio St.3d 25, 635 N.E.2d 1248, 1254 (Ohio. 1994); *State v. Harold*, 109 Ohio App. 3d 87, 671 N.E.2d 1078, 1080 (Ohio App. 1996).

There should be a substantial connection between the illegal use and the real property. Factors relevant in finding a substantial connection include:

- Large quantities of drugs on the premises;
- Drug records documenting a large customer base;
- Witness testimony documenting long-term sales at the residence;
- Scales and packaging material indicative of drug sales;
- Marked bills from prior undercover drug sales; and
- Admissions of prior sales from the location.

See *In re Forfeiture of 5118 Indian Garden Road*, 253 Mich. App. 255; 654 N.W.2d 646, 648 (Mich. App. 2002); *In re Forfeiture of One 1978 Sterling Mobile Home*, 205 Mich. App. 427; 517 N.W.2d 812, 814 (Mich. App. 1994).

An alternative basis of forfeiture for real property is under the proceeds theory that it is "a thing of value" traceable to the exchange of a controlled substance. *See* 21 U.S.C. § 881(a)(6). All states provide for proceed theory forfeitures, so in jurisdictions that do not permit facilitation theory forfeitures, real property may still be forfeited on the proceeds theory.

Forfeiting real property on the theory that it is a "container" intended for use in controlled substances offenses has been rejected because most statutes specifically exclude real property from the definition of "container." *Cal. Health & Safety Code* § 11470(c); *In re Forfeiture of 30800 Grandview*, 178 Mich. App. 434; 444 N.W.2d 547, 549 (Mich. App. 1989); *People v. 8120 Ravine Road, Alamo Twp.*, 151 Mich. App. 358; 390 N.W.2d 242, 244 (Mich. App. 1986); *People v. 2850 Ewing Road*, 161 Mich. App. 266; 409 N.W.2d 800, 802 (Mich. App. 1987).

C. Seizure of Real Property

Generally, a claimant is not entitled to preseizure notice or a hearing before property is seized for civil forfeiture. *See Calero-Toledo v. Pearson Yacht Leasing,* 416 U.S. 663, 678–79 (1974). However, in *United States v. James Daniel Good Real Property,* 510 U.S. 43, 57 (1993), the U.S. Supreme Court departed from this position and made an exception for real property. Because of the important privacy interests inherent in real property, the Court ruled that, unless exigent circumstances are present, the due process clause requires notice and a meaningful opportunity to be heard prior to seizing real property for civil forfeiture. *See James Daniel Good,* 510 U.S. at 62.

The *Good* decision has been codified in CAFRA Section 7, 106 Pub. L. No. 185, 114 Stat. 202, 214, with the addition of new procedures governing the civil forfeiture of real property. *See* 18 U.S.C. § 985; Supplemental Rule G(3)(a). Two states, California and Florida, have joined suit. *See Cal. Health & Safety Code* § 11471(e); *Fla. Stat. Ann.* § 932.703(2)(b).

Under CAFRA, the government initiates a civil real property forfeiture action by filing the complaint for forfeiture, posting a notice of forfeiture on the property, and serving the property owner with the complaint and notice. *See* 18 U.S.C. § 985(c)(1). Constructive notice is permitted if the party is a fugitive, resides outside the country, or cannot be located with due diligence efforts. *See* 18 U.S.C. § 985(c)(2). This is a distinctive procedure from other civil forfeiture actions in that it replaces the requirement of obtaining an arrest warrant *in rem* to establish jurisdiction over the property. *See* 18 U.S.C. § 985(c)(3).

To protect its interest, the government may file a lis pendens against the property and obtain a writ of entry to conduct an inventory of the premises. *See* 18 U.S.C. § 985(b)(2); *United States v. Woods,* 436 F. Supp. 2d 753, 755 (E.D.N.C. 2006) (lis pendens); *United States v. Residence (24227 Gulf Bay Road),* 2006 WL 2091764 (S.D. Ala. 2006) (writ of entry). Because these actions are neither a seizure nor restraint they do not require prior notice or an adversarial hearing. *See James Daniel Good,* 510 U.S. at 58; *United States v. Land, Winston County,* 163 F.3d 1295, 1301 (11th Cir. 1998); *United States v. Real Property (429 South Main Street),* 906 F. Supp. 1155, 1158 (S.D. Ohio).

If the government determines that seizure is necessary to protect its interest in the property, it must either notify the court and hold an adversarial hearing or make an ex parte application for seizure based on probable cause and exigent circumstances. *See* 18 U.S.C. § 985(d)(1). Exigent circumstances require a showing that less-restrictive measures such as a lis pendens, restraining order, or bond are insufficient to preserve the property, *see* 18 U.S.C. § 985(d)(2), and prevent sale, *see United States v. Real Property Located at 1184 Drycreek Road*, 174 F.3d 720, 730 (6th Cir. 1999), destruction, or continued unlawful use of the property. *See United States v. All Right, Title and Interest (Kenmore Hotel)*, 888 F. Supp. 580, 582–83 (S.D.N.Y. 1995); *United States v. Puello*, 814 F. Supp. 1155, 1164 (E.D.N.Y. 1993); *United States v. All Right Title and Interest in Real Property Titled in the Name of Taipei Partners*, 927 F. Supp. 1324, 1329 (D. Haw. 1996).

If the ex-parte application is granted, a prompt post-seizure hearing must be held where the property owner will have the opportunity to contest the basis for the seizure. *See* 18 U.S.C. § 985(e); *Tellevik v. Real Property*, 120 Wash.2d 68; 838 P.2d 111, 121 (Wash. 1992), *clarified at* 845 P.2d 1325.

Pre-CAFRA courts held that the adversarial hearing should be limited to whether the government has probable cause to believe that the property is subject to forfeiture. *See James Daniel Good*, 510 U.S. at 78; *United States v. Quintana-Aguayo*, 235 F.3d 682, 684 (1st Cir. 2000); *United States v. One Parcel of Property Located at 194 Quaker Farms Road*, 85 F. 3d 985, 988 (2d Cir. 1996). Post-CAFRA cases also limit the issues to probable cause or whether exigent circumstances exist. *See United States v. Certain Real Property Located at 263 Weatherbrook Lane*, 202 F. Supp. 2d 1275, 1276 (N.D. Ala. 2002; *United States v. Real Property in Section 9*, 308 F. Supp. 2d 791, 813 (E.D. Mich. 2004).

In lieu of actual seizure and in addition to filing a lis pendens clouding title to the property, the government may obtain a restraining order to require that the property is properly maintained and insured, and that mortgage and property tax payments remain current. *See* 18 U.S.C. § 985(f)(3).

D. Statutory Protections

The federal government and states have adopted various methods to grant enhanced protections to the civil forfeiture of real property. For example, the federal drug statute limits facilitation forfeiture to felony offenses, *see* 21 U.S.C. § 881(a)(7), and most states have the same restriction. *See Fla. Stat. Ann.* § 932.701(2)(a)(6); *Idaho Code* § 37-2744A(a); *Mont. Code Ann.* § 44-12-102(1)(i); *Okla. Stat. Ann.* § 63-2-503A.8; *Va. Code Ann.* § 19.2-386.22A.

A few states increase the level of proof to beyond a reasonable doubt when real property is being forfeited. *See Ky. Rev. Stat. Ann.* § 218A.410(1)(j); *N.Y. Civil Practice Law* § 1311.3; *Tenn. Code Ann.* § 53-11-452(d)(1)(E). The federal government and two states have enacted separate statutory procedures that govern real property forfeitures. *See* 18 U.S.C. § 985; *Idaho Code* § 37-2744A; *Tenn. Code Ann.* § 53-11-452. Two states shift the burden of proof for the innocent owner exemption on real property forfeitures from the claimant to the state. *See Ala. Code* § 20-2-93(h); *Ky. Rev. Stat. Ann.* § 218A.410(1)(j).

To insure that there is a substantial connection between the criminal offense and the real property, some jurisdictions have enacted minimum thresholds based on the quantity of drugs possessed, *see Mass. Ann. Laws* Ch. 94C § 47(c)(4) (10 lbs. of marijuana); *S.D. Codified Laws Ann.* § 34-20B-70.1 (10 lbs. of marijuana), dollar value of drugs sold, *see Minn. Stat. Ann.* § 609.5311 Subd. 3(b) ($1,000); *Utah Code Ann.* § 58-37-13(2)(i) ($1,000 within two-month period); *Wash. Rev. Code Ann.* § 69.50.505(1)(h) (five marijuana plants or one lb.; 40 grams of drugs or $100 value), or number of drug transactions conducted. *See Mass. Ann. Laws* Ch. 94C § 47(c)(3) (three sales); *Tenn. Code Ann.* § 53-11-452(a)(1) (three sales within 60-day period).

However, the primary protection for claimants in real property forfeiture is contained in the various federal and state innocent owner exemptions.

CAFRA Section 2, 106 Pub. L. No. 185, 114 Stat. 202, 206, enacted a uniform innocent owner exemption for civil forfeitures that is especially applicable to real property forfeitures. For pre-existing ownership interest, a claimant may defeat forfeiture if he or she can prove that: (1) he or she did not know of the conduct giving rise to the forfeiture; OR (2) upon learning of the conduct, did all that reasonably could be expected under the circumstances to terminate the illegal use. *See* 18 U.S.C. § 983(d)(2)(A). Examples of reasonable acts to terminate the illegal use include giving timely notice to law enforcement, revoking permission to use the property, or consulting with law enforcement to discourage or prevent the illegal use. *See* 18 U.S.C. § 983(d)(2)(B). The second prong of this innocent owner defense is pertinent to real property forfeitures involving rental property or leasehold interests where the illegal conduct is not ascribed to the title owner. *See United States v. 16328 South 43rd East Avenue,* 275 F.3d 1281, 1286–87 (10th Cir. 2002).

For property interests that arose after the illegal conduct, CAFRA requires that the innocent owner be a (1) bona fide purchaser for value AND (2) did not know AND (3) was reasonably without cause to know that the property was subject to forfeiture. *See* 18 U.S.C. § 983(d)(3)(A). This basically is the same innocent owner defense for criminal forfeitures, *see* 21 U.S.C. § 853(n)(6)(B), and excludes anyone who is not a purchaser of the property.

To prevent undue hardship of the bona fide purchaser requirement on families and other dependents, Congress enacted a limited exception for real property if *all* of the following conditions apply:

(1) The property is the primary residence of the claimant;
(2) Forfeiting the property would deprive the claimant of the means to provide reasonable shelter in the community for him or her and all dependents;
(3) The property is not traceable to drug proceeds; and
(4) The claimant acquired his or her interest through marriage, divorce or legal separation, or inheritance. *See* 18 U.S.C. § 983(d)(3)(B).

The exemption will be denied if the claimant does not establish all four elements. *See United States v. One Single Family Residence at 2200 SW 28th Avenue,* 204 F. Supp. 2d 1361, 1365 (S.D. Fla. 2002).

Many states have enacted similar protections for primary or family residences by exempting family residences from forfeiture, *see Cal. Health & Safety Code* § 11470(g); *Vt. Stat. Ann.* Title 18 § 4241(a)(5), requiring a criminal conviction, *see Md. Ann. Code Crim. Proc.* § 12-103(d); N.Y.C.P.L.R. § 1310 (4)(a); *Tenn. Code Ann.* § 53-11-452(a)(2), or shifting the burden of proof on the innocent owner exemption from the claimant to the state. *See Me. Rev. Stat. Ann.* Tit. 15 Ch. 517 § 5821.7.

E. Homestead Exemption

Several states have constitutional provisions that exempt homestead property from forced sale under process of court. *See Fla. Const.* Art. X , § 4. Five state courts have ruled that the homestead exemption precludes the forfeiture of real property that qualifies as a homestead. *See Butterworth v. Caggiano,* 605 So. 2d 56, 61 (Fla. 1992); *People v. One Residence Located at 1403 East Parham St,* 251 Ill. App. 3d 198; 621 N.E.2d 1026, 1031 (Ill. App. 1993); *In re Bly,* 456 N.W. 2d 195, 200 (Iowa 1990); *State ex. Rel. Braun v. Tract of Land in the Northwest Quarter of Section Four,* 840 P.2d 453, 455 (Kan. 1992); *State ex. rel. Means v. 10 Acres of Land,* 877 P.2d 597, 601 (Okla. 1994). Therefore, the homestead exemption may be a complete defense to a state real property forfeiture in these jurisdictions.

However, other courts have determined that the state homestead provision does not exempt state real property forfeitures. *Matter of Smith,* 176 B.R. 221, 223 (Bankr. N.D. Ala. 1995); *Matter of Parcel of Real Property Known as 1632 N. Santa Rita, Tucson,* 166 Ariz. 197; 801 P.2d 432, 437 (Ariz. App. 1990); *In re Forfeiture of 5118 Indian Garden Road,* 253 Mich. App. 255; 654 N.W.2d 646,

650 (Mich. App. 2002); *Lot 39, Section C, Northern Hills Subdivision, Grayson County Texas v. State,* 85 S.W.3d 429, 432 (Tex. App. 2002).

Further, a state homestead exemption is not a defense to a federal real property forfeiture case because the federal supremacy clause preempts the state exemption. *See United States v. Lot 5, Fox Grove,* 23 F.3d 359, 363 (11th Cir. 1994); *United States v. Curtis,* 965 F.2d 610, 616 (8th Cir. 1992); *United States v. Wagoner County Real Estate,* 278 F.3d 1091, 1096 (10th Cir. 2002); *United States v. 817 N.E. 29th Drive, Wilton Manors,* 175 F.3d 1304, 1311 n.14 (11th Cir. 1999).

Therefore, in jurisdictions with state homestead exemptions, law enforcement will use the federal forfeiture system for any real property that may be exempted under the state statute.

F. Mortgagee/Lienholder

The rights of mortgagees, lien holders, and other secured creditors are protected under various provisions of the real property forfeiture statutes. CAFRA states the basic rule that the rights of an innocent owner's interest in property shall not be forfeited under any civil forfeiture statute. *See* 18 U.S.C. § 983(d)(1). An owner is further defined to include a person with a lien, mortgage, or recorded security interest, *see* 18 U.S.C. § 983(d)(6)(A), and is entitled to protection under the innocent owner exemption. *See United States v. Harris,* 246 F.3d 566, 568 (6th Cir. 2001); *In Re Metmor Fin. Inc.,* 819 F.2d 446, 449 (4th Cir. 1987). A security interest must be recorded to be exempt from forfeiture. *In re Forfeiture of U.S. Currency $91,357.12,* 595 So. 2d 998, 999 (Fla. App. 1992).

When forfeiture proceedings are initiated against real property, a mortgagee or lien holder has several options to consider.

The claimant may apply for an expedited settlement of his or her security interest. This is specifically provided for in federal forfeitures in the booklet, *A Guide to Interlocutory Sales and Expedited Settlement,* issued by the U.S. Department of Justice in July 2007. To qualify, the party must have a perfected lien or mortgage and meet the criteria of the statutory innocent owner defense. *See Guide to Interlocutory Sales,* at I-5. The claimant files a claim and an answer in the civil action or agrees to file a petition in the ancillary hearing in a criminal forfeiture, and sends a request for expedited settlement to the U.S. Attorney, including copies of all documents that substantiate the interest. *See Guide to Interlocutory Sales,* at I-4. By agreeing to this expedited procedure the claimant agrees to relinquish his or her right to foreclose on the property. *See Guide to Interlocutory Sales,* at I-6.

If the request is accepted, upon sale of the property, the claimant is paid principal plus interest to the date of payment. Attorney fees under CAFRA Section 4, 28 U.S.C. § 2465, are waived, but other attorney fees recoverable under contract law may be available. See Section G, *infra,* for a discussion of attorney fees in the context of real property forfeitures.

Another alternative is to apply for remission or mitigation of the forfeiture. *See* 28 C.F.R. § 9.5(a). A lien holder is entitled to remission if he or she is innocent within the provision of the innocent owner statute. *See* 28 C.F.R. § 9.5(a)(1). If remission is granted, the claimant will receive unpaid principal plus interest at date of seizure plus post-seizure interest. No attorney fees will be included. *See* 28 C.F.R. § 9.2(k).

If the property is at risk of depreciation, default, or foreclosure, an interlocutory sale should be considered. The property is ordered sold, and the proceeds are deposited into a special fund pending the final order of forfeiture. The interlocutory sale can be by stipulation of the parties, *see United States v. Real Property at 3097 S.W. 111th Ave, Miami, Florida,* 699 F. Supp. 287, 288 (S.D. Fla. 1988); *United States v. Real Property Located at 22 Santa Barbara Drive,* 264 F.3d 860, 866–67 (9th Cir. 2001), or court order if one of the parties contests the sale. *See United States v. One Parcel (Lot 41, Berryhill Farm),* 128 F.3d 1386, 1389–90 (10th Cir. 1997); *United States v. Pelullo,* 178 F.3d 196, 198–99 (3d Cir.1999); *Aguilar v. United States,* 1999 WL 1067841 (D. Conn. 1999); *United States v. 2540 Chadwick Way,* 2005 WL 2124539 (N.D. Ill. 2005). The legal authority for an interlocutory sale is found in the customs laws, 19 U.S.C. § 1612, federal supplemental Rule G(7)(b), as well as several state statutes. *See Ariz. Rev. Stat. Ann.* § 13-4310.G; *Cal. Health & Safety Code* § 11492(a)(3); *Kan. Stat. Ann.* § 60-4108(e). Guidance for this procedure in the federal system is found in the government publication entitled *A Guide to Interlocutory Sales and Expedited Settlement,* printed by the U.S. Department of Justice in July 2007.

There is no right to foreclose in a federal criminal forfeiture action because the statute specifically prohibits any legal or equitable action being untaken to litigate an interest in the property subsequent to the criminal forfeiture filing. *See* 21 U.S.C. § 853(k).

The right to foreclose in a federal civil forfeiture is unclear. Several courts point to 28 U.S.C. § 2409a(b) for authority that the property cannot be foreclosed while the forfeiture is still pending. *See United States v. Parcel of Real Property Known as 708-710 West 9th Street,* 715 F. Supp. 1323, 1327 (W.D. Pa.

1989); *United States v. Real Property Constituting Approximately Fifty (50) Acres,* 703 F. Supp. 1306, 1312 (E.D. Tenn. 1989); *United States v. Real Property Titled in the Name of Shashin, Ltd.,* 680 F. Supp. 332, 335 (D. Haw. 1997). A contrary opinion is expressed in *In re Newport Savings and Loan Assn,* 928 F.2d 472, 477–79 (1st Cir. 1991).

However, if a foreclosure does proceed, it could have deleterious consequences for the government because it may trump the relation back doctrine under 21 U.S.C. § 881(h) and make the government's forfeiture action a junior encumbrance to the foreclosed note. *See United States v. Real Property at 2659 Roundhill Drive,* 194 F.3d 1020, 1026–27 (9th Cir. 1999). Therefore, the government should never stipulate to a foreclosure sale, and every effort should be exerted to work out an agreement between the government and the lien holder to recognize the interest and eventual payment. *See Tenn. Code Ann.* §§ 39-11-710(a)–(d).

G. Costs

There are various costs relating to real property forfeitures that must be assumed, and hopefully reimbursed, at the conclusion of the litigation. These include property management and sales expenses, *see* 28 U.S.C. § 524(c)(1)(A), payoffs of mortgages and liens, *see* 28 U.S.C. § 524(c)(1)(D), and state and local property taxes. *See* 28 U.S.C. § 524(c)(1)(H).

Payment of attorney fees may also be required. Although attorney fees generally are not recoverable, *see United States v. One 1989 Harley Davidson Motorcycle,* 743 F. Supp. 589, 591–92 (C.D. Ill. 1990), they may be awarded to a mortgagee or lien holder if expressly specified in the underlying mortgage or trust deed. *See In Re Metmor Fin. Inc.,* 819 F.2d 446, 448 (4th Cir. 1987); *United States v. Real Property Located at 41741 National Trails Way,* 989 F.2d 1089, 1092 (9th Cir. 1993).

Also, when a party prevails in the real property action and the government's position was not substantially justified, attorney fees and costs may also be available under the Equal Access to Justice Act ("EAJA"). *See* 28 U.S.C. § 2412. Real property cases where EAJA fees have been awarded include *United States v. Real Property Known as 22249 Dolorosa Street,* 190 F.3d 977, 981 (9th Cir. 1999), and *United States v. Real Property at 2659 Roundhill Drive, Alamo, California,* 283 F.3d 1146, 1153 (9th Cir. 2002).

Under CAFRA Section 4, 106 Pub. L. No. 185, 114 Stat. 202, 212, a provision for attorney fees and costs in civil forfeiture actions was added at 28 U.S.C. § 2465. If a claimant substantially prevails in the forfeiture action, he or she may recover reasonable attorney fees and costs, including post-judgment interest and interest on any proceeds from an interlocutory sale. *See* 18 U.S.C. § 2465(b)(1).

Finally, under CAFRA Section 3, 106 Pub. L. No. 185, 114 Stat. 202, 211, the government may be liable for damage or loss to the real property if it was seized by law enforcement and was not forfeited, remitted, or mitigated, and the claimant was not convicted of the underlying crime subjecting the property to forfeiture. *See* 28 U.S.C. § 2680(c).

H. Summary

The forfeiture of real property can be a daunting task, confronting the litigator with complex legal issues, property management concerns, and mounting costs and expenses. When considering initiating a real property forfeiture action, the wise practitioner should consider the following questions:

(1) What is the statutory basis for the forfeiture of this property?
(2) Who is the title owner? Is he or she involved in the underlying criminal activity?
(3) How is title held in the real property (i.e., joint tenancy, tenancy in common, community property, etc.)?
(4) Are there occupants on the premises?
(5) What legal exemptions or defenses may apply to this property?
(6) What is the fair market value of the property?
(7) What liens are secured against the property and what is their total liability?
(8) What is the net equity of the property?
(9) Will it be necessary to seize and manage the property?
(10) What are the estimated costs of property management and sale?

One of the practical considerations of real property forfeitures is that there must be sufficient equity in the asset to pay off all existing liens and costs. Consequently, the federal government has set a minimum equity threshold of $20,000, or 20% of the appraised value, whichever is higher, as the benchmark for determining whether to adopt a real property action. *See Guide to Equitable Sharing,* at 4. Higher thresholds may be set at the discretion of the U.S. Attorney. However, the government may depart from the minimum threshold if the real property will be retained for law enforcement use or there are other compelling law enforcement interests justifying the forfeiture.

12 Constitutional Protections

A. Introduction

"We continue to be enormously troubled by the government's increasing and virtually unchecked use of the civil forfeiture statutes and the disregard for due process that is buried in those statutes." *See United States v. All Assets of Statewide Auto Parts, Inc.,* 971 F.2d 896, 905 (2d Cir. 1992).

This statement from the Second Circuit typifies some of the underlying concerns expressed about the increasing use of the asset forfeiture power by the federal and state governments. Criticism of asset forfeiture may be categorized into three basic areas: (1) constitutional rights must be recognized and honored; (2) property rights must not be infringed; and (3) protection must be provided for innocent parties.

This section will discuss the constitutional and statutory safeguards applicable to asset forfeiture actions.

B. Eighth Amendment Excessive Fines Clause

1. Federal Litigation

For over 200 years the excessive fines clause was an almost forgotten part of the Eighth Amendment of the U.S. Constitution because the U.S. Supreme Court had little occasion to review it. That all changed in 1993 when it issued two landmark cases relating to the excessive fines clause and asset forfeiture.

In *Alexander v. United States,* 509 U.S. 544 (1993), the defendant was convicted of federal obscenity and racketeering charges in the operation of several stores and theatres dealing with sexually explicit materials. The jury found that four magazines and three videotapes were obscene. The defendant was sentenced to six years in prison and fined $100,000. Additionally, the court criminally forfeited all of the defendant's interest in his wholesale and retail businesses and almost $9 million in moneys acquired through racketeering activity. Alexander appealed, asserting that the forfeiture violated the Eighth Amendment excessive fines clause. The Court determined that an *in personam* criminal forfeiture action was punishment no different than a traditional fine and was subject to the Eighth Amendment excessive fines clause, and remanded the case to the appellate court to consider the excessiveness issue. *Id.* at 559.

The same day, the court issued its ruling in *Austin v. United States*, 509 U.S. 602 (1993). In this matter, the defendant sold two grams of cocaine to a state undercover agent. The agent's declaration stated that the defendant obtained the drugs from his mobile home and the sale took place at his body shop. The defendant pled guilty to state charges of possessing drugs for sale and received a seven-year state prison sentence. The federal government then filed civil *in rem* forfeiture charges against the mobile home and auto body shop under the facilitation theory.

The U.S. Supreme Court held that the excessive fines clause also applies to a civil action if it is, in part, punishment. After evaluating the language of the federal civil drug forfeiture statutes for conveyances, *see* 21 U.S.C. § 881(a)(4), and real property, 21 U.S.C. § 881(a)(7), on a facilitation theory the court found that these statutes are punitive and subject to the excessive fines clause. *Austin*, 509 U.S. at 622. However, rather than articulate a test for excessiveness, the court deferred on that issue and remanded it back to the lower courts. *Id.* at 623.

Over the next five years, the lower federal courts developed a dizzying array of tests for excessiveness, such as the "substantial connection test," *see United States v. Myers*, 21 F.3d 826, 830–31 (8th Cir. 1994); "quantitative test," *see United States v. Premises Known as RR # 1*, 14 F.3d 864, 874 (3d Cir. 1994); "nexus test," *see United States v. Chandler*, 36 F.3d 358, 365 (4th Cir. 1994); "multi-factor test," *see United States v. Real Property Located at 6625 Zumirez Drive*, 845 F. Supp. 725, 732 (C.D. Cal. 1994); and the "two-prong nexus and proportionality test," *see United States v. Real Property Located in El Dorado County*, 59 F.3d 974, 982 (9th Cir. 1995). Some tests limited their review to objective elements demonstrating the nexus of the property to the offense, *see Chandler*, 36 F.3d at 365, while others considered subjective factors, such as harshness to insure that the forfeiture was proportional to the offense. *See El Dorado County*, 59 F.3d at 985. A few circuits adopted a test that incorporated all of the factors articulated by the other circuits and directed their courts to select the most appropriate under the circumstances. *See United States v. Certain Real Property (11869 Westshore Drive)*, 70 F.3d 923, 930 (6th Cir. 1995); *United States v. 829 Calle De Madero*, 100 F.3d 734, 739 (10th Cir. 1996).

Obviously, this led to a situation where results were fact driven and contingent on the law of the circuit where the case was litigated, preventing practitioners from having any certain guidelines to determine when a forfeiture action would be excessive.

The U.S. Supreme Court finally articulated a test of excessiveness in *United States v. Bajakajian*, 524 U.S. 321 (1998). The defendant and his family were preparing to board an international flight out of Los Angeles but failed to report that they were carrying over $357,144 on their person and baggage. Bajakajian was charged with failing to report that he was carrying over $10,000 of currency outside of the United States, *see* 31 U.S.C. § 5316(a), and criminal forfeiture of the currency. *See* 18 U.S.C. § 982(a)(1). He pled guilty to the criminal charge and was sentenced to three years probation and a $5,000 fine. However, rather than forfeit the entire $357,144, the court reduced the forfeiture to $15,000. The government appealed, contending that the statute required forfeiture of the full amount.

The U.S. Supreme Court held that, because this was a criminal *in personam* forfeiture, it was punishment and subject to the excessive fines clause. *Bajakajian*, 524 U.S. at 328. It then held that a punitive forfeiture violates the excessive fines clause if it is grossly disproportional to the gravity of the defendant's offense. *Id.* at 334. Under this test, the lower court must conduct a proportionality review by comparing the amount of the forfeiture to the gravity of the defendant's offense. *Id.* at 336–337.

Although *Bajakajian* was a criminal forfeiture case, it has been equally applied to civil forfeiture actions. *United States v. Collado*, 348 F.3d 323, 328 (2d Cir. 2003); *United States v. Six Negotiable Checks*, 389 F. Supp. 2d 813, 823 (E.D. Mich. 2005).

In view of the *Bajakajian* case, there are certain general rules that may be stated pertaining to excessive fines challenges. The first is that there are certain forfeiture actions that should never be excessive under the Eighth Amendment excessive fines clause, including (1) contraband; (2) instrumentalities; (3) proceeds; (4) smuggled goods; and (5) substitute assets.

Contraband forfeitures are never excessive because they are merely removing property that is illegal to possess, such as illegal drugs or weapons. *See United States v. 89 Firearms*, 465 U.S. 354, 364 (1984); *Austin*, 509 U.S. at 621.

Instrumentality forfeitures are not excessive because they are limited to the actual property that has been used to commit the offense, such as money involved in a money laundering violation, *see United States v. Ahmad,* 213 F.3d 805, 814 (4th Cir. 2000); *United States v. Ely,* 468 F.3d 399, 403 (6th Cir. 2006) (bulk cash smuggling); *United States v. Jose,* 499 F.3d 105, 111 (1st Cir. 2007) (bulk cash smuggling), or money sent to fund terrorist activities. *See United States v. One 1997 E35 Ford Van,* 50 F. Supp. 2d 789, 808 (N.D. Ill. 1999). Therefore, they are already proportional to the offense because they are limited to the actual amount involved and no more. *See Bajakajian,* 524 U.S. at 333, n.8.

Proceed forfeitures are not excessive because they are remedial, not punitive, and merely take away the illicit profits from the defendant, which he or she had no legal right to possess. Therefore, they are always proportional to the offense. This was the law before *Bajakajian, see United States v. Ursery,* 518 U.S. 267, 291 (1996); *United States v. Tilley,* 18 F.3d 295, 300 (5th Cir. 1994); *United States v. Alexander,* 32 F.3d 1231, 1236 (8th Cir. 1994), reaff'd after remand, 108 F.3d 853, 858 (8th Cir. 1997); *United States v. Wild,* 47 F.3d 669, 676 (4th Cir. 1995); *United States v. One Parcel (Lot 41, Berryhill Farm),* 128 F.3d 1386, 1395 (10th Cir. 1997), and after *Bajakajian. See United States v. Real Property Located at 22 Santa Barbara Drive,* 264 F.3d 860, 874–75 (9th Cir. 2001); *United States v. One Parcel of Real Estate Located at 1948 Martin Luther King Drive,* 91 F. Supp. 2d 1228, 1245 (C.D. Ill. 2000); *United States v. Loe,* 248 F.3d 449, 464 (5th Cir. 2001); *United States v. Betancourt,* 422 F.3d 240, 250–51 (5th Cir. 2005).

Customs forfeiture for illegally smuggled goods or contraband also are not excessive, as the court has determined that they are considered liquidated damages for costs borne by the government and society for violation of the statute and thus proportional to the offense. *See One Lot of Emerald Cut Stones v. United States,* 409 U.S. 232, 237 (1972); *United States v. $273,969.04 U.S. Currency,* 164 F.3d 462, 466 (9th Cir. 1999); *United States v. An Antique Platter of Gold,* 184 F.3d 131, 140 (2d Cir. 1999).

Forfeiture of substitute assets is never excessive because it is proportional to the value of the money judgment entered. *See United States v. Shepherd,* 171 Fed. Appx. 611, 616 (9th Cir. 2006).

Forfeitures litigated on a facilitation theory are subject to the excessive fines clause. This is because facilitating property is not unlawful to possess, may have been purchased with legitimate funds, and the value of the property may substantially exceed the illegal use or the cost or damages suffered by society in enforcing the law. *See Austin,* 509 U.S. at 621. Therefore, whenever an excessive fines challenge is brought against a facilitation forfeiture case, the court must conduct a test for excessiveness under *Bajakajian.*

In addition to the constitutional protection of the Eighth Amendment, statutory protection against excessive forfeitures has now been enacted by the passage of the Civil Asset Forfeiture Reform Act ("CAFRA") Section 2, 106 Pub. L. No. 185, 114 Stat. 202, 209–10). This adds 18 U.S.C. § 983(g) and provides procedures for the court to follow in determining whether a forfeiture is constitutionally excessive. *See* 18 U.S.C. § 983(g)(1).

The burden of proof is on the claimant to establish that the forfeiture is grossly disproportional to the offense by a preponderance of the evidence, *see* 18 U.S.C. § 983(g)(3); *United States v. Ahmad,* 213 F.3d 805, 816 (4th Cir. 2000); *United States v. Ladum,* 141 F.3d 1328, 1349 (9th Cir. 1998); *United States v. 829 Calle De Madero,* 100 F.3d 734, 738 (10th Cir. 1996); *United States v. One Parcel of Property Located at 32 Medley Lane,* 372 F. Supp. 2d 248, 258 (D. Conn. 2005); *United States v. DeGregory,* 480 F. Supp. 2d 1302, 1304 (S.D. Fla. 2006), and the hearing is before the court without a jury. *See* 18 U.S.C. § 983(g)(3); *United States v. Derman,* 211 F.3d 175, 184 (1st Cir. 2000). The claimant must also demonstrate a legal ownership in the property to establish standing to object to the forfeiture under the excessive fines clause. *United States v. Cochenour,* 441 F.3d 599, 601 (8th Cir. 2006).

The court must conduct a balancing test comparing the value of the forfeiture to the gravity of the offense underlying the forfeiture. *See* 18 U.S.C. § 983(g)(2).

Some of the factors that the courts have utilized in this balancing test include:

(1) The value of the property versus the maximum fine available under the criminal offense. *See United States v. 817 N.E. 29th Drive, Wilton Manors,* 175 F.3d 1304, 1309 (11th Cir. 1999); *United States v. One Parcel of Property Located at 1512 Lark Drive,* 978 F. Supp. 935, 940 (D.S.D. 1997); *United States v. Reiner,* 397 F. Supp. 2d 101, 114 (D. Me. 2005); *United States v. Heldeman,* 402 F.3d 220, 223 (1st Cir. 2005); *United States v. Cekosky,* 171 Fed. Appx. 785, 788 (11th Cir. 2006); *United States v. Ford Motor Company,* 442 F. Supp. 2d 429, 437 (E.D. Mich. 2006) (a forfeiture 31 times the amount of the fine was excessive); *United States v. Ortiz-Cintron,* 461 F.3d 78, 82 (1st Cir. 2006); *United States v. Carpenter,* 317 F.3d 618, 627 (6th Cir. 2003).

(2) The value of the drugs sold. *United States v. One Parcel (45 Claremont St.)*, 108 Fed. Appx. 651, 657 (1st Cir. 2004); *United States v. 817 N.E. 29th Drive, Wilton Manors*, 175 F.3d 1304, 1310 (11th Cir. 1999); *United States v. One 1995 Grady White 22' Boat*, 415 F. Supp. 2d 590, 595 (D. Md. 2006).

(3) The scope and duration of the related criminal activity. *See United States v. Wyly*, 193 F.3d 289, 303 (5th Cir. 1999); *United States v. Real Property Known as 415 East Mitchell Ave.*, 149 F.3d 472, 477 (6th Cir. 1998); *United States v. One Parcel of Real Property Known as 16614 Cayuga Rd*, 69 Fed. Appx. 915, 919 (10th Cir. 2003) (large-scale marijuana operation); *United States v. Hosseini*, 504 F. Supp. 2d 376, 382 (N.D. Ill. 2007) (car dealerships involved in multi-year, multi-million dollar gang racketeering and money laundering conspiracy).

(4) The harm caused. *See United States v. 3814 N.W. Thurman Street,* 164 F.3d 1191, 1198 (9th Cir. 1999); *United States v. Bollin*, 264 F.3d 391, 417 (4th Cir. 2001); *United States v. Collado*, 348 F.3d 323, 328 (2d Cir. 2003) ($20 million in drug sales from the building); *United States v. DeGregory*, 480 F. Supp. 2d 1302, 1304–05 (S.D. Fla. 2006) (illegally transported radioactive material in and out of country).

(5) The relationship of the property to the offense. *See United States v. Real Property (40 Clark Road)*, 52 F. Supp. 2d 254, 267 (D. Mass. 1999); *United States v. One 1990 Ford Ranger Truck*, 888 F. Supp. 1170 (1995) (transportation of personal use quantities of mushrooms); *Von Hofe v. United States*, 492 F.3d 175, 188 (2d Cir. 2007) (use of home in cultivation was "lengthy and extensive").

(6) The owner's culpability. *See Yskamp v. DEA*, 163 F.3d 767, 773 (3d Cir. 1998); *United States v. One 1997 Ford Expedition*, 135 F. Supp. 2d 1142, 1146 (D.N.M. 2001); *United States v. One Parcel (45 Claremont St.)*, 108 Fed. Appx. 651, 657 (1st Cir. 2004) (directly involved in criminal activity); *United States v. Lot Numbered One of the Lavaland Annex*, 256 F.3d 949, 958 (10th Cir. 2001); *United States v. One Parcel (10380 SW 28th Street)*, 214 F.3d 1291, 1295 (11th Cir. 2000) (criminal conviction and sentence); *United States v. $3,124,977.28 in U.S. Currency*, 239 Fed. Appx. 335, 338 (9th Cir. 2007) (court considered the gravity of the offense, not the specific culpability of the parties).

The U.S. Department of Justice has promulgated a test for excessiveness that focuses on three factors:

(1) The criminal activity involving the property has been sufficiently extensive in terms of time and/or spatial use of the property, OR

(2) The role of the property was integral or indispensable to the commission of the crime in question, OR

(3) The particular property was deliberately selected to secure a special advantage in the commission of the crime. *See* U.S. Department of Justice, *Government Response to Forfeiture Challenges Under the Excessive Fines Clause in Light of Austin/Alexander*, Jan. 1994, at 18.

This test directs the analysis to the nexus of the property to the offense and the manner in which the property is utilized in the underlying offense, and away from subjective factors.

An excessive fines challenge is an affirmative defense that must be pled in the claimant's answer to the complaint. Supplemental Rule G(8)(e)(1); Fed. R. Civ. Pro. 8. It is a post-judgment motion because it cannot be raised until the government establishes that the property is forfeitable under the statute and a judgment has been entered. *See United States v. Funds in the Amount of $170,926.00*, 985 F. Supp. 810, 814 (N.D. Ill. 1997); *United States v. $633,021.67 in U.S. Currency*, 842 F. Supp. 528, 535 (N.D. Ga. 1993); *United States v. One Parcel of Real Estate Located at 13143 S.W. 15th Lane*, 872 F. Supp. 968, 974 (S.D. Fla. 1994). Therefore, it should only be heard after a trial on the merits, or summary judgment motion is filed. *See United States v. 47 West 644 Route 38*, 190 F.3d 781, 783 (7th Cir. 1999); *United States v. One Parcel (2526 Faxon Avenue)*, 145 F. Supp. 2d 942, 952–53 (W.D. Tenn. 2001). If raised during a summary judgment motion, the court has the discretion to reopen discovery to allow additional evidence to be received on this issue. *See* Supplemental Rule G(8)(e)(ii); *United States v. $100,348 U.S. Currency*, 157 F. Supp. 2d 1110, 1119 (C.D. Cal. 2001).

If a court finds that the forfeiture is grossly disproportionate to the offense, it has the option of either reducing, *see United States v. Real Property Located in El Dorado County*, 59 F.3d 974, 986 (9th Cir. 1995); *United States v. Bieri*, 21 F.3d 819, 824–25 (8th Cir. 1994); *United States v. $100,348*, 354 F.3d 1110, 1118 (9th Cir. 2004), or eliminating it. *See* 18 U.S.C. § 983(g)(4); *United States v. Real Property 835 Seventh Street*, 820 F. Supp. 688, 696–97 (N.D.N.Y. 1993); *United States v. 4641 Shelby County Rd. 361*, 857 F. Supp. 935, 940–41 (N.D. Ala. 1994). Notice that the cases that generally are in line for dismissal are real property forfeitures where the criminal activity is tangential to the value of the property. Most other cases involving currency and other assets are more amenable to mitigation of the forfeiture. *See United States v. Bajakajian*, 84 F.3d 334, 338 (9th Cir. 1996).

State Excessive Fines Litigation

The U.S. Supreme Court has never held that the Eighth Amendment excessive fines clause applies to the states through the Fourteenth Amendment, *see Browning-Ferris v. Kelco Disposal,* 492 U.S. 257, 276 n.22 (1989), and prior U.S. Supreme Court cases were uniform in recognizing that the Eighth Amendment's excessive fines clause does not apply to the states. *See Pervear v. Commonwealth,* 72 U.S. 475, 480 (1867); *Eilenbecker v. District Court of Plymouth County,* 134 U.S. 31, 34–35 (1890); *O'Neil v. Vermont,* 144 U.S. 323, 332 (1892); *Waters-Pierce Oil Co. v. Texas,* 212 U.S. 86, 111 (1909); *Knapp v. Schweitzer,* 357 U.S. 371, 379 n.5 (1958). Therefore, before a state prosecutor concedes that a state forfeiture is controlled by the *Austin* or *Bajakajian* cases, he or she should thoroughly review the state constitution and forfeiture statute. *See State v. Meister,* 866 S.W. 2d 485, 488 (Mo. App. W.D. 1993).

However, most state courts have concluded that their forfeiture statutes are governed by either the federal or state excessive fines clause. See Table 12-1. Additionally, several states provide for statutory protection against excessive fines in their forfeiture statues. See Table 12-1.

Table 12-1
State Constitutional Protections
Eighth Amendment Excessive Fines Clause

State	Test	Authority
Alabama	Grossly disproportional	*Dorough, Ex Parte*, 773 So.2d 1001, 1005 (Ala. 2000)
Arizona	Grossly disproportional	*State v. Leyva*, 195 Ariz. 13, 19-21; 985 P.2d 498 (Ariz. App. 1998); *In re One Residence 319 E. Fairgrounds Dr.* 71 P.3d 930, 937 (Ariz. App. 2003)
Colorado	Grossly disproportional	Colo. Rev. Stat. § 16-13-303 5.1(a.5)(I)
Florida	Instrumentality & Proportionality	*Town of Jupiter v. Garcia*, 698 So.2d 871, 872 (Fla. App. 1997); *In re Forfeiture of 1990 Chevy Blazer*, 684 So.2d 197, 199 (Fla. App. 1996); *In re: One 1993 Dodge Intrepid*, 645 So.2d 551, 552 (Fla. App. 1994)
Georgia	Instrumentality & Proportionality	*Rabern v. State*, 221 Ga. App. 874; 473 S.E.2d 547; 552 (Ga. App. 1996); *Thorp v. State*, 264 Ga. 712; 450 S.E.2d 416, 419 (Ga. 1994); *State v. Evans*, 225 Ga.App. 402; 484 S.E.2d 70, 73 (Ga. App. 1997)
Hawaii	Grossly disproportionate	Hawaii Rev. Stat. § 712A-5.5
Idaho	Grossly disproportionate	*Nez Perce County Prosecuting Attorney v. Reese*, 142 Idaho 893; 136 P.3d 364 (Idaho App. 2006)

Table 12-1 (continued)
State Constitutional Protections
Eighth Amendment Excessive Fines Clause

State	Test	Authority
Illinois	Instrumentality & Proportionality	*Peo ex. Rel. Waller v. 1989 Ford F350 Truck,* 162 Ill.2d 78; 642 N.E.2d 460, 466 (Ill. 1994); *People v. $5,970 U.S. Currency,* 279 Ill.App.3d 583; 664 N.E.2d 1115, 1122 (Ill. App. 1996)
Indiana	Grossly disproportional	*$100 v. State,* 822 N.E.2d 1001, 1011 (Ind. App. 2005)
Iowa	Grossly disproportionate	*Matter of H.E.W., Inc.,* 530 N.W.2d. 460, 464 (Iowa. App. 1995); *Matter of Property Seized from Chiodo,* 555 N.W.2d 412, 416-17 (Iowa 1996); *In re Property Seized from Terrell,* 639 N.W.2d 18, 21 (Iowa 2002)
Kansas	Grossly disproportionate	Kansas Stat. Ann. § 60-4106(c)
Kentucky	Grossly disproportionate	*Harbin v. Com.,* 121 S.W.3d 191, 197 (Ky. 2003); *Hinkle v. Com.,* 104 S.W.3d 778 , 782 (Ky. App. 2002)
Maryland	Instrumentality & Proportionality	*Aravanis v. Somerset County,* 339 Md. 644, 664 A.2d 888 , 893-94 (Md. 1995)
Michigan	Proportionality	*In re Forfeiture of $25,505,* 220 Mich.App. 572; 560 N.W.2d 341, 347 (Mich. App. 1996)
Minnesota	Gross Disproportionality	*City of Worthington Police Dept. v. One 1988 Chevrolet Berreta,* 516 N.W.2d 581, 584 (Minn. App. 1994)

Table 12-1 (continued)
State Constitutional Protections
Eighth Amendment Excessive Fines Clause

State	Test	Authority
Mississippi	Instrumentality & Proportionality	*One (1) 1979 Ford 15V v. State ex re. Mississippi Bureau of Narcotics*, 721 So.2d 631, 636 (Miss. 1998); *One (1) Charter Arms, Bulldog 44 Special v. State ex rel. Moore*, 721 So.2d 620, 625 (Miss. 1998)
Missouri	Proportionality	*State v. Meister*, 866 S.W.2d 485, 490 (Mo. App. 1993)
Nevada	None articulated	*Levingston v. Washoe County Sheriff*, 112 Nev. 479; 916 P.2d 163, 169 (Nev. 1996)
New Hampshire	1 – Substantial connection; 2 – Extensive criminal activity; 3 – Value of property outweighs a. value of drugs b. costs of investigation c. harm caused by criminal conduct.	N.H. Rev. Stat. § 318-B:17-b IV (e)
New Jersey	Instrumentality	*State v. Williams*, 286 N.J. Super. 507; 669 A.2d 867, 874 (N.J. Super.L. 1995)
New Mexico	Value of property does not exceed: a) pecuniary gain derived or sought to be derived from crime; b) pecuniary loss caused or sought to be caused by the crime or; c) the value of the convicted owner's interest in the property	N.M. Stat. Ann. § 31-27-6.E

Table 12-1 (continued)
State Constitutional Protections
Eighth Amendment Excessive Fines Clause

State	Test	Authority
Ohio	Totality of circumstances; Proportionality	*State v. Hill,* 70 Ohio St.3d 25; 635 N.E.2d 1248, 1256 (Ohio. 1994); *Rice v. Logan Cty. Bd. Of Commrs.,* 114 Ohio App.3d 198; 682 N.E.2d 1106, 1109 (Ohio App. 1996); *State v. Harold,* 109 Ohio App.3d 87; 671 N.E.2d 1078, 1082 (Ohio App. 1996)
Oregon	Proportionality	Ore. Rev. Stat. §§ 131.585; 475A.100
Pennsylvania	Grossly disproportional	*Com. v. Real Property and Improvements,* 574 Pa. 423; 832 A.2d 396, 402 (Pa. 2003)
South Carolina	Instrumentality	*Medlock v. One 1985 Jeep Cherokee,* 322 S.C. 127; 470 S.E.2d 373, 377 (S. C. 1996)
Tennessee	Proportionality	*Stuart v. State Dept. of Safety,* 963 S.W.2d 28, 36 (Tenn. 1998)
Texas	Grossly disproportional	*One Car v. State,* 122 S.W.3d 422, 428 (Tex. App. 2003)
Utah	Proportionality	Utah Code Ann. § 24-1-14; *State v. 392 South 600 East, Nephi,* 886 P.2d 534, 541 (Utah 1994)
Washington	Instrumentality & Proportionality	*Tellevik v. Real Property,* 83 Wash.App. 366; 921 P.2d 1088, 1093 (Wash. App. 1996); *State v. Clark,* 124 Wash.2d 90; 875 P.2d 613, 619 (Wash. 1994)
Wisconsin	Grossly disproportional	*State v. Boyd,* 238 Wis.2d 693; 618 N.W.2d 251, 256 (Wis. App. 2000); *State v. Hammad,* 212 Wis.2d 343; 569 N.W.2d 68, 73 (Wis. App. 1997)

States uniformly have found that, because proceeds forfeitures merely disgorge the illicit profits from the offender, they are remedial, proportionate, and do not violate the Eighth Amendment excessive clause. *State ex rel. Napolitano v. Gravano*, 204 Ariz. 106; 60 P.3d 246, 256 (Ariz. App. 2002); *In re Forfeiture of $25,505*, 220 Mich. App. 572; 560 N.W.2d 341, 347 (Mich. App. 1996); *State v. Meister*, 866 S.W.2d 485, 491 (App. W.D. 1993); *Stuart v. State Dept. of Safety*, 963 S.W.2d 28, 34 (Tenn. 1998).

2. States Follow Various Tests to Evaluate the Excessive Fines Challenge

Most states use the "grossly disproportional" standard from the U.S. Supreme Court *Bajakajian* case. *See Dorough, Ex Parte*, 773 So. 2d 1001, 1004 (Ala. 2000); *$100 v. State*, 822 N.E.2d 1001, 1011 (Ind. App. 2005); *Com. v. Real Property and Improvements*, 574 Pa. 423; 832 A.2d 396, 403 (Pa. 2003). Others focus on the relationship of the property to the illegal activity under the "instrumentality" test. *State v. Williams*, 286 N.J. Super. 507; 669 A.2d 867, 874 (N.J. Super. L.1995); *Medlock v. One 1985 Jeep Cherokee*, 322 S.C. 127; 470 S.E.2d 373, 377 (S.C. 1996). Other states consider subjective elements in their analysis under a "proportionality" test. *State v. Evans*, 225 Ga. App. 402; 484 S.E.2d 70, 72 (Ga. App. 1997) (family home has intangible value); *People v. $5,970 U.S. Currency*, 279 Ill. App. 3d 583; 664 N.E.2d 1115, 1122 (Ill. App. 1996) (society places higher value on real property); *Nez Perce County Prosecuting Attorney v. Reese*, 142 Idaho 893; 136 P.3d 364, 371 (Idaho App. 2006) (effect of forfeiture on third parties character of property as a residence, claimant's economic circumstances).

Some of the factors states courts have considered in determining excessiveness include:

- • Nature and extent of criminal activity, *State v. Harold*, 109 Ohio App. 3d 87; 671 N.E.2d 1078, 1083 (Ohio App. 1996) (multiple transactions near school); *Com. v. Schill*, 164 Pa. Cmwlth. 594; 643 A.2d 1143, 1146 (Pa. Cmwlth. 1994) (multiple transactions); *In re King Properties*, 535 Pa. 321; 635 A.2d 128, 133 (Pa. 1993) (base of ongoing drug operation); *One (1) 1979 Ford 15V v. State ex rel. Mississippi Bureau of Narcotics*, 721 So. 2d 631, 637 (Miss. 1998) (large amount of drugs involved);
- • Value of drugs, *Howard County v. One 1994 Chevrolet Corvette*, 119 Md. App. 93; 704 A.2d 455, 463 (Md. App. 1998) (personal amounts only); *State v 392 South 600 East, Nephi*, 886 P.2d 534, 542 (Utah

1994) (personal amounts only); *State v. Evans*, 225 Ga. App. 402; 484 S.E.2d 70, 73 (Ga. App. 1997) (small amount of drugs);

- Value of property, *Com. v. Mitchell*, 833 A.2d 1220, 1223 (Pa. Cmwlth. 2003) (car value less than maximum fine); *State v. Hammad*, 212 Wis.2d 343; 569 N.W.2d 68, 73 (Wis. App. 1997) (same);
- Prior criminal history, *Thompson v. Grindle*, 113 Md. App. 477; 688 A.2d 466, 472 (Md. App. 1997) (no prior record); *One (1) Charter Arms, Bulldog 44 Special v. State ex rel. Moore*, 721 So. 2d 620, 625 (Miss. 1998) (same);
- Harm caused by criminal conduct, *State v. One House*, 346 N.J. Super. 247; 787 A.2d 905, 910 (N.J. Super. A.D. 2001) (cultivation for personal use only); *One Car v. State*, 122 S.W.3d 422, 427 (Tx. App. 2003) (misdemeanor conviction only); and
- Nexus between the property and offense, *Rabern v. State*, 242 Ga. App. 804; 531 S.E.2d 373, 376 (Ga. App. 2000) (plants in shed attached to house).

C. Fifth Amendment Double Jeopardy Clause

The double jeopardy clause prevents multiple punishments for the same offense, *see North Carolina v. Pearce*, 395 U.S. 711, 717 (1969), and the U.S. Supreme Court had previously held that the double jeopardy clause was inapplicable to a civil *in rem* forfeiture action. *See United States v. One Assortment of 89 Firearms*, 465 U.S. 354, 361 (1984). However, between 1989 and 1996, the federal and state courts took a bumpy detour in the application of the double jeopardy clause to civil forfeiture actions.

In *United States v. Halper*, 490 U.S. 435 (1989), the defendant was charged with 65 counts of filing false Medicare invoices. He had overcharged the government $9 per bill for a total out-of-pocket loss of $585. He was convicted of all 65 counts and received a criminal sentence of two years in prison and a $5,000 fine. The government then brought a civil action pursuant to 31 U.S.C. §§ 3729–3731, which provided for a civil penalty of $2,000 per count, or $130,000. Halper appealed, claiming that the civil penalty violated the double jeopardy clause.

The U.S. Supreme Court ruled that a civil action that cannot fairly be said to serve a remedial purpose, but rather can only be explained as also serving either retributive or deterrent purposes, is punishment. *Halper*, 490 U.S. at 448. Consequently, a defendant who has already been punished in a criminal prosecution may not be subjected to an additional civil sanction that may not fairly be characterized as remedial without violating the double jeopardy clause. *Id.* at 449.

In 1993, the Court issued its decision in *Austin,* 509 U.S. 602 (1993), holding that the excessive fines clause of the Eighth Amendment applies to a civil as well as a criminal action if the civil action was, in part, punitive. In its decision, the Court quoted *Halper,* stating that civil actions must be remedial and rationally related to making the government whole. *Id.* at 610.

In 1994, the U.S. Supreme Court heard the case of *Department of Revenue of Montana v. Kurth Ranch,* 511 U.S. 767 (1994). The defendant was charged with possession of drugs for sales to which he pled guilty and was sentenced to state prison. The county attorney also brought a civil *in rem* forfeiture action against currency and equipment, and the defendant entered into a stipulated settlement of that action. Thereafter, the Montana Department of Revenue assessed a tax pursuant the state drug tax in the amount of almost $900,000. The defendant appealed, charging that the drug tax assessment violated the double jeopardy clause.

The majority ruled that a drug tax assessed in a separate proceeding after a criminal conviction was punitive and barred by the Fifth Amendment double jeopardy clause. *Kurth Ranch,* 511 U.S. at 778.

In September 1994, the Ninth Circuit dealt federal prosecutors a major setback when it released its opinion in *United States v. $405,089.23 U.S. Currency et al.,* 33 F.3d 1210 (9th Cir. 1994), which set aside the civil forfeiture of almost one million dollars of property seized and forfeited as drug proceeds as a second "punishment" in violation of the double jeopardy clause because the defendants had already been previously convicted in a "separate proceeding." *Id.* at 1222. The civil *in rem* forfeiture action was dismissed because it was the second punishment. The Ninth Circuit cited as authority for its decision the U.S. Supreme Court decisions in *Halper, Austin,* and *Kurth Ranch.*[1]

In August 1995, the Sixth Circuit joined suit with the Ninth Circuit and set aside a federal criminal conviction of manufacturing marijuana and a sentence of 63 months imprisonment because the defendant previously had resolved a civil forfeiture action by paying $13,250 in lieu of forfeiture. The Sixth Circuit reasoned that the civil forfeiture constituted "punishment" for double jeopardy purposes and set aside the criminal conviction and sentence because they were the second punishment in a separate proceeding. *See United States v. Ursery,* 59 F.3d 568, 576 (6th Cir. 1995).

A massive increase in double jeopardy litigation ensued with defendants attempting to set aside civil forfeiture judgments based on previous criminal convictions or obtain dismissal of criminal convictions on account of the prior resolved civil forfeiture action.[2] Many state courts followed the *$405,089.23* and *Ursery* appellate decisions and found that their state forfeiture provisions were punitive and that separately filed civil forfeiture actions violated the double jeopardy clause. *People v. Towns,* 269 Ill.App.3d 907; 646 N.E.2d 1366 (1995); *rev.,* 169 Ill.2d 260; 661 N.E.2d 329, *vacated,* 518 U.S. 1031; *State v. 1979 Cadillac DeVille,* 632 So. 2d 1221 (La. App. 1994), *vacated,* 667 So. 2d 510 (1996); *Stratemeyer v. State,* 107 Md. App. 420; 668 A.2d 948 (1995); *State v. Rosenfeld,* 540 N.W.2d 915 (Mn. App. 1995); *Wright v. State,* 112 Nev. 391; 916 P.2d 146 (Nev. 1996); *Levingston v. Washoe County By and Through Sheriff of Washoe County,* 112 Nev. 479; 916 P.2d 163 (Nev. 1996); *State v. One Lot of $8,560 in U.S. Currency,* 670 A.2d 772 (R.I. 1996); *State v. Romero,* 907 S.W.2d 858 (Tex. App. 1995); *Ex parte Ariza,* 913 S.W.2d 215 (Tex. App. 1995), *set aside,* 934 S.W.2d 393; *State v. Davis,* 903 P.2d 940 (Utah App. 1995), *rev'd,* 972 P.2d 388 (Utah 1998); *State v. Catlett,* 81 Wash. App. 791; 916 P.2d 975 (Wash. App. 1996); *rev'd,* 133 Wash.2d 355; 945 P.2d 700 (Wash. 1997).

Double jeopardy challenges were not limited to civil forfeiture statutes, but defense attorneys were using the *$405,089.23* and *Ursery* cases to argue dismissal of criminal charges based on separate impositions of such diverse sanctions as revocation of professional licenses, *see Loui v. Board of Medical Examiners,* 889 P.2d 705 (Haw. 1995), imposition of prison discipline, *see State v. Walker,* 646 A.2d 209 (Conn. App. Ct. 1994), *appeal denied,* 648 A.2d 159 (Conn. 1994), and suspension of drivers licenses. *See Baldwin v. Department of Motor Vehicles,* 35 Cal. App. 4th 1630 (1995).

The U.S. Supreme Court granted consolidated review of the *$405,089.23* and *Ursery* cases, and in *United States v. Ursery,* 518 U.S. 267 (1996), made the following findings:

(1) *In rem* civil forfeiture is neither punishment nor criminal for purposes of the double jeopardy clause. *Id.* at 292.

(2) *In rem* forfeiture is a remedial civil sanction distinct from potentially punitive *in personam* civil penalties and does not constitute punishment for double jeopardy. *Id.* at 284–286.

(3) *Halper* refers to civil *in personam* penalties and its case-by-case balancing test is inapplicable to civil *in rem* forfeiture. *Id.* at 284.

(4) *Austin* is limited to the Eighth Amendment excessive fines clause *Id.* at 287.

(5) Civil *in rem* forfeiture is not per se exempt from the double jeopardy clause, and whether a civil action is punitive is determined by the following test:

a) Did Congress intend the proceedings to be criminal or civil?

b) Are the proceedings so punitive in fact that they must be considered criminal rather than civil? *Id.* at 288.

(6) Only the "clearest proof" will suffice to demonstrate that an *in rem* forfeiture action is so punitive as to be equivalent to a criminal prosecution. *Id.* at 289, n.3; *United States v. Ward,* 448 U.S. 242, 248 (1980).

The *Ursery* opinion did much to resolve the confusion concerning the application of the double jeopardy clause to civil asset forfeiture cases and to quell the mounting number of appeals on that issue.

The final turn in the double jeopardy forfeiture journey occurred with the court's opinion in *Hudson v. United States,* 522 U.S. 93 (1997). Federal banking officials imposed civil monetary penalties against the defendant for illegal loans that had been issued. When the government later criminally indicted him for the same conduct, he alleged a double jeopardy violation.

The U.S. Supreme Court granted certiorari to resolve novel double jeopardy claims made in the wake of *Halper.* The court basically relegated the *Halper* test to history calling it "ill considered" and "unworkable," *Id.* at 106 (J. Scalia, concurring), and instead reaffirmed the test of *United States v. Ward,* 448 U.S. 242, 248 (1980), limiting the inquiry to two questions: (1) whether the legislature intended the statute to be criminal or civil; and (2) whether the statute is so punitive in purpose or effect as to make it criminal rather than civil. *Hudson,* 522 U.S. at 96.

Thus, the double jeopardy-civil asset forfeiture merry-go-round has now returned to its starting gate, and challenges based on violations of the double jeopardy clause have virtually disappeared in the federal and state jurisdictions as courts are following *Ursery. See United States v. Real Property (Parcel 03179-005R),* 287 F. Supp. 2d 45, 56 (D.D.C. 2003) (no double jeopardy violation for civil forfeiture based on prior criminal conviction for same offense); *Com. v. Wingait Farms,* 547 Pa. 332; 690 A.2d 222, 226 (Pa. 1997) (claimant failed to show by clearest proof that forfeiture proceedings were punitive).

Table 12-2 is a list of state cases relating to the application of the double jeopardy clause to civil forfeiture actions. In the aftermath of *Ursery,* virtually all states have found that their civil forfeiture statutes are not punitive and do not offend the Fifth Amendment double jeopardy clause.

Table 12-2
State Constitutional Protections
Fifth Amendment Double Jeopardy Clause

State	Punitive	Not Punitive	Authority
Alabama		X	*Money v. State*, 717 So.2d 38, 46 (Ala. Cr. App. 1997); *Wilhite v. State*, 689 So.2d 221, 224 (Ala. Cr. 1996)
Arkansas		X	*State v. Rice*, 329 Ark 219; 947 S.W.2d. 3, 4 (Ark. 1997); *Sims v. State*, 326 Ark. 296; 930 S.W.2d 381, 382 (Ark. 1996)
Arizona		X	*State v. Geotis*, 187 Ariz. 521; 930 P.2d 1324, 1326 (Ariz. App. 1996)
California		X	*People v. $4,413 U.S. Currency*, 47 Cal. App. 4th 1631, 1637 (1996); *People v. Shanndoah*, 49 Cal. App. 4th 1187, 1191 (1996); *People v. Nazem*, 51 Cal. App. 4th 1225, 1233 (1996)
Colorado		X	*People v. Ferrel*, 929 P.2d 65, 67 (Colo. App. 1996); *People v. Milton*, 732 P.2d 1199, 1204 (Colo. 1987); *People v. Coolidge*, 953 P.2d 949 , 951 (Colo. App. 1997)
Delaware		X	*In re: 1982 Honda, Delaware Registration No. 83466*, 681 A.2d 1035, 1038 (Del.Supr. 1996)
Florida		X	*Town of Jupiter v. Garcia*, 698 So.2d 871 (Fla. App. 1997); *In re Forfeiture of 1986 Pontiac Firebird*, 600 So.2d 1178, 1179 (Fla. App. 1992); *State v. Sobieck*, 701 So.2d 96, 102 (Fla. App. 1997); *State v. Llewellyn*, 682 So.2d 1242, 1243 (Fla. App. 1996); *State v. Powelson*, 680 So.2d 1089, 1090 (Fla. App. 1996)

Table 12-2 (continued)
State Constitutional Protections
Fifth Amendment Double Jeopardy Clause

State	Punitive	Not Punitive	Authority
Georgia		X	*Cuellar v. State*, 230 Ga. App. 203; 496 S.E.2d 282, 283 (Ga. App. 1998); *Murphy v. State*, 267 Ga. 120, 475 S.E.2d 907, 908 (Ga. 1996)
Hawaii		X	*State v. Tuipuapua*, 83 Haw. 141; 925 P.2d 311, 323 (Hawaii 1996)
Idaho		X	*State v. Ayala*, 129 Idaho 911; 935 P.2d 174, 182 (Ida. App. 1996); *State v. Ross*, 129 Idaho 380; 924 P.2d 1224, 1225 (Idaho 1996); *State v. McGough*, 129 Idaho 371; 924 P.2d 633, 637 (Idaho App. 1996)
Illinois		X	*People ex re. Neal v. Ryan*, 284 Ill.App.3d 318; 672 N.E.2d 47, 50 (Ill. App. 1996); *In re P.S.*, 175 Ill.2d 79; 676 N.E.2d 656, 661 (Ill. 1997); *People v. Daniels*, 283 Ill.App.3d 958, 670 N.E.2d 1223, 1228 (Ill. App. 1996)
Indiana		X	*$100 v. State*, 822 N.E.2d 1001, 1010 (Ind. App. 2005); *Davis v. State*, 819 N.E.2d 863, 869 (Ind. App. 2004); *Willis v. State*, 806 N.E.2d 817, 823 (Ind. App. 2004); *C.R.M. v. State*, 799 N.E.2d 555, 561 (Ind. App. 2003)
Iowa		X	*State v. Predka*, 555 N.W.2d 202, 213 (Iowa 1996)
Kansas		X	*State v. Yeoman*, 24 K.A.2d 639; 951 P.2d 964, 966 (Kan. App. 1997)
Kentucky		X	*Smith v. Com.*, 205 S.W.3d 217, 223 (Ky. App. 2006)

Table 12-2 (continued)
State Constitutional Protections
Fifth Amendment Double Jeopardy Clause

State	Punitive	Not Punitive	Authority
Louisiana		X	*State v. Johnson*, 667 So.2d 510, 519 (La. 1996);
Massachusetts		X	*Com. v. Vieira*, 671 N.E.2d 531, 533 (Mass. App. 1996)
Maryland		X	*Jones v. State*, 111 Md.App. 456; 681 A.2d 1190, 1204-05 (Md. App. 1996); *One 1984 Ford Truck v. Baltimore County*, 111 Md.App. 194; 681 A.2d 527, 533 (Md. App. 1996)
Michigan		X	*In re Forfeiture of $25,505*, 220 Mich.App. 572; 560 N.W.2d 341, 347 (Mich. App. 1996)
Minnesota		X	*Freeman v. Residence Located at 1215 21st Street, Minneapolis*, 552 N.W.2d 275, 277 (Minn. App. 1996)
Mississippi		X	*State v. Fleming*, 726 So.2d 113, 115 (Miss.1998); *Luckett v. State*, 797 So.2d 339, 345 (Miss. App. 2001)
Nebraska	X		*State v. One 1987 Toyota Pickup*, 233 Neb. 670; 447 N.W.2d 243, 249 (Neb. 1989)
Nevada		X	*Levingston v. Washoe County*, 114 Nev. 306; 956 P.2d 84, 88 (Nev. 1998)
New Hampshire		X	*In re 1994 Chevrolet Cavalier*, 142 N.H. 705; 708 A.2d 397, 400 (N.H. 1998)

Table 12-2 (continued)
State Constitutional Protections
Fifth Amendment Double Jeopardy Clause

State	Punitive	Not Punitive	Authority
New Jersey		X	State v. $3,000 in U.S. Currency, 292 N.J.Super. 205; 678 A.2d 741, 744 (N.J. Super.A.D. 1996)
New Mexico	X		State v. Nunez, 129 N.M. 63; 2 P.3d 264, 273 (N.M. 1999); State v. Tijerino, 135 N.M. 313; 87 P.3d 1095, 1097 (N.M. App. 2004)
New York		X	People v. Edmonson, 300 A.D.2d 317; 751 N.Y.S.2d 280, 281 (N.Y. A.D. 2002)
Ohio*	X		State v. Casalicchio, 58 Ohio St.3d 178; 569 N.E.2d 916, 921 (Ohio 1991)
Oklahoma		X	Lozoya v. State, 932 P.2d 22, 27 (Okl. Cr. App. 1996)
Pennsylvania		X	Com. v. Wingait Farms, 547 Pa. 332; 690 A.2d 222, 226 (Pa. 1997); Com. v. Trayer, 452 Pa.Super. 1; 680 A.2d 1166, 1168 (Pa. Super. 1996)
Rhode Island		X	State v. One 1990 Chevrolet Corvette, 695 A.2d 502, 507 (R.I. 1997)
South Dakota		X	State v. Kienast, 553 N.W.2d 254, 256 (S.D. 1996)
Tennessee		X	State v. Blackmon, 984 S.W.2d 589, 592 (Tenn. 1998); Stuart v. State Dept. of Safety, 963 S.W.2d 28, 33-34 (Tenn. 1998)

* Although the Ohio Supreme Court determined in State v. Casalicchio, 58 Ohio St.3d 178, 569 N.E.2d 916 (1991) that the Ohio forfeiture statute was punitive and double jeopardy precludes a civil forfeiture filed after criminal sentencing, it is a pre-Ursery decision. Other states have declined to follow it. Smith v. Com., 205 S.W.3d 217, 220 (Ky. App. Feb. 10, 2006)

Table 12-2 (continued)
State Constitutional Protections
Fifth Amendment Double Jeopardy Clause

State	Punitive	Not Punitive	Authority
Texas		X	*Romero v. State,* 927 S.W.2d 632, 635 (Tex. 1996); *Johnson v. State,* 931 S.W.2d 314, 317 (Tex. Cr. App. 1996); *Fant v.. State,* 931 S.W.2d 299, 308 (Tex. Cr. App. 1996); *Prear v. State,* 933 S.W.2d 643, 646 (Tex. App. 1996)
Utah		X	*State v. Davis,* 972 P.2d 388, 391 (Utah 1998); *State v. One Hundred Seventy-Five Thousand Eight Hundred Dollars,* 942 P.2d 343, 349 (Utah 1997); *State v. One 1980 Cadillac,* 21 P.3d 212, 216 (Utah 2001)
Washington		X	*State v. Catlett,* 133 Wash.2d 355; 945 P.2d 700, 703 (Wash. 1997); *State v. Lynch,* 84 Wash. App. 467; 929 P.2d 460, 473 (Wash. App.1996)
West Virginia		X	*State v. Greene,* 196 W.Va. 500; 473 S.E.2d 921, 925 (W.Va. 1996)

There are two notable exceptions to states following the *Ursery* case. In Nebraska, the supreme court has determined that the state drug forfeiture statute is a criminal statute; consequently, forfeiture actions there must be filed in the same proceeding as the criminal case. *See Nebraska v. Juan Franco, Jr.,* 257 Neb. 15; 594 N.W.2d 633, 642 (Neb. 1999).

Under our system of federalism, a state constitution may provide constitutional protections beyond that guaranteed by the federal Constitution. *See State v. Zerkel,* 900 P.2d 744, 751–52 n.4 (Ala. App. 1995). In New Mexico, the supreme court has ruled that the double jeopardy clause in the state constitution contains higher protections than the federal Constitution and hence refused to apply *Ursery,* finding that separately filed civil forfeiture actions under the Controlled Substances Act are punitive and violate the state double jeopardy clause. *See State v. Nunez*, 129 N.M. 63; 2 P.3d 264, 275 (1999). A legislative fix to this problem appears to have been enacted given that new legislation now consolidates civil *in rem* forfeiture narcotic actions with pending criminal cases to provide for a single proceeding. *See N.M. Code Ann.* § 31-27-6C.

However, the New Mexico Supreme Court has upheld the civil forfeiture of vehicles seized from repeat offender, driving-under-the-influence offenders and revoked driver's licenses on a nuisance theory, reasoning that the city ordinance was remedial. *See City of Albuquerque v. One 1984 White Chevy*, 132 N.M. 187; 46 P.3d 94, 99 (2002). This is consistent with other post-*Chavez* appellate cases that upheld the revocation of bail and denial of prison good-time credits, finding they were administrative acts that were remedial. *See State v. Astorga*, 129 N.M. 736, 738; 13 P.3d 468 (2000); *State v. Elliott*, 131 N.M. 390, 399; 37 P.3d 107 (2001). The message to practitioners in New Mexico appears to be that the ruling of *Chavez* is extremely narrow and will not be applied wholesale to other areas without a finding that the statute is punitive.

Other state courts that have examined the federal and state double jeopardy clauses have found that they provide the same protection, and that separately filed civil forfeitures do not violate the double jeopardy clause. *See People v. $4,413.00 U.S. Currency*, 47 Cal. App. 4th 1631, 1639 (1996).

Overall, significant litigation under the double jeopardy clause does not appear to be likely in future asset forfeiture actions.

D. Fifth and Fourteenth Amendment Due Process Clause

Under the Fifth and Fourteenth Amendments, the federal and state governments may not deprive a person of life, liberty, or property without due process of law. The due process clause is founded on principles of basic fairness that a person has a right to reasonable notice and an opportunity to contest the proceedings. For example, after the Civil War, the U.S. Supreme Court set aside a forfeiture entered against property owned by a confederate officer and a forced tax sale executed against the Arlington home of General Robert E. Lee on due process grounds. *See McVeigh v. United States*, 78 U.S. 259 (1870); *United States v. Lee*, 106 U.S. 196 (1882).

Four issues that commonly arise in asset forfeiture litigation relating to the due process clause are:

1) Seizure of property;
2) Promptness in initiating the forfeiture action;
3) Notice of the proceedings; and
4) Protection of innocent parties.

1. Seizure of Property

Generally, the due process clause does not require a preseizure notice or a hearing before property subject to civil forfeiture is seized. *See Calero-Toledo v. Pearson Yacht* Leasing, 416 U.S. 663, 678–79 (1974); *United States v. Eight Thousand Eight Hundred & Fifty Dollars ($8,850) in United States Currency,* 461 U.S. 555, 563 n.12 (1983); *United States v. Monsanto,* 491 U.S. 600, 615 (1989). There are extenuating circumstances that justify seizure without notice, such as the need of the government to exercise *in rem* jurisdiction over the property, curtail the continued use of the property in the illicit activity, and prevent it from being removed from the jurisdiction or being destroyed or concealed. *See Calero-Toledo,* 416 U.S. at 679–80.

However, the court has found that due process requires a noticed hearing and an opportunity to be heard before real property may be seized for forfeiture. *See United States v. James Daniel Good Real Property,* 510 U.S. 43 (1993). This is based on the higher expectation of privacy in real property, the lower need for immediate seizure of the property, and the availability of less-intrusive legal procedures to preserve the government's interest. *Id.* at 62. However, the government may seize real property without notice upon a showing of exigent circumstances. *Id.*

This same constitutional exemption for real property has now been codified into the federal statute. *See* 18 U.S.C. § 985(b).

2. Promptness

Because property may be seized for forfeiture without notice, due process requires that the claimant have an opportunity for a post-seizure hearing at a meaningful time. *See Fuentes v. Shevin,* 407 U.S. 67, 80 (1972). However, if the agency seizes the property but fails to timely initiate forfeiture proceedings, the claimant will be denied a post-seizure hearing during that time. *See Krimstock v. Kelly,* 306 F.3d 40, 48 (2d Cir. 2003), *cert. denied,* 539 U.S. 969 (2003).

In evaluating whether a substantial delay in initiating forfeiture proceedings violates due process, the U.S. Supreme Court in *United States v. Eight Thousand Eight Hundred Fifty Dollars ($8,850) in United States Currency,* 461

U.S. 555, utilized the four-prong balancing test contained in *Barker v. Wingo,* 407 U.S. 514, 530 (1972), by looking at such factors as: (1) the length of the delay; (2) the reason for the delay; (3) claimant's assertion of a right to a hearing; and (4) the prejudice to the claimant due to the delay. *See $8,850 in U.S. Currency,* 461 U.S. at 564. Using this test, the court found that a delay of 18 months was not constitutionally excessive.

Statutory protections enacted by Congress in CAFRA Section 2, 106 Pub. L. No. 185, 114 Stat. 202, are much more restrictive in that they require initiation of nonjudicial civil forfeiture actions "as soon as practicable" and no more than 60 days from the date of seizure, *see* 18 U.S.C. § 983(a)(1)(A)(i), or 90 days on adoptive forfeitures. *See* 18 U.S.C. § 983(a)(1)(A)(iv). Furthermore, the case must be filed within the applicable statute of limitations, i.e., five years from discovery of the offense or two years from the discovery of the involvement of the property in the offense. *See* 19 U.S.C. § 1621.

United States v. Eight Thousand Eight Hundred & Fifty Dollars ($8,850) in United States Currency, 461 U.S. 555, is the standard used by state and federal courts in evaluating due process claims for delay. *See Jones v. Takaki,* 153 F.R.D. 609, 611–12 (N.D. Ill. 1993); *In re Forfeiture of $109,901,* 210 Mich. App. 191; 533 N.W.2d 328, 329 (Mich. App. 1995); *Escamilla v. Tri-City Metro Drug Task Force,* 100 Wash. App. 742; 999 P.2d 625, 630 (Wash. App. 2000); *People v. One 1979 Chevrolet C-20 Van,* 248 Ill. App. 3d 640; 618 N.E.2d 1290, 1294–95 (Ill. App. 1993); *State v. One 1986 Subaru,* 120 N.J. 310; 576 A.2d 859, 862 (N.J. 1990); *State v. One Black 1989 Cadillac,* 522 N.W.2d 457, 462 (N.D. 1994).

Significant delays have been upheld based on the defendant's conduct in causing the delay, failure to request a hearing, or show prejudice. *Jones v. Greene,* 946 S.W.2d 817, 826 (Tenn. App. 1996) (41-month delay); *Com. v. Two Parcels of Land,* 724 N.E.2d 739, 746 (Mass. App. 2000) (4½-year delay); *State v. $107,156 U.S. Currency,* 935 So. 2d 827, 834 (La. App. 2006) (11-month delay). Conversely, seizing a vehicle and delaying initiation of the forfeiture may prejudice the claimant by depriving him or her of use of the property as well as with costs of depreciation, car payments, and storage fees. *In re Forfeiture of One 1983 Cadillac,* 176 Mich. App. 277; 439 N.W.2d 346, 348–49 (Mich. App. 1989); *State v. One (1) Ford Van, Econoline,* 154 N.J. Super. 326, 381 A.2d 387, 392–93 (N.J. Super. A.D. 1977). The primary question that should be resolved is whether the claimant's right to a meaningful hearing has been violated. *State v. Nourallah,* 726 So. 2d 923, 926 (La. App. 1998).

3. Notice

Due process requires that a party receive notice and have an opportunity to be heard before being deprived of his or her property. *See United States v. James Daniel Good Real Property*, 510 U.S. 43, 48 (1993). This means that the government must take steps "reasonably calculated" to give notice of the proceedings. *See Mullane v. Central Hanover Bank & Trust Co.*, 339 U.S. 306, 314 (1950); *United States v. Gonzalez-Gonzalez*, 257 F.3d 31, 35–36 (1st Cir. 2001).

There are a few general rules that pertain to service of notice of the forfeiture action.

First, the government must give notice to any party who appears to have an interest in the property. *See* Supplemental Rule G(4)(b)(i); 19 U.S.C. § 1607; *Upshaw v. U.S. Customs Service*, 153 F. Supp. 2d 46, 51 (D. Mass. 2001); *United States v. Colon*, 993 F. Supp. 42, 44 (D.P.R. 1998).

Second, actual notice or receipt of notice is not required. *See Dusenbery v. United States*, 534 U.S. 161, 170 (2002); *Mesa Valderrama v. United States*, 417 F.3d 1189, 1197 (11th Cir. 2005).

Third, service of the notice of forfeiture in the English language is sufficient. *See Toure v. United States*, 24 F.3d 444, 446 (2d Cir. 1994); *Hong v. United States*, 920 F. Supp. 311, 316 (E.D.N.Y. 1996).

Fourth, any service of process performed as authorized by the statute is sufficient, provided it is "reasonably calculated" to apprise the claimant of the proceedings and the requirements are "just and reasonable." *See* Supplemental Rule G(4)(b)(iii)(A); *Mullane*, 339 U.S. at 315; *United States v. Wade*, 230 F. Supp. 2d 1298, 1306 (M.D. Fla. 2002).

Effective service includes actual service, Supplemental Rule G(4)(b)(v); mail at the address given by the claimant to the arresting or seizing agency, Supplemental Rule G(4)(b)(iii)(D)–(E); *Lobzun v. United States*, 422 F.3d 503, 508 (7th Cir. 2005), or claimant's place of incarceration, Supplemental Rule G(4)(b)(iii)(C); *Chairez v. United States*, 355 F.3d 1099, 1101 (7th Cir. 2004), or service on claimant's attorney. Supplemental Rule G(4)(b)(iii)(B); *Nunley v. Department of Justice*, 425 F.3d 1132, 1139 (8th Cir. 2005).

Mailed notice received and signed at the claimant address is assumed to have reached the claimant. *Collette v. DEA*, 386 F. Supp. 2d 1120, 1137 (D. Alaska 2005). However, if the government becomes aware that prior service efforts were ineffective, it must take reasonable additional steps to serve the notice to comply with due process. *Jones v. Flowers*, 547 U.S. 220, 236–37 (2006) (certified mail returned unserved); *United States v. Ritchie*, 342 F.3d 903, 910 (9th Cir. 2003) (same).

A claimant is entitled to a hearing to determine whether the agency's efforts were reasonably calculated to reach him or her. *Taylor v. United States,* 483 F.3d 385, 390 (5th Cir. 2007). The court will look at the "totality of the circumstances" in determining whether due process was satisfied. *United States v. One Star Class Sloop Sailboat,* 458 F.3d 16, 24 (1st Cir. 2006).

Due process is violated if a claimant who appears to have an interest in the property does not receive notice of the hearing, and the forfeiture judgment should be vacated. *See United States v. Marolf,* 973 F. Supp. 1139, 1148 (C.D. Cal. 1997). The remedy for ineffective service is to permit a new filing of either an administrative or civil forfeiture action. *See Muhammed v.* DEA, 92 F.3d 648, 654 (8th Cir. 1996); *United States v. Giraldo,* 45 F.3d 509, 512 (1st Cir. 1995); *Barrera-Montenegro v. United States,* 74 F.3d 657, 661 (5th Cir. 1996). Before CAFRA, if the time for the statute of limitations had expired, the federal courts took two different approaches. Some courts allowed the trial court to hold a trial on the merits of the claim, *see Boero v. United States,* 111 F.3d 301, 307 (2d Cir. 1997), while others dismissed the action and prohibited a new filing, ruling it was barred by the statute of limitations. *See Clymore v. United States,* 164 F.3d 569, 574 (10th Cir. 1999); *United States v. Marolf,* 173 F.3d 1213, 1217 (9th Cir. 1999).

Congress resolved this conflict with CAFRA Section 2, 106 Pub. L. No. 185, 114 Stat. 202, 207–08, which permits the filing of a new administrative action within 60 days or a judicial filing within six months of the order irrespective of the expiration of the statute of limitations. *See* 18 U.S.C. § 983(e)(2).

State courts have found due process violations when: (1) the information contained in the forfeiture notice was inadequate; or (2) all potential interested parties have not been served.

Federal and state forfeiture statutes require that certain information be contained in the forfeiture notice such as:

- A description of the property;
- The violation of law associated with the forfeiture of the property;
- Instructions for filing and serving a claim; and
- The deadline for filing a claim and/or answer.

See Supplemental Rule G(4)(b)(ii); *Cal. Health & Safety Code* § 11488.4(j).

If a forfeiture notice fails to contain all of the required information, it is defective, and the court will set aside the forfeiture order. *Nasir v. Sacramento County Off of DA,* 11 Cal. App. 4th 976, 987 (1992) (missing property value); *State v. Property Located at No. 70 Oakland Street,* 727 So. 2d 1240, 1243 (La. App. 1999) (missing date of seizure); *State v. 1978 LTD II,* 216 M 401; 701 P.2d 1365, 1368 (Mont. 1985) (missing deadline to file claim).

Any person who reasonably appears to be a potential claimant has a right to notice and an opportunity to be heard at each stage of the forfeiture action. *City of Ft. Lauderdale v. Baruch*, 718 So. 2d 843, 847 (Fla. App. 1998); *Byrom v. Gallagher*, 609 So. 2d 24, 26 (Fla. 1992). Thus, if the government fails to send notice to all potential claimants, the forfeiture judgment will also be set aside. *In re Magone v. Froehlich*, 270 M 381; 892 P.2d 540, 546 (Mont. 1995) (wife who claimed interest not served); *Johnson v. City of Fairfax, Com of Va.*, 394 F. Supp. 387, 390 (D.C. Va. 1972) (part owner not served); *Harbin v. Com.*, 121 S.W.3d 191, 195 (Ky. 2003) (incarcerated claimant not served).

Whether the method of service used complies with due process will be evaluated under the "reasonably calculated" to give notice standard. *State v. $4200 U.S. Currency*, 809 So. 2d 302, 305 (La. App. 2001).

Actual notice is not required. *State v. $1,480.00 in U.S. Currency*, 637 So. 2d 1255, 1257 (La. App. 1994). Notice sent by certified or regular U.S. mail should be sufficient, *City of Hoisington v. $2,044 in U.S. Currency*, 27 K.A.2d 825; 8 P.3d 58, 62 (Kan. App. 2000); *State v. $1,480.00 in U.S. Currency*, 637 So. 2d 1255, 1257 (La. App. 1994), unless the government is aware that the claimant is not at the mailed location. *People ex rel. Devine v. $30,700.00 U.S. Currency*, 199 Ill. 2d 142; 766 N.E.2d 1084, 1095–96 (Ill. 2002) (claimant in custody); *State v. U.S. Currency in Amount of $3,743*, 25 K.A.2d 54, 60; 956 P.2d 1351, 1355 (Kan. App. 1998) (same). If the mailed notice is returned unserved, the government must take additional steps to give notice. *In re Forfeiture of $2,354.00 U.S. Currency*, 326 Ill. App. 3d 9; 760 N.E.2d 565, 571 (Ill. App. 2001). Published service may also be sufficient. *State v. Tuipuapua*, 83 Haw. 141; 925 P.2d 311, 316 (Hawaii 1996).

Even if the claimant fails to receive the prescribed notice, if he or she has actual knowledge of the proceeding and contests it, the claimant has not been prejudiced, and there is no due process violation. *Matter of 1977 Mercury Coupe*, 129 Ariz. 1; 969 P.2d 166, 171 (Ariz. App. 1997).

If the court determines that the service was inadequate, the forfeiture judgment is set aside, and the parties litigate the matter on the merits. *Gonzalez v. City of Hollywood*, 805 So. 2d 58, 59–60 (Fla. App. 2002).

4. Innocent Owner Exemption

In *Bennis v. Michigan*, 516 U.S. 442 (1996), the state forfeited an automobile jointly owned by the petitioner and her husband under the state nuisance statute. Although the Michigan statute contained no innocent owner exemption, the petitioner alleged that forfeiting her interest violated her due process rights because she was neither involved in the underlying criminal activity nor consented to it. The U.S. Supreme Court upheld the forfeiture judgment, holding that there is no constitutional requirement for an innocent owner exemption under the due process clause. *Bennis,* 516 U.S. at 446.

To mitigate the impact of forfeiture on parties who have legitimate legal interests in the property but no involvement in the criminal activity, Congress and state legislatures have enacted statutory exemptions. The categories of protected individuals include: (1) owners; (2) interest holders; and (3) bona fide purchasers for value.

An owner is a person who has a legal or ownership interest in the property. *See Ariz. Rev. Stat. Ann.* § 13-4301.4; *Iowa Code Ann.* § 809A.1.

An interest holder is a secured creditor who files and records his or her security interest to perfect his or her interest as required by law. *See Hawaii Rev. Stat.* § 712A-1; *Kan. Stat. Ann.* § 4102(c).

A bona fide purchaser is a party who buys property in good faith for valuable consideration. *See Ga. Code Ann.* § 16-13-49(e)(1); *La. Rev. Stat. Ann.* § 40:2605(1).

Federal and state civil forfeiture statutes contain exemptions for claimants who demonstrate a valid ownership interest within these three categories, provided they did not acquiesce to the illegal conduct. This intent usually is defined in the statute with a knowledge or consent prong.

Federal and state forfeiture exemption statutes preclude forfeiture if the party had no knowledge of the illegal conduct. *See* 18 U.S.C. § 983(d)(2)(A)(i); Table 7-4. The knowledge requirement is expressed in such terms as "actual knowledge," *see Md. Ann. Code Crim. Proc.* § 12-103(a); *Ohio Rev. Code Ann.* § 2925.42(F)(5)(b); *Utah Code Ann.* § 24-1-6(2), "did not know or could not reasonably have known," *see Conn. Gen. Stat. Ann.* § 54-36h(c), and "knew or should have known." *See Fla. Stat. Ann.* § 932.703(6)(a); *Mass. Ann. Laws* Ch. 94C § 47(d).

Most statutes also prohibit civil forfeiture if there was a lack of consent to the unlawful use. See Table 7-4. The consent element includes "taking reasonable steps to prevent the unlawful use," *see* 18 U.S.C. § 983(d)(2)(A)(ii); *Minn. Stat. Ann.* §§ 609.5311 Subd. 3(d), (e); *N.J. Stat. Ann.* § 2C:64-5b, but prohibits "willful blindness." *See Nev. Rev. Stat.* § 179.1164 2.

Most innocent owner exemption statutes are in the disjunctive, so the party may prove either lack of knowledge OR consent, *see* 18 U.S.C. § 983(d)(2); *Ala. Code* § 20-2-93(h); *Mont. Code Ann.* § 44-12-204, but some are in the conjunctive requiring both knowledge AND consent. *See* 725 *Ill. Comp. Stat.* 150/8; *N.H. Rev. Stat. Ann.* § 318-B:17-b III(a). Also, although most statutes place the burden on proof on the claimant, *see* 18 U.S.C. § 983(d)(1); *Mo. Ann.*

Stat. § 195.140 2(1); *S.D. Codified Laws Ann.* § 34-20B-70.1, others shift that burden to the state. *See Fla. Stat. Ann.* § 932.703(6)(a); *N.Y. Civil Practice Law* § 1311.3(b)(ii); *Ore. Constitution* Art. XV § 10(4).

Many innocent owner exemptions are written into the statutory grounds for forfeiture, so the scope of the defense will depend on the theory of forfeiture. *See Ark. Code Ann.* § 5-64-505(a)(4) (conveyance facilitation); (a)(6) (proceeds); (a)(7) (real property facilitation); *D.C. Code Ann.* §§ 48-905.02(a)(4)(B), (a)(7)(A), (a)(8)(A). A current trend is to enact a separate uniform innocent owner exemption that applies to all theories of forfeiture. *See* 18 U.S.C. § 983(d); *Co. Rev. Stat.* § 16-13-303(5.2); *Utah Code Ann.* § 24-1-6(2).

The correlation between the relation back doctrine and statutory innocent owner exemption merits discussion. Under the relation back doctrine, the government's interest in seized property vests upon commission of the act, giving rise to the forfeiture. *See* 21 U.S.C. § 881(h); 21 U.S.C. § 853(c). The purpose of the relation back doctrine is to prevent defendants from transferring forfeitable property to third parties to circumvent the forfeiture action. *Johnson v. Equip. Used to Cultivate Marijuana*, 271 M 500; 898 P.2d 1200, 1202–03 (Mont. 1995) (relation back doctrine defeats preforfeiture complaint quitclaim deed). Most federal and state forfeiture statutes contain relation back provisions. *See Cal. Health & Safety Code* § 11470(h); *La. Rev. Stat. Ann.* § 40:2611.I.

In *United States v. A Parcel of Land (92 Buena Vista Avenue)*, 507 U.S. 111 (1993), the U.S. Supreme Court dealt with the conflict between the application of the relation back doctrine with the innocent owner exemption. The claimant purchased a house with funds she received as a gift from her companion that the government asserted were proceeds traceable to a drug offense. She claimed an innocent owner exemption under 21 U.S.C. § 881(a)(6) alleging she did not have knowledge or consent to the illegal acts. The government countered that, under the relation back doctrine, the government's interest vested in the property when the money was exchanged for drugs. Because that was prior in time to when the defendant gave his companion the money as a gift to purchase the residence, it cut off her right to claim the innocent owner exemption.

The court determined that the relation back doctrine is not self-executing and therefore does not occur until entry of the forfeiture judgment. *Id.* at 126. Consequently, the innocent owner defense at issue could be asserted by any party with an ownership interest irrespective of the fact that it had been acquired after the illegal act. *Id.* at 128. By this reasoning, the innocent owner defense trumped the relation back provision.

It is significant to note that, under CAFRA Section 2, the innocent owner exemption examined in the *Buena Vista* case was deleted, *see* 21 U.S.C. §

881(a)(6), and the new uniform federal innocent owner exemption limits the innocent owner exemption for interests acquired after the conduct giving rise to forfeiture to bona fide purchasers who did not know and were reasonably without cause to believe the property was subject to forfeiture. *See* 18 U.S.C. § 983(d)(3)(A). Although there is a limited real property exemption for non-bona fide purchasers, it excludes proceeds property. *See* 18 U.S.C. § 983(d)(3)(B)(iii). Therefore, the results of the *Buena Vista* case under CAFRA would be a government victory.

With the enactment of CAFRA Section 2, 106 Pub. L. No. 185, 114 Stat. 202, 206, there is now a uniform innocent owner exemption that applies to *all* federal civil forfeiture actions. *See* 18 U.S.C. § 983(d)(1). Comparable protections are contained in the federal criminal forfeiture statutes. *See* 21 U.S.C. § 853(n)(6); 18 U.S.C. 1963(l)(6). Also, *all* 50 states and the District of Columbia have statutory exemptions contained in their civil (see Table 7-4) or criminal forfeiture statutes. *See* Neb. Rev. Stat §§ 28-431(4)(a)-(c); N.C. Gen. Stat. §§ 90-112(a)(4)(a)–(d).

E. Conclusion

In response to critics with concerns that asset forfeiture is unchecked by constitutional provisions, Chief Justice Rehnquist wrote the following:

> Finally, it should be noted that some of the ills at which *Halper* was directed are addressed by other constitutional provisions. The due process and equal protection clauses already protect individuals from sanctions which are downright irrational. *Williamson v. Lee Optical of Okla., Inc.,* 348 U.S. 483, 99 L. Ed. 563, 75 S. Ct. 461 (1955). The Eighth Amendment protects against excessive civil fines, including forfeitures. *Alexander v. United States,* 509 U.S. 544, 125 L.Ed. 2d 441, 113 S. Ct. 2766 (1993); *Austin v. United States,* 509 U.S. 602, 125 L. Ed. 2d 488, 113 S. Ct. 2801 (1993).

See Hudson v. United States, 522 U.S. 93, 103 (1997).

Bolstering these constitutional provisions are the federal statutory protections contained in CAFRA and exemptions or remission procedures[3] for innocent owners, interest holders, and bona fide purchasers drafted into all 50 state statutes and the District of Columbia.

Contrary to critic assertions, asset forfeiture is not an unbridled governmental power but is kept in check by constitutional law and sound statutory enactments. Recognizing the constitutional parameters of forfeiture and enforcing the statutory provisions will insure that individual property rights are respected.

Notes

1.   This material was previously published in two articles, the first of which I wrote for the California District Attorneys Association entitled *Double Jeopardy Challenges—A State Perspective,* PROSECUTORS BRIEF, Vol. XIX, No. 1, at 17–22, and the second for the National Association of Attorneys General entitled *Post-Ursery—A State Perspective,* NAAG FINANCIAL CRIMES REPORT, Dec. 1996/Jan. 1997, at 1–4.

2.   The Washington State Supreme Court noted that the number of federal and state courts examining double jeopardy and forfeiture cases increased from 40 in 1980 to 146 in 1994. *See* State v. Cole, 906 P.2d 925, 932 n.5 (Wash. 1995).

3.   The remission procedures are discussed in Chapter 4D.

---

13 Ethical Considerations

A. Introduction

"LICENSE TO STEAL—TAKE IT AWAY;"[1]
"SEIZURE OF ASSETS LEAVES CASUALTIES IN WAR ON DRUGS;"[2]
"SHERIFF UNDER INVESTIGATION—STATE LOOKING INTO
MISUSE OF DRUG PROBE MONEY."[3]

These headlines are typical of national press articles critical of the asset forfeiture laws.

The U.S. Department of Justice Executive Office for Asset Forfeiture published a report in July 1993 entitled *Summaries of Federal Asset Forfeiture Cases Criticized by the News Media*, which revealed that the complaints came from every part of the country and included such national publications as *Newsweek, New York Times, Washington Post, Los Angeles Times,* and the *Wall Street Journal* and broadcast media presentations in *60 Minutes, 20/20,* and *Larry King Live.*[4] This chapter will review the ethical concerns involving asset forfeiture litigation and discuss national standards of conduct for the asset forfeiture program.

B. Areas of Concern

Critics of asset forfeiture programs tend to focus on three basic areas: (1) Corruption; (2) Fairness; and (3) Accountability. Each is discussed separately below.[5]

Corruption is concerned with dishonest acts by law enforcement officers tempted by greed and the allure of large cash seizures to commit unlawful acts to obtain money for their personal use or their agency. The conviction of 19 Los Angeles Sheriffs Deputies from the elite Major Violators Two team between 1990 and 1992 in the federal money-skimming operation known as

Operation Big Spender is a tragic example of this type of corruption.[6] Other allegations are that illegal seizures are condoned,[7] and that law enforcement agencies are more interested in generating money than in crime detection and prevention.[8]

Prosecutors are not immune from allegations of corruption in connection with asset forfeiture cases. In 1996, Somerset County New Jersey prosecutor Nicholas Bissell, Jr., was convicted of federal charges of fraud and extortion, several involving misconduct in relation to forfeiture cases, and committed suicide rather than surrender to federal authorities.[9] Filing cases with insufficient evidence in the hope that the claimant will default on the forfeiture case,[10] coercing settlements with claimants by making them buy back their assets,[11] and plea bargaining a forfeiture case with an off-the-record payment to reduce a criminal charge [12] are some of the charges leveled at prosecutors.

Another controversial aspect of asset forfeiture cases is the potential unfairness that they have on innocent owner property rights. The intent of civil asset forfeiture is not to punish the truly innocent owner, and both federal and state statutes have provisions to protect them, but what process must innocent parties go through in order to preserve their interests? The denial of a claim for early release of property to bona fide innocent owners and lien holders can seriously impact property rights by depriving the owner of the use of the asset, allowing it to depreciate and incur storage and maintenance costs, and requiring the owners to hire lawyers at great expense to get their property back.[13] The problem of fairness has received attention and criticism in the national and local press.[14]

The final issue of accountability concerns the auditing of the expenditures of asset forfeiture funds and the use of property, such as vehicles that have been awarded to agencies for law enforcement use. Charges are asserted that appropriate accounting and auditing practices are not followed, unauthorized expenditures are made, and established inventory procedures are not observed.[15]

C. Ethical Guidelines

In 1993, in response to the mounting public criticism and concerns, two sets of national guidelines were promulgated for the development and conduct of asset forfeiture programs.

The United States Department of Justice Executive Office for Asset Forfeiture began drafting a set of guidelines in the latter part of 1991[16] that was published in 1993 as the *National Code of Professional Conduct for Asset Forfeiture.*[17] It consists of 10 principles and is known by the federal agencies as the "ten commandments." The National Code of Professional Conduct for Asset Forfeiture is now published in *A Guide to Equitable Sharing of Federally Forfeited Property for State and Local Law Enforcement Agencies,* by the U.S. Department of Justice, and all state and local agencies who intend to participate in the federal asset forfeiture sharing program are required to sign an annual certification that they are in compliance with the Code.[18] In 2000, the National Code was amended to add article II prohibiting racial profiling.[19] See Table 13-1.

Table 13-1

Comparison of Ethical Codes for Asset Forfeiture

U. S. Dept of Justice National Code of Professional Conduct for Asset Forfeiture	National District Attorneys Association Guidelines for Civil Asset Forfeiture	California Health & Safety Code § 11469
I. Law enforcement is the principal objective of forfeiture. Potential revenue must not be allowed to jeopardize the effective investigation and prosecution of criminal offenses, officer safety, the integrity of ongoing investigations, or the due process rights of citizens.	1. The removal of unlawfully obtained proceeds of criminal activity and the elimination of the instrumentalities used to commit crimes are the principal goals of asset forfeiture. Potential revenue must not be allowed to jeopardize the effective investigation or prosecution of criminal offenses. 2. Where multiple agencies in a geographic region have jurisdiction to pursue asset forfeiture every effort should be made to cooperate to advance the public interest. 14. Agencies receiving forfeiture funds should make annual budget requests based on agency funding needs without regard for anticipated or projected asset forfeiture revenues.	(a) Law enforcement is the principal objective of forfeiture. Potential revenue must not be allowed to jeopardize the effective investigation and prosecution of criminal offenses, officer safety, the integrity of ongoing investigations, or the due process rights of citizens
II. The Constitution and Federal statutes prohibit the improper use of personal characteristics such as race, color, national origin, gender, or religion to target individuals for law enforcement action.	15. Nor should a prosecutor improperly consider the race, gender, social or economic status of any person in deciding whether to initiate or dismiss a forfeiture proceeding	*See Cal. Pen.* Code § 13519.4(e) A law enforcement officer shall not engage in racial profiling.

Table 13-1 (continued)
Comparison of Ethical Codes for Asset Forfeiture

U. S. Dept of Justice National Code of Professional Conduct for Asset Forfeiture	National District Attorneys Association Guidelines for Civil Asset Forfeiture	California Health & Safety Code § 11469
III. No prosecutor's or sworn law enforcement officer's employment or salary shall be made to depend upon the level of seizures or forfeitures he or she achieves.	12. Salaries and personal benefits of any person influencing or controlling the selection, investigation, or prosecution of forfeiture cases must be managed in such a way that employment or salary does not depend upon the level of seizures or forfeitures in which they participate.	(b) No prosecutor's or sworn law enforcement officer's employment or salary shall be made to depend upon the level of seizures or forfeitures he or she achieves.
IV. Whenever practicable, and in all cases involving real property, a judicial finding of probable cause shall be secured when property is seized for forfeiture. Seizing agencies shall strictly comply with all applicable legal requirements governing seizure practice and procedure.	4. Absent exigent circumstances, a judicial order is advisable for all seizures of real property. When real property in residential use is sought to be forfeited, the least intrusive means that will preserve the property for forfeiture and protect the public should be employed. A notice of *lis pendens* or an order restraining alienation should suffice to preserve the government's interest in forfeiture pending final judicial determination of the forfeiture action.	See *Cal. Health & Safety Code* § 11471(e) Real property subject to forfeiture may not be seized, absent exigent circumstances, without notice to the interested parties and a hearing to determine that seizure is necessary to preserve the property pending the outcome of the proceedings. At the hearing, the prosecution shall bear the burden of establishing that probable cause exists for the forfeiture of the property and that seizure is necessary to preserve the property pending the outcome of the forfeiture pro-ceedings. The court may issue seizure orders pur-suant to this section if it finds that seizure is war-ranted or pendente lite orders pursuant to Sec-tion 11492 if it finds that the status quo or value of the property can be preserved without seizure.

Table 13-1 (continued)
Comparison of Ethical Codes for Asset Forfeiture

U. S. Dept of Justice National Code of Professional Conduct for Asset Forfeiture	National District Attorneys Association Guidelines for Civil Asset Forfeiture	California Health & Safety Code § 11469
V. If no judicial finding of probable cause is secured, the seizure shall be approved in writing by a prosecuting or agency attorney or by a supervisory-level official.	3. Every government entity with the authority to seize property should ensure that its asset forfeiture program provides for: a) Prompt prosecutorial review of the circumstances, and propriety of the seizure;	See *Cal. Health & Safety Code* § 11488.2. Law enforcement to refer forfeiture case in writing to prosecutor within 15 days after the seizure.
VI. Seizing entities shall have a manual detailing the statutory grounds for forfeiture and all applicable policies and procedures. The manual shall include procedures for prompt notice to interest holders, the expeditious release of seized property where appropriate, and the prompt resolution of claims of innocent ownership.	3. Every government entity with the authority to seize property should ensure that its asset forfeiture program provides for: b) Timely notice of seizure to interest holders of seized property; and c) Expeditious resolution of ownership claims and a rapid release of property to those entitled to the return of the property. 11. Every prosecutor should establish procedures to insure expeditious resolution of ownership claims if challenges to the asset forfeiture proceeding are made and timely return of the property to the known owner or interest holders if the forfeiture action is dismissed or is unsuccessful.	(d) Seizing agencies shall have a manual detailing the statutory grounds for forfeiture and all applicable policies and procedures. The manual shall include procedures for prompt notice to interest holders, the expeditious release of seized property, where appropriate, and the prompt resolution of claims of innocent ownership.
VII. Seizing entities retaining forfeited property for official law enforcement use shall ensure that the property is subject to internal	5. Every entity retaining forfeited property for official law enforcement use should ensure that the property	(g) Seizing agencies shall not put any seized or forfeited property into service.

Table 13-1 (continued)
Comparison of Ethical Codes for Asset Forfeiture

U. S. Dept of Justice National Code of Professional Conduct for Asset Forfeiture	National District Attorneys Association Guidelines for Civil Asset Forfeiture	California Health & Safety Code § 11469
controls consistent with those applicable to property acquired through the normal appropriations processes of that entity.	is subject to controls consistent with those applicable to property acquired through the normal appropriations process.	
VIII. Unless otherwise provided by law, forfeiture proceeds shall be maintained in a separate fund or account subject to appropriate accounting controls and annual financial audits of all deposits and expenditures.	8. Forfeiture proceeds shall be maintained in a separate fund or account subject to appropriate accounting controls and annual financial audits of all deposits and expenditures.	(h) Unless otherwise provided by law, forfeiture proceeds shall be maintained in a separate fund or account subject to appropriate accounting controls and annual financial audits of all deposits and expenditures.
IX. Seizing agencies shall strive to ensure that seized property is protected and its value preserved.	6. No seized property should be used without judicial authorization and/or supervision. A use order may be obtained from the court in appropriate circumstances. Otherwise the property should not be used unless the forfeiture action has been completed and title to the property has vested in the receiving agency. Forfeited property not used in an undercover capacity should be sold or added to the regular inventory of the agency. All property should be used and disposed of in a manner consistent with the use and disposition of similar property by that agency.	(i) Seizing agencies shall ensure that seized property is protected and its value preserved.

Table 13-1 (continued)
Comparison of Ethical Codes for Asset Forfeiture

U. S. Dept of Justice National Code of Professional Conduct for Asset Forfeiture	National District Attorneys Association Guidelines for Civil Asset Forfeiture	California Health & Safety Code §11469
	9. Every seizing agency should maintain seized property to preserve value for successful claimants as well as the taxpayers.	
X. Seizing entities shall avoid any appearance of impropriety in the sale or acquisition of forfeited property.	7. The disposition of forfeited property retained by the law enforcement agency should not be determined by any person who directly supervised or exercised discretion in its forfeiture. 13. Agency employees and their families should be prohibited from purchasing forfeited property directly or indirectly from the agency, or any property forfeited by any other agency, if the employee participated in any aspect of the investigation or litigation involving that property	(f) Seizing agencies shall avoid any appearance of impropriety in the sale or acquisition of forfeited property.
	10. To the extent possible, civil forfeiture actions should be initiated as independent cases which are not controlled or influenced by the criminal prosecution. Prosecutors should avoid plea agreements in a criminal case which involve	(c) Whenever appropriate, prosecutors should seek criminal sanctions as to the underlying criminal acts which give rise to the forfeiture action. See *Cal. Health & Safety Code* § 11488.4(i)(3), (5) which require a joint trial unless waived.

Table 13-1 (continued)
Comparison of Ethical Codes for Asset Forfeiture

U. S. Dept of Justice National Code of Professional Conduct for Asset Forfeiture	National District Attorneys Association Guidelines for Civil Asset Forfeiture	California Health & Safety Code §11469
	agreements to dismiss forfeiture proceedings. The converse is also true. Prosecutors should avoid settlements in a forfeiture case which involve concessions in a criminal proceeding.	
		(e) Seizing agencies shall implement training for officers assigned to forfeiture programs, which training should be ongoing.
	15. Prosecutors should pursue forfeiture actions to further the remedial goals set forth above. A prosecutor should not consider any personal or political advantages or disadvantages, or gains or losses that the initiation of a forfeiture action may bring to the prosecutor or the prosecutor's office in deciding whether to initiate or dismiss a forfeiture proceeding.... This guideline should not be read to preclude the initiation of forfeiture proceedings which contribute to the fulfillment of the official mission of the prosecutor's office.	(j) Although civil forfeiture is intended to be remedial by removing the tools and profits from those engaged in the illicit drug trade, it can have harsh effects on property owners in some circumstances. Therefore, law enforcement shall seek to protect the interests of innocent property owners, guarantee adequate notice and due process to property owners, and ensure that forfeiture serves the remedial purpose of the law.

In March 1993, the National District Attorneys Association ("NDAA") is-sued *Guidelines for Civil Asset Forfeiture*. It was drafted by a task force com-mittee of nine prosecutors selected from across the country and was unani-mously adopted by the full board of the NDAA. The guidelines contain the following preamble that explains the purpose of asset forfeiture:

> Crime in America is a multi-billion [dollar] industry that has a devas-tating effect on legitimate economic enterprise by diverting money from lawful commerce while rewarding and financing ongoing ille-gal activity. Asset forfeiture destroys the money base necessary for the continuation of illegal enterprises and attacks the economic in-centive to engage in organized criminal activity. Asset forfeiture also deters individuals from using their property to facilitate criminal ac-tivity. Forfeiture programs then rededicate the money from illegal activity to the public good. The National District Attorneys Associa-tion strongly believes that law enforcement agencies and prosecu-tors should aggressively pursue forfeiture actions to eliminate the in-strumentalities of crime and to confiscate the proceeds from criminal acts. To encourage such efforts it is important that forfeiture laws con-tinue to allow most of the proceeds from forfeitures to be returned to the law enforcement community responsible for initiating these ac-tions to be used to further their law enforcement efforts. These guide-lines are designed to assist in the exercise of prosecutorial discretion in administering and enforcing statutorily authorized forfeiture pro-grams.

The NDAA Guidelines contain 15 general standards and procedures to assist in the conduct of asset forfeiture programs.

Some states have adopted the National Code of Professional Conduct for Asset Forfeiture as part of their state forfeiture statute. For example, in Sep-tember 1993, the California legislature enacted a new state forfeiture law, Stats.1994, C. 314 (A.B.114), Sec 1, and incorporated 10 ethical standards into a new section located at Health & Safety Code 11469 entitled *Guide-lines for Utilization of Seizure and Forfeiture Laws*. Other states that have taken similar action include Colorado,[20] Florida,[21] Iowa,[22] Louisiana,[23] and New Hampshire.[24]

D. Comparison of Ethical Guidelines

A comparison of the federal National Code of Professional Conduct for Asset Forfeiture, the National District Attorneys Association Guidelines for Civil Asset Forfeiture and California Health & Safety Code § 11469 is found in Table 13-1. It reveals some interesting contrasts among the three ethical standards that will be discussed in the next section of this chapter.

The federal National Code of Professional Conduct for Asset Forfeiture has adopted standards to respond to the issues of corruption, fairness, and accountability, which are the three basic areas for criticism of asset forfeiture laws.

To combat corruption, the National Code emphasizes that law enforcement is the principal objective of forfeiture, not revenue (I.); that employment and salary shall not be dependent on the level of seizures achieved (III.); and seizing agencies should avoid any appearance of impropriety in the sale or acquisition of forfeited property (X.).

To encourage fairness, the National Code forbids racial profiling (II.). It also provides for strict compliance with legal requirements concerning seizure practice and procedure and encourages a judicial finding of probable cause whenever possible, and mandates it in all cases of real property (IV.). If there is no judicial finding of probable cause, the seizure must be approved in writing by a prosecuting or agency attorney or by a supervisory-level official (V.). Prompt notice to interest holders, expeditious release of seized property where appropriate, and prompt resolution of innocent owner claims are also advocated (VI.).

Professionalism and accountability are promoted in the National Code by four provisions that require agencies to maintain policy and procedure manuals (VI.); deposit seized funds in separate accounts subject to financial audits (VIII.); protect and preserve the value of seized property (IX.); and establish internal controls for forfeited property retained for law enforcement use (VII.).

Thirteen of the 15 NDAA Guidelines are comparable to the U.S. Department of Justice National Code of Professional Code for Asset Forfeiture, see Table 13-1, but there are a few unique provisions. It encourages multiple agencies to work together to advance the public interest (2), mandates annual budgeting without regard to anticipated or projected asset forfeiture revenue (14), forbids the use of seized property prior to forfeiture absent a judicial order (6), prohibits agency employees or family members from purchasing forfeited property (13), and discourages dismissal of criminal or forfeiture actions as part of plea bargaining (10).

California Health & Safety Code § 11469 basically is patterned after the U.S. Department of Justice Code of Professional Conduct in that it adopts six of the 10 federal standards. See *Cal. Health & Safety Code* § 11469, sections (a), (b), (d), (f), (h), and (i). Although the California code does not adopt the federal standards relating to judicial findings of probable cause prior to seizure (IV.) and prosecutorial reviews (V.), it has specific statutes that relate to those issues. *See Cal. Health & Safety Code* §§ 11471(e), 11488.2. The only other area in which the California code differs from the federal code is in the area of retention of property for law enforcement use, which the federal code approves (See VII.), but the California code does not. *See Cal. Health & Safety Code* § 11469(g). This is a response by the California legislature against perceived abuses of property retained for law enforcement use that actually was used for personal benefit.[25] California addresses the issue of racial profiling with mandatory law enforcement training, *see Cal. Penal Code* § 13519.4, similar to other states. *See Fla. Stat. Ann.* § 932.706.

The states that have incorporated ethical guidelines into their program include all or part of the National Code of Professional Conduct for Asset Forfeiture. Additionally, there are other states that have enacted specific provisions concerning the conduct of asset forfeiture without adopting the entire federal code of ethics. The next portion of this chapter will review some of the major ethical issues that are confronted by asset forfeiture practitioners.

E. Purpose of Forfeiture

All of the national and state ethical guidelines emphasize that law enforcement is the principle objective of forfeiture. See Table 13-1, National Code I, NDAA Guideline 1, *Cal. Health & Safety Code* § 11469(a). Note that this is the first ethical principle in every national and state ethical code. The Minnesota forfeiture statute aptly articulates the purposes of asset forfeiture in the following language: "[The forfeiture statute] must be liberally construed to carry out the following remedial purposes:

1) To enforce the law;
2) To deter crime;
3) To reduce the economic incentive to engage in criminal enterprise;
4) To increase the pecuniary loss resulting from the detection of criminal activity; and

5) To forfeit property unlawfully used or acquired and divert the property to law enforcement purposes." *See Minn. Stat. Ann.* § 609.531 Subd. 1a.

Of significance is the lack of emphasis on revenue production. All of the national and state ethical guidelines specifically caution that potential revenue must never be allowed to jeopardize the effective investigation of criminal offenses, officer safety, the integrity of ongoing investigations, or the due process rights of citizens. See Table 13-1; National Code I, NDAA Guideline I, *Cal. Health & Safety Code* § 11469(a); *Fla. Stat. Ann.* § 932.704(1). These guidelines admonishing against governmental overreaching and revenue production have been acknowledged with approval in federal case law. *See Krimstock v. Kelly,* 306 F.3d 40, 63 n.25 (2d Cir. 2003).

One of the major criticisms of national press articles concerns law enforcement utilizing the federal forfeiture system merely to obtain a higher share under the federal equitable sharing program.[26] Whenever a state or local law enforcement agency intends to submit a case for federal adoption, it should be able to articulate the basis for the federal adoption request:

(1) State laws are inadequate, making a successful forfeiture action unfeasible or unsuccessful;
(2) The seized item poses unique property management problems;
(3) State laws will result in a delay in the forfeiture that may lead to significant diminution in the value of the asset; and
(4) The state or local prosecutor has declined to initiate forfeiture proceedings. *See Asset Forfeiture Policy Manual* (1996) Chap. 6, Sec. I, at 6-3 through 6-4.

Additionally, if the state statute contains specific restrictions limiting the turnover of assets to the federal system, the state provisions should be strictly adhered to. See Chapter 3, Section J, and Table 3-3.

All personnel involved in the asset forfeiture program must remember that, when making any decision relating to the filing of an asset forfeiture action, law enforcement, not revenue production, is the primary objective of forfeiture.

F. Use of Forfeited Funds

When the Illinois legislature enacted the Drug Asset Forfeiture Procedure Act, it issued this declaration of legislative intent: "While forfeiture may secure for State and local units of government some resources for deterring drug abuse and drug trafficking, *forfeiture is not intended to be an alternative means of funding the administration of criminal justice." See 725 Ill. Comp. Stat.* 150/2 (emphasis added).

This is consistent with other national provisions that provide that salaries or benefits should not be contingent upon the level of seizures achieved, *see* Table 13-1, National Code III; NDAA Guideline 12; *Cal. Health & Safety Code* § 11469(b), and that agencies should make annual budget requests without regard to anticipated or projected forfeiture revenue. See Table 13-1, NDAA Guideline 14.

Two states have specific provisions that forbid forfeited funds being used to supplement salaries of any public employees or officers and funds awarded to any agency may not supplant other local, state, or federal funds appropriated for staff or operations. *See Tenn. Code Ann.* § 39-11-713; *Ga. Code Ann.* § 16-13-49(u)(4)(D)(i). This is also discussed in Chapter 10, Section D.

G. Audit

Whenever money is involved, fraud and theft are potential concerns.[27] Therefore, the national and state guidelines require that funds be kept in separate accounts, subject to accounting controls and annual financial audits. See Table 13-1, National Code VIII, NDAA Guideline 8, *Cal. Health & Safety Code* § 11469(h). Misuse of federally shared funds may also form the basis of criminal prosecution for embezzlement. *See United States v. Kranovich,* 244 F. Supp. 2d 1109, 1112 (D. Nev. 2003); "Judge Gives Ex-Sheriff a Choice in Sentencing," *Fayette Observer* (N.C.) May 31, 2008.

The federal government and many states also require annual reports and audits for oversight of the program. *See* 28 U.S.C. § 524(c)(6); 31 U.S.C. § 9703(f); *Cal. Health & Safety Code* § 11495; *Pa. Consol. Stat. Ann.* tit. 42 § 6801(i); *Tx. Code of Crim. Proc.* § 59.06(g). Failure of the state or local law enforcement agencies to comply with the annual report requirement can lead to allegations of misconduct and reform of the statute.[28]

H. Property Management

Damaged or depreciated property is the bane of forfeiture programs. Law enforcement agencies have a duty to properly maintain all seized property. *Gadson v. Hembree,* 364 S.C. 316; 613 S.E.2d 533, 536 (S.C. 2005). Protecting and preserving seized assets is mandated in all national and state ethical codes. *See* National Code IX, NDAA Guideline 6; *Cal. Health & Safety Code* § 11469(i). This provision has taken on greater significance with the Civil Asset Forfeiture Reform Act of 2000 ("CAFRA") Section 3, 106 Pub. L. No. 185, 114 Stat. 202, 211, by making the government liable for damage or loss if property was seized for forfeiture, and the claimant's interest was not forfeited, remitted, or mitigated, or the claimant was not convicted of a crime subjecting the property to forfeiture. *See* 28 U.S.C. § 2680(c).

Avoiding the appearance of impropriety in the sale of forfeited assets also is advocated in the national and state guidelines. *See* National Code X, NDAA 13; *Cal. Health & Safety Code* § 11469(f). The NDAA guidelines specifically prohibit agency personnel or their family members from purchasing forfeited assets either directly or indirectly if the agency employee participated in the investigation or litigation involving that property. *See* NDAA Guideline 13. The purchase of forfeited assets likewise is forbidden in federal practice by policy and regulation. *See* 28 C.F.R. § 45.735-18(a)–(b); *Asset Forfeiture Policy Manual* (1996) Ch. 5 Sec. V, at 5-20. A few states have comparable prohibitions. *Colo. Rev. Stat.* § 16-13-302(g); *Mont. Code Ann.* § 44-12-205(2)(a).

I. Settlement

Global settlement of criminal cases and forfeiture actions can be potentially troublesome for prosecutors in that allegations of impropriety and overreaching by the government may be asserted.[29] Civil rights lawsuits have been brought against agents and prosecutors who forfeited assets in lieu of criminal prosecution. *Giuffre v. Bissell,* 31 F.3d 1241, 1253 (3d Cir. 1994) (prosecutor not entitled to absolute immunity).

The NDAA Guidelines recommend that civil forfeiture actions and criminal prosecutions should be independent cases, and plea bargains should be avoided that involve dismissal or concessions of the interrelated cases. *See* NDAA Guideline 10. Although the National Code does not contain a provision for settlement of forfeiture actions, the federal government does have a settlement policy with a "critical principle . . . that civil forfeiture, either judicial or administrative, should not be used to gain an advantage in a criminal case." *See Asset Forfeiture Policy Manual* (1996) Ch. 3, Sec. I.A, at 3-1. In language similar to the NDAA guidelines, the federal policy emphasizes that: "The government should *not* agree, however, to release property subject to forfeiture (civil or criminal) in order to *coerce* a guilty plea on the substantive charges, nor should the government agree to dismiss criminal charges in order to *coerce* a forfeiture settlement." *See Asset Forfeiture Policy Manual* (1996) Ch. 3, Sec. I.A at 3-5. (Emphasis in original.)

A few states have specific guidelines pertaining to joint resolution of criminal and civil actions setting forth the following rules:

(1) Global settlement of criminal and civil forfeitures is not prohibited. *Com. v. Alston,* 722 A.2d 161, 164 (Pa. Super. 1998) (fosters "efficiency and judicial economy"). However, joint settlement negotiations should be at the request of the claimant-defendant or his or her attorney. *See Ore. Rev. Stat.* § 475A.055(7).

(2) Settlement of the civil forfeiture action should not be conditioned upon a disposition of the criminal charges, *see Kan. Stat. Ann.* § 60-4107(i), or an agreement to defer the criminal charges, obtain a guilty plea, or affect sentencing recommendations. *See Mo. Ann. Stat.* § 513.617.3.); *United States v. Dean,* 80 F.3d 1535, 1540 (11th Cir. 1996) (court had power to modify terms of global settlement of criminal and civil *in rem* forfeiture where imposition of full civil forfeiture would have been punitive and violate Eighth Amendment excessive fines clause).

(3) The state must not accept any monetary payment or thing of value for release of the property in lieu of forfeiture or settlement of the criminal charges. *See Mo. Ann. Stat.* § 513.617.3; *Giuffre v. Bissell,* 31 F.3d 1241, 1250–51 (3d Cir. 1994) (transfer of two real property lots in lieu of criminal prosecution); *Clift v. State,* 708 P.2d 342, 343 (Okla. Cr. 1985) (payment by defendant into county drug fund invalid); *State v. Hendrix,* 944 S.W.2d 311, 313–14 (Mo. App. 1997) (funds voluntarily surrendered in lieu of forfeiture should be included as part of forfeiture settlement); *Rice v. Logan Cty. Bd. of Commrs.,* 114 Ohio App.3d 198; 682 N.E.2d 1106, 1108–09 (Ohio App. 1996) (transfer of real property after dismissal of criminal charges was de facto plea agreement subject to court scrutiny).

(4) Forfeited personal property should be sold at auction. However, as part of a settlement agreement, an agency has the discretion to sell a

seized asset back to a claimant, provided the funds paid are forfeited and distributed pursuant to the forfeiture statute. *Boyd v. Hickman,* 114 Md. App. 108; 689 A.2d 106, 117 (Md. App. 1997) (option to sell vehicle back to defendant within discretion of agency provided money is forfeited).

(5) All settlement agreements must be in writing, *see 725 Ill. Comp. Stat.* 150/11, and approved by the prosecuting attorney and judge, *see Kan. Stat. Ann.* § 60-4107(k); *State ex rel. Haynes v. Sixteen Thousand, Eight Hundred Dollars ($16,800.00),* 990 P.2d 334, 337 (Okla. Civ. App. 1999); *Com. v. Alston,* 722 A.2d 161, 165 (Pa. Super. 1998), unless waived and unrepresented parties advised of their right to counsel. *See Fla. Stat. Ann.* § 932.704(7).

(6) It is not a conflict of interest for a prosecutor to initiate a forfeiture matter where a portion of the forfeited funds will be returned to his or her office. The prosecutor has no personal interest in the funds, and the distribution and use of the proceeds are restricted by state law. *State ex rel. County of Cumberland v. One 1990 Ford Thunderbird,* 371 N.J. Super. 228;852 A.2d 1114, 1120 (N.J. Super. A.D. 2004).

(7) There is no violation of the separation of power doctrine in permitting a law enforcement official to serve as an administrative hearing officer in a forfeiture matter in which his or her agency has a pecuniary interest. *Smith v. Mount,* 45 Wash. App. 623; 726 P.2d 474, 477 (Wash. App. 1986). The hearing officer has no personal interest in the outcome, and the claimant has the authority to remove the matter to a judicial court and to appeal the verdict. *Lowery v. Nelson,* 43 Wash. App. 747; 719 P.2d 594, 597 (Wash. App. 1986).

(8) Law enforcement agents involved in the seizure of the property are prohibited from negotiating settlement agreements in forfeiture actions on behalf of their agency. Such authority generally is limited to the chief administrative officer or his or her designee. *Tenn. Code Ann.* § 40-33-212.

Although there is no easy answer to the ethical dilemma raised by global settlements of criminal and civil cases, prosecutors should be advised that all plea agreements should be able to withstand scrutiny under the "totality of the circumstances" test.[30]

J. ABA Statement of Principles Regarding Asset Forfeiture

In February 1996, the House of Delegates of the American Bar Association adopted a statement of principles on asset forfeiture.[31] Table 13-2 lists the 13 principles approved by the ABA and shows the subsequent enactment of legislation or judicial rules in response to the stated concern. It is apparent from Table 13-2 that virtually *all* of the proposals relating to civil forfeiture have been enacted into law, leaving only two provisions concerning the restraint of assets of third parties or substitute assets in criminal forfeiture actions unfulfilled. Request for simplicity of procedures, a uniform innocent owner defense, definition of terms, enhanced burden of proof, and increased use of criminal forfeiture have all been addressed by CAFRA in 2000. *See* Pub. L. No. 106-185, 114 Stat. 202. This demonstrates that the law enforcement community can work together with respected legal organizations and critics to resolve areas of concern and improve the viability of the program for all concerned.

Table 13-2

ABA Statement of Principles Regarding Asset Forfeiture

Statement	Statutory Provision
1. Uniformity and Simplicity. The statutory procedures regarding administrative, civil and criminal forfeiture are mutually inconsistent and unnecessarily complex. In revising these statutes, Congress should simplify the procedures and make them as uniform as possible.	1. CAFRA Section 2 See 18 U.S.C. § §983(a)
2. Terms used to describe what is forfeitable. Likewise, the statutory language describing what property is subject to forfeiture should be amended to avoid use of confusing and inconsistent terms such as "proceeds," "gross receipts" and "gross proceeds" in favor of uniform, well-defined terms.	2. CAFRA Section 20 See 18 U.S.C. § 981(a)(2)
3. Innocent Owner Defense. Congress should enact a uniform innocent owner defense applicable to all civil and criminal forfeitures.	3. CAFRA Section 2 See 18 U.S.C. § 983(d)
4. Forfeiture as a law enforcement tool. The seizure and forfeiture of the proceeds and instrumentalities of criminal acts is an important and appropriate tool of federal law enforcement. Congress should encourage the continued use of both civil and criminal forfeiture not only to deter and diminish the capacity of the criminal to commit future criminal acts, but to provide a means of restoring criminal proceeds to victims.	
5. Burden of proof. Civil forfeiture statutes should be amended to provide that the government bears the burden of proof regarding the forfeitability of property at trial. That is, the government should be required to prove, by a preponderance of the admissible evidence, that the crime giving rise to the forfeiture occurred, and that the property bears the required relationship to the offense.	5. CAFRA Section 2 See 18 U.S.C. § 983(c)
6. Time Limits. To enhance the ability of property owners to contest forfeiture actions, Congress should extend and make uniform the time limits for filing claims in civil and administrative proceedings.	6. CAFRA Section 2 See 18 U.S.C. § 983(a)

Table 13-2 (continued)

ABA Statement of Principles Regarding Asset Forfeiture

Statement	Statutory Provision
7. Third party interests in criminal cases. Congress should amend the provisions of the criminal forfeiture statutes regarding pretrial restraining orders to provide a mechanism for addressing the interests of third parties in a manner that does not unduly interfere with the criminal trial.	8. CAFRA Section 4 See 28 U.S.C. § 2465 (Post-judgment attorney fees)
8. Attorney fees. The civil and criminal forfeiture statutes should contain a mechanism by which the court may make an early determination as to whether seized or restrained property may be made available to a criminal defendant to pay attorney's fees.	
9. Restraint of substitute assets. If Congress provides for the pre-trial restraint of substitute assets in criminal cases, it should exempt assets needed to pay attorney's fees, other necessary cost of living expenses, and expenses of maintaining the restrained assets.	
10. Forfeiture of criminal proceeds. No person has a right to retain the proceeds of a criminal act. Accordingly, Congress should provide for the civil and criminal forfeiture of the proceeds of all federal criminal offenses, and it should authorize the government to restore forfeited property to the victims of the offense. In particular, this change in the law will eliminate the overuse of the money laundering statutes to forfeit proceeds and restore property.	CAFRA Section 20 See 18 U.S.C. § 981(a)(1)(c)
11. Scope of criminal forfeiture. To avoid the necessity of filing and defending successive criminal and civil forfeiture proceedings arising out of the same course of conduct when property is held jointly by defendants and non-defendants, Congress should provide a mechanism for adjudicating the forfeitability of the non-defendant's interests in the forfeited property as part of the ancillary proceeding n criminal cases.	11. Fed. Rules Crim. P. Rule 32.2(c).
12. Facilitating property. When property used to facilitate the commission of a criminal offense is made subject to forfeiture, Congress should enact a standard defining the required nexus between property and the offense.	12. CAFRA Section 2 See 18 U.S.C. § 983(c)(3)

Table 13-2 (continued)
ABA Statement of Principles Regarding Asset Forfeiture

Statement	Statutory Provision
13. Availability of criminal forfeiture. Current law outside of the drug enforcement context requires the government to bring most forfeiture actions as civil actions. The statutes should be amended to give the government the option, in all instances where civil forfeiture is presently authorized, of bringing a criminal forfeiture action as part of the criminal indictment in accordance with the standard rules for criminal forfeiture.	13. CAFRA Section 16 See 28 U.S.C. § 2461(c)

K. Conclusion

The ethical provisions found in the National Code of Professional Conduct for Asset Forfeiture and the National District Attorneys Association Guidelines contain important standards and procedures to guide prosecutors and law enforcement in the implementation of asset forfeiture programs. All asset forfeiture practitioners should become familiar with and abide by these ethical standards. The observance of these guidelines may help prevent the conflict and controversy that have hindered the asset forfeiture program in the past and renew public support for the use of civil remedies and criminal forfeiture by law enforcement.

As summarized by the ABA in the Statement of Principles Regarding Forfeiture:

> The seizure and forfeiture of the proceeds and instrumentalities of criminal acts is an important and appropriate tool of federal law enforcement. Congress should encourage the continued use of both civil and criminal forfeiture not only to deter and diminish the capacity of the criminal to commit future criminal acts, but to provide a means of restoring criminal proceeds to victims.

Notes
1. NATIONAL REVIEW, Feb. 20, 1995, at 45.
2. LOS ANGELES TIMES, Oct. 14, 1992, at A1.
3. THE CITIZEN (Auburn NY), Dec. 20, 2001, at A1.

4.   In 1994, the volume of anti-forfeiture articles decreased but the pejorative approach did not. *See* David Heilbroner, *Is It Police Work or Plunder?*, Readers Digest, Apr. 1995, at 181–188, condensed from his article *The Law Goes on a Treasure Hunt*, N.Y. Times Mag., Dec. 11, 1994.

5.   This section is based on an article that I wrote in 1995 and was published by the California District Attorneys Association entitled *Ethical Considerations in Civil Asset Forfeiture Litigation*, XVII Prosecutor's Brief 3 (1995).

6.   *The Slide From Cop to Criminal*, L.A. Times, Dec. 1, 1993.

7.   *PRESUMED GUILTY—The Law's Victims in the War on Drugs*, Pittsburgh Press, Aug. 1991, reprint p. 4, at 11–16.

8.   *The Forfeiture Racket*, San Jose Mercury News, Aug. 29, 1993.

9.   *From Swagger to Suicide*, Newsweek, Dec. 9, 1996.

10.   *The Forfeiture Racket*, San Jose Mercury News, Aug. 29, 1993.

11.   Pittsburgh Press, *supra* note 7, at 31–32.

12.   *Prosecutor Dealt Away Charge on Marijuana for $3,000.00*, St. Louis Post Dispatch, Oct. 10, 1991.

13.   *See* Krimstock v. Kelly, 306 F.3d 40, 56 (2d Cir. 2002).

14.   *Police Profit by Seizing Homes of Innocent*, Pittsburgh Press, *supra* note 7, at 16–19; Cash Seizures by Police Prompt Court Fights, NPR, June 17, 2008, http://www.npr.org/templates/story/story.php?storyId=91555835.

15.   *The Thin Green Line*, California Lawyer, Sept. 1994, at 50–51; *Police Ask for Audit of Records*, Las Vegas Rev.–J., Mar. 24, 2001; Sheriff Under Scrutiny Over Drug Money Spending, NPR, June 19, 2008, http://www.npr.org/templates/story/story.php?storyId=91638378.

16.   National Asset Forfeiture Quality Assurance Program: Draft Principles and Commentary, *National Association of Attorneys General Civil Remedies in Drug Enforcement Report*, Dec./Jan. 1992, at 8–9.

17.   *National Code of Professional Conduct for Asset Forfeiture*, The Police Chief, Oct. 1993, at 86–88.

18.   The National Code of Professional Responsibility has also been adopted by the U.S. Department of Treasury for asset forfeiture cases under its jurisdiction. *See Guide to Equitable Sharing for Foreign Countries and Federal, State, Local Law Enforcement Agencies*, October 1, 1993, Executive Office for Asset Forfeiture, Office of the Assistant Secretary (Enforcement).

19.   The racial profiling provision was added as article II and old articles V & VI were combined into one provision as article V. Thus the number of ethical guidelines still remains at 10.

20.   Colo. Rev. Stat. § 16-13-302.

21.   Fla. Stat. Ann. § 932.704(11)(a).

22.   Governor's Alliance on Substance Abuse Grant Funded Multi-jurisdictional Drug Law Enforcement Task Forces Code of Professional Conduct for Asset Forfeiture, July 1, 1994.

23.   House Concurrent Resolution No. 156, HLS 97-3693.

24. N.H. REV. STAT. ANN. § 318-B:17-e.

25. *Embattled Police Chief Drove Seized Mercedes Benz*, L.A. TIMES, Nov. 1992.

26. *See Taking Cash into Custody—A Special Report on Police and Drug Money Seizures, available at* www.kcstar.com/projects/drugforfeit/.

27. *Auditors probing police fund in Warwick*, PROVIDENCE (R.I.) J., Aug. 5, 1998.

28. *Bill to target forfeiture law*, DENVER POST, Mar. 19, 2002.

29. *Critics Contend Asset Forfeiture in Drug Cases Rewards Successful Criminals*, L.A. DAILY J., Mar. 20, 1996.

30. *See Ethics and Responsibility for the California Prosecutor*, California District Attorneys Association, 3d edition (1992), Sec 4.6, Case Settlement, at 107–08.

31. *ABA Issues Statement of Principles on Forfeiture*, ASSET FORFEITURE NEWS, Jan. /Feb. 1996, at 1.

Table of Authorities

Cases

Statutes

United States Code

Rules

Supplemental Rules

Selected Bibliography

California District Attorneys Association. *California Seizure and Forfeiture Manual.* Sacramento, Cal., 2006.

Cassella, Stefan D. *Asset Forfeiture in the United States.* Huntington, N.Y.: Juris Publishing, 2006.

Kessler, Steven L. *Civil and Criminal Forfeiture Federal and State Practice.* St. Paul, Minn.: West Group, 2000.

Smith, David B. *Prosecution and Defense of Forfeiture Cases.* New York: Lexis Publishing, 2000.

U.S. Department of Justice. Criminal Division Asset Forfeiture and Money Laundering Section. *A Guide to Interlocutory Sales & Expedited Settlement.* Washington, D.C., July 2007.

___. *Asset Forfeiture Law and Practice Manual.* Washington, D.C., June 1998.

___. *Asset Forfeiture Policy Manual.* Washington, D.C., July 1996.

___. *Civil and Criminal Forfeiture Procedure.* Washington, D.C., May 2007.

___. *Federal Money Laundering Cases.* Washington, D.C., April 2007.

___. *Legislative History Civil Asset Forfeiture Reform Act (CAFRA) of 2000.* Washington, D.C., May 2000.

___. *Money Laundering Statutes and Related Materials.* Washington, D.C., May 2006.

___. *Selected Federal Asset Forfeiture Statutes.* Washington, D.C., May 2006.

___. Executive Office for Asset Forfeiture. *A Guide to Equitable Sharing of Federally Forfeited Property for State and Local Law Enforcement Agencies.* Washington, D.C., March 1994.

U.S. Department of Treasury. Executive Office for Asset Forfeiture. *Guide to Equitable Sharing for Foreign Countries and Federal, State, Local Law Enforcement Agencies.* Washington, D.C., October 1993.

Index

S

seizure orders/warrants 48
service of process 85
settlement 129–30 191, 299
Sixth Amendment right to counsel 189
standing 87–93
   jurisdictional 88–94
   statutory 87–88
state administrative forfeiture 35
state civil *in personam* forfeiture 36
state civil *in rem* statutes 35
state criminal forfeiture 36, 204
state distribution 224–35
state nuisance forfeiture statutes 39
state summary judgment motion 130
statute of limitations 109–10
statutory protections 245–47
substitute assets 189, 195
summary forfeiture 3, 19
summary judgments 126–29

T

terminology 1–21
   administrative forfeiture 3, 19
   civil forfeiture 8–12
   civil *in personam* forfeiture 20
   civil *in rem* forfeiture 20
   contraband forfeiture 12–16
   criminal forfeiture 5, 19
   enterprise forfeiture 16
   facilitation forfeiture 13–16
   jurisdiction 1–2
   proceeds forfeiture 12–13
   summary forfeiture 3, 19
trial defenses
   innocent owner 163
   insufficient nexus 159
   legitimate source defense 161
trial setting 132
turnover orders 60–62

U

USA PATRIOT Act 24

W

warrant, criminal seizure 189
warrantless seizure 51, 186

About the Author

Dee R. Edgeworth is the manager partner of Edgeworth & Associates. His firm provides litigation and training expertise in federal and state asset forfeiture actions. He was a Deputy District Attorney for the San Bernardino County California District Attorney's Office for 25 years, serving as the lead attorney of the Asset Forfeiture Unit from 1990 through March 2008. He was also a Special Assistant United States Attorney with the Central District of California for three years. In his new firm he continues to actively prosecute federal and state asset forfeiture actions.

A graduate of Brigham Young University (B.A. History, cum laude 1974) and Western State University College of Law (J.D. 1981), he is the author of the California District Attorneys Association *California Seizure and Forfeiture Manual* (2006) and has written numerous articles on asset forfeiture published by national and state prosecution associations.

A frequently requested instructor, he teaches for several federal law enforcement agencies, including the U.S. Department of Justice, Criminal Division, Asset Forfeiture and Money Laundering Section; Federal Bureau of Investigation; Drug Enforcement Administration; and U.S. Department of the Treasury. He has also taught for national law enforcement entities, including the National District Attorneys Association, National College of District Attorneys, National Association of Attorneys General, National Sheriffs Association, International Association of Chiefs of Police, and numerous state and local prosecution and law enforcement organizations. He is the current chairman of the California District Attorneys Association Asset Forfeiture Training and Education Committee. He is the recipient of several professional awards, including the California District Attorneys Association Instructor of the Year (1996), United States Department of Justice Exceptional Service Award (1996) and (2008), and National College of District Attorneys Lecturer of Merit Award (2002).